D1500295

Conscription and the Search for Modern Russian Jewry

THE MODERN JEWISH EXPERIENCE

Paula Hyman and Deborah Dash Moore, editors

Conscription and the Search for Modern Russian Jewry

Olga Litvak

INDIANA UNIVERSITY PRESS
BLOOMINGTON AND INDIANAPOLIS

305.8924047
L78c

PUBLISHED WITH THE GENEROUS ASSISTANCE OF THE KORET FOUNDATION.

THIS BOOK IS A PUBLICATION OF

INDIANA UNIVERSITY PRESS
601 NORTH MORTON STREET
BLOOMINGTON, INDIANA 47404-3797 USA

HTTP://IUPRESS.INDIANA.EDU
Telephone orders   800-842-6796
Fax orders   812-855-7931
Orders by e-mail   IUPORDER@INDIANA.EDU

Cav

LIBRARY OF CONGRESS CATALOGING-IN-PUBLICATION DATA

LITVAK, OLGA.
CONSCRIPTION AND THE SEARCH FOR MODERN RUSSIAN JEWRY / OLGA LITVAK.
P. CM. — (MODERN JEWISH EXPERIENCE)
INCLUDES BIBLIOGRAPHICAL REFERENCES AND INDEX.
ISBN-13: 978-0-253-34808-1 (CLOTH : ALK. PAPER)
ISBN-10: 0-253-34808-0 (CLOTH : ALK. PAPER) 1. JEWS — RUSSIA — HISTORY.
2. DRAFT — RUSSIA. 3. JEWS — RUSSIA — INTELLECTUAL LIFE. 4. RUSSIA — ETHNIC RELATIONS.
I. TITLE. II. SERIES: MODERN JEWISH EXPERIENCE (BLOOMINGTON, IND.)
DS135.R9L54 2006
305.892'4047 — DC22
2006015064

1   2   3   4   5   11   10   09   08   07   06

To
Polina Moiseevna Slizinova (1915–1975)
Hanan Ayzikovich Portnoi (1906–1981)

Moisei El'kunovich Litvak (1919–1943)
Vitya L'vovna Kaushanskaia (1917–1986)
my past

and
to Abigail Hannah Litvak (b. July 31, 2002)
my present

A Jewish boy and his father are walking down the street. The boy is thin and pale. He wears thick glasses and carries a book under his arm. They pass a uniformed Russian soldier, tall, broad, and muscular — a picture of gentile health and strength. The father looks down at his son and says: "See, Moishe, if you don't study, you're going to look like that."
Russian-Jewish joke

I'd like to underline the fact that the state's power (and that's one of the reasons for its strength) is both an individualizing and a totalizing form of power.
— Michel Foucault, "The Subject and Power"

The "proper stuff of fiction" does not exist; everything is the proper stuff of fiction, every feeling, every thought; every quality of brain and spirit is drawn upon; no perception comes amiss. And if we can imagine the art of fiction come alive and standing in our midst, she would undoubtedly bid us break her and bully her, for so her youth is renewed and her sovereignty assured.
— Virginia Woolf, *The Common Reader,* 1925

Contents

A NOTE ON TRANSLITERATION

In transliterating Hebrew and Russian, I have followed the Library of Congress rules, except that I have eliminated most diacritical marks. Yiddish terms are generally romanized according to the standards of the YIVO Institute for Jewish Research. All translations from Hebrew, Yiddish, and Russian are my own, except where indicated.

Place and personal names are usually offered in their Russian form unless there is a familiar English variation. The transliteration of Jewish personal names follows their original Russian spelling; hence Abramovich, not Abramovitsh.

ACKNOWLEDGMENTS

This book initially emerged at Columbia University's Department of History. I owe the most profound debt to my teachers there, especially to Yosef Hayim Yerushalmi, whose patient, clear-eyed guidance and near-prophetic wisdom steered me toward a career as a historian of Eastern European Jewry. Thanks also go to Richard Wortman for discerning a topic in a very preliminary and inchoate proposal and for asking me all those difficult questions. I am very grateful to Mark Von Hagen for helping me to approach the social and cultural role of the military in new ways, and to Elliot Wolfson, whose strong readings of rabbinic texts continually reassert themselves in my own analytical inclinations. My profound thanks to Dan Miron for teaching me how to think with literature. The enthusiasm and critical acumen of the other members of my committee, Abraham Ascher and David Roskies, saved me from despair and countless mistakes.

While at Columbia I was blessed with the wonderful company of fellow graduate students who have since become fast friends and treasured colleagues. I am deeply thankful to Nils and Jennifer Roemer, Dan Unowsky, Marc Miller, Robert Crews (who keeps leaving every place just as I get there), and Margaret Sena for the shelter of their enduring affection. My thanks to Nancy Sinkoff for breaking ranks to talk to me when I was still an undergraduate, and for remaining, ever since, a steadfast member of our mutual admiration society. I thank Yaacob Dweck for all the unearned but much needed applause. And most of all I thank Avi Matalon, my best pal and partner-in-crime, for generously sharing your mind when I felt like I was losing mine; and thank you, sweetheart, for 9 June 2002.

This book could only have been conceived at Columbia but it could only have been written at Princeton where I have spent seven very productive years. The mentoring of my colleagues at the history department and in the Program of Judaic Studies helped me to find my way toward these pages. Laura Engelstein's guidance was instrumental in shaping the direction of the project. She gave generously of her time, and provided acutely constructive criticism and an immensely fruitful exchange of ideas. Thanks to Tony Grafton for an eye-opening conversation about Jewish counter-history, to Dan Rodgers for a comparative perspective on the problem of the Anglo-Saxon genitive, and to Andy Rabinbach, for linking East and West. Three people in the department fearlessly undertook the task of reading the entire manuscript and providing copious and immeasurably useful, heartening notes. I am grateful to Bill Jordan, Dirk Hartog, and Michael Gordin for taking time away from their own work and for seeing things clearly before I did. Thanks to Cormac Ò Gráda, Davis Center fellow in 2003–2004, for sharing my enthusiasm for the nineteenth century and for a truly cross-disciplinary conversation. My warmest thanks to Angela Creager for leading by example, and to Molly Greene for always keeping her office door open.

I am deeply grateful to Leora Batnitzky, a constant source of intellectual and personal support, and to Barbara Hahn whose perfect company I sorely miss. My thanks to Froma Zeitlin for her passionate interest in Jewish Eastern Europe and for her generous and warmhearted welcome to Princeton. Peter Schaefer, in his inimitably calm and penetrating way, helped me to embrace the imbrication of literature and history which is central to this book. Thanks to his invaluable intervention and advice, I finally stopped agonizing about my sources. I thank all my students at Princeton, especially the HIS281 fan club and Vance Serchuk, Boris Fishman, Anne O'Donnell, Adina Yoffie, Amos Bitzan, Mark Schwartz, Marissa Troiano, Amy Widdowson, and Joe Skloot, for all the ways in which their own brilliant readings of the Jewish past helped to inspire my work (but mostly for laughing at all my jokes).

I am immensely grateful to my colleagues in the field of Eastern European Jewish history who gathered together at the Center for Advanced Judaic Studies at the University of Pennsylvania in 2002–2003. My thanks to David Ruderman, its guiding spirit. I am deeply in debt to Ben Nathans for his engaging and sympathetic reading of my manuscript. His friendship and unparalleled analytical skills have made all the difference. I am grateful to John Klier, Adam Teller, Ken Moss, Marcus Moseley, Bat-Sheva Ben-Amos, David Engel, Zvi Gitelman, and Moshe Rosman for their challenging questions, and to Ruth Wisse, Gabriella Safran, and Misha Krutikov for fielding my own dumb ones about Yiddish literature. My thanks to Steve Zipperstein and Amir Weiner for hosting me at Stanford and for providing a critical and much needed opportunity to discuss my ideas in a stimulating and congenial setting; ditto Sheila Jelen and Eliyana Adler at the University of Maryland, Lis Tarlow at the Davis Center at Harvard University, and Seth Schwartz at the Jewish Theological Seminary. And thank you Benjamin Gampel for your indispensable help with 1492. My thanks to Alice Nakhimovsky for her judicious pioneering work in Russian-Jewish literature and for all her help with the *odessity*. I am profoundly thankful for the rocklike support of Elisheva Carlebach; throughout the last decade she has steadily watched over and encouraged my progress. Her own scholarship serves as a model of conceptual rigor and literary creativity.

This book would have been impossible without the help of the staff at Firestone Library, Princeton University; my thanks to Nancy Pressman, Nina Shapiro, Joel Burlingame, and all the members of the Interlibrary Loan Department for fulfilling every obscure request with speed and care. I am immeasurably grateful to Yohanan Petrovsky-Shtern for taking on all the aspiring Jewish genealogists who called to ask me about Grandpa's fate in the imperial army. My thanks to Janet Rabinowitch — who took a chance on me when I had only thirty pages and no other editor would give me the time of day — and Rita Bernhard at Indiana University Press for all their work on the manuscript and to the anonymous readers whose penetrating comments guided the final revisions.

I owe an incalculable debt of gratitude and admiration to my family and friends. My parents, Tanya and Gregory Litvak, had the courage and foresight to leave the USSR for America in 1979. In giving me the gift of freedom, they made possible everything that came after. I am thankful that I get to share the planet (and a few chromosomes) with my brother, Paul. Thank you for being curious, and in possession of enough patience, good cheer, and unconditional love to tolerate all the aborted phone calls, unreturned messages, and bouts of unaccountable bad humor that were the unfortunate by-products of this book. By the way, I apologize. To my own personal cheering section — John Efron, Noam Elcott, Rebecca Kobrin, Alyssa Quint, Emily Rose, and Jeff Shandler — thank you for never doubting and for listening to all the stories that went into the making of this book.

Finally, this book, and indeed my entire intellectual career, have grown out of an ongoing conversation that first began in the fall of 1992 when I was a senior at Columbia College. From that day to this, Michael Stanislawski has been my adviser, my friend, my colleague, my constant reader, my ally, and my sometimes conscience. From him I have learned everything I know about what it means to be both a teacher and a student. His professional integrity and sense of engagement with the past have shaped my own scholarly commitments. When I undertook to write about conscription, he warned me not to associate too closely with his own work on that subject. I can only repeat now what I said then: that it would be my proudest achievement to be in such company. Every good idea in this manuscript belongs as much to him as to me. All the goofs, howlers, errors of content and infelicities of style are, of course, mine alone.

Conscription and
the Search for
Modern Russian Jewry

INTRODUCTION

THE LITERARY RESPONSE TO CONSCRIPTION AND THE PERSISTENCE OF ENLIGHTENMENT IN RUSSIAN-JEWISH CULTURE

MIRIAM'S MIND

The image of Russia's first Jewish soldiers, drafted into the army of Nicholas I between 1827 and 1855, has entered contemporary culture as one of the preeminent examples of Jewish hardship under the tsars. Descendants of Russian-Jewish immigrants in such diverse places as Dublin and New York continue to invoke fear of conscription as one of the most important reasons for their grandfathers' and great-uncles' flight from Eastern Europe.[1] Together with the pogrom, conscription regularly features in the repertoire of stories about the unremitting horrors of Russian anti-Semitism.

Here, for instance, is the American-Jewish writer Johanna Kaplan, in a recent story titled "Sickness," narrated by Miriam, a girl at home with the measles and a stack of Jewish books at her bedside:

> In such a study house, in just such a *shtetl* (for so these villages were called), a tailor, Mottel, and his five sons sat poring over the Holy Writ as the afternoon deepened into evening. Suddenly amidst the dull hum of men's voices chanting the Scriptures and disputing over the commentaries, a

great clatter was heard at the door soon followed by an icy blast of chill air. It was the red-headed beadle, a lantern swaying on his arm, as he cried in a terror-filled voice, "Brothers! Brothers! Bestir yourselves! Hide! Run! Save yourselves and your sons!"

"What is it, Beadle?" asked the tailor. "A pogrom?"

"Not that," the beadle replied, his voice still shaking. "Oh, hurry, brothers, hurry! It's the Snatchers, the Tsar's kidnappers, and with them ride an army of Cossack soldiers." [. . .]

The evil purpose of these kidnappers was to snatch little Jewish lads, not more than seven or eight years of age, tear them from their mothers and their homes, and send them to peasant Christian families in distant reaches of the Tsar's vast realm, where in hapless servitude they would daily be forced to go against the teachings of their faith. For twenty-five long years such captivity was theirs to endure, the latter part to be spent, as unwilling conscripts in the Tsar's brutal army. By that time, gloated the ruthless Tsar, all ties with their heritage and origin would be forgotten.[2]

In Kaplan's dark fantasy, the evil tsar plots to break up Jewish families and destroy the faith of Jewish children. Refracted through the eyes of Miriam, the narrator, Jewish history becomes a kind of "sickness," a series of hallucinations brought on by fever and too much reading. The cure for Miriam's literary nightmares is more Nancy Drew mysteries, suggests the well-meaning but obtuse Dr. Lichtblau. Miriam, however, is not interested in any light reading or, for that matter, in reading anything lightly. The Jewish past lodges in her consciousness as the source of an incurable psychosomatic affliction.

The "sickness" of Kaplan's Miriam points to the complicated ways in which Jewish literature continues to figure as the battleground for the modern Jewish mind.[3] Invoking conscription, Kaplan stands at the end of a long line of Jewish writers who sought to turn this episode in the history of Russia's Jews into a distinctly Jewish story. In "Sickness," Miriam herself is the locus of this transformation. Her acute sensibility creates its own Jewish country, governed exclusively by the power of her personal engagement with the text and texture of the Jewish past. Through the intensity of her absorption, Miriam moves from being a Jewish reader to being a Jewish author in her own right. The work of cultural signification here takes place not in the study house or in the synagogue — not even in the kitchen — but exclusively within the interior landscape created by Kaplan's precocious heroine. In a way, *Conscription and the Search for Modern Russian Jewry* is about how conscription entered into Miriam's mind; more precisely, it is about how the treatment of history in Jewish literature has shaped the history of the Jewish imagination.

GETTING HISTORY WRONG

In her imaginative obsession with the Jewish past, Miriam — the arche-typal Jewish constant reader — gets conscription history all wrong. Nicholas I was not "ruthlessly" plotting to destroy the Jews; he did not employ Cos-sacks or "Snatchers" to kidnap seven- and eight-year-old Jewish children from their beds; and there were no pogroms in Russia during his reign. Of course, Miriam is hardly alone in her particular affliction. One memoirist has recently asserted that her grandfather, who came to Dublin from "Riga in Lithuania," had been "conscripted into the Russian Army at the age of twelve, but ran away to escape a pogrom."[4] Riga is located in Latvia, not in Lithuania; it has never witnessed a pogrom; and by the time the first wave of urban riots hit the Pale of Settlement in 1881–1882, children of twelve had not been conscripted into the Russian army for twenty-five years.

Few aspects of Jewish experience under the tsars defy the distinction between fact and fiction as manifestly as the fate of Russia's first Jewish soldiers. Instituted in 1827 by Nicholas I (r. 1825–1855), the Jewish recruit-ment statute set the draft age for eligible male Jews at twelve to twenty-five. Implementation of the decree was left to the leadership of the Jewish com-munities, presented with official quotas to fill either with able-bodied young men, aged eighteen to twenty-five, or with adolescent boys, aged twelve to eighteen. The former would serve out the regular twenty-five-year term of service in the ranks; the latter, known as military cantonists, would be placed in special training battalions to be reared within the general population of soldiers' children, and upon reaching the age of eighteen transferred into regular ranks to serve out their full twenty-five-year term. Although the military authorities showed no marked preference for recruiting Jewish minors in place of adults, Jewish communal leaders found themselves be-tween a rock and a hard place. On the one hand, young men of draft age often had families of their own to support. The alternative presented the gruesome spectacle of having to tear children away from their parents. The situation bred abuse to which the young, the poor, and the marginal fell victim. Contemporaries placed the blame almost exclusively at the feet of Jewish communal leaders rather than the Russian government; the prob-lem, intoned a chorus of Jewish voices, was that "God was high above and the tsar far away."[5]

Resistance to the decree expressed itself chiefly in acute social friction rather than in antagonism toward the monarchy. Nothing focused Jewish ire against the established elites like the notorious khappers or lovchikes, agents that communities employed to gather prospective recruits in the last years of the Nicholaevan reign when the quotas were stepped up. In fact, the hiring of enforcers became necessary because, unlike peasant communes that also had to choose recruits from among their own, Jewish communities lacked the resources to compel their members to do the government's bidding.[6] The same calculus of desperation explains the choice to draft children in place of adults.

Nicholas I died in 1855, in the midst of the Crimean War. A year later, his son Alexander II (r. 1855–1881) abolished the drafting of minors. By that time, seventy thousand Jews had been recruited into Nicholas's army. Two-thirds had entered the ranks as cantonists. Their experience, among the general population of soldiers' children, vagrants, orphans, and sons of criminal exiles, was markedly different from that of adult Jewish soldiers. Whereas the former were expressly permitted to pray in public as Jews and given leave to celebrate the Jewish holidays, Jewish cantonists were subject to strenuous conversionary pressure. Life in cantonist ranks was exceedingly difficult for Jews and non-Jews alike. Corporal punishment was ubiquitous, brutal, and often arbitrary, relieved only, it seems, by the fortuitous show of mercy or by the intervention of well-placed patrons. No one escaped the physical rigors and mind-numbing routine for which the pre-reform Russian army was justly infamous.

Informed by the literary preeminence of Nicholaevan conscription, vernacular memory consistently confuses the kind of experience the immediate forebears of present-day descendants of Russian Jews might have actually faced in the Russian army with features of the draft peculiar to the Nicholaevan regime, particularly the twenty-five-year term of service and the drafting of minors. Cantonist battalions were disbanded in 1856. With the introduction of universal conscription, a general lottery administered by a locally elected draft board replaced the communal quota system; after 1855, there were no more khappers. The term of service was reduced to six years, generally consistent with the practice of contemporary European states. Thus no grandfather or great-uncle of any living Jewish person of Eastern European descent could possibly have encountered the dangers that his immediate progeny see fit to locate at the heart of their personal family mythology.

The confusion, I think, speaks directly to the ways in which the literary construction of Eastern European Jewry has displaced the history of actual Jews who lived in a real place called Russia. Even in the late imperial period, most Jews encountered the horrors of the Nicholaevan regime chiefly in Jewish literature. Today, what people know or claim to know about Jewish conscription in Russia also comes almost entirely from conscription literature. Anticipating the first attempts at writing conscription history by more than fifty years, conscription literature actively shaped not only the vernacular memory of the Jewish experience in the Russian army but also the substance of the scholarship on Russian Jewry.

The central role of conscription literature in the creation of Russian-Jewish history raises broader questions — who, precisely, determines the shape of the past? And, more important, to what end? This line of inquiry is not new to historical scholarship. From the moment that modern history actively dissociated from the rhetorical arts and entered into the domain of the social sciences, historians have asserted their professional claims to be in exclusive possession of objective truth about the past. Literary construction in the subjunctive mood — how it might or ought to have been — gave way to the reconstruction of "how it really was," stated boldly in the declarative. But the historian's craft did not displace the art of making history afresh; novelists, filmmakers, journalists, and artists continue to give scholars a run for their money.[7]

Partly in response to the radical uses and abuses of history by twentieth-century ideologues, professional historians have maintained a consistent concern with the conventions which inform history writing.[8] In the last twenty years, however, occasional ruminations by eminent figures in the field on the "idea of history" or the "historical imagination" have given way to a steady stream of books on the production and consumption of historical knowledge.[9] Shaken by postwar skepticism about the reach of human reason as well as by the linguistic turn of neighboring disciplines in the humanities, historians can no longer afford merely to assert that the past yields easily to their quest for accuracy and perfect likeness. The contention that history comes in the form of a *story*, subject to its own particular narrative logic no less than to the evidentiary standards of proof, has fueled interest in the styles of historical discourse that are peculiar to a specific time and place, styles that render the past continually relevant to the present. An enduring awareness that (in the words of William Faulkner) the "past is not dead, it is not even past," new scholarship tells us, is not entirely, not even mostly, the fruit of a lone archival search for the facts but an expression of what the sociologist Maurice Halbwachs first termed "collective memory."[10]

The concept of "collective memory" presupposes a dichotomy between the social construction of a common past and the self-consciously analytic reconstruction of historical experience. The former locates the past in public monuments, schoolbooks, imaginative literature, even language itself; the latter takes the form of scholarship, grounded in the critical interpretation of primary sources. Following in Halbwachs's footsteps, historians working in a variety of fields have explored the complicated often impossibly fraught relationship between these two projects.[11] For historians of the Jews, the distinction between history and memory has offered a new perspective on the secularization of Jewish culture in the modern era. In his groundbreaking *Zakhor: Jewish History and Jewish Memory* (1982), Yosef Hayim Yerushalmi first considered the tension between the impulse to write Jewish history and the "social reality" of collective Jewish memory, sustained by the liturgical and ritual elevation of Jewish suffering. While the former is, according to Yerushalmi, a relatively recent and limited, even idiosyncratic occupation, the latter has sustained Jewish life in the diaspora for two thousand years. For all the efforts of "history" to undermine the sway of "memory" by subjecting Jewish knowledge of the past to the impartial authority of source criticism, Yerushalmi says, the teleological connection between the travails of Exile and the promise of redemption continues to inform the common perception of Jewish history. In fact, even avowedly secular Jews remain perfectly comfortable in the embrace of the idea that the history of the Jews constitutes a dramatic tale of patient endurance in the face of unrelenting persecution in *galut* (exile), a faithful echo of the biblical promise of Jewish chosenness and divinely assured collective survival.[12]

Focusing on the case of nineteenth- and early-twentieth-century Russian Jews — the forebears of the largest number among today's Jewish population in Israel, the U.S., and countries of the former Soviet Union and, in the nineteenth century, the largest concentration of Jewish readers and writers in the world — this book addresses the role of literature in the creation of a common Jewish past. Inspired by the questions first posed by Yerushalmi in *Zakhor*, as well as by the outpouring of scholarship on the various forms of collective memory in other fields, I investigate the ways in which the literature of the Jewish Enlightenment (Heb. *Haskalah*) served to mobilize the Jewish memories of readers who, under the impact of emancipation, abandoned the public expression of their increasingly private religious commitments. This did not happen only in Russia, of course; but conscription literature offers a particularly rich case study of the relationship between Jewish literature and the emergence of modern Jewish conscience.

THE PERSISTENCE OF ENLIGHTENMENT IN
THE AGE OF EMANCIPATION

Conscription emerged as a theme in Russian-Jewish writing directly under the impact of the dual image of Nicholas I as both the father of the Jewish recruitment statute and the author of the Jewish Enlightenment in Russia, the author, as it were, of Jewish modernity. Under the leadership of Nicholas's minister of education, S. S. Uvarov (1786–1855), the autocracy sponsored Russia's first network of Jewish schools where secular subjects were taught alongside a new enlightened Jewish curriculum. Under Uvarov's aegis, the 1840s saw the creation of two rabbinical seminaries and the introduction of laws that limited social practices which Jewish enlighteners (Heb. *maskil*, pl. *maskilim*) deemed obnoxious and arcane, such as early marriage. The government hired its own Jewish experts from the ranks of the maskilim, supported the publication of Jewish Enlightenment tracts, and encouraged the "productivization" of the Jewish population by opening up the southern frontier to Jewish agricultural settlement.[13] The broad sweep of the Nicholaevan project, known as "official enlightenment," inspired and nourished the hopes of the maskilim. Most of them actively sought government employment and patronage in order to realize their own aspirations for Russian Jewry. Conscription literature came into being precisely at the moment when the future of this vision first came into question, under the impact of a shift in Jewish policy from "official enlightenment" to "selective integration," that is, the emancipation of Russian Jews into the Russian estate structure.

From the end of the eighteenth century, when Russia first acquired its Jewish population in the course of the Polish Partitions (1772–1795), Russian-Jewish residence had been restricted to the western borderlands, an area that became known as the Pale of Jewish Settlement. Deeply provincial, Jewish life remained circumscribed by local ties, religious discipline, and traditional status hierarchies; communal autonomy was guaranteed and maintained by the state. Exceptions existed only at the margins; in the pre-reform era, select individuals who had provided some outstanding service to the state were permitted the privilege of living outside the Pale and beyond the boundaries of communal authority.

In the 1860s and 1870s, as part of his efforts to direct the course of modernization, Alexander II implemented a policy known as "selective integration," aimed at expanding personal privileges, including the right to move beyond the Pale, on the basis of estate rather than confession, to entire categories of Jews.[14] These categories included merchants with sufficient capital to enroll in the first guild (1859); university graduates holding advanced degrees, particularly doctors and lawyers (1861); craftsmen such as brewers, mechanics, and distillers (1865); army veterans (1867); and, finally, pharmacists and veterinarians as well as university graduates without advanced degrees (1879). A new cohort of Jewish men and women now associated the experience of modernity not with the Jewish enlightenment but with their emancipation from the jurisdiction of the Jewish community and, possibly, with the abandonment of all forms of Jewish filiation. Jewish enlighteners observed this generational shift with both exhilaration and a mounting sense of anxiety. Their ambivalence expressed itself in a critique of emancipation and provided the impetus for the emergence of conscription literature.

The long journey through a variety of genres, languages, styles, characters, and plots that culminated in Miriam's "sickness" began back in Russia in the era of the Great Reforms, precisely at the moment that the Nicholaevan draft, with its twenty-five years of service, the drafting of minors, and the attempts to convert Jewish children, had become history. In 1856 Alexander II began to dismantle his father's military regime and initiated the long bureaucratic trek toward reform that culminated in the introduction of universal conscription in 1874. In 1859 Osip Rabinovich published "The Penal Recruit," the first of a stream of conscription stories that by the end of the century grew into a virtual flood. The relationship between the end of Nicholaevan *rekrutchina*, in fact, and its beginning in fiction is hardly fortuitous. Its closest parallel lies in the imaginative recasting of the peasant in Russian culture following the emancipation of the serfs in 1861. In both cases the creation of a literary commonplace promoted an ideal of the common life, just as the social, economic, and confessional foundations of community began to shift under the impact of Alexander's "unserfment" (Rus. *raskreposhcheniie*) of Russian society.

Russian writers began alternatively to exoticize and to idealize pre-reform peasant life precisely at the moment that former serfs, drawn to economic and social prospects available in the cities, began to leave their villages and, in the process, radically transformed Russia's urban landscape as well as the villages they left behind.[15] For the Russian *intelligentsia,* emancipation was at once the cure for Russia's persistent political backwardness and the cause of its present disorder. The unintended consequences of sexual and economic freedom for the vast rural population of the empire unleashed a public debate which implicated the contemporary condition of the "rural people" in the ostensible decline of piety, family harmony, social discipline, and physical and mental health, not to mention the troubling rise of criminality and mass culture.[16] Imaginary peasants became most other just as their historical counterparts were becoming increasingly modern, provokingly similar in aspirations and desires to the educated professionals who were so invested in the collective fate of the folk.[17]

Just like their Russian counterparts, Jewish intellectuals initially envisioned the prospect of emancipation under Alexander II as the culmination of a process of political and cultural development that would result in the wholesale transformation of society. In the reign of Nicolas I Jewish enlighteners saw a direct connection between their efforts to improve the state of Russian Jewry and the civic enfranchisement of the Jews still to come.[18] In both cases — the Russian and the Jewish — the realities of emancipation tested and finally shattered the political teleology of enlightenment. Just as the emancipation of the serfs failed to usher in a well-ordered and stable social order composed of loyal, productive, and responsible citizen-subjects, the emancipation of Russian Jews, under Alexander's policy of "selective integration," did not lead to the reformation of the Russian-Jewish community *tout court.* In fact, the opposite occurred; the liberation of the Russian Jew exacted heavy social, economic, and cultural costs, and placed into doubt the future of Jewish enlightenment. The heady promises of emancipation, extended not to Russian Jewry in the collective — still largely confined to the Pale — but to Russian Jews as individuals, undermined institutional discipline, rewarded ambition at the expense of communal responsibility, unsettled the patriarchal order, and encouraged the cultivation of personal desire. All this only served to deepen the post-emancipation malaise of Jewish enlighteners who, like their Russian fellows, remained wedded to the romantic ideal of social harmony in an age characterized by the ambiguities of freedom.

Conscription literature developed in the course of the expansion of

Russian-Jewish culture in the late imperial period, defined by the anxieties and opportunities that accompanied emancipation. Just as Russian educated society celebrated the figure of the peasant as a way of coping with the contradictory effects of modernity, the purveyors of Jewish Enlightenment turned to the figure of the pre-reform conscript in order to resolve the contemporary contradiction between the messianic yearning for community and the historical vicissitudes of emancipation. Each in his own way, the peasant and the recruit exemplified an integral vision of pre-reform peoplehood, the historical reality of which the lives of their post-reform creators so manifestly belied. The casting of Russian Jewry in the role of the Nicholaevan recruit involved the self-conscious re-vision of contemporary history. The collapse of the present into an imagined past lay at the heart of the conservative revolution in the course of which modern Russian Jews created a Russian Jewry for all time. At the center of a new secular scripture, the iconic image of the Nicholaevan recruit provided a foil for the post-emancipation awakening of Jewish national consciousness.

LITERATURE AND COUNTER-HISTORY

Like the literature on Russia's "rural people," conscription stories comprise an enlightened counter-history of emancipation. Drawn together by more than their common subject, they do not provide the reader with a faithful record of the Nicholaevan period in Russian-Jewish history. Conscription literature constitutes a Jewish discourse, polemically charged by the post-emancipation commitments on the part of Russian maskilim to the collective future of Russian Jewry. To put the matter as plainly as possible, conscription literature is not a history of conscription; it is, after a fashion, a history of the persistence of the *Haskalah* in Russian-Jewish culture.[19]

Historians have conventionally attributed the end of the Jewish Enlightenment in Russia and the turn toward so-called post-liberal Jewish politics — nationalism and socialism — to the disappointment with the end of emancipation and the incapacity of the Russian autocracy to sustain its political promises against the forces of reaction and resurgent popular anti-Semitism.[20] The treatment of conscription, a key theme in Russian-Jewish writing, polemically aimed at the emancipated Russian-Jewish reader, shows that both the historical and the ideological relationship between the aspirations toward enlightenment and the fruits of emancipation were not nearly so straightforward.[21] The emancipation of the Jews, no matter how carefully managed by the authorities, Russian and Jewish alike, did not necessarily result in the enlightenment of the Jews or of Judaism. Against the specter of increasing social conflict, economic dislocation, and the erosion of religious faith and praxis, Russian-Jewish writers embraced the memory of Nicholas's experiment in Jewish social engineering as the symbol of a lost opportunity for creating an enlightened Russian Jewry. The imaginary return to conscription past spoke to the difficulties of measuring the realities of emancipation against the harmonious vision of collective improvement. In light of the continuing literary investment in the conscription theme, it becomes possible to understand the turn toward Jewish politics as immanent in the counter-historical discourse of the Haskalah.

Principally concerned with the emergence and flowering of conscription literature in the post-Nicholaevan period, I begin with a chapter that examines Nicholaevan conscription as the point of intersection between the state's investment in the idea of Russian-Jewish reform and the emergence of the Haskalah not as social process — the adaptation of cultural mores to socioeconomic realities — but as an intellectual project. The meeting of the minds between Nicholaevan state officials and the founders of the Russian-Jewish Enlightenment has always been something of an embarrassment to Jewish historians, especially given the grim realities of child recruitment and rampant corruption.[22] As chapter 1 demonstrates, the faith in the power of government authority to effect change was, however, neither entirely instrumental nor politically misplaced. In the Nicholaevan reign, both maskilim and Russian state functionaries were equally inclined to overestimate the state's capacity to instantiate far-reaching social improvements and to administer a widely disparate and often refractory imperial population. The bureaucratic effort to implement Nicholas's conscription program demonstrates the extent to which state-sponsored reform consistently ran aground of innumerable practical obstacles. Thus Nicholas's successor, his son Alexander II, began his reign with scrapping his father's costly and inefficient military-pedagogical regime in favor of a lottery-based universal conscription more consistent with the general "unserfment" of Russian society from the tutelary state. Not coincidentally, Nicholas's program of "official enlightenment," which had nurtured the personal and social aspirations of the maskilim, would soon follow.

For the Nicholaevan cohort of Jewish enlighteners, raised on the potential of the reforming state as an article of faith, the crowning of the new tsar brought a heightened sense of expectation. The glorious vision of Jewish emancipation flowered under the impact of the abolition of serfdom, the cornerstone of the most far-reaching revolution from above since the reign of Peter the Great. The new Jewish literature declared its allegiance to the autocracy by invoking this connection explicitly; in Lev Levanda's Russian-Jewish novel, *Hot Time* (Rus. *Goriachee vremia*, 1871–1873), set against the background of the Polish revolt of 1863, a Russian maskil wrote:

> We must never forget that it was *barbarous* Russia and not *civilized* Poland which first began to concern itself with our education and development. The awakening of our self-consciousness we owe to Russia and not to Poland. In a certain sense, emperor Nicholas I was for us, the Jews, what Peter

I was for the Russians. What did prince Czartoryski ever do for our education? We did not exist, as far as he was concerned. But exist we did for Count Uvarov. He invented us [the maskilim] for the sake of Russia's education.[23]

The rise of Jewish liberal consciousness during the early years of the Great Reforms era is the subject of the second chapter, which treats the conscription stories of Osip Rabinovich as political allegories of the imagined link between Nicholaevan and Alexandrine projects of creating a modern Russian Jewry. Ironically Russian-Jewish reformers who, like Rabinovich (and Levanda) came of age in the Nicholaevan period, saw the state's attempts to direct the course of Jewish emancipation not as the liberal departure from the regime of "official enlightenment" but rather its logical — and ideological — fulfillment. In the work of Rabinovich, Nicholaevan conscripts became symbolic of the state's mission to manage the ostensible inner chaos of modern Russian-Jewish life, signified by the urban backyard of Odessa. The tension between the idealized depiction of Nicholas's Jewish soldiers and Rabinovich's jaundiced vision of his secular Jewish contemporaries points to the conservative tenor of Russian-Jewish literature, which would become all the more evident in the conscription stories of Isaac-Meir Dik, Grigorii Bogrov, and Judah-Leib Gordon, all of whom engaged the conscription theme in a potent critique of Russian-Jewish embourgeoisement.

In chapter 3 the conscription stories of Dik, Bogrov, and Gordon exemplify the growing cultural significance of Russian-Jewish literature as the new locus of Jewish enlightenment. In the 1870s to the early 1880s, as the state pulled back from its institutional commitment to the Haskalah, Jewish enlighteners sought different ways to fashion a model Russian Jewry. Authorship itself became a sort of social mission and literature the focus of the reformist imagination. At the same time that the personal fortunes of increasing numbers of Russian Jews became radically disengaged from the historical fate of Russian Jewry, the conscription story became wedded to the maskilic fantasy of collective improvement. Enshrined in the Nicholaevan mythology of Sh. J. Abramovich, popularly known by the name of his literary persona, Mendele the Bookpeddler, the conscription story, in fact, spoke both to the hopes and the missed opportunities of Jewish enlighteners in the age of emancipation.

The fourth chapter, devoted to the subject of conscription in the prodigious oeuvre of Abramovich, links the cultural politics of the Haskalah in the age of emancipation with the conservative tilt toward populism, a momentous ideological shift that shaped the ethos of Jewish nationalism. Abramovich, the progenitor of the so-called Hebrew renaissance, enters into the picture as the first Jewish enlightener-turned-populist. The singular importance of conscription in his attempt to fix the cultural significance of Russian-Jewish literature informs the ways in which a subsequent generation of younger writers, working in Hebrew and Yiddish and associated in various ways with modern Jewish politics, continued to use the conscription story in their attempts to rewrite the history of modern Jewish experience.

In chapter 5 I treat the conscription tales of the Hebrew renaissance as the enlightenment subtext of the Jewish nationalist movement. Through the close reading of stories written by M. Z. Feierberg, Ben-Ami, I. L. Peretz, and Judah Steinberg, I arrive at a typology of the conscription story as a potent myth about the imminent rebirth of the Jewish nation from the muck and mire of Russian soil. I locate the paradigm of conscription at the intersection between the expansion of Jewish literary culture and the rise of nationalism; to the extent that the political authority of the latter actually derived from the moral authority of the former, nationalism itself became the newest manifestation of the maskilic interest in reforming Russian Jewry. In fact, the nationalist paradigm of the conscription tale constituted a polemical thrust against the unprecedented phenomenon of a secular imperial Jewish subculture, the creators of which had their own conscription stories to tell. At the turn of the century it was possible to discern these different strains in the tension between the likes of Feierberg, Steinberg, Ben-ami, and Peretz and those of Sholem-aleichem, Joseph Brenner, and Grigorii Arieli-Orlov, the first Russian-Jewish writers whose conscription fictions pointedly disavowed the link between the commitments of the Haskalah and modern Russian-Jewish writing. But by the first quarter of the twentieth century, as Russian Jewry dispersed into its various diasporas, it was the normative version of the conscription story as the originary tale of Jewish enlightenment that entered into history.

The last chapter treats the way that the enlightenment project persisted in various historical re-creations of Jewish conscription. From autobiography to scholarship, the conscription theme became central to the retelling of the Russian-Jewish past as a moral fable about the heroic resistance of Russian Jewry against the ravages of modern life. The narrative roots of this historiographical paradigm, still prevalent in the academic writing of Eastern European Jewish history, go all the way back to the work of Osip Rabinovich and his literary followers, who invoked imagined counter-histories of conscription as parables of their own historical struggles on behalf of Jewish enlightenment in the age of emancipation.

1

STEPCHILDREN OF THE TSAR:
JEWISH CANTONISTS AND THE
OFFICIAL ORIGINS OF RUSSIAN JEWRY

MAKING RUSSIAN JEWRY

In the second half of the nineteenth century Russian-Jewish writers raised the figure of the Nicholaevan recruit to the status of an icon, the cultural signifier of the difficult origins of Russian Jewish Enlightenment. Through their imaginative mediation, the story of Jewish conscription into the army of Nicholas I came to exemplify the defining moment in the creation of a common Russian-Jewish past. The singular dedication of post-Nicholaevan Jewish intellectuals to investing the conscription tale with contemporary meaning in an attempt to distill a modern Russian-Jewish *ethnos* out of the tangle of social, economic, and cultural differences that defined the lives of Jewish men and women in the Pale of Settlement emerged against the background of its precedent in tsarist policy. In fact, the nature and extent of the Russian government's investment in constructing Russian Jewry, a project dictated more by the changing definition of imperial *raison d'état* than by any Jewish agenda, anticipated and informed the concerns of the Russian-Jewish intelligentsia long past the age of Nicholas I down to the fall of the Romanov empire.

The imposition of the conscription decree in 1827 marked the inception of the state's ambitious program of social engineering, a project that aimed at using Russia's extensive military resources to transform a generation of Jewish boys into a model Russian Jewry. Reared at the expense of the state, Jewish minors, drafted first into *cantonist* battalions and then, once they came of age, into regular army ranks, exemplified to their superiors both the reach and the limits of the government's ambitious efforts to reform its Jewish subjects. The ambiguities implicit in this situation found reflection in official discourse before Nicholaevan conscription became a commonplace in the repertoire of Jewish storytellers. The earliest version of the conscription tale appeared in the form of a bureaucratic narrative that chronicled the struggle of the military administration, specifically the Department of Military Settlements (DMS) to realize, in spite of substantial difficulties of principle and practice, the tsar's uncompromising vision of Jewish manhood reborn in Nicholas's own image.

Driven by the growing discrepancy between ends and means, the official story of Jewish conscription under Nicholas I stands up to historical scrutiny far more consistently than its normative Jewish version given to posterity and retold in a variety of ways to the present day. This, for a number of reasons: first, the bureaucratic narrative concerns the immediate realities of Nicholaevan conscription. Conscription literature, produced almost in its entirety by Jewish authors in the post-reform period, is, to the same extent, contemporary; that is, it subordinates the interest in the Nicholaevan past to the cultural concerns of its *own* moment; Jewish conscription literature derives its historical character precisely from its imaginative relationship to the past, from all of the ways, in other words, that it gets history wrong. Second, the bureaucratic narrative reproduces a variety of different, competing voices. These voices include the tsar, the local command, the administration, regimental priests, the minister of war, parents of Jewish recruits, sometimes even the recruits themselves. Conscription literature, contrary to the contemporary notion that its essential truthfulness is rooted in the authenticity of Jewish vernacular memory ostensibly undisturbed by the passage of time between the reign of Nicholas I and the end of the imperial period, developed and changed in accordance with the power of individual authorial control. Unselfconsciously polyphonic, the bureaucratic narrative often speaks against the avowed interest of the state which it ostensibly serves. At such moments, it gets closest to the historical contingencies of conscription, vastly more complicated and confusing than its expressly ideological — normative — representation, either in the tsar's law or in Jewish literature, allows. The bureaucratic narrative emerges as a kind of historical, secular, we might say, commentary on the programmatic confessional and political interest of the autocracy, enunciated in the tsar's decree. Conscription literature, by contrast, constitutes its narrative teleology against the grain of secular historical experience. Every single one of its Jewish authors read the Nicholaevan past as past in relation not only to his (it is, without exception, his and not hers, in itself a critical aspect of the story I tell in this book) own present but also to the Jewish literary tradition in which he located the enduring cultural significance of his work. In fact, the post-reform work of making the Russian-Jewish encounter into an exemplary Jewish tale cannot be divorced from the attempt of Nicholas's disciplinary state to make Russian Jewry.

Under Nicholas I, the Russian military reached its apotheosis as the state's laboratory for social discipline and integration, and thus an ideal site for the creation of Russian Jewry.[1] The subject of the imposition of military conscription as emblematic of imperial Jewish policy and the high point of Nicholas's particular interest in the Jews is not new to students of Russian-Jewish history; but, in the past, the scholarly treatment of Russian political aims vis-à-vis the tsar's Jewish subjects relied almost exclusively on codified legislation and the rhetorical pronouncements that emerged out of seemingly interminable ministerial debates over the notorious Jewish question.[2] Such sources by their very nature imply and promote a rigid hierarchical view of imperial administration, a staple in the commonplace view of the autocracy as a political monolith, unrelentingly hostile to Judaism and Jews. In fact, the state's Jewish agenda developed within a highly contested bureaucratic arena where the will of the tsar collided with the extent to which his servitors proved willing and able to carry it out. The imperial ideal often clashed with administrative realities and, for all the plans carefully laid out in St. Petersburg, the palpable contradictions between *ukaz* and *prikaz*— between legislation and execution, law and order — manifest an attitude of official ambivalence toward implementing any radical change that might challenge the authority or strain the capacity of established government institutions.

A closer look the bureaucratic fate of the tsar's momentous decision to dedicate the imperial army to the reformation of Russian Jews exposes the fissures between explicit endorsement of Nicholas's magisterial pedagogical aims and tacit resistance against using the military to pursue what rapidly proved to be a costly and confusing experiment, the results of which consistently fell short of royal expectations. The orderly absorption into Russian ranks of some fifty thousand Jewish children presented a formidable prospect. Charged with the task, the staff of the Department of Military Settlements left a substantial paper trail of the Russian military bureaucracy beset by the difficulties which, from the beginning, dogged any attempt to turn the Jews of Russia into Russian Jewry.

FROM PARTITION TO CONSCRIPTION

Between the period of the Polish Partitions (1772–1795) and the end of the reign of Nicholas I, the policy of the Russian government vis-à-vis its Jewish subjects wavered between a vision of radical reform and the reality of social and administrative conservatism heavily laced with Judaeophobia.[3] Despite the persistence of the latter, throughout the half-century between partition and conscription, the autocracy demonstrated in various ways its commitment to forging a well-ordered Russian Jewry out of the welter of economic distinctions, regional variations, and social frictions that constituted the "patchwork" of Jewish life in the former Polish-Lithuanian Commonwealth.[4] However, Russia's Jewish policy, aimed at replacing the lingering chaos of Polish self-rule with its own hegemonic vision of imperial uniformity, consistently suffered from a fundamental contradiction. Legislative measures promoted the gradual erosion of Jewish autonomy and the parallel integration of Jews into the Russian estate structure even as the state continued to support the corporate confessional discipline of the Jewish community for the collection of taxes and the preservation of order. Catherine II (r. 1762–1796), for instance, instituted new laws that made Jews voting members of the urban strata to which they belonged in accordance with their economic position, residence, and occupation. At the same time she undercut the impact of such a bold move by explicitly endorsing the authority of local Jewish communities over its members. While every Russian subject simultaneously belonged to an estate and a confession, only in the case of the Jews did membership in the one implicitly undercut the power of the other.[5] The Jewish policies of Catherine's immediate imperial successors never resolved this problem of dual jurisdiction, either in theory or practice. While Russia's first official statute on Jews, passed by the government of Alexander I in 1804, encouraged individual Jews to enroll in Russian institutions of higher learning as a way of moving from one estate category to another, the new law did not vitiate the formal power of Jewish leadership, both religious and lay, that remained invested for social and theological reasons in combating the potential allure of secular education as a means of departure from the community. Deepening the tension still further, the statute encouraged Jews to turn to municipal courts for settling internal disputes even as it backed the legal power of communal bodies, effectively bolstering the system of local Jewish self-government that reform-minded Russian bureaucrats themselves deplored as unregenerate, corrupt, and exploitative. The state explicitly favored the Jewish individual at the expense of the Jewish community, associated in the Russian administration with a whole host of persistent evils, but the prospect of abolishing communal authority raised the "specter of insolvency" and the still more difficult problem of local tax collection, an effort beyond the straitened resources of the imperial administration.[6] Thus the statute of 1804 not only tightened the prerogatives of the rabbis and the lay elders elected to the local board of governors (Heb. *kahal*) but confirmed in law the previously ad-hoc residential restrictions that confined Jews to the fourteen western provinces known collectively as the Pale of Jewish Settlement. Under these conditions, Jewish life in Russia could hardly be expected to transcend the social and cultural limitations imposed by its own provincialism. Not surprisingly, the statute of 1804 aroused strong religious opposition particularly within the nascent Hasidic movement and inspired few Jews to take the high road to St. Petersburg.[7]

The trouble with the "phantom" of reform that hovered over the statute of 1804 was that the Russian state remained heavily dependent on the social status quo to ensure the orderly execution of its laws.[8] Jewish communities in the post-partition age were no exception in this regard. Throughout the course of its imperial advance between the eighteenth and the mid-nineteenth century, Russian state power had consistently maintained, even strengthened, existing hierarchies and backed established authority of rival faiths, even as it claimed its new territories in the name of Holy Russia.[9] Russia experienced its greatest period of territorial expansion between the reigns of Catherine II and Nicholas I; during this period, Russian civilian and military authorities, charged with the administration of conquered territories, continually strained for personnel. Forced to co-opt non-Orthodox, occasionally hostile elites — an enterprise fraught with the potential for subversion of imperial aims — for the purposes of governing its ever expanding frontiers, the Russian bureaucracy nevertheless aspired toward juridical uniformity and social transparency.[10] The disparity between reach and grasp that characterized tsarist policy toward Russia's recently acquired Jewish population resulted in new social and cultural divisions being superimposed upon old ones.

Instead of fostering homogeneity and reform, the state's support of a dual system of jurisdiction actively exacerbated internal division and promoted a sense of religious entrepreneurship, hardly consistent with the bureaucratic vision of order. For example, competition for state patronage and access to government power aggravated the most important split in the spiritual life of Eastern European Jews, the late-eighteenth-century conflict between Hasidism and its rabbinic opponents. In Vilna, both the followers of the new pietism and their opponents (Heb. *mitnagdim;* sing., *mitnagged*) took turns denouncing each other to the state; effectively institutionalizing the dispute, the statute of 1804 formally sanctioned the existence of Hasidic conventicles (Heb. *minyanim*) alongside established synagogues and study houses.[11] At the same time the mythology attached to the St. Petersburg imprisonment and official vindication of R. Shneur Zalman of Liady, the founder of the Habad branch of Hasidism, in connection with this case endowed the movement with substantial cultural cache. The subsequent popularity of Habad Hasidism derived, at least in part, from the perpetuation of its sense of political triumph over its competitors.[12]

Thus, despite its rhetorical commitment to the idea of "gathering its Jews" under a single legal and social rubric, prior to the accession of Nicholas I, the Russian state succumbed to the countervailing needs of policing that made the notion of a Russian-Jewish administrative ingathering practically untenable, even though most Russian Jews already lived in a single territory. The preamble to the new "general" Jewish statute of 1835, already in the works during the last years of the reign of Alexander I but officially passed under his successor, affirmed as much: "With the putting of this statute [of 1804] into practice, *local* difficulties were uncovered, indicating from the very beginning the need for several modifications. In the aftermath of such difficulties, specific needs and occurrences eventually led to the enactment of a variety of particular measures regarding the Jews."[13] Such were the first official inklings of a divide between the designs of St. Petersburg and the "local" realities of bureaucratic administration, a divide that would widen into a chasm during Nicholas's reign. In fact, the more ambitious the plans conceived in high places, the greater the possibility for resistance and ambivalence at the level of their implementation.

Nicholas's departure from the Jewish policy of his predecessors did not, in fact, constitute a profound structural shift. Rather, the break manifested itself as part of the general movement during the last years of Alexander's reign away from an Enlightenment-inspired faith in legislative solutions to the problems of social integration that bedeviled the expanding imperial landscape. This turn reflected a mounting sense of disappointment with so-called constitutional experiments that developed in Russian official circles in the wake of the Napoleonic wars.[14] With respect to the Jewish population, Orthodoxy now rose to the fore as a disciplinary alternative to civic integration; the last years of Alexander I saw the earliest government attempts to evangelize actively among the Jews.[15] At the same time the political faith in the Russian nation-at-arms that became attached to the cultural memory of 1812 dovetailed with Alexander's personal interest in the use of the military as a school of citizenship, specifically the plan, first contemplated in 1810, to transform state peasants into a stable hereditary caste of soldier-farmers.[16]

During the last years of the reign of Alexander I, the notion that the army could function as an experimental school of citizenship for Russia's enserfed rural population gave rise to the creation of a network of military settlements — cantons — composed of state peasants and their families, living on individual homesteads. All male children were classified as "military cantonists" and legally became the property of their fathers' regiment. From the age of eight military cantonists were required to undergo military training in the special schools created for them in each district. Many of the military settlements would be dismantled following the settlers' revolt in 1831, but the regimental schools would continue to function as the institutional foundation for Nicholas's reformed cantonist battalions.

Under Nicholas I, the idea of combining military and confessional discipline to foster obedience and uniformity among the lower orders developed into a principle of social policy.[17] Partly in response to the 1831 revolts that discredited the original function of military settlements as a model of peasant life, Nicholas substantially expanded their disciplinary function.[18] Five newly established educational brigades — composed of seventeen battalions, nine half-battalions, and two companies — came under the control of special commanders who reported directly to the newly created Department of Military Settlements that, in turn, took its orders from the minister of war and the tsar himself. The enrollment age was raised from eight to twelve; more important, in addition to educating the children of soldiers, cantonist battalions now became the repository of vagrants, orphans, youthful criminals, as well as children of populations deemed subversive or suspicious by the Russian state. In the aftermath of the Polish rebellion of 1831, this last category, consisting initially of gypsies and Old Believers, would also come to include the male offspring of Polish nobility. And, as of the passage of the conscription decree of 1827, cantonist battalions would also be used as a mechanism for missionizing among Jewish minors drafted into cantonist battalions.

Under Alexander I, children of military settlers — cantonists — went into the army because of their fathers; under his successor, children often entered cantonist ranks because they were marked fatherless.[19] Acting in loco parentis, the state promoted the idea that the military could be the site of an effective rebirth into the bosom of the imperial family; freed from his own problematic parentage, the cantonist would become a stepchild of the tsar. At the start, the social and political function of military settlements actually reified the link between traditional peasant patriarchy and the well-ordered police state. A Russian play, written by the minor dramatist Nikolai Il'in (1770–1823), and presented at the tsar's own theater on 13 November 1803 idealized the symbiosis between the patriarchal authority of the commune and the political power of the state explicitly by reference to conscription.[20] This pastoral drama, ostensibly drawn directly from the life of the folk, thematizes the endless capacity of the Russian peasant for service and sacrifice. The benevolent peasant elder Abram Makarov speaks in the voice of autocratic authority and hands down to the rank and file a courtly code of honorable conduct in war. Here are his parting words to his son, Ippolit, about to be conscripted. Note the author's anxiety about potential plots hatched in the ranks; patriarchal forbearance here not only supports the authority of the state but inoculates the peasant-warrior against political resistance to injustice.

> Should you happen to be in battle, do not retreat. Better to leave the battlefield without an arm than to wander the whole of your life without your good name to the shame of your family. But should the enemy ask for mercy, dare not touch him [. . .] And here is another order [Rus. *prikaz*] for you. I have heard from old soldiers that in time of war some conspire against wicked officers. Dare not enter into any such conspiracy. Tell your commander the truth bravely, but do not plot against his life. To kill in stealth is the business of the highwayman, but to tell truth to wickedness is to keep one's own soul. But for a good commander, do not spare yourself. You shall save not only him but a thousand others. A good commander lights the way like the moon in the sky; in his light, all the little stars shine, too.[21]

The sentimental view of peasant life in Il'in's conservative fantasy echoed the ideology of state which informed the creation of military colonies; but all sentimentality evaporated in the wake of the colonists' revolt in 1831. Il'in apparently had every reason to be nervous about political subversion in the ranks. Serf culture did not, as Il'in's strenuous efforts to assert the contrary intimated, make for more obedient soldiers. Partly in response to the events of 1831 — not to mention the more dangerous Decembrist precedent of 1825 where the high command actively marshaled the lower ranks against the state — Nicholas's government would directly assume the authority that Alexander I had been willing to delegate to peasant-soldiers in his attempt to rear a new generation of dutiful citizen-subjects.

Nicholas's cantonist system, in contrast to Il'in's ideal of the happy merger between family, community, and state, actively disrupted the system of unquestioned paternal obedience on which communal authority, not just among the peasants but among all of Russia's various social and confessional groups, explicitly albeit imperfectly relied. This was especially true with regard to Jewish cantonists who were, as a rule, expected to abjure the faith of their fathers and embrace the regnant faith of their fatherland.[22] The contradiction between the state's reliance on Jewish patriarchy, familial and communal, to produce recruits for its army and its desire to turn those recruits fatherless in the process was not lost on the tsar's Jewish subjects. In a petition addressed to Count Chernyshev, the tsar's minister of war, thirteen Jewish householders from the district of Vitebsk whose sons were drafted into cantonist battalions in 1851 registered not only their anxiety about the spiritual fate of their offspring but also their understanding of the basic link between filial and political allegiances which informed the effective exercise of social control in the empire:

> Before the party of Jewish recruits departed [. . .] each of us, fathers, made sure to supply his son with everything that Jewish law requires for participating in prayer services and other rites. Blessing our sons to have a good journey, we were entirely confident that our children, when they found themselves in the service of the sovereign, provided with the appropriate parental injunction to uphold firmly the rules of their inherited (Rus. *prirodnaia*, lit. natural) religion, would always remain useful soldiers, since faith is the basis for loyalty to the government.[23]

Just as the creation of military settlements implied their model character for the future transformation of all serfs into agricultural-military servitors, so, too, did the fate of various marginal groups who came together in the barracks of cantonist battalions become exemplary of the pedagogic function of the state. Military service was meant to redeem not only the Jewish cantonists themselves but also to foster an all-embracing vision of effective Jewish integration. Yet, even as the project promoted the notion that Jewish individuality would be dissolved in the vast Russian sea of the imperial army, the administration of the conscription decree, left to individual Jewish communities, exacerbated Jewish difference and fractured Jewish life as never before.[24]

For the recruits themselves, army life often served a similarly contradictory purpose. While it is true that a common military experience transcended existing confessional and social boundaries, this experience could also serve the expression of Jewish individuality, fostering the recruit's sense of apartness from both his fellow Russian soldiers and his former co-religionists—the last thing the tsarist administration wanted. To be sure, the military was the largest and most powerful institution of imperial socialization. Twenty-five years of service certainly helped to efface markers of native ties that differentiated Russian peasants from one another; speech, manner, custom, and all sorts of regional peculiarities gave way to a sense of exclusive belonging to the military estate which had cultural and social peculiarities all its own.[25] This, in large measure, happened through the experience of acculturating into the norms of military society. It was not a goal actively pursued by the high command. But the prevalent model of an unself-conscious erosion of serf identity in the ranks did not sit well with conversion. Conversion demanded not merely forgetting one's past but also the self-conscious, volitional displacement of that past in favor of new memories. Regardless of the extent of collective pressure implicit in the military regimentation of belief, conversion, as defined by the Orthodox Synod (the authoritative governing body of the Russian church) in response to the inquiries of the DMS and to the increasing dismay of military authorities charged with the task of converting Jewish recruits, required active and voluntary consent on the part of the new Christian.

Indeed, the conversion option could also serve to heighten Jewish self-awareness, because it placed Jewish children who accepted the fact of their Jewishness as natural into a position to grapple, perhaps for the first time, with the unsettling idea that confessional identity could be a matter of choice. Thus, in resisting the state's effort to convert them, Jewish cantonists became not merely Russians but Russian *Jews*, initiated into their religion not by their elders but, effectively, by their regimental commanders. The results of this self-realization, often measured in the course of years, were ambivalent in the extreme. As we shall see, the Russian military fostered an acute awareness of Jewish individuality at the expense of both the tsarist vision of Jewish difference erased in the ranks and Jewish communal authority derived from the tsarist regime which itself supported Jewish confessional discipline.

The tension between stated ends and unexpected consequences brings us back to the bureaucratic narrative which duly records a gradual attenuation of the tsar's original program of sweeping social transformation through military discipline and its displacement by the idea of individual integration into the body politic through education. The critical shift occurred in the 1840s and 1850s, when the bureaucratic commitment to Jewish conversion in the ranks began to crack under the weight of its own contradictory character; commanders and cantonists alike proved increasingly willing to challenge both the role of the military in the process of Jewish conversion and the effects of that process on the converts themselves. In the last years of Nicholas's reign, the bureaucratic investment in Jewish conversion became secondary to a general reform of military training for the lower orders.[26] In fact, the concomitant rise in the importance of education began to displace the crucial link between military discipline and conversion. Starting in 1849, the DMS requested and received regular reports from regimental commanders of cantonist battalions regarding the "educational and moral progress" of underage recruits.[27] According to these detailed cantonist report cards, the general curriculum included not only military drill but also basic literacy and numeracy, drawing, geography, cartography, sometimes Russian history and military law, as well as a wide variety of crafts such as carpentry, metallurgy, veterinary, bookbinding, sewing, and cobbling. Commanders noted carefully how many Jewish recruits had been excused from the generally mandatory lesson in Orthodox catechism (Rus. *zakon bozhii*). Given the programmatic emphasis on conversion, the numbers of officially recognized Jewish abstainers are striking, all the more so, since the DMS always made strenuous efforts to underplay the number of "unconverted Jews" in cantonist ranks. As late as 1854, the cantonist battalion attached to the Third Regiment stationed in New Russia had 295 "unconverted Jews" out of a total of 1,263 cantonists who did not attend catechism class; in the Orenburg battalion of military cantonists, 171 did not do so, and in the Saratov battalion, 95 likewise did not.[28] In the much smaller and selective St. Petersburg battalion, 15 Jewish cantonists, along with 35 Catholics, 33 Lutherans, and 1 Muslim, all being trained to serve as military musicians, were not required to attend catechism class.[29] This sort of recordkeeping, alongside the reports of the number of conversions which the DMS dutifully collected and sent back to the tsar, shows that the department's educational program actually competed with the stated goal of drafting Jewish minors. Ironically the far more expensive pedagogical experiment helped to undo the DMS no less than the social and political costs of the conversion program.

Not coincidentally, the same decade (the 1840s) that saw the military turn to education as a vehicle of imperial integration also witnessed the institutionalization of "official enlightenment" of the Jews. Promulgated by Nicholas's energetic minister of national enlightenment, S. S. Uvarov, the program established a network of government-sponsored schools where secular subjects were taught alongside a reformed Jewish curriculum as well as two rabbinical seminaries, in Vilna and in Zhitomir. In addition, Uvarov's ministry extended personal patronage to reform-minded Jewish activists, attempted to pass a series of measures against traditional Jewish customs that both the government and Jewish reformers associated with backwardness, and encouraged Jewish productivization through resettlement in specially created agricultural colonies in the southern provinces of the Pale. All these measures involved the active participation and support of an enlightened Russian-Jewish elite committed to the ideals of the Haskalah, newly empowered by the state and armed with unprecedented access to the Jewish community as an object of their own re-vision.[30] Like Jewish cantonists, Jewish enlighteners remained acutely self-conscious about the role the state played in their lives; the latter, like the former, associated their sense of Jewish difference — from the established Jewish order, largely hostile to their efforts at reform — with the Russian state. Unlike the cantonists, however, Jewish enlighteners actively promoted the Nicholaevan reformation of Russian Jewry, the same disciplinary ideal which had originally inspired the conscription of Jewish children and which, a little more than a decade later, had brought "official enlightenment" into being.

Nicholas's policies nurtured hopes for the success of the Haskalah on an unprecedented scale; in the nineteenth century Russian Jews comprised the largest Jewish population in the world. From the perspective of the maskilim, a small and frequently embattled minority, the possibilities of success seemed nothing short of miraculous, even messianic. In a letter to a fellow member of the Nicholaevan maskilic fraternity, the Vilna enlightener S. J. Fuenn (1818–1890) wrote, in 1840, that "the benevolent emperor" would heal the wounds and end the tribulations of the Jewish people: "Now our master, the emperor, has taken upon himself to be the tiller of our soil, to uproot from it all rank and bitter weeds, to cleanse the hearts of the Jewish people of all evil schemes and to sprinkle blessed dew upon thirsting, yearning soil."[31] Fuenn's aggressive rhetoric evinces the profound sense of identification with state power that served to mobilize Jewish maskilim during the Nicholaevan reign. In the 1840s the image of Nicholas I dominated the intellectual landscape of the Jewish Enlightenment; the abortive legacy of "official enlightenment" continued to haunt Russian-Jewish reformers throughout the era of selective integration which saw the disengagement of the government from the project of making Russian Jewry. The divorce of the Haskalah from the state in the post-Nicholaevan era helps to explain why the first cohort of maskilim who witnessed the realities of Jewish conscription personally produced virtually no conscription literature, protest or otherwise, whereas every subsequent generation continually returned to the theme.

During the Crimean War, the inadequacy of the Nicholaevan army against French and British forces plainly in evidence, it became clear that the cantonist regime had failed to live up to its political promise. Owing in part to the latest expansion of its pedagogic function, it had also grown prohibitively expensive. Even before the death of Nicholas I, the Department of Military

Settlements was preoccupied with dismantling its own administration. In 1856 Alexander II formally abolished the cantonist battalions, initiating the process of the formal reassessment of the social role and administrative structure of the Russian military that culminated in the introduction of universal conscription in 1874. Moving away altogether from the vision which had informed the Nicholaevan project of making Russian Jewry, the so-called tsar-liberator instead turned to the programmatic encouragement of Russian-Jewish difference. At once capitalizing on and fostering the ever-widening gaps within Russian-Jewish life, the state embraced a program of emancipation, more consistent with Catherine's original legislative aim of integrating individual Russian Jews into the existing estate structure than with the Nicholaevan vision of reforming Russian Jewry as a whole. Selective integration made the release of Jewish persons from Jewish communal discipline contingent upon education, money, or service, promoting their effective departure — both geographic and cultural — from the Pale. In fact, the state's turn toward the liberation of Russian Jews at the expense of Russian Jewry during the reign of Alexander II derived its impetus precisely from the tension between the letter of autocratic fiat and the spirit of bureaucratic compromise that first manifested itself in Nicholaevan chancelleries.[32] In the late imperial period it would be left to Jewish enlighteners, heirs to Nicholas's uncompromising social vision of comprehensive Jewish reform if not to his Orthodox zeal, to seek a Russian Jewry where the government had found its first Russian Jews.

"WITH ALL DUE MEEKNESS"

In December 1843 Major Titkov, the commander of the Revel (now Tallinn, Estonia) half-battalion of military cantonists wrote an aggrieved letter to the DMS. Titkov complained that, despite the best efforts of the company priest Ioann Golubov to follow military orders requiring regimental clergy to "sway cantonists of the Jewish faith to convert to Orthodoxy with all due meekness and gentle persuasion," all such attempts were in vain and, what was more, were destined to remain so.[33] Titkov pointed to a fundamental contradiction between the conversionary mission entrusted to him and military protocol which required that all recruits, including Jews, be allowed to "fulfill the rites of their religion" unimpeded. The DMS responded in characteristically convoluted language that there was no conflict of interest between permitting Jewish servicemen to celebrate the Sabbath and other Jewish holidays while zealously pursuing "without force" the conversion of as many Jewish cantonists as possible. The DMS instructed Titkov that military protocol applied exclusively to adult soldiers from whose company underage Jewish recruits should be carefully isolated.[34] Acting under the impact of a recent case, the DMS affirmed the importance of peer pressure in the successful conversion of Jewish cantonists. That same year a remarkable 571 Jewish cantonists converted to Orthodoxy in the Voronezh battalion, under the impact of the conversion of one Yudko Shtemberg, "gifted with extraordinary mental abilities and a clear grasp of Jewish law, and enjoying great respect among all the other Jewish recruits."[35] Of course, this case also implied the alternative: the very same peer pressure could have had the opposite effect and move Jewish recruits to affirm collectively the faith of their fathers. Such ambiguities continued to frustrate the goals of the conversion program.

Thus, although the DMS addressed Titkov's specific concerns, the bureaucracy failed to confront the tensions within the conversion policy to which his criticism alluded. While the conversion program directed at Jewish cantonists implied that it was the duty of every officer to work toward the eradication of Judaism in Russian Orthodox ranks, army policy also required the very same military commanders to use the resources of military discipline to safeguard the Judaism of adult recruits. In one particularly striking case, also dating from the 1840s, the DMS demoted to the rank of private one Second Lieutenant Efremov who, declaring himself "the destroyer of the yids" (Rus. *istrebitel' zhidov*), caused a series of disturbances during High Holiday worship in his regiment.[36] The DMS took a dim view of such local "initiatives" and punished the lieutenant for "insubordination."[37] Fearing that Efremov's religious fervor would inspire others to similar violations of the military code, the DMS reissued its order that all Jewish soldiers were to be allowed either to conduct holiday celebrations in the barracks or be given special leave to do so with their co-religionists in nearby Jewish communities.[38]

The DMS not only punished the physical excesses of Efremov but resisted the slightest hint of rhetorical violence against Judaism. In 1854 Lieutenant-Colonel Desimon of the Kiev battalion of military cantonists interceded on behalf of the local archdeacon, Efim Remizov, who had written a work which he hoped might be adapted by the DMS as part of its conversion program. The DMS sent an extract of Remizov's composition for review to the St. Petersburg Ecclesiastical Academy, attached to the Holy Synod, and the response was less than enthusiastic. The Synod noted dryly that the author's "arguments," which focused mostly on the alleged uses of Christian blood in Jewish ritual, were not only "unclear" but also "unconvincing" in their blatant bias against the Jewish religion.[39] At the heart of both the Efremov case and the rejection of Remizov's book lay the problem of trying to instill the spirit of evangelical Christianity in military personnel without violating the letter of military law. Sometimes this ambiguity resulted in the creation of more new Christians, some more reluctant than others; but it could also lead, with unexpected consequences, to the official recognition of the tsar's Jewish stepchildren as fully constituent members of the multi-confessional imperial family. Instead of instilling in Jewish recruits the humility proper to a Russian soldier, Orthodoxy itself proved a powerful tool of subversion in the ranks.

From the initial implementation of the Jewish conscription decree in 1827, Nicholas I took an active interest in the fate of underage Jewish recruits. Even though the wording of the decree made no principled distinction between drafting Jewish adults and Jewish minors, in ministerial correspondence, the tsar affirmed his preference for the latter as the surest way toward the conversion of Russian Jewry. Before the creation of the DMS in the mid-1830s, all orders related to the disposition of Jewish cantonists went through the tsar's personal chancellery and were cosigned by his adjutant. Following the formation of the DMS, Nicholas personally requested that the department issue monthly reports on the success of his mission to the Jewish cantonists and apprise him directly on the numbers of converts in each regiment.

Nicholas remained intimately concerned with the fate of Jewish cantonists. In 1831 he penciled in the proposed destination of 2,558 Jewish minors, expected in the upcoming ninety-seventh levy.[40] Upon his direct orders, Jewish minors were to be dispatched either to so-called educational brigades, attached to the battalions and half-battalions of military cantonists — a designation which until this point referred exclusively to the male children of soldiers and military colonists who were, in accordance with their membership in the military estate under the auspices of the army — or handed over to be raised in the homes of Russian military settlers. The reported conversion rates in the latter were much higher than in the former.[41] It is not difficult to understand why: despite the evidence of the isolated Shtemberg case, Jewish children as a group proved less vulnerable to proselytizing efforts than individual children living in soldier-peasant households. But Nicholas was uneasy from the start about the prospect of Jewish children living in Christian homes and preferred to rely on the army's own educational facilities. In 1827 the tsar issued a special personal order that underage Jewish recruits were not, under any circumstances, to be quartered in residential apartments either in cities or villages.[42] By 1831 the option of settling Jewish recruits in military colonies was no longer available anyway; following the revolt in the fall of that year, most military settlements were gradually liquidated, their settlers absorbed into the regular draft. The government, both by choice and necessity, expanded the scope of its educational system and created the DMS to administer, under its purview, the growing number of cantonists, a category that now included both children of soldiers and those recruits who were drafted as minors. While most non-Jewish cantonists were children of soldiers who continued to live with their parents or with relatives, Jewish cantonists were sent to special educational battalions, usually attached to regiments stationed in the interior or in the North, far away from areas of dense Jewish settlement. By October 1853 the DMS counted under its jurisdiction 307,529 Christian cantonists living with parents or relatives and 35,669 cantonists—2,557 Jewish and 4,510 newly converted—enrolled in special cantonist regiments and other military educational institutions for the lower ranks.[43] The stark disparity here reflects the impact of economic reality on the decisions of the DMS. It was much cheaper for the army to quarter cantonists in private homes; most cantonists were, in fact, children of soldiers and lived where their fathers were stationed. Jewish cantonists always served far away from home. A small number of those who converted may have eventually been adopted by Christian families. Barracks, built and maintained at the direct expense of the DMS, housed the minority that, for ideological or practical reasons, could not be quartered with relatives or in hospitable Christian families.

In a set of special instructions drafted in 1830, the minister of war placed responsibility for the conversion of Jewish minors exclusively with regimental priests, who were supposed to appeal to the individual sensibilities of Jewish cantonists, rewarding and celebrating each successful conversion as an act of military valor. The minister advised that even if the convert chose a Christian denomination other than Orthodoxy, he was to be initiated into his new faith in public, with great pomp, preferably on a Sunday or on a name day of a saint or a member of the royal family.[44] The splendor of the occasion not only obscured dismally low conversion rates but implicitly heightened the visibility of Jewishness which army life was meant to efface. In the summer of that year, the commander of the Kazan battalion of military cantonists reported on the initiation of a group of recent converts into the holy sacrament of communion by the archbishop himself at the Kazan Cathedral of Annunciation on the anniversary of the crowning of His Imperial Majesty. The list of godparents and sponsors of the new Christians reads like a who's who of Russian provincial society: the city governor and state counselor (Rus. *statskii sovetnik*) Zhevano, Baroness Pirkh, retired chamberlain Musin-Pushkin, the wife of the vice-governor Filipov, Major-General Bulygin, the wife of Professor Leontovsky, the chief of police Lieutenant-Colonel Stan, the chairman of the municipal chamber of deputies Rudanovsky, collegiate assessor (Rus. *kollezhskii assessor*) Kirilov, a nobleman named Osokhin, the district magistrate Sontsov, Count Apraksin, and other local notables. Virtually the entire urban elite devoted itself to the conversion of twenty Jewish minors.[45] Altogether this regiment registered 105 conversions out of a total of 623 Jewish recruits, an uncharacteristically *high* rate; in the same year, other regiments registered as few as 1 out of 584, 5 out of 272, and 12 out of 201.[46]

To improve on these low numbers, the DMS undertook measures at once to untie the hands of regimental priests to baptize Jewish recruits without asking in each and every case for the permission of Synod authorities.[47] The bureaucracy was quick to recognize that the success of the conversion program depended less on ceremony and more on the effectiveness of integrating it into the existing system of military discipline. Despite the minister's emphasis on the public recognition of the individual recruit, the bureaucracy sought to transform conversion from an *extraordinary* act of personal piety, an event in the life of the convert, the regiment, and Russian society, into a *regular* feature of military indoctrination. The tsar himself, bound to the ideal of converting cantonists "with all due meekness," strenuously resisted the one measure that would have led to the possibility of mass baptism in the ranks; despite all the lobbying of the DMS, Nicholas I refused to issue an order that would permit regimental priests to baptize Jewish recruits on their own authority. As late as 1853, commanders were still requesting in specific cases that regimental priests forego having to ask permission from the episcopate before baptizing Jewish recruits.[48]

The business of conversion continued to be plagued by the tension between military discipline and the element of personal choice introduced into the process by the tsar himself. Nothing confirmed this tension more powerfully than the dubious practice of inducing Jewish minors to convert by offering them monetary incentives. In September 1829 the tsar's own chancellery issued an ukase which would plague the cost-conscious officials of the DMS for the rest of Nicholas's reign: the emperor ordered that every Jewish recruit who exhibited an inclination toward baptism would be given twenty-five rubles.[49] Despite the flood of requests for money for the noble purpose of converting Jews that inundated the DMS between 1837 and 1856, the numbers of new Christians did not seem to justify the expense; in addition, even though the lash-and-cash method produced results, the tsar himself remained ambivalent about such inducements and continued to stress the importance of effective religious persuasion. By 1843 Nicholas acknowledged that the realities of Jewish conversion in the ranks failed to live up to his ideal. In April of that year he instructed the minister of war to write to the DMS asking again to be kept informed monthly about the numbers of Jewish cantonists converting in each regiment.[50] The DMS responded immediately with a report regarding the conversion rates for January 1843. That month a total of 93 out of 4,702 Jewish recruits had converted; conversion rates, as reported by the DMS, remained extremely uneven, varying between 3.5 percent for 1842–1843 to 65 percent for 1854.[51] Moved by the twin incentives of lash and cash, some 30–40 percent of the roughly 50,000 Jewish cantonists drafted into Nicholas's army converted in the ranks.[52] The results of the conversion program thus fell far short of the tsar's stated goal of converting every Jewish cantonist "with all due meekness."

Apprised of the initial problems attending conversion, the tsar noted on the 1843 report that the time had come to "set about converting them [Jewish cantonists] to Christianity through the efforts of reliable priests, supplementing each regiment with additional priests if necessary, and ordering for that purpose a set of special instructions from the Synod."[53] At the same time the head of the DMS, Baron Korf, informed Chernyshev, that he himself had received personal instructions from the tsar regarding the means by which this laudable goal was to be attained:

> [In] the matter of inclining toward Orthodoxy the Jews enrolled in the battalions of military cantonists, special care ought to be taken, all actions pursued with the utmost caution and mildness without the slightest hint of compulsion. Before appointing priests to this task, the Ober-Procurator of the Synod should be consulted.[54]

This kind of formulation, while fully consistent with Christian principles, flew in the face of both rigid military protocol and military discipline; the former required perfect obedience and the latter depended almost entirely on the threat of corporal punishment. The Nicholaevan army proved inhospitable to the art of gentle persuasion. Furthermore, the practice of offering bribes to perspective converts now bore some unsavory fruit.

The discrepancy between low conversion figures and the barrage of requests for reward money raised not a few eyebrows among the personnel of the DMS. The investigation of a number of particularly egregious cases led to the conclusion that many of the requests were based on the fraudulent reports of conversions that did not, in fact, take place. Officers were simply pocketing the money themselves.[55] By this point the DMS had to contend not only with the unconscionable behavior of such dishonest and dishonorable commanders but also with conscientious objectors like Titkov. More disturbingly still, by the 1850s Jewish cantonists themselves had grown increasingly bold in accusing their superiors of using force to compel their conversion. Thus, even as the institutional ground beneath the conversion program began to totter, Jewish cantonists were coming of age as a small but self-conscious and assertive constituency within the Russian military system. The internal crisis spelled both the demise of the cantonist regime *and* the birth of the tsar's Jewish stepchildren, at once victims and beneficiaries of the Nicholaevan experiment in social engineering.

STEPCHILDREN OF THE TSAR

In the 1850s the DMS confronted two cases of complaints brought by Jewish cantonists against their regimental command. In both instances the recruits alleged that their conversions had been forced upon them. Although in neither case did the DMS take the side of the recruits against their superiors—which would have been tantamount to a violation of the army's strict principle of subordination—the outcome was nonetheless ambiguous. DMS correspondence reveals that the charges of the cantonists put the bureaucracy on the defensive and forced the administration into the position of having to consider the merits of the cantonist regime as a whole.

Plausible enough to merit a serious investigation, the accusations directly contributed to discrediting the idea of using the imperial army to create a Russian Jewry by autocratic fiat. In the reforming reign of Alexander II, the bureaucracy would rewrite the Nicholaevan narrative of radical integration and promote instead the political gradualism of individual emancipation.

In March 1849 Chernyshev dispatched Colonel Lubianovskii, chief adjutant to the general in charge of the tsar's personal headquarters, to the city of Perm to look into a series of complaints filed by five Jewish cantonists against their company commander.[56] The recruits claimed not only that their own conversions had been forced but that, in fact, the recourse to physical force to get Jewish cantonists to convert was a persistent and regular feature of life in the barracks. To the distress of the DMS, what had begun with five malcontents from the Perm battalion had spread through cantonist ranks into the Kazan battalion, notable for containing the second largest population of Jewish cantonists (only the Voronezh battalion had more). By the conclusion of the investigation in February 1851, not 5 but 110 converted Jewish cantonists from both Perm and Kazan were alleging the improper use of force in their conversion.

Lubianovskii reported that the claims of the five "instigators" were entirely without foundation. The minister of war accepted his conclusion without demur and ordered that the original troublemakers be immediately transferred into penal regiments where their observance of all the rites of the Christian religion "which they accepted voluntarily" would be carefully monitored. At the same time the minister of war warned the DMS that "in order to preclude in the future any possible cause for such complaints, the measures used in the conversion of Jewish cantonists to Christianity must not include any form of compulsion which violates the spirit of Christian teaching." Moreover, wrote the minister, Jewish recruits must be given sufficient time to consider the gravity of their decision so that there would be no chance of eventual backsliding.

The tension between the actual disposition of the case and the directive the minister issued to the DMS reveals that the high command took such complaints seriously both because they threatened military discipline and potentially undermined "the spirit of Christian teaching." After twenty-five years of converting Jewish cantonists, the DMS still had not found a way to deal with the potential contradictions between the former and the latter. And now Jewish recruits themselves had begun to feel sufficiently empowered by the "spirit of Christian teaching" to assert its principles of "meekness" against army protocol. Christianity, in effect, had made these recruits fully aware of their Jewish condition. The consequences of this blurring of confessional boundaries would be fully borne out in another, still more problematic instance of cantonists alleging the use of force in their conversions.

One of the last cases handled by the DMS before it was finally dismantled in 1856 was the investigation of a complaint waged by ninety-two formerly

Jewish sailors, stationed with the imperial fleet in Kronstadt, who, as cantonists attached to the Archangel'sk regiment, had been converted to Orthodoxy by force.[57] As a result, they categorically refused to consider themselves
Christian and petitioned the naval ministry to be allowed to return to Judaism officially so that they could practice the rites of their religion alongside
other Jewish sailors in Kronstadt who had entered the army as adults. Here,
the former cantonists not only vigorously pursued the blatant discrepancy
between the active toleration of Judaism in the ranks and the army's conversionary program but implied that the Christian principles of that program
now made their return to Judaism necessary and just. According to the
witnesses interviewed in the case, the commander of the Arkhangel'sk cantonist battalion had systematically violated the tenets of Orthodoxy and
direct military orders, coercing Jewish cantonists to convert and in one case
driving a boy almost to the point of suicide. The cantonists showed a remarkable tenacity and presence of mind in their determination to retain their
Jewish faith. They affirmed that, on their way to Arkhangel'sk, they had
already heard that officers in cantonist battalions "take away prayer books
and other ritual objects, and for this reason they had buried these things in
the ground just before reaching Arkhangel'sk. Afterward, on their way to St.
Petersburg to join the imperial fleet, they retrieved them and took them
along" presumably expecting to reclaim their Jewish faith as adults.[58] Their
conversion thus appeared to be entirely instrumental, exposing the folly of
the original lash-or-cash method that lured cantonists to the font either with
the threat of a beating or the promise of money. In this case at least, this
method made for Christians who now publicly identified themselves as Jews.
The army had no institutional means to deal with such discrepancies.

The Kronstadt case made the DMS even more uncomfortable than its
predecessor in Perm and Kazan. The unaccountable behavior of the Jewish
sailors and their willingness to make their commitment to their former faith
a matter of record revealed the possibility that religious identity could defy
any form of established institutional, even strictly confessional, discipline —
a fact that Jewish communities, riven by the conflict between Hasidism and
its opponents, exemplified only too well. Unwilling to tolerate the show of
insubordination and set an official precedent for accepting the word of a
private over that of his commanding officer, the ministry once again equivo-
cated, instructing that the "instigators" of the complaint be severely punished with military prison terms and forbidding converted recruits from
practicing Judaism in secret. However, General Vrangel', personal adjutant
to the minister of the navy, Grand Duke and Admiral-General Constantine
Nikolayevich (the brother of Nicholas I and the heir's uncle), sent out to
investigate the matter, conveyed in the strongest possible terms the dis-
pleasure of the high command that the DMS still had not taken sufficient
precautions against such charges being brought. In the future, warned
Vrangel', all military commanders who would presume to violate the express

provision of the emperor to convert Jewish cantonists using only methods of mild verbal persuasion would be prosecuted by military tribunal and punished to the fullest extent of the law.

Speaking on behalf of the navy, the branch of the Russian military most invested at the highest levels of command, in the project of reforming the Nicholaevan system, Vrangel' effectively rang the death knell of the DMS.[59] Indeed, by this time — July 1856 — Vrangel' knew that no more cantonists would be drafted, that the DMS was on its way to being dismantled, and that the entire conversion program would be quietly dropped; at the end of August the tsar issued a manifesto abolishing the conscription of minors altogether. All underage recruits presently under the jurisdiction of the DMS were to be sent home to their parents. Although this case surely helped to seal the fate of the conversion program, the military establishment never took a stand, one way or another, on its own signal contribution to complicating the relationship between baptism as a political rite of passage into Russian society and its significance in the spiritual life of the believer. In fact, until 1865 the military persisted in rewarding conversions in the ranks as if they constituted acts of military valor. By this point the fate of converted Jewish cantonists had become a matter of public debate about the status of Russian Jews in the law. As shall become clear, the bureaucratic struggle over the claim of forced conversion as a basis for reverting to one's former faith impinged directly on the social effects of the contradiction, going all the way back to the partition period, between the formal juridical independence of the individual Jew and his confessional status as a member of the Jewish collective.

The case of the cantonists showed that, as long as conversion to Orthodoxy constituted a kind of political sacrament which conferred the privileges of citizenship, its juridical effects could not be undone even if the conversion could be abjured upon well-established theological grounds, that is, because it was the result of compulsion. Indeed, until "The Law on Religious Toleration" of 1905 active apostasy from the regnant faith constituted a political crime.[60] Therefore the cantonist who desired as an adult to return to Judaism on the basis of a legitimate claim of force, remained a Christian in the law even if he still considered himself a Jew. This position effectively segregated him from both his former co-religionists and his fellow Orthodox Christians. Worse still from the perspective of the state, Russia's first Jewish Christians lived not on the margins of a less-than-neutral society but in the military, the institutional heart of the autocracy. For Jewish reformers of the post-Nicholaevan era, their predicament dramatized the highly unstable relationship between the Russian Jew, treated by the state as an autonomous member of his estate where his religion presumably remained a private matter of conscience, and Russian Jewry, a confessional body with ambiguous legal standing and continually eroding, if still formally recognized, disciplinary powers over its members.

The life story of the cantonist Itskovich, one of the sailors who served in the Arkhangel'sk battalion between 1853 and 1857 demonstrates the extent to which the state both empowered and constrained the expression of Jewish individuality not merely as a theoretical legal possibility but in actual administrative practice.[61] Itskovich had been converted in the ranks shortly after being kidnapped and drafted; according to his mother's subsequent testimony, he was only seven at the time.[62] His attempt, as an adult, to resolve through legal means the conflict between his public status as a Christian and his private desire to remain a Jew spoke to the absence of a secular legal sphere in which Jewishness could be disengaged from the dual jurisdiction of confession and estate in which it had been embedded since the partition period. The resolution of the Arkhangel'sk case left Itskovich profoundly disappointed because it only deepened the gulf between his formal confession and the reality of his life as a new Christian, a commitment he apparently took seriously, at least at first. What he could not bear, he says, were the continuing insults of his fellow soldiers, members of his new regimental "family" who accused him of converting for material gain, invoking the proverb: "A baptized yid is a wolf who's been fed" (Rus. *zhid kreshchennyi — volk kormlennyi*). No less than Jewish recruits, Christian soldiers sensed the moral ambiguities involved in the army's lash-or-cash system of religious persuasion; whether his own self-doubt reflected or inspired such taunts, Itskovich leaves unclear. Unable to bear the contradiction, Itskovich "swore to himself to secure justice and, without fear of legal consequences or retribution, to restore to himself the right to live as a Jew."[63]

In 1860 Itskovich entered into regular ranks as a scribe, moved to a regiment stationed in Moscow where he was soon promoted to officer rank; along with two other formerly Jewish officers whom he considered his "brothers," he served in his new company for ten years. In 1872, just before he was to be discharged from the army, Itskovich transferred to Tomsk, in Western Siberia; upon his arrival he informed his military superiors by letter that he no longer wished to be considered a Christian, since, as he termed it, he had been "turned into one" by force.[64] Undeterred by the threat of a military trial, even capital punishment, for his crime of "high treason" — even for civilians, the renunciation of Orthodoxy constituted a serious criminal offence, subject to trial by the state — Itskovich submitted a memorandum to the military governor-general of Tomsk in which he declared that "even though [he] was not who his army record said he was, i.e. that his name was not his own, he had honestly and diligently served the tsar for twenty years." Using the language of property rights, he demanded "that the military authorities return to him that which they had forcibly taken" — his Jewish name (64). After repeated and vain attempts on the part of the regiment priest to convince the newly self-possessed Itskovich — who "smiling, insisted that he was no longer a child of seven but a man of twenty-six" — not to abjure Orthodoxy, the army finally gave up on him. On 23 October 1873 the Tomsk military authorities discharged Itskovich, allowed him to reclaim his Jewish name, and conceded not to take any legal action against his public renunciation of Christianity, even though it was a serious and flagrant violation both of civil and military penal statutes. Handing Itskovich quietly over to the civilian administration, the military sought to evade its responsibility in muddling the religious and social distinctions which gave shape and meaning to the estate structure of Russian life. The singularly confusing legal and confessional status of the cantonist Itskovich was nothing if not the creation of the Nicholaevan regime, dedicated explicitly to effacing all markers of Jewish particularity. Although his autobiography declared that "the scribe of the artillery chancellery, formerly known as Sergeev, Arkhipov, and Beilin" was now living openly "under his own Jewish name — Ilia Isaevich Itskovich," in law he remained an "apostate," a liminal figure, tacitly tolerated by the state but vulnerable any time to prosecution as a renegade Christian.

The social and legal marginality of the cantonist Itskovich thus yielded a peculiar sense of freedom from all forms of institutional discipline, Jewish and Russian. Itskovich's indeterminacy, and that of his fellow stepchildren of the tsar, would become a touchstone in the reconsideration of Jewish legal status during the era of the Great Reforms. In the 1870s the cantonist became a symbol of the estate system which pinioned the Russian Jew between the political paternalism of an Orthodox Russian state and the social despotism of the Jewish community. No one was more sensitive to this dilemma than Ilia Grigorievich Orshanskii (1846–1875), one of Russia's first Jewish lawyers and an outstanding exponent of Western-style juridical individualism.[65] Orshanskii was the first to outline the conflict between state law and social discipline, specific to the context of Russian life, as an instrumental force in shaping Russian-Jewish identity. In his work on the legal condition of Russian Jewry, Orshanskii gave wider political purchase to the questions attending the status of converted cantonists.

In his essays, collected in a posthumously published volume entitled *Russian Law on the Jews,* Orshanskii argued that Russian state law had from the beginning constituted Jewishness as both a confessional and a social category.[66] Although the law assigns to Jews the same civic obligations as their Christian counterparts, on an individual basis, according to their membership within a particular estate category — town dweller, guild merchant, or honorary citizen — Jews fulfill their obligations, consisting principally of taxation and discharge of military duty, collectively, through the "confessional" mediation of the Jewish community, supported and empowered by the state (11–15). Thus, according to Orshanskii, the state effectively creates Russian-Jewish individuals but then subjects them to the legal despotism of the community (Rus. *obshchestvo*) which, like the peasant commune, constitutes a "world" (Rus. *mir,* which also means "commune") of its own

(11). But, unlike the peasant *mir,* the Jewish *obshchestvo* identified with the *kahal* bears a religious character interpreted *against* the Russian "state interest," identified with Orthodoxy. For this reason, the Jewish community, even though maintained by the state, always remains liable to the charge of Jewish conspiracy, a product of legal prejudice; for this same reason the law's recognition of Jewish "exceptions" — individuals who render an extraordinary service to the "state's interest" now identified with the treasury or in more broadly secular terms — implicitly undermine the confessional privileges of Judaism (197). In fact, the only Jewish individual to whom the state grants complete civic equality is a convert to Orthodoxy (6).

The system makes no room for the claims of Jewish individuals who wish to remain Jewish outside the bounds of communal discipline, even though the fact of dual jurisdiction is precisely what makes this kind of social revolt possible. Pitting individuals against the community diminishes respect for the law and makes Jews seeking justifiably to escape the vicious circle of "mutual responsibility" (Rus. *krugovaia poruka*) look like criminals — tax evaders and draft dodgers — in the eyes of the state, inclined to be prejudiced against Jews in the collective. Orshanskii dramatized this impossible condition in a conscription tale called "Story of an Exemption." Deemed too radical for publication during the author's lifetime, "Story of an Exemption" relates the struggle of a young man attempting to establish his rights of residence against a corrupt Jewish *obshchestvo* trying to get him drafted.[67] Orshanskii registers the attempt to *evade* conscription as exemplary, civic-minded behavior, a form of righteous protest against the infernal "deal" (Rus. *sdelka*) for the mutual "gain" of the Jewish community and the Russian state, conspiring together against the rights of those "unfortunate" Russian Jews who are "helpless against the encroachments" of collective discipline.[68] Orshanskii's explicit attack on the venality of Jewish communal leadership implicitly challenged the prerogatives of the autocracy, from which the former derived its coercive power; the polemical image of the Russian state in cahoots with Jewish society directly countered the contemporary Judaeophobic charge of Jewish subversion, embodied in both the alleged Jewish penchant for draft dodging and in the *kahal* as a Jewish cabal.[69]

For Orshanskii, the Jewish victims of Nicholaevan conscription policies emblematized the fate of every Russian Jew. Nicholas's recourse to the military in its attempt to gain converts to the ruling faith reflected, as far as Orshanskii was concerned, the fundamental tension between the secular integration of the Russian Jew into the estate structure of the empire, which presumably required the equitable distribution of responsibilities, and the religious conversion of Russian Jewry, the unspoken object of all tsarist legislation. Orshanskii saw evidence of the "conversionary bias" in every aspect of the Nicholaevan attempt to reform Jewish society, including the fight against traditional Jewish customs — dress, beards, early marriage —

and even the state's investment in "official enlightenment."[70] He argued that the alleged "abuses" of military discipline in the Nicholaevan army, linked to the overzealous pursuit of conversion, did not constitute an aberration of the conversion program but its most logical outcome (24–25). For Orshanskii, Efremov's personal "war against the yids," demonstrated the ramifications of confusing the project of socializing the Jews into the fabric of Russian life through legal institutional means with the evangelical mission of Orthodox Christianity. In fact, Efremov's religious "initiative" on behalf of the regnant faith was a form of Orthodox resistance against the secular prerogatives of the state, here embodied in military protocol that expressly *permitted* Jewish communal worship in the ranks; Efremov found the contradiction between the conversion program and the persistence of collective Jewish visibility unbearable. His defense of the political privileges of Orthodoxy paralleled the "initiative" of baptized cantonists who, in seeking to return to Judaism, undermined the ostensible legal and social transparency of Russia's confessional categories. As a foil for the case of Efremov, Orshanskii discussed the contemporary trial of the cantonist Katsman, as it unfolded on the pages of the *Judicial Herald* (Rus. *Sudebnyi vestnik*), the official journal of the recently reformed Ministry of Justice (49–58).

Private Katsman had been christened during his army service as a cantonist; apparently he had never ceased to practice Judaism in secret, for which he was finally tried. A Moscow district court acquitted him, citing a law of 1862 prohibiting the conversion of minors under the age of fourteen without parental consent. The court further argued that since Katsman never actually accepted the faith into which he had been baptized and observed Jewish law the entire time, he had never really been Orthodox. The Moscow court of appeals overturned the verdict; the judges agreed with the prosecutor that the law of 1862 was not retroactive. Katsman, they said, had indicated his consent to the "sacrament of baptism"; his laxity afterward was no indication to the contrary. Accordingly, he ought to have gone to church regularly and attended catechism class. The court ruled that Katsman be sent back to the church to be "confirmed" in his faith. Until he had done so to the court's satisfaction, his property would be impounded. This rider left Katsman in a kind of legal limbo, a Christian-in-the-making. Noting the inconsistency, the Senate in St. Petersburg eventually overturned the decision of the Moscow court; however, according to Orshanskii's argument against the position taken by the legal correspondent for the *Judicial Herald*, Katsman's personal status remained ambiguous (55). Here is why.

Since Orthodoxy effectively stood for citizenship, baptism conferred upon the believer a form of legal, as well as spiritual, grace. The sacramental effect of this rite, once performed, could not be reversed on the grounds of conscience, even when, as in the case of Katsman, there was sufficient legal basis for doing so. He would have had to reconvert to Judaism which, until the 1905 Law on Religious Toleration, remained prohibited. Converted cantonists, even if they could effectively prove compulsion, were Christians with regard to all issues of civil status even though they, like Katsman, may have considered themselves Jewish. This problematic condition served to segregate them from both Russian and Jewish life. Katsman could not, as a matter of conscience, marry a Christian woman, and the law barred him from marrying a Jewish woman because he was considered to be a Christian. He could not raise his children as Jews or be buried in a Jewish cemetery. The ultimate perversity of Russian law, Orshanskii charged, lay in its patent refusal to take responsibility for its role in the creation of legal outcasts like Katsman. The state continued to treat them as if they were "exceptions" when, in fact, their sense of alienation from the Orthodox state and from collective Jewish life dramatized the legal homelessness of the Jewish individual in imperial Russia caught in an "enchanted circle" of restrictive legislation that liberated him as a person and imprisoned him as a Jew, all in the name of the "state's interest" (152–153).

> It is time for us to grasp [Orshanskii concluded] the simple truth that the Jew has the right to live and to earn a lawful living, regardless of whether his doing so might be useful to the cadets in Polotsk, the military officers in Odessa, the vodka distillers in Kursk, the landowners in Lifland, or anyone else. We repeat: to justify every expansion of Jewish civil rights by reference to a special "interest" of one sort or another means to see the Jews as things and not as individuals, a principle which modern jurisprudence cannot sustain. (236–237)

Orshanskii's comparison between the juridical disembodiment of the converted cantonist and the political disability of the Russian Jew reverberated in the lives of Russian-Jewish intellectuals who found themselves both empowered and oppressed by the autocratic exercise of the "state's interest." Like the cantonists, they saw themselves as stepchildren of the tsar, reared and educated in the name of the Nicholaevan vision of a radically transformed Russian-Jewish society. Like the cantonists, too, they resisted the uncompromising anti-Judaic character of that vision, even as their understanding of Judaism grew progressively distant from the piety of their own co-religionists. Their Jewishness was of their own making, in many ways just as alien to their Jewish fathers as it was to the state that had adopted them. In the case of Orshanskii, the strain of self-conscious subversion, both of Jewish communal power and state authority, in the name of uncompromising Jewish individualism induced a pointed sense of identification with the cantonist as the Russian-Jewish individual par excellence.

Within the discourse of the Russian-Jewish intelligentsia, Orshanskii's radical Jewish individualism proved to be an exception. Where his reform-minded contemporaries wished to see the makings of modern Russian Jewry, Orshanskii saw only Russian Jews, living under the fiat of the autocracy and the petty tyranny of rabbis acting like government bureaucrats; for

him, Jewish communal life and religious culture in imperial Russia functioned exclusively as social hypostases of the "state's interest" in policing its
population (83). Nothing symbolized Orshanskii's lack of investment in the
collective future of Russian Jewry more than his open advocacy of civil
marriage between Jews and non-Jews as the most effective means of integrating the various "tribes" of the empire into a secular *Rechtsstaat* (101–102).
For Jewish reformers, seeking in their own disciplinary vision of Russian
Jewry a viable alternative to the sociopolitical order which Orshanskii dismissed in principle as pernicious to the freedom of the Russian Jew, the
cantonist signified not the impossibility of personal liberation from the
"state's interest" but the possibility of collective redemption from the risks
of emancipation.

MAKING RUSSIAN JEWS

In September 1853 the director of the DMS wrote to the army inspector-
ate regarding the urgent matter of quartering the latest party of thirty-eight
hundred Jewish cantonists: "At present," reported Major-General Danilov,
"there does not appear to be any possibility of placing even half this number
of underage Jewish recruits in the already overcrowded educational facilities designated expressly for this purpose."[71] Contrary to the tsar's personal
order of 1831, said Danilov, they are currently being billeted in villages,
"which results in terrible inconveniences, as far as both the health of the
recruits and their military training are concerned." In view of these difficulties, he suggested tentatively, perhaps the DMS ought not to accept any
more underage Jewish recruits. This extraordinary show of bureaucratic
initiative apparently in tension with the monarch's will went all the way to
the minister of war, Count Dolgorukov. By October — relatively quickly,
given the usual pace of DMS correspondence — Dolgorukov responded with
nothing short of an order directly from the tsar himself that the DMS find a
place for the seven hundred Jewish recruits not yet billeted, adding, moreover, that "in the opinion of His Royal Highness, underage Jewish recruits, if
properly supervised and educated, might in time prove useful in military
service."[72]

In light of the tsar's long-standing interest in the conversion of Jewish
cantonists, this avowal constituted an admission that the purely political —
secular and civic — ideal of rearing "useful" soldiers superseded the state's
evangelical mission to the Jews. By then, of course, it was already apparent
that the immediately available means did not justify such distant ends. Given
the exigent nature of Russia's current military situation — the Crimean War
was raging — the army could not spend its limited funds on training recruits
who would "in time," as adult soldiers, be in a position to prove their usefulness. This, in fact, was just as true with respect to non-Jewish minors being

educated at the expense of the army—more so, in fact, since there were a great many more of them.

The demise of the Nicholaevan conversion program was therefore not the result of the miraculous triumph of Alexandrine liberalism but rather part of the general retrenchment of Russian military resources that took place in the wake of the Crimean debacle. Alexander II himself actively embraced the idea of Jewish "utility" which emerged directly from the inner tension between imperial reach and administrative grasp that shaped the policy of Jewish conscription under his father. The half-hearted admission that, in fact, the "state's interest" might be better served by the "utility" of the Jews than by the conversion of Russian Jewry highlights the historical relationship, obscured in contemporary historiography, between the "transformation of Jewish society" by the government of Nicholas I and the "Jewish encounter with late imperial Russia," initiated by the emancipatory policies of his son.[73]

The secular rhetoric of Jewish "utility," the terms of which obviously vitiated the radically transformative agenda of the conversion program, had, in fact, been available to Russian bureaucrats throughout the Nicholaevan period. Before "selective integration" institutionalized the practice and turned it into a matter of policy, the state regularly set apart its "useful" Jewish subjects from the unregenerate body of Russian Jewry, construed exclusively, it seems, in order to objectify both the urgency of reform and the need for continued residential and occupational restriction.[74] Affirming the potential "usefulness" of Jewish cantonists as a matter of course, Nicholas allowed for the possibility that *all* Russian Jews could be so distinguished, especially "if properly educated." That being the case, the government's investment in the creation of a model Russian Jewry—embodied in both the conversion program and in "official enlightenment"—seemed quite beside the point; Nicholas's remark intimated that, given the incentive and the time, "properly educated" Russian Jews would prove their own usefulness in the ranks or, for that matter, elsewhere.

In fact, the tension between the confessional *project* aimed at reforming Russian Jewry and the social *process* that produced "useful" Russian Jews found expression in the ambiguous results of "official enlightenment," which, like the conversion program, started as the former but ended up encouraging the latter. The student bodies of the two government-sponsored rabbinical seminaries founded in Vilna and Zhitomir in 1847 provide a case in point. Expressly created as training institutions for a modern rabbinate, the seminaries instead functioned more as gateways into Russian institutions of higher learning and out of the Pale of Settlement altogether. Like cantonists, seminary graduates ordained as "crown rabbis" were supposed to represent and anticipate the reformation of Russian Jewry as a whole. Indeed, Uvarov and P. D. Kiselev, the head of the tsar's Jewish Committee, saw the education of a new "clerical estate" as instrumental in the "organization (Rus. *ustroistvo*) of the Jewish people (Rus. *evreiskogo naroda*) in Russia."[75] A new cadre of teachers and religious leaders would presumably emerge from the seminaries to displace the corrupt, and after 1844 formally defunct, *kahal* with the government's own well-ordered vision of Jewish *obshchestvo*. But things did not quite work out as planned: first, despite the ambitious dual curriculum of Jewish and secular studies, "the standard of religious education was low." Graduates failed to "establish their authority" within the Jewish community and had a difficult time securing appointments. Even when they did, their congregants perceived them merely as bureaucrats in the state's employ and continued to engage "spiritual rabbis" for moral and religious guidance.[76] Thus the institution of the "crown rabbinate" instantiated in a different form the same confusing system of dual jurisdiction that it was meant to rectify. Second, because enrollment brought a coveted exemption from conscription and because graduates were eligible to apply to universities, seminaries began to serve as preparatory schools for aspiring Jewish professionals, who, once they received their diplomas, acquired the personal status that enabled the move, both geographic and intellectual, beyond the Pale. Graduates of rabbinical seminaries not only merged into the Russian student society but in many cases became the founders of modern Russian-Jewish culture and politics.[77] Graduates of rabbinical seminaries contributed to the rise of the Jewish "diplomaed" intelligentsia in the era of the Great Reforms; following the decree in November 1861 that granted Jewish university graduates the "rights and privileges of their Gentile counterparts — including unrestricted residence and occupation," they joined the growing stream of Jews flocking to Russian universities.[78] It is significant that such privileges were not extended to graduates of rabbinical seminaries who did not go on to matriculate, another indication of the way the government remained committed to its program of Jewish Enlightenment even while actively encouraging the (individual) enlightenment of the Jews. Here, as in the case of the conversion program, the latter outlasted the former; in 1873 the government transformed the seminaries into pedagogical institutes, claiming that the seminaries had outlived their purpose.[79] Meanwhile, Jewish students continued to flock to Russian institutions of higher learning — and beyond the Pale — in greater and greater numbers.[80] The "transformation of Jewish society" had paved the way toward the "Jewish encounter with late imperial Russia," official enlightenment toward emancipation.

Alexander II substantially expanded the Nicholaevan concept of Jewish "utility." The policy of "selective integration" of Jewish individuals into the Russian estate structure took its cues from a novel idea that emerged at the end of the Nicholaevan reign, the attempt at the "reclassification" (Rus. *razbor*, lit. "selection") of Russian Jews based on their individual "usefulness."[81] First proposed to the tsar by Kiselev in the early 1840s, the idea of selection originally carried a punitive connotation; Jews who failed to register themselves as "useful" guild merchants, licensed artisans, farmers, or townsmen with a permanent occupation would be subject to higher draft quotas and other measures—including forced resettlement—meant to make them so.[82] Because the government lacked both the reliable data on the estate membership of the Jews to implement such a scheme and the resources to administer the program even if such information were available, the idea of the *razbor* was moot in practice, if not in theory.

During the era of the Great Reforms, the notion of "selection" returned as the motive principle behind the policy of "selective integration." The new program explicitly rewarded Jewish individuals for their "usefulness" by a host of privileges, the most important being the freedom to leave the Pale of Settlement. Categories of "useful" Jews now included merchants of the first guild (1859), university graduates (1861), guild-registered artisans, and non-university-trained physicians and medics (1865), veterans (1867), and, finally, all graduates of institutions of higher education, including veterinarians, dentists, pharmacists, and midwives (1879).[83] The policy represented the fullest expression of the state's tendency to privilege Russian Jews at the expense of Russian Jewry. As the government extended the range of categories of personal achievement that rendered individual Jews eligible for "selective integration," a new set of fissures rent the economic and cultural fabric of Jewish society. Jewish life beyond the Pale took on its own characteristic cast; the Jewish elites of St. Petersburg, for instance, both insisted on their own distinctiveness and vied to represent the collective interests of their co-religionists in the western provinces.[84] At the same time the Pale of Settlement, its boundaries eroding from within under the strain of increasing economic pressure, social dislocation, and cultural polyglotism, remained the last, tenuous vestige both of collective oppression and of the pre-reform ideal of a well-ordered Russian Jewry.

Under the impact of selective integration, the ideal of engineering modern Russian Jewry acquired the status of a mythology which continued to exercise Russian-Jewish enlighteners, heirs to the sweeping vision of Nicholas I. Although beneficiaries of his heir's investment in the selective integration of Russian Jews, Russian *maskilim*, more than ever divided by geography, education, class, language, and even politics, derived a sense of collective identity from their joint commitment to complete the abortive Nicholaevan project of remaking Russian Jewry. Throughout the course of the late imperial period, they revisited again and again the troubling pre-reform origins of the *maskilic* desire to discipline an increasingly fractious and fractured Jewish population. Like the Russian bureaucrats who anticipated their efforts, they proved vulnerable to the distance between ideological reach and practical grasp. In the *maskilic* versions of the cantonist tale, first told by Russian bureaucrats, the recruit embodied the aspiration toward Jewish Enlightenment, a polemical thrust against the visible effects of emancipation.

2

GREAT EXPECTATIONS: THE BEGINNINGS OF CANTONIST LITERATURE AND THE EMANCIPATION OF RUSSIAN-JEWISH CONSCIOUSNESS

The singular experiences of Russia's first Jewish soldiers in the army of Nicholas I emblematized the immediate difficulties facing Russia's Jewish enlighteners as they made the transition into the era of the Great Reforms. The distance of former cantonists like Katsman and Itskovich both from Russian civil society and Jewish communities, and their fraught relationship to organized Jewish life and to the military, bespoke simultaneously the promise of state-sponsored programs of social engineering and their heavy social costs. The effects of this tension on the Jewish loyalties of cantonists themselves remained irrelevant to the enlightenment mythology of Nicholaevan conscription that began to accumulate in Russian-Jewish literature in the subsequent reign. The autobiographies of Jewish cantonists exhibited the radical possibility of being Jewish without acting Jewish, and articulated the powerful pull of Jewish self-identification absent Jewish observance and Jewish obedience. In the immediate aftermath of the Great Reforms, Jewish literature about Nicholaevan recruitment first emerged to defy the cultural effect of such historical ambiguities — evident no less in the lives of the reformers themselves than in the lives of the conscripts — to shore up the gap between the increasingly secular concience of the Russian Jew, emancipated by the tsar-liberator, and the confessional ideal of Russian Jewry that informed the policies of his father.

Produced by O. A. Rabinovich (1817–1869), a Russian *maskil* and one of Odessa's first Jewish cultural entrepreneurs, the earliest literary treatment of Jews in the Russian military registered the conflict between the desires of the one and the needs of the many.[1] Rabinovich's own experience of the tension between official enlightenment and personal liberation in the reign of Nicholas I anticipated the unexpected risks of freedom enjoyed and debated by increasing numbers of Russian Jews in the first decade of the Great Reforms. But in his conscription stories, Rabinovich explicitly linked the passing of Nicholaevan *rekrutchina* to a common Russian-Jewish past and turned the figure of the Jewish soldier into a paradigm of collective Jewish renewal in the reign of the tsar-liberator. This chapter explores the tension between this recasting of conscription history as a Jewish story and the personal history of V. N. Nikitin (1839–1908), a converted cantonist whose personal transformation into a Russian writer and public figure was similarly informed by the promise of emancipation.

A small number of Nikitin's fellows eventually emerged as adult authors of their own experiences, their stories collected and published in the journal *The Jewish Heritage* (Rus. *Evreiskaia starina*) during the first decade of the twentieth century.[2] Long before that, however, their literary counterparts, of whom there were a great many more, began to figure as epic heroes of an imagined Russian-Jewish past, star players in the mythology of Russian-Jewish origins, the projection of Jewish enlighteners' desire for social power, cultural prestige, and civil autonomy precisely at moments when the position of the *maskilim* as authors and arbiters of contemporary Jewish mores and tastes would become increasingly contested. Nikitin's reform-era story of the Russian Jew in cantonist ranks, in fact, anticipated the thematization of individual autonomy and historical contingency that informed the writing of cantonist memoirs. At the same time Rabinovich's disciplinary *maskilic* fictions of Russian-Jewish integration foreshadowed the continuing relevance of Nicholas's homogenizing vision to the imaginative evolution of Russian Jewry. In the heroic deaths of his recruits, Rabinovich instantiated the significance of Russian-Jewish culture that purportedly transcended the increasingly secular lives of Russian Jews between the era of Nicholaevan discipline and the ensuing decade of Alexandrine liberation. Nikitin — a lucky survivor of the former — lived, worked, and wrote under the radical sign of his own difference, a difference amplified by the "unserfment" of Russian society.

TWICE-BORN: JEWISH IDENTITY AS REFORMING CONSCIOUSNESS

During the era of the Great Reforms, Nikitin, who converted to Orthodoxy in the ranks at the age of nine, parlayed his Jewish origins into a successful career as a progressive public official involved in the critical tasks of perestroika and a distinguished literary vocation as a Jewish author working in the spirit of glasnost.[3] The link between Nikitin's fixation on his Nicholaevan childhood and his quest for individual autonomy not *from* but *through* the reforming state highlights the ways in which the autocracy continued, despite a compelling interest in rendering Jewishness both socially invisible and juridically transparent, to enable unexpected possibilities for leading a thoroughly unconventional Jewish private life in the Russian public sphere.[4] Particular in the extreme, Nikitin's biography speaks eloquently to the emancipation of Jewish difference in the age of "unserfment." Nikitin's literary investment in the traces of his long-lost Jewishness, a commitment he cultivated on a par with both his confessional allegiance to Orthodox Christianity and his professional dedication to reform, signifies the way in which personal emancipation served to place Jewish self-expression beyond the boundaries of religious discipline and social control. In his singular attachments Nikitin was, therefore, hardly unique. The Nicholaevan experiment in Jewish enlightenment created a new generation of Russian Jews whose sense of themselves *as Jews* grew not in opposition to Russian state and society but precisely out of their direct "encounter with imperial Russia," unmediated by the authority of Jewish scripture and Jewish community.[5] The interplay between Nikitin's various public selves shows that the displacement of the latter by the former neither entailed nor presupposed the abandonment of Jewish identity in favor of its Russian counterpart, as if these were mutually contradictory categories of self-ascription. On the contrary, in the absence of established textual and social controls, Jewishness not only persisted but began to take on new significance as a Russian cultural style. The genesis of Nikitin's authorial persona exemplifies the process of self-translation that rendered Jewishness into secular Russian terms.

A ward of the Russian military, reared in its institutions, Nikitin embarked on his public career with *The Long-Sufferers* (Rus. *Mnogostradal'nye*) the first treatment — part literature, part archival record, part memoir — of life in a cantonist regiment. Initially serialized in the leading journal of the Russian populists (Rus. *narodniki*), *Notes of the Fatherland* (Rus. *Otechestvennye zapiski*) in 1871, the book came out in a separate edition, under the journal's own imprint, a year later.[6] Despite the avowal of documentary realism — corroborated by the editorial posture of *Notes of the Fatherland* — Nikitin's narrator here emerged as a self-conscious and highly cultivated literary voice whose rhetorical mediation predominated over the matter of objective description.[7] The so-called sketches or studies (Rus. *ocherki*) drawn, as it were, straight from the "everyday life of cantonists" (Rus. *byta kantonistov*) were hardly the observations of a naïve informant. Indeed, the illusion of immediate access to the pre-reform past in itself constituted a virtuoso performance of Nikitin's Nicholaevan double, who served expressly to authenticate his creator's reform-era ideological commitments.

The studied return to the Nicholaevan past initiated in *The Long-Sufferers* informed the recuperation of Nikitin's Jewish connections. In a short story, thematically linked to *The Long-Sufferers*, Nikitin invented a set of new Jewish memories that linked him explicitly to the Russian-Jewish press, a new arena for the public articulation of Jewish selfhood.[8] Published in 1873 in the recently founded St. Petersburg journal *The Jewish Library* (Rus. *Evreiskaia biblioteka*), "To Live a Life Is No Easy Matter" (Rus. *Vek-perezhit' — ne pole pereiti*) positioned Nikitin's self-conscious recovery of Judaism in an ambiguous space between his own conversion, in fact, and his hero's open defiance of the Nicholaevan system in fiction. As in *The Long-Sufferers*, in "To Live a Life," the relationship between Nikitin the narrator and Nikitin the author remained uncertain; was Nikitin projecting his own anxiety about his Orthodoxy onto his narrator, or was he expressing appropriately Christian empathy with those who were forced into the position he had chosen voluntarily? Was he himself a hidden Jew or was his protagonist an entirely secular literary creation, detached from whatever personal loyalties Nikitin was inclined to feel? Such questions became publicly negotiable in the era of Alexandrine openness; but the initial source of the interesting confusion between Russianness and Jewishness lay at the heart of the "transformation of Jewish society" wrought by the Nicholaevan project of social engineering. From his position within the bureaucracy, Nikitin understood very well the dialectical effects of freeing Jewishness from internal modes of signification, a process that began in cantonist ranks and picked up pace under the impact of the Great Reforms.

In Nikitin's case, the various hypostases of his Nicholaevan self-consciousness foregrounded the social process of emancipation through which he created himself anew in the ranks of the reform-era civilian bureaucracy. Nikitin dropped his narrative double to complete the evolution from Jewish cantonist to Russian official in a personal history of his time published in 1906–1907. Polemically positioning the authochthonous tradition of autocratic reformism against the post-1905 Western-inspired model of parliamentary government and civil liberty, the pointedly named journal *Russian Heritage* (Rus. *Russkaia starina*) featured Nikitin's memoirs in a series that idealized the efforts of prominently placed bureaucrats who had engaged in the work of the Great Reforms.[9] An imperial prototype for the *Jewish Heritage*, which just a few years later published its own selection of Jewish cantonist memoirs, *Russian Heritage* thus provided Nikitin with an opportunity to marshal the official discourse of emancipation in the performance of authenticity.

45

Nikitin entered the cantonist regiment of Nizhnii Novgorod in 1848 at the age of nine. In his memoirs he describes a steadily upward movement through the ranks of the military and civilian bureaucracy. He registers his induction into the ranks as the moment of birth. Indeed, the person of Victor Nikitin did not seem to have existed before the age of nine; his Jewish origins find no place in the artful reconstruction of a public life. He does not describe his conversion, implicit only in the mention of his new god-parents, through whom Nikitin acquired a new genealogy. His well-placed godfather, in fact, was himself "from among the cantonists." His god-mother, a childless general's widow, alluding to the total displacement of Nikitin's birth family, referred to him as "her little orphan."[10] Whether in fact he had been an orphan upon entering the ranks remained beside the point; his godparents comprised Nikitin's new military family who, in this capacity, acted both as parents and as representatives of military authority. Exemplifying the potential conflict between these roles, their personal intervention allowed their son to escape most of the horrors perpetrated by the state upon its charges, horrors Nikitin so graphically described in *The Long-Sufferers*. Personal privilege placed him in a "false position" of witnessing the suffering of other "less fortunate" recruits and endowed with redemptive urgency his self-appointed publicistic mission on behalf of Russian prisoners, similarly placed in government custody and located at the margins of civil society.[11]

Nikitin's reforming self is the product of his so-called false position in the ranks; in the cantonist-turned-bureaucrat, the Nicholaevan state effectively fathered its own rebel son, his posture of resistance to the regime an expression of his institutional conscience. Indeed, Nikitin's life as a writer began not in opposition to the strictures of military discipline but when, at the ripe age of thirteen, he transferred into the regimental chancellery for training as a scribe. Just as his official family displaced his biological Jewish family, this transition provided a foil for a lost coming-of-age ceremony. As a bar mitzvah (lit. "son of the commandment"), the thirteen-year-old Nikitin would have been initiated into Jewish manhood by displaying his mastery of the Torah's teachings and his responsibility to obey them. As a child of the state, he was called upon to immerse himself in regimental logs and orders, the commanding texts of his official life. An encounter with the regimental inspector, a highly placed St. Petersburg official, boded well for Nikitin's future. Hinting at the promise of advancement, the inspector compelled Nikitin to recite Suvorov's famous dictum, "Poor is the soldier who does not aspire to the rank of the general."[12] A. V. Suvorov (1730–1800), the military idol of the Catherinian wars of imperial conquest credited with the creation of a national school of martial arts, became, in the Nicholaevan period, the subject of popular adulation, associated with the tsar's own stern but benevolent paternalism that ensured steady promotion through the military hierarchy.[13] The invocation of Suvorov's well-known aphorism pointed to the role of Nikitin's own military patrons, who recognized the talents of this so-called orphan and determined the course of his orderly advancement through the ranks.

Parallel to his professional success, Nikitin recorded the progress of his cultural education, interrupted in 1854 when the Crimean War broke out. The military crisis of the Nicholaevan regime actually fit well into the teleology of success that informed the construction of Nikitin's professional persona. The war occasioned Nikitin's first railway journey from Moscow to St. Petersburg, a formative event in the life of a future bureaucrat. The railroad journey, an ambiguous signifier of Russian modernity in late imperial literature, portended here Nikitin's break with the legacy of Nicholaevan militarism and his transition to a civilized — and civilian — future of progress and reform. The transition abounds with irony; Nikitin, rhetorically invested in the break from his Nicholaevan past, obscured more patent historical continuities. It was the Nicholaevan state that initially sponsored and financed railroad building in Russia. Such projects, associated with the modernizing efforts of Alexander II, actually expanded the ambitious state-building program that first began under his father. Indeed, the St. Petersburg reforming bureaucracy toward which Nikitin himself aspired first developed in the shadow of Nicholas's court, not in opposition to it.

Nikitin's initial sojourn in the imperial capital occasioned his first promotion from the least prestigious rank of cantonist into the regular army, even though he was only sixteen. At the conclusion of the war in 1856, while the rest of his regiment returned to Nizhnii Novgorod, the eighteen-year-old Nikitin, the "little hero" (who did not get anywhere near the frontlines), was "summoned" to St. Petersburg to work in the Department of Military Settlements, just as it was being dismantled in the wake of Alexander's dispatch of the cantonist system.[14] Nikitin's participation in the dismembering of the Nicholaevan state coincided with a personal moment of reckoning that foreshadowed the emergence of his social conscience. At the train station Nikitin saw a convoy of prisoners, a vision which he says "plant[ed] the seeds of a lifelong empathy." His desire to help "these wretched people" eventually translated into a devastating exposé of prison conditions in Russia.[15]

Quickly promoted to "scribe of the third class," Nikitin experienced the unexpected pleasure of pinning gold braid to his uniform "having barely reached the age of eighteen."[16] When the cantonist regiments were finally dissolved, he was offered a discharge but decided to stay on because his "future seem[ed] promising."[17] The military bureaucracy presented ready opportunities for an ambitious and capable young man without established social connections. In fact, Nikitin quickly acquired a new patron and, as a result, expanded his social horizons beyond the barracks. To supplement his income, he became the personal secretary to Count Orlov-Davydov, who introduced him into St. Petersburg high society. Under Orlov-Davydov's tutelage, Nikitin became acquainted with the "enlightened" circles of reform-minded nobility, frequented by his employer. Eventually Orlov-Davydov went abroad and discharged his secretary. By this time Nikitin's earnings had made him financially secure at a very young age.

Nikitin's experience of enlightened noble patronage laid the foundation for his next promotion in 1858, to the Department of Irregular Forces in charge of the administration of Cossack regiments. For the first time Nikitin's job offered him more than merely secretarial responsibilities. In his new position as departmental archivist, responsible for updating the collection of newspapers and books owned by the department, he made rapid progress in his cultural education, devouring the poetry of Pushkin, Lermontov, and Koltsov, the pleiade of Nicholaevan literary luminaries found in the department's library. At the age of twenty-two he was promoted to the rank of officer. Once again the attainment of a professional milestone was punctuated by a parallel step toward the making of a literary career. Encouraged by the editor of the military journal *Military Anthology* (Rus. *Voennyi sbornik*), Nikitin attempted for the first time to write fiction.

In 1863–1864 Nikitin gradually shed the last vestige of his obscure Nicholaevan origins. In 1863 he petitioned for a discharge into the civil service and received a transfer into the Ministry of State Domains, where he occupied an unranked position of "chancellery servitor of the third grade."[18] After passing his required examination in literature (Rus. *slovesnost'*), a cultural rite of passage for Russian bureaucrats, he received another, more substantial promotion. In 1865 Nikitin began his advance through the ranks of civilian bureaucracy from collegiate registrar (Rus. *kollezhskii registrator*), the lowest rung of the fourteen in the Table of Ranks; he wrote proudly that his promotion set an important official precedent for the civil service advancement of former cantonists.[19] In the 1870s he achieved his biggest professional coup when he came to the attention of D. A. Miliutin, the tsar's minister of war and the man responsible for the military reform of 1874, the capstone of Alexander's program to forge Russian civil society within the military, the traditional crucible of autocracy.[20] On Miliutin's personal request, Nikitin compiled a report on the state of Russian military prisons. In 1871, based on the research he collected on his state-sponsored expedition, Nikitin published his acclaimed exposé of prison conditions in St. Petersburg.[21] In the next three decades he continued his steady rise through the ranks at the Ministry of State Domains, thanks to Miliutin's patronage and to his own increasing public prominence as an advocate of prison reform, a cause célèbre in Russian high society throughout the 1870s.[22] By 1904, four years before his death, Nikitin celebrated fifty years in government service, having attained the fifth rank, the civilian equivalent to the military rank of brigadier. He worked as the assistant to the minister of state domains, in charge of the minister's personal chancellery.

Nikitin ended his memoir in the 1870s; he died in 1908, before he could complete his assignment for *Russian Heritage* and bring his reminiscences up to date. In 1904 a progressive Jewish weekly in St. Petersburg pointedly called *The Future* (Rus. *Budushchnost'*) paid tribute to Nikitin's jubilee in government service, glossing over his conversion entirely.[23] The article seamlessly combined the celebration of Nikitin's achievements in service with praise of his publicistic work on Jewish agricultural colonies as well as his active interest in the "world of society's outcasts."[24] The capital's Russian-Jewish public noted the Nicholaevan beginnings of Nikitin's illustrious public persona, identifying the achievements of the "former cantonist" (and former Jew) with its own emancipation from the pre-reform past.

Significantly the editors of *The Future* had a more ambiguous version of Nikitin's life at their disposal. In his literary work, Nikitin continually tested the boundaries of his carefully crafted official personality. In *The Long-Sufferers,* for example, he used his official voice to tell a story about the role of state institutions in the life of the individual, which undermined the tenor of his own biography. As the self-appointed historian of the cantonist regiments and the implicit subject of the memoir, Nikitin spoke in the name of state authority on behalf of himself as its victim rather than its beneficiary. This contradiction would bear cultural fruit in his literary attempt to come to terms with his conversion, the necessary "false step" on his road to personal freedom and artistic truth and, implicitly, the symbol of the Nicholaevan origins of the liberated society of the Great Reforms era.

Nikitin organized his story of the "long-sufferers" according to the days of the week to encapsulate the entire dreary life of the cantonist, for whom every week was just like another "monotonous, stupefying, mind-numbing week," stretching out into year after year.[25] The form of the narrative mirrored its central theme — the routinization of suffering and the systematic denigration of the individual by the military machine which resulted in the absolute loss of self. Nikitin depicted a life that reduced people to the status of things. The body of the cantonist was continually objectified, ceaselessly beaten, and publicly displayed in a spectacular theater of cruelty, meant to instruct its audience in the virtues of submission. "Birch-branches" (Rus. *rozgi*) used for whipping constituted an inexorable part of the décor in the barracks; without them, "nothing [could] be done" (25–26). Their ominous presence sent cantonists into convulsions of fear. Flogging itself became subject to an elaborate ritual of punishment meant to maximize the victim's pain and humiliation which everyone was required to watch.

Every aspect of life in a cantonist regiment fell pattern to the same kind of brutal and brutalizing routine. Nikitin emphasized the absurdity of military discipline as pure ritual, rooted in pathological exhibitionism devoid of meaning. He insisted in satirizing this tendency to the point of absurdity; often his descriptions achieve a supreme comic effect that undermines the avowal of unadulterated realism. In one case, the passion for military exercises drove one Captain Tarakanov (Cockroach) to forget the difference between soldiers and dining room furniture:

Tarakanov's passion for muster reached the point of madness. He could not live a single day without military exercises [. . .] On Sundays and holidays, when all muster was categorically prohibited, he was inspired to invent a most original method of conducting military exercises at home. Let us say, for example, that it is Sunday. He can hardly wait until his wife leaves for church and the housekeeper straightens up all the rooms. As soon as they do, he quickly dons his frock coat, buttons it up, moves all the chairs into the middle of the dining room in three rows, approaches them from the side and begins to command them, shouting louder and louder: "Third man from the left, half a step back! Fifth man, eyes to the right! Look sharp! Seventh row, stand still or I'll bust up your mug! Aha! You think it's all fun and games, do you? I'll give you what for!" All of a sudden he runs up to the chair and begins to pound it with his fist. (60–61)

Most of the commanders shared Tarakanov's fateful inability to distinguish between people and things. In the same spirit, the cantonists were taught to shoot and display nonexistent rifles. While their superior, Sviniev (Swine), wholly gave himself over to the ritual of the parade ground, the cantonists rebelled heroically against the cruel "unreality" of the experience: "You can beat me till I die, your Excellency, but it still won't make a rifle appear in my hand. So you're hitting me for nothing" (106). The cantonist here summed up the illogic of the entire system; the education of the cantonist, Nikitin suggests, was all about hitting people for nothing. The perversion of pedagogy actually had an even more baleful effect on the teachers who somehow internalized its meaningless rules and thereby lost all sense of humanity. Like Tarakanov enthralled by the illusion of military exercises, Sviniev succumbed entirely to his own mirage and, even after the drill was over, continued to "imagine that he [was] in a real battle" (107). Every one of the teachers seems to have had his particular obsession which he would pursue to the point of madness. In the contrary world of the cantonists as Nikitin imagined it, any official who treated his charges with even a shred of reason or humanity had clearly found himself "in the wrong place" (81), ultimately rendered fit for nothing but drunken oblivion or suicide.

The derogation of the individual, reflected in the comic depiction of the regimental personnel, echoes the effects of military transparency upon the cantonists themselves. The same system that makes Nikitin into a person also has the capacity to unmake the personhood of his fellow cantonists; his public persona actually evolves as a result of the initial loss of selfhood in the ranks. The autocracy's power to erase the individual indelibly marks its capacity to induce and enable the process of self-fashioning. Nikitin makes precisely this point in a harrowing tale of a cantonist who became one with the lash used to beat him. The cantonist Mesarev made repeated attempts to flee but was always caught, returned to the regiment, and whipped. All his attempts to reason with the authorities, to complain, to appeal to pity were apparently to no avail. The frequency and the cruelty of beatings eventually had what Nikitin calls an "unnatural" effect on Mesarev's personality: he came to embrace punishment and actively to seek it out. Rather than signifying his escape from oppression, his last, seemingly successful, attempt to run away fulfills the masochistic scenario and results in the total obliteration of his identity; one day Mesarev simply vanishes, beaten, as it were, into nonexistence (138–141). But, in fact, Mesarev's disappearance is no less complete than Nikitin's own; their lives represent two possible outcomes of the state's program of converting marginal persons into Russian citizens. Between the high price of defiance and the enormous rewards of perfect obedience lay an abyss of possibilities for social and cultural self-expression. Unlike Nikitin and his literary foil, Mesarev, most cantonists, and most Russian Jews, inhabited the morally and politically ambiguous space in between the two extremes.

In depicting so graphically the state's attempt to break down every vestige of the cantonist's resolve, Nikitin effectively revealed the full scope of the power of political socialization, grotesque in its capacity for destruction, formidable as an agent of change. Nikitin's story of his own cantonist past, like his book about prison conditions, was not the protest manifesto of a perennially embittered outsider, alienated from an oppressive government; rather, these works marked his increasing sense of public responsibility and his rising stature in Russian civil circles during the era of the Great Reforms. In speaking on behalf of the oppressed, Nikitin assumed the self-assurance of a respectable member of the Russian bureaucratic establishment, committed to the Russian state as a force for social progress. But between his bureaucratic autobiography and the horrors depicted in *The Long-Sufferers* — which, as we know, he experienced only as a witness — Nikitin's own inner life remained obscure. The elusive nature of an identity beyond the barracks and beyond the Ministry of State Domains emerged in his only acknowledgment of his Jewish past, the short story "To Live a Life Is No Easy Matter" (Rus. "Vek prozhit' ne pole pereiti").

Published in the St. Petersburg annual *The Jewish Library* (Rus. *Evreiskaia biblioteka*) in 1873, "To Live a Life," linked Nikitin's own cantonist past with the post-reform ambiguities of the Russian-Jewish condition. The fate of Nikitin's narrator, a Jewish soldier and survivor of service in Nicholas's cantonist regiments, alluded to the uneasy fit between the author's Nicholaevan beginnings, shrouded in the oppressive mystery of his origins, and his adult self, explicitly linked with the promise of the Great Reforms. Unlike his author, destiny's happy prodigy, the protagonist acknowledged that he was, from the beginning, accursed, destined — unlike his author — to remain a Jew. This is the seed of the apparent paradox at the heart of Nikitin's success; his protagonist's curse proved, in Nikitin's case, to be the ultimate blessing. A Jewish cantonist was the only Jew who could be "orphaned," whether or not his parents or relatives were still alive, in order to be re-fathered in the image of the Russian Orthodox tsar. No other Russian Jew, similarly emancipated by the grace of autocratic fiat, could so completely escape his Jewish connections in the embrace of the state. Yet for all its obvious enticements, Nikitin did not altogether internalize his new political faith; his open connection to Jewish society, his filiation with Russian-Jewish culture, his continuing literary engagement with the Jewish question — all his elective Jewish affinities served, rather than vitiated, by the public standing of his well-heeled Russian persona — bespoke the unexpected consequences of Nicholas's effort to make Russian Jews.

In "To Live a Life," Nikitin's Jewish protagonist symbolizes political and social nonconformity. His resistance to the state-sponsored program of conversion indicates his saintly purity and his heroic posture of self-renunciation. His staunch refusal to be baptized contrasted with the actual conversion of his creator, an act of complicity with authority that paved the way toward success. Nikitin's empathic depiction of his protagonist, like his sense of identification with his fellow cantonists and with St. Petersburg's prisoners, implicitly acknowledged that the development of a reforming conscience started with a "false step." At the same time the convert's admiration for his Jewish hero complicated the totalizing logic of emancipation from Judaism that Nikitin's own life so plainly conveyed. Paradoxically Nikitin's public voice as a proper Russian subject here served the invention of a private Jewish alter ego, a tension always already implicit in the education of Jewish cantonists. As we have seen (chapter 1), cantonist regiments, while in the business of remaking Jews into Russians, were actively making Russian Jews.

In "To Live a Life," Nikitin offered his own version of a Jewish coming-of-age as an alternative to the story of the awakening of his own professional conscience and to the bar mitzvah, both of which highlight the assumption of collective responsibility. Nikitin — and an increasing number of his Russian-Jewish contemporaries — were, in fact, engaged in turning Jewishness into a psychological force, rejecting its theological claims and social duties. Tellingly Nikitin's cantonist-hero initiates himself into adulthood by means of a tortuous process of introspection, not through the assumption of the public yoke as a loyal state servitor or, for that matter, a bar mitzvah. Marking the recovery of Jewishness, he resurrects his Jewish name, transformed from the bookbinder's apprentice "Lyovka," a diminutive of the name Lev, into the sonorous "Lev Abramovich."[26] The assumption of this patronymic, derived from the name Abram or Abraham, not only reminds him of his own long-lost Jewish father but evokes a more distant biblical parentage. He is, as he has always been, the progeny of Abraham — a Jew. Implicitly putting the efficacy of his own conversion into question, Nikitin imagines his protagonist's Jewish awakening as a conversion *to* Judaism — every convert becomes a son of Abraham — an act of the author's symbolic auto-emancipation from the state.

In becoming Jewish, Lev Abramovich also comes into possession of his manhood. The fruit of his sexual empowerment lies in the discovery of true love, the ultimate test of his forbearance and his capacity to resist the state's efforts to remake him:

> As a child, I was torn away from my family, from my faith. From the age of nine, they tormented my body, destroyed my health, and now when I am an adult, they shatter my heart into tiny pieces [. . .] Why do these blows keep falling upon me? A Jew is forbidden even to love. (345)

But, in fact, the greatest obstacle to his happiness with Natasha, the Russian girl he loves, stems neither from the legal prohibition against intermarriage —a reality in imperial Russia—nor from any religious or ethnic taboo. Natasha, in fact, tells her agonized suitor that the empire is large and full of all kinds of people, "Frenchmen, Germans, Finns, all of them marry Russians [. . .] And, if he suits me, why can I not marry a Jew?" (349). They can never be married, the protagonist responds, because the authorities will not allow it. Cantonists "do not marry" since they belong, body and soul, to the state.

While Natasha's cosmopolitan sentiments point to the radical social possibilities of imperial geography, Lev Abramovich calls her back to the politics of imperial rule, the way that the government imposes its own vision of order upon the human landscape of the Russian lands. In Nikitin's story, it is these official aspirations toward administrative uniformity and social control rather than popular anti-Jewish sentiments that ultimately doom the hero to remain forever a wandering Jew, an avatar of the unfulfilled utopian ambitions of the reforming Romanovs. Ejected by his master for ruining Natasha—his ward—the hero bemoans his bitter fate:

> I finally understood that a person who belongs to the state (Rus. *kazennyi chelovek*) and a Jew especially does not dare to have a heart or feelings [. . .] And so I dragged myself along the road, tortured by guilt and by unremitting questions about Natasha's fate and my own, destined as I was to wander the earth without direction, without the hope of finding a place of refuge. (350)

The image of exile here points to the persistence of the Pale of Settlement, the lingering vestige of Nicholaevan order in the liberating chaos of emancipation and a symbol, as I. G. Orshanskii argued, of the politically parlous condition of reform-era Russian Jews. Nikitin's protagonist does, in fact, find his own peculiar haven outside the Pale where the cantonist Jewboy Lyovka meets Lev Abramovich, (literally) the son of his Jewish father and (figuratively) a stepson of his imperial majesty. After the Crimean War, Nikitin's reluctant hero receives his medical discharge and returns to St. Petersburg. Eventually he acquires his own bindery; for the first time in his life he is his own master. Like Nikitin, he attains his independence through the written word, but the disquieting echo of the Nicholaevan past resounds in the age of glasnost. Occasionally his erstwhile regimental commander— the same man who used to flog him—joins him for a cup of tea and some

reminiscing about old times. The pronounced ambiguity of this reconciliation hints at Nikitin's own service career, an irresistible embrace of social
privilege at the expense of Jewish memory.

The cantonist's dilemma here mirrored the historical situation of the
Russian maskil, similarly positioned to see the Nicholaevan state as the author of his ambiguous liberation from the strictures of piety and society.
Indeed, under Nicholas I, the state became the most active proponent of
Jewish enlightenment in the Pale and, more significantly still, the agent of
individual emancipation from the sticky provincialism of Russia's Jewish
geography. In the ambient glow of the Great Reforms new opportunities
made the promise of ultimate redemption from the state's own system of
social discipline that much more seductive and, as long as the state refused
to abolish the Pale of Settlement, visibly out of reach. The Pale remained the
signifier of the political contradiction that bound the majority of Russian
Jews to a communal regime which the government, in its immediate commitment to the selective integration of Jewish individuals, simultaneously
undermined. The paradox, always already implicit in the Alexandrine scenario of the autocrat as liberator, exacerbated existing tensions in Jewish
society between the one and the many, and engendered competing concep-
tions of what the emancipationist rhetoric of the Great Reforms meant for
the future of Judaism and for Russia's Jews.[27] While St. Petersburg Jewish
elites maintained their commitment to the conservative notion of expanding residential privileges, vocal provincials within the Pale now asserted
their residential rights.

Increasingly the conflict took on a distinctive geographical cast, marked
by the array of differences that divided the Jewish North from the Jewish
South; not surprisingly, the debate over the relationship between enlightenment and emancipation became implicated in the struggle for leadership
between rival Jewish elites in Vilna and St. Petersburg, on the one hand, and
in Odessa, on the other. In the Jerusalem of Lithuania, Jewish enlighteners,
together with their well-heeled merchant patrons in the capitol, placed
their faith in the logic of the political narrative that the Nicholaevan state set
in motion when it began to make Russian Jews. Direct beneficiaries of state
support and government concessions, northerners advocated the principle
of "selective integration" as a form of state patronage extended on the basis
of individual distinction by service, education, or economic standing.[28] In
Odessa, the cultural center of Russia's New South, Rabinovich an enterprising journalist, publisher and editor of *The Dawn* (Rus. *Razsvet*), Russia's first
Russian-language Jewish periodical, offered an original rationale for collective emancipation, inspired to a great extent by his own cultivation of a
southern style. In pointed contrast to the ideal of personal achievement,
advocated by the northern elites and their supporters who "favored direct
ties to the Great Russian center" Rabinovich called for the legal recognition
of an indigenous Russian Jewishness, constituted precisely by the "popu-

lations of the peripheries" that Jewish St. Petersburg disowned.[29] From Odessa, Rabinovich saw and celebrated the Russian empire as a hothouse of ethnic difference; a northern perspective, he claimed, imprisoned Russian Jewry in its own parochial vision of a well-ordered bourgeois paradise where a select few spoke schoolbook Russian and wrote perfectly turned neo-classical Hebrew quatrains. Rabinovich's Jews communicated in a mélange of Yiddish, Russian, Ukrainian, Polish, Greek, and French that mirrored the natural condition of life in the empire's balmy southern backyard, closer, in the imagination if not in fact, to Palestine and Constantinople than to chilly St. Petersburg or, for that matter, Vilna.

Rabinovich wrote conscription stories about Russian Jewry's Nicholaevan past that read like political fables about the momentous transition into the reign of the tsar-liberator. His recruits embodied not the status anxieties of individual Russian Jews struggling with the social costs and benefits of eman-cipation but rather the political commitments of their creator to the contro-versial idea that, in the southern cradle of the empire, Russian Jewry was born. In fact, Rabinovich's imaginative claims on behalf of southern Jewry mirrored the poetic invention of the southern frontier as the ancient link between the Russian Orient and western Europe.[30] In both instances, the modern literature of colonization served the invention of a historical ro-mance between land and people. Thus, while Rabinovich asserted in his fiction that Russian Jewry was native to the South, the vicissitudes of his own life testified to the contingency of Russian-Jewish geography. His own pains-taking efforts at self-fashioning — much like those of Nikitin — demonstrated that Russian Jews were made, not born, and through their efforts trans-formed the landscape they inhabited.

HOW IT WAS DONE IN ODESSA

Rabinovich's Jewish life informed his Jewish fiction in a complicated way; just as in the case of Nikitin, the tension between experience and expression required the mediation of a strong authorial persona, distinct from both the private person of the writer and the public presence of his characters.[31] Rabinovich cultivated a distinctive southern sensibility that functioned as a controlling fiction, a personal literary genealogy. Nikitin's official voice ul-timately and paradoxically served his vocation as supreme defender of the impoverished ego, broken and silenced by the state, that graced Nikitin himself with the gift of speech. Rabinovich's authorial ego similarly fore-grounded the nearly messianic significance he attached to the Great Re-forms as the happy outcome of Nicholas's Jewish reformation. Rabinovich's identity as a Jewish writer, in fact, rendered explicit the ambivalence that began to inform the maskilic romance with the autocracy, as Jewish re-formers began to think about the opportunities of emancipation. Like Nikitin, Rabinovich derived his politics from his "false position" as the beneficiary of the Nicholaevan project in social engineering. In the Alexandrine possibilities of collective liberation he foresaw an urgent means of resolving the conflict between the grand design of "official enlightenment" and its disruptive effects on Jewish social life.

From the beginning, Rabinovich associated his literary vocation with a polemical revision of maskilic geography.[32] Implicating Jewish enlightenment in the imperial civilizing project, he linked the settlement of Russia's New South, acquired under Catherine II and formally integrated into the Pale of Settlement by Nicholas's Jewish statute of 1835, with the military subjugation of the eastern frontier.[33] Rabinovich appropriated the homology between the southern and the eastern borderlands of the empire that famously inspired Russia's most famous romantic, Alexander Pushkin, in order to create an image of a Jewish southland ancient in its eastern exoticism and hypermodern in its artful pursuit of the vernacular. Rabinovich established his personal cultural genealogy (Yid. *yikhes*) in the form of a poetic homage to Pushkin, in whose name he issued an open challenge to the northern Hebraism of his maskilic contemporaries. Embarking on his literary career with a Russian translation of a Hebrew poem about chess, written by the professional reformer and amateur mathematician Jacob Eichenbaum (1796–1861), Rabinovich expressly sought to point acolytes of Jewish enlightenment away from the Lithuanian Jerusalem.

The enlightened North, while geographically marked by the imagined cultural nexus of Vilna, Berlin, and St. Petersburg, was, of course, not geographically determined. Although a Talmudic prodigy, Eichenbaum himself had few personal or professional connections to the capitals of the Haskalah. Like Rabinovich, he shared with the Jewish intelligentsia of Russia's New South both his recent Galician origins and the self-consciousness of a cultural parvenu, made, as it were, by the state. A rallying figure for aspiring Jewish intellectuals in the southwestern town of Zamosc, Eichenbaum proudly served Jewish enlightenment in his official capacity as the government-appointed inspector of the Zhitomir Rabbinical Seminary.[34] For Rabinovich, Eichenbaum's poem, entitled "The Battle" (Heb. *Ha-krav*), enshrined the excessively dry, abstract aspects of the Haskalah which, in his own quest after the "freedom and freshness" of the South, his Russian translation sought explicitly to disavow.[35] In fact, Eichenbaum's poem is a striking example of studied maskilic medievalism, the conservative tendency to derive justification and precedent for cultural experiments from the philosophic and linguistic achievements of Iberian Judaism.[36] Poems about chess had appeared first in the secular repertoire of Jewish poets of medieval Christian Spain. One such poem, apparently recovered in the nineteenth century and known to Eichenbaum, was "A Song of Chess," attributed to the twelfth-century exegete and versifier Abraham Ibn Ezra.[37] Ibn Ezra set the action in a legendary East, where chess was supposed to have originated. Comparing the game to armed combat between "Ethiopian" and "Edomite" kingdoms—that is, between black and white chessmen—Ibn Ezra drew attention to the supremacy of the battle of wits over the battle of swords. Eichenbaum's neo-medieval poem was, in turn, intended as a spirited defense of Ibn Ezra's rationalism, a contribution to the contemporary scholarly controversy regarding Ibn Ezra's character and exegetical methodology between the Venetian proponent of *Wissenschaft des Judentums* (Science of Judaism), S. D. Luzzatto (1800–1865), and his Galician colleague, S. J. Rapoport (1790–1867).[38]

Following Ibn Ezra, Eichenbaum highlighted both the preeminence of intellectual over physical combat and the non-European—Eastern?—origins of chess:

> This is not a war of vengeance, wrath, and anger
> But an intellectual quarrel, of thought and discernment [...]
> This war with all its laws
> Both the plan of the field and the number of troops
> A wise man from India once devised [...][39]

While the content of Rabinovich's translation remained faithful to the stated purpose of the Hebrew original, the spirit of his Russian version derived in part from his striking appropriation of Pushkin's imperial theme. Composed in iambic tetrameter, the predominant meter of the romantic *poema*, both the form and content of Rabinovich's translation evoked Pushkin's southern poems: *The Fountain of Bakhchisarai* (1823), *The Captive of the Caucasus* (1821), and *The Gypsies* (1824), written when the Russian poet was living as a provincial exile in Odessa and Kishinev.[40] In fact, in order to translate Eichenbaum's scene into the local register of Pushkin's Crimea, Rabinovich expanded the description of the romantic Eastern setting, at which Eichenbaum only hinted. Rabinovich added an additional introductory passage that located the chess match against the background of a lush exotic landscape:

> In the land of poetry and flowers
> Where the golden sun rises
> Where the generous gifts of heaven
> Fill an entire ever-flowing sea
> Where nature delivers to the people
> The whole year through, a blooming spring
> And blood flows wildly
> In the veins of a fiery people
> Where in the evening hours
> A wave of fragrant scent flows through the air
> In a land which from the beginning of time
> We have called the East [...][41]

Rabinovich recast Eichenbaum's enlightened Jewish East in the image of Pushkin's romantic Russian South.

Unlike Eichenbaum, who identified more with the implied maskilic reader of the poem than with the "wise man from India" who allegedly invented the game, Rabinovich invoked the mythical Eastern origins of chess as a foil for the invention of a native southern Jewish style. The idea of a southern literary imagination that emerged so powerfully in his Russian translation of northern Hebraism continued throughout the Nicholaevan period to shape Rabinovich's reforming consciousness; in the wake of the Great Reforms, his southern persona served the transition to a new politics of emancipation, embodied in the figures of Jewish recruits. Rabinovich, the gadfly of Odessa's Jewish bourgeoisie, now became the epic voice of benighted Jewish peoplehood. This transformation highlights the importance of maskilic anxiety about the secular effects of emancipation, already in evidence in Rabinovich's early Odessa stories, for an understanding of the cultural mission of the Jewish enlightener-turned-writer in the era of "unserfment." At the same time Rabinovich's literary investment in Russian-Jewish ingathering, articulated in his emancipation-era conscription tales tellingly grouped under the title *Scenes from the Past,* reveals the extent to which Russian-Jewish writers remained invested in the Nicholaevan fantasy of creating Russian Jewry.

Rabinovich's precocious appropriation of the imperial lingua franca as a regional vernacular reflected the influence of the Ukrainian renascence of the 1840s, associated with Kharkov University, which Rabinovich attended between 1840 and 1845.[42] Born in 1817, in Kobeliaki, a small settlement in Poltava Province, Rabinovich grew up during a time when few Jews attended Russian universities and fewer still participated in the cultural life of the Russian provinces beyond the western borderlands. Kharkov, located on the border between eastern and western Ukraine, remained just outside the Pale and tantalizingly off-limits to Jews. Like his enterprising merchant father who attempted to make a living in an area sparsely populated by Jews and bereft of organized communal life, Rabinovich was willing to venture alone beyond the Pale. In fact, he was one of the first Russian Jews to study at the university in Kharkov: in 1841, a year after Rabinovich first enrolled, there were only four Jews among a population numbering between 450 and 500 students.[43] Economic opportunities brought a heterogeneous mix to the city, a "special cross between Great Russians and Little Russians."[44] The makeup of the student body and the faculty mirrored the ethnic and cultural diversity that characterized the city. About half the students were Polish and a large number were of local origin. The language of instruction was Russian, but many of the students were bilingual and textbooks were often in Polish.[45]

In the 1840s the liberal arts faculty dominated Kharkov University and enjoyed enormous prestige among the students. Literature and history were favored by a student population that disdained its fellows in St. Petersburg and Moscow as career-oriented and single-minded. Professors and students alike embraced the historical novels of Sir Walter Scott and the philosophical legacy of German idealism. At the same time the contagious literary enthusiasm of the critic "furious Vissarion" Belinskii (1811–1848) produced an interest in the literary vocation as a serious pursuit and promoted a turn toward a more direct prose style, as well as an interest in contemporary life. Kharkov University proved to be a hospitable environment for the development of a bilingual, distinctively "southern" — that is to say, regional — literature, as well as of a rising interest in the ethnography and folklore of southern Russia. In the 1840s Kharkov University not only nurtured the talents of the future Ukrainian historian N. I. Kostomarov (1817–1885) but also saw the beginning of the academic career of I. I. Sreznevskii (1812–1880), one of the first Russian experts on the history of Slavic literature and dialectology and an early proponent of "comparative slavistics," who later went on to take up a distinguished academic post in St. Petersburg.[46] During these years Kharkov also saw the efflorescence of the southern school of Russian romantic poetry. Characterized by a self-conscious bilingualism, this literary movement flourished within small, informal circles, composed both of university students and faculty members. The poets of the "southern school" were interested in bringing the Ukrainian language and southern themes into the Russian literary mainstream. Their most important concern was to overturn the genre hierarchy which relegated southern ethnographic details or folkloric material to the burlesque, the primitive, and the fantastic. They strove to create a southern style that would stand up to the criteria set forth by their Russian contemporaries for the formation of an aesthetically and morally significant national literature.[47] Continuing in this tradition the founders of modern Ukrainian culture — the poet Taras Shevchenko (1814–1861), the literary critic Panteleimon Kulish (1819–1897), and the historian Kostomarov — wrote in both Ukrainian and Russian, asserting that it was the latter tongue which bound the two peoples together.[48]

In Kharkov Rabinovich formed a lasting literary friendship with the poet Nikolai Shcherbina (1821–1869). Their relationship nourished a common interest in translating a regional southern idiom into the imperial vernacular. Shcherbina's personal and literary background was, in many respects, representative of the cultural diversity of the city where he and Rabinovich first met. Of Greek descent on his maternal side and of Cossack stock on the paternal, Shcherbina grew up near the town of Taganrog, in a house where both Greek and Ukrainian were spoken. His poetic evocation of an imaginary Hellenic heritage in an anthology of "Greek poems" in Russian, published in Odessa in 1850 with the help of Rabinovich, was meant "to touch an audience to whom the Greek world was completely foreign."[49] Following the romantic poets of the Kharkov school, both Shcherbina and Rabinovich made a choice to write in Russian because they wished to bridge the distance between their own families and communities and the Russian literary establishment at the imperial center. Like Shcherbina, Rabinovich also assigned an important social function to Russian that transcended its purely literary qualities. In an editorial for *The Dawn,* on the cultural potential of the Russian language, Rabinovich described Russian as the future "mediating agent" (Rus. *posrednik*) of *Jewish* enlightenment. For Rabinovich, the creation of Russian Jewry depended on the common embrace of Russian: "How pleasant it is to dream of a time when the resonant Russian language will flow through all the layers [of the population] of our co-religionists in the Russian Empire."[50] This was clearly a fantasy of linguistic ingathering, ambiguously cast in the subjunctive; the reality, as Rabinovich himself acknowledged in the same article, was that Russia's Jews throughout the first half of the nineteenth century were more likely to employ Hebrew, French, or German as the primary languages of self-cultivation.

In 1845, because of straitened financial circumstances, Rabinovich left Kharkov without getting his degree and moved to Odessa. He earned his living first as a clerk in a law office and eventually as a self-employed notary public. Like most maskilim, and, for that matter, most contemporary Russian writers, Rabinovich turned to literature as a vocation, not as a way to make a living. Between the last decade of the Nicholaevan period and the first years of Alexander's reign, his literary treatment of Jews and Judaism shifted away from a critical interest in the small deeds of contemporary provincial life toward the creation of a master Russian-Jewish narrative, a self-consciously conservative rereading of his own earlier fictions. In his initial attempt at handling a Jewish theme, the short story "Moritz Sefardi," published in 1850 in an Odessa journal dedicated to local talent, the short-lived *Literary Evenings* (Rus. *Literaturnye vechera*) which Rabinovich edited together with Shcherbina, Rabinovich brought the full weight of his southern imagination to bear on a devastating critique of the bourgeois ideal of maskilic manhood, imported into Odessa by German-speaking merchants from Galicia—cultural speculators and carpetbaggers, northerners masquerading as southerners who assumed the outward trappings of culture in pursuit of money and sex.

A comparison between the southern locals of "Moritz Sefardi" and the southern Jewish recruits in Rabinovich's reform-era conscription story, "A Family Candlestick," highlights the ways in which the promise of emancipation conditioned the explicitly Jewish turn in Rabinovich's work. Moving away from both the imperial exotic of *The Battle* and from the secular uses of fiction as social criticism, "A Family Candlestick" exemplified the potential public significance of literature for the constitution of regional Jewish identity in the absence of clearly marked boundaries of social, economic, confessional, and civic space. This interest in the disciplinary function of literature evolved out of Rabinovich's nearly messianic certitude that the Pale of Settlement would shortly disappear by the same force of autocratic magnanimity that had emancipated the serfs. Rabinovich's Jewish South, distributed between "Moritz Sefardi" and "A Family Candlestick," paradoxically stood for both the attrition of Jewish enlightenment by the emancipation of desire — already precociously evident in Nicholaevan Odessa — and the liberation of maskilic self-consciousness in the era of the Great Reforms.

The image of the title character of "Moritz Sefardi," a German-Jewish arriviste whose *gebildete* (cultured) façade masks the nature of a crass opportunist, presents a stark contrast to Odessa's native Jewish types, the poor family of the tailor Henokh Khmel'nik whose daughter Sefardi almost seduces after his pursuit of a local Galician heiress comes to naught. For all the detail that went into this early attempt at social criticism, Rabinovich's Odessa types had less to do with the realities of Jewish life in that city and more with the programmatic distinction between North and South that informed Rabinovich's reforming politics. In fact, Odessa had no native Russian-Jewish past and no indigenous Russian-Jewish culture except that which was created by Galician drifters like Sefardi, precisely during the period that "Moritz Sefardi" was written. Founded in 1795, Odessa was home to a new kind of Jewish community; its Jews were recent immigrants riding the wave of opportunity that trailed Russian colonization of the New South. The frontier of Jewish embourgeoisement, Odessa attracted those with ambition and business acumen, often accompanied by a smattering of culture; by mid-century the newcomers turned their commercial talents to civic life. They patronized Odessa's opera theater, subscribed to its first newspaper, and attended its recently built liberal synagogue, one of the first in the Russian Empire. And in the process of becoming Russian Jews, the so-called port Jews of Odessa created what was arguably the most visibly Jewish city in Russia.[51] By the end of the imperial period, Jews were so closely allied with the spirit of the place that in Russian the terms "Odessite" (Rus. *odessit*) and "Jew" became virtually interchangeable; the same could hardly be said for more venerable sites of Russian-Jewish settlement — like Vilna, for instance — that had at least as many Jews. The ultimate irony, of course, was that the creator of the despicable comer Moritz Sefardi was himself an immigrant who, equipped with little more than his initiative and a budding (some might say superficial) literary talent, came to the southern port in search of its "freedom and freshness."

Sefardi's name serves as a primary marker of his essential falseness, a pregnant sign of his incongruity, revealed in the course of his failed courtship. Attempting to establish his social and financial credentials, Sefardi pins his hopes on an advantageous alliance with the daughter of a German-Jewish banker, another recent immigrant to Russia's wild South. A foil for the ironically named anti-hero, Sefardi's rival, a Dr. Flax from Jena, represents an authentic Sephardi, that is, a de-Orientalized Oriental Jew, fully at home in Western Europe. Flax's genealogy embodies the "myth of Sephardic supremacy," according to which Iberian Jewry represented the noble ancestry of enlightened German Jews, a fictive kinship that ostensibly distinguished the latter from their unruly Eastern European Ashkenazi neighbors and relatives.[52] Appropriately his noble character and medical education reflect badly on Sefardi's superficial accomplishments and glib demeanor. Unlike the upstart Sefardi, Dr. Flax is described by his prospective father-in-law as "an excellent, most erudite person [. . .] from a very ancient stock [. . .] His family is well-known among learned people. He is a scion of the famous [medieval Jewish traveler] Benjamin of Tudela and a close relative of the scholar Dr. Achs, the preacher of the modern synagogue in Cologne."[53] Flax's illustrious pedigree torments Sefardi, because the young doctor stands for everything Sefardi himself desires but cannot have: "I'm going to go and show that fool of a father, gone crazy over all those ancestors and relatives of Flax's, that I despise them all," exclaims Sefardi after learning that Flax has wed the girl of his tortured dreams (430). In the aftermath of this self-revealing moment, Sefardi emerges as a fraud in every aspect of his life. As the juxtaposition of the German name Moritz and the appelation Sefardi ironically reveals, its bearer is a pretender, a permanent immigrant without roots. His portable nobility is a sham; German Jews, like their Russian counterparts, ought to stay where they are, Rabinovich implies. The good Dr. Flax, in marrying the daughter of the slightly seedy Galician speculator, reclaims her for German Jewry and redeems her father's ill-gotten wealth. Himself a parvenu, Sefardi cannot take his bride back to Cologne, back to her native land and to all those distinguished relatives.

Thus, although Sefardi appears to possess all the cultural advantages of enlightenment, without a sense of rootedness his intelligence, taste, and appreciation for the German classics serve only to underscore his duplicity. His "priceless *I*" (369), his faith in his own power to rise above his station at the end, deserts Sefardi, leaving him "alone, a superfluous, contemptible zero" (439). Sefardi shatters on the rocks of his own unbounded egoism and extravagant ambitions. His is a failure of the bourgeois ideal in the sense that his determination and his efforts at self-improvement do not bring him fulfillment or happiness. In fact, he recoils from the ultimate prize of bourgeois aspirations, a proper Jewish "bürgerfrau" (bourgeois wife) (299). The comforts of a placid middle-class existence taunt Sefardi in the form of a "samovar which seemed to him to have turned into an apparition dressed in an enormous bonnet and yellow housecoat, a revolting fat-bellied specter" (311–312). Rabinovich's paradoxical image of a well-fed ghost highlights the artificial — spectral — character of bourgeois Jewish comfort bought, as it were, on spec. Rabinovich's authentic Russian Jews may be undernourished but they are distinguished by their vitality; poor and thin in body, they are nevertheless solid, firmly planted in time and space.[54]

Sefardi's alienation stands out against the idealized picture of the Khmel'nik family, Odessa's Jewish natives. Khmel'nik, the patriarch, compared to Sefardi, appears ignorant and rude, and his wife superstitious, narrow-minded, and a nag. Nonetheless, the couple presents a paradigm of family harmony. The source of their redemption from the crass commercialism of their surroundings lies in their simple unconditional affection for each other. Their love finds its most powerful outlet in their daughter, the beautiful ingenue Margala, the jewel (*margala* is Hebrew for pearl) of her parents' impoverished home. A true *odessit*, Khmel'nik is neither learned nor particularly pious; but, unlike Sefardi, he is sympathetic in his duplicity, a sign of innocence rather than guile. His name alludes both to his fondness for alcohol—*khmel'* is the Russian word for hops and a metonym for drunkenness—and to that of the "southern" hero, the Cossack rebel Bohdan Khmel'nytsky. Certainly Khmel'nik prefers drink to work, and leaves the support of his family to God and to his wife and daughter. At the same time, Khmel'nik is Rabinovich's initial effort at creating a southern Jewish hero, a distant kin both to his seventeenth-century Ukrainian namesake and a progenitor of Odessa's most famous Jewish Cossacks, the Moldavanka gangsters (Rus. *razboiniki*) invented by Isaac Babel in his *Odessa Tales* (1920–1930).

The genealogical link between Khmel'nik and Khmel'nytsky alludes to the former's hypermasculinity, a virtue singularly lacking in Sefardi, in pointed defiance of the liturgical memory of martyrdom, the peculiar talent of Eastern European Jews and their crusade-era predecessors. Rabinovich's southern Jews are neither pseudo-Sephardim like Moritz nor the obedient progeny of pious Ashkenazim. The figure of Khmel'nik incarnates a radically *secular* view of Jewish peoplehood (Rus. *narodnost'*), here conceived as a Russian cultural style. In the wake of the Great Reforms, Rabinovich substantially attenuated the subversive potentialities of this depiction. Embracing the possibility of playing a prominent role in speaking directly to Jewish educated society (Rus. *obshchestvo*) through the Russian-Jewish press, he became much more invested in Jewish fiction. It was precisely in his role as an advocate of Jewish emancipation that Rabinovich discovered the uses of Jewish literature as a medium of auto-colonization. Shifting the scene from cosmopolitan Odessa to the imperial port of Nikolaev, Rabinovich created a new family of Jewish southerners, distinguished chiefly by the virtue of perfect obedience.

IN THE TOWN OF N.

Rabinovich wrote two conscription stories grouped under the subtitle "Scenes from the Past" (Rus. "Kartiny proshlogo"), an explicit reference to the imaginative "pastness" of the Nicholaevan period. The stories share an elegiac, monitory tone unprecedented in Rabinovich's pre-reform fiction. Here is the opening of "Penal Recruit" (Rus. "Shtrafnoi"), published in 1859:

> From the gloom of the past, shadows rise before me, but not those long-forgotten, as is commonly said — rather, those which have long slumbered deep within my memory. I had seldom called up these unhappy reminiscences because they torture my soul. Everyday worries, worldly concerns, but above all egoism which compels us to chase, as far away as possible, sad images and impressions in order to avoid poisoning our lives, disturbing our sleep — these were the reasons that I buried the torture-filled memories in my heart and was afraid of awakening them too often [. . .] Being incapable of relieving those conditions under the influence of which these appalling events occurred — events of which hardly anyone took notice except those for whom the words "man" and "brother" have real meaning — I understood that my every impulse would be nothing but poison for myself and no good to others [. . .] But now when the present takes on such bright forms, when my heart [. . .] has rested a bit from the tension into which it was plunged by the uncertainty of each passing day, I begin to feel the pain of old wounds.[55]

Appearing in the moderately liberal and widely read Moscow journal *Russian Bulletin* (Rus. *Russkii vestnik*), "Penal Recruit" recounted the life and death of a Jewish community leader caught between his obligations to the state and his responsibility to his fellow Jews.[56] Unable to fulfill government recruitment quotas, the "penal recrruit" ends up being drafted himself, his family destroyed in the process.[57] Framed as an object lesson for the narrator, a callow Jewish youth of some means and education, the life story of the old soldier was meant to inspire the moral awakening of the secular Russian and Jewish reader.[58] The most recent historian of Jewish conscription aptly refers to the unnamed "penal recruit" as an "enlightener in uniform"; indeed, Rabinovich's hero consistently sounds the "program of the Haskalah," without explicitly saying so.[59] At the same time the patriarchal voice of Rabinovich's "enlightener in uniform" undercuts the critical edge of maskilic social and cultural criticism:

> "My children! [he calls out on his deathbed] Man's pride is ridiculous and worthless, that of a worm feeling pride before his Creator! Grumbling at fate is the greatest of sins . . . This is rebellion against the Creator and a sign of unbelief in His justice . . . Do not complain so that you may not destroy your own soul . . . Everything has a purpose under Heaven and one cannot change it. Fulfill honestly the laws of man. Accept everything with love, and love will be returned unto you. Do not cry . . . tears lead to grumbling. Pray, pray . . . prayer, not tears, are given to strengthen us."[60]

The "penal recruit" creatively misreads the key text of the Haskalah, Moses Mendelssohn's *Jerusalem,* in the same devotionary spirit: " 'Yes, Mendelssohn was a great man [. . .] His *Jerusalem* is balm for my cruel wounds. Oh, Yerushalaim, Yerushalaim, how your mighty have fallen! Is there any sorrow equal to theirs?' "[61]

The slippage here from Mendelssohn's German title to the Hebrew

"Yerushalaim" collapses the philosopher's vision of freedom from religious constraint — this is the controversial subject of Mendelssohn's 1783 treatise — into the originary site of the Jewish diasporic consciousness. Displacing Mendelssohn's new Jerusalem, the memory of Yerushalaim lodges in the post-Nicholaevan conscription story, reformulated as a cure for the psychic travails of liberation.

On the eve of the Great Reforms, Rabinovich's depiction of Jewish suffering in the bondage of the Nicholaevan military acquired the same political resonance as the literary treatment of serfdom.[62] However, calling for Jewish emancipation on the basis of the Job-like Jewish patience of the "penal recruit" presented a certain paradox. It is hardly a coincidence that I. S. Aksakov (1823–1886), a staunch Slavophile, Russian nationalist, the eventual founder of pan-Slavism, and hardly a fan of Russian Jews, embraced the story as a compelling *conservative* justification for emancipating Rabinovich's "co-religionists." Confusing the virtues of the "penal recruit" with the literary talents of his decidedly un–Job-like creator, Aksakov wrote to Rabinovich: "If it is indeed the case that a Jew can Russify himself to such an extent, then I can no longer have anything against the emancipation of your co-religionists. Insofar as it depends on me, I will apply myself to [this task]. This is the duty of every Russian who loves his country."[63] No less ironic was the Jewish embrace of Rabinovich's "Penal Recruit" as a form of liturgy. According to Rabinovich's biographer, the Russian-Jewish historian Iulii Gessen, readers of "Penal Recruit" included even those too pious or too poor to read Russian periodicals; Yiddish translations supposedly circulated in manuscript and in families that experienced the taking of a son into the Nicholaevan army, ritually declaimed on the anniversary of the event. Contemporaries compared it to the Passover Haggadah. It could be found, Gessen claimed, "even in homes where there were no other secular books."[64] And that is precisely the point: "Penal Recruit," although written by a secular Jew, was hardly secular.

With "Penal Recruit," maskilic literature began to blur the line between fiction and history in the name of "commemoration," a code word for the persistence of religious values in the guise of secular writing.[65] In fact, no one, not even the skeptical practitioners of *Wissenschaft des Judentums*, doubted either the facticity or the moral import of "Penal Recruit" for modern Jews. The first German historian of the Jews, Isaak-Markus Jost (1799–1860), had the story translated into German and published it as a faithful — in every sense of the word — rendering of Russian-Jewish reality.[66] For Rabinovich himself, "Penal Recruit" opened the door to recognition as a writer and publicist, even as the little story intimated the social and cultural potential of a "big" Russian-Jewish literature.[67] In the wake of his triumph, he received permission from the Odessa censor to bring out a new Russian periodical devoted to issues of Jewish interest; his *Dawn*, though short-lived, served the public discussion of Jewish reform in the provinces and offered an initial forum for all sorts of experiments in regional self-assertion.[68] As the author of "Penal Recruit," Rabinovich now acquired sufficient visibility to endow the local with imperial significance.

"Family Candlestick," the second of his two conscription stories, was serialized in *Dawn* in 1861; bringing his pre-reform southern style to the telling of Jewish suffering, Rabinovich turned a post-Crimean critique of Nicholaevan policy into a myth of common Russian-Jewish origins. Like "Penal Recruit," "Family Candlestick" explored the tragic social consequences of Nicholaevan restrictions on Jewish residence and occupational choice, rendered especially poignant in light of the Jewish recruits' loyal service to the tsar. Rabinovich placed the tale of conscription without emancipation into the framework of the biblical paradigm of Jewish travail in exile. While "Family Candlestick" called for Russian Jewry's collective departure from the native diaspora of the Pale of Settlement, the story imaginatively relocated *galut* (exile) into the heart of the Jewish domestic order; displacing the enfeebled Jewish paternity of the "penal recruit," the matriarchy of "Family Candlestick" was now charged with keeping the home fires burning. The image of the "family candlestick" objectified the durability of Jewish enlightenment, its weight born by chaste Jewish daughters, loyal Jewish wives, and devoted Jewish mothers.

"Family Candlestick" takes up the fate of two generations of Jewish sailors who fall in the Crimean War, defending the southern naval town of "N." or Nikolaev, the city of Nicholas. Here, as in "Penal Recruit," Rabinovich extrapolated fiction from fact. According to Nicholaevan military statute, as long as Jewish soldiers continued to serve, their families were permitted to live with them outside the Pale of Settlement; however, once their term of service was complete, their residential status as Jews was once again put into question. This problem manifested itself with particular poignancy in the proximate southern ports of Sevastopol and Nikolaev, cities within the geographic boundaries of the Pale where permanent Jewish settlement was restricted in 1834. Because a substantial number of Jewish sailors was stationed in these cities, the Nicholaevan military was forced to consider the situation of their wives and children, who, in effect, now belonged officially to the military estate rather than to any recognized Jewish community. Unwilling to extend Jewish residential rights any further than was absolutely necessary, in 1837 the government made an exception only for the mothers of Jewish sailors stationed in Nikolaev. Under Alexander II, Nicholaevan veterans stationed in Nikolaev were the first group to experience legal emancipation; in 1860 they were granted permanent residence in the city, a lifelong privilege extended also to their families. In the aftermath of the Crimean War, the principle of residential restriction collided with the legacy of Jewish participation in the defense of Sevastopol, a city where Jews were not allowed to live. In 1866 a royal decree incorporated Nikolaev (but not neighboring Sevastopol) into the Pale of Settlement.[69] This Jewish liberation of Nikolaev—in place of Jewish emancipation *from* the Pale—signified the persistence of the piecemeal approach to dismantling Jewish disabilities. In 1860, when Rabinovich wrote "Family Candlestick," the emancipation of the veterans of Nikolaev portended the importance of the South as the place where modern Russian Jewry began.

The Jewish tragedy of "Family Candlestick" picked up at the end of the Crimean War; the widows of Rabinovich's sailors lose the legal right to live in "N." after the heroic deaths of their husbands. Unable to come up with enough money to propitiate the constable, the two women are expelled from the town and forced to wander in search of a new home, like the long-suffering biblical matriarch Naomi and her obedient daughter-in-law, Ruth; all they have left of their meager possessions is a "family candlestick." The plot emphasized the worrying persistence of Nicholaevan inequity in the state's reluctance, under Alexander II, to abolish the Pale. Rabinovich drew attention to the ambiguous legal status of the families of Jewish servicemen, stationed throughout the empire, as paradigmatic of the unresolved legal condition of Russian Jewry as a whole. The "city of N." symbolized the Pale, both the cradle of Russian-Jewish life and its grave, the place where hopes for collective emancipation had come to die in the long Nicholaevan winter, destined to be reborn in the springtime of reform. The exile Ruth, according to biblical genealogy, was, after all, the great-grandmother of King David, the progenitor of the messianic line; in Rabinovich's story, the image of an infant daughter similarly gestures at the possibility of Jewish redemption. The gender shift is not, as we will see, incidental to Rabinovich's conception of the familial origins of modern Russian-Jewish consciousness.[70]

Rabinovich emphasized the larger significance of general residential restrictions by drawing attention to the liminal character of the Jewish community in the town of "N.," centered around the lodging house of the sailor-protagonist, who offers a refuge for traveling Jewish businessmen. The stories told by the various guests at the sailor's table recapitulate the theme of geographic and social discrimination of Russian Jewry under the sway of Nicholaevan restrictions: one guest tells the story of his short and troubled sojourn in Moscow, a city that was officially closed to Jews but where they could, at great cost and effort, attain temporary residence. Through the voice of the oldest character in the story who provides an eyewitness account of the 1831 expulsion of the Jews from the city of Nikolaev, Rabinovich rehearsed the biblical motif of exile in order to mobilize the Jewish "memory" of his Odessa readers.[71]

The old man's artful version of events occasions the following intervention from the narrator: "Fortunately, we can note here that all this belongs to scenes *from the past*. Official permission, which restored the right to our co-religionists to settle in this city [Nikolaev] along with other cities, fills our hearts with gratitude and obligates us to forget the past."[72] The author's point in this ironic remark is precisely the opposite of its stated message. In writing the story, Rabinovich reminded his secular readers of the principled value of recalling Nicholaevan oppression, fully integrated into the drama of *galut*. "Family Candlestick" thus provided Russian Jews with both an argument for political emancipation and a compelling picture of an imagined Russian-Jewish past, a potent narrative of collective survival that mitigated the claims of personal desire and ambition bedeviling Rabinovich's modern Jewish hero, Moritz Sefardi.

Even as the theme of exile emphasized the acute legal alienation of Russian Jewry, Rabinovich's virtuoso command of the linguistic variety that characterized Russia's border regions expressed the reverse — Russia was an empire and Jews were an imperial people. The language of "Family Candlestick" alternated between detached third-person description and first-person colloquial speech, peppered with regional idioms, proverbs, and Yiddish and Ukrainian words. The reproduction of direct discourses that renders the story virtually untranslatable (this is *not* the case with "Penal Recruit," written in exceedingly formal, even slightly stilted Russian) reflects the fundamental contradiction between the ideal of autocratic order and the social reality of imperial hybridity, particularly evident in Rabinovich's depiction of his native South. In the process of expanding the empire, tsarist policy effectively created individual Russian Jews whom, in the name of confessional hierarchy, it refused to recognize as fully constituent subjects.

For Rabinovich, the anomalous legal status of the Jewish recruit represented a form of accidental citizenship, an unstable and equivocal position that developed out of the contradiction between Russian Jews and Russian Jewry and pitted the ambitions of the one against the many. By contrast, the association between the integrity of the Jewish family, embodied in the selflessness of Jewish wives, and the service ideal, personified by the patriotic devotion of their soldier-husbands, intimated for Rabinovich the future happy marriage between emancipation and enlightenment. Rabinovich's Jewish recruits represented a kind of domesticated heroism, consisting of patrimonial dignity, maternal devotion, and filial respect, and fully embedded in pious Jewish observance. These virtues, by dint of their association with military life, acquired a political significance, expressed in the names of Rabinovich's characters, demonstrating the author's conviction that the accidental Jewish citizens, created in the course of Nicholaevan conscription, would become true children of the tsar under his successor.

Rabinovich named the young sailor, Aaron Malkin's only son, Sender, the Yiddish diminutive of the name Alexander, and his wife, Malkin's ward, Masha, a diminutive of Maria; these names refer to the first names of the Russian royal couple. The family name of Malkin, possibly derived from a creative concatenation of the Hebrew word *melekh,* meaning "king," and the Russian word *maly,* meaning "small," "diminutive," or "junior," served to underscore the homology. The household of the old Jewish sailor was the Russian royal household writ small; the younger generation signified the family of the ascendant monarch. The names allude to the pregnant moment of "transition" between Jewish enlightenment under Nicholas I and Jewish emancipation under his son; indeed such historical ripeness, argued Rabinovich in a contemporary editorial for *Dawn,* was all.[73] The courtship of Sender and Masha—a "transition" from elective affinity to legal union— dramatizes the tension between the opportunities for enlightenment as a form of "service" to the Russian state and the deferral of emancipation. When the young man seeks his father's approval of his attachment, he confesses that he has kissed his intended "by force" four times:

> "I, you know, stood straight up, stuck my chest out, placed my hands at my sides like so. 'You love me, don't you Masha?' I said. 'With my whole soul,' she says. 'You'll marry me, won't you?' say I. 'If not you, then no one,' says she. 'So kiss me, Masha-sweetheart!' say I. But she says 'Nothing doing, Sender-sweetheart, Auntie [Zelda] has not given her consent. When she does and the engagement is announced, then maybe [...]' While she, you know, is standing there, a *picture,* her lips begging, just begging [...] I couldn't hold back. I grabbed her with both hands and kissed her right then and there."[74]

Sender's spontaneously aggressive sexuality presents a pointed contrast to his military stance at the beginning of the scene, when he stands up straight with his hands at his sides and extracts merely verbal assurances from his beloved. But the conflict between discipline and desire exists only in Masha's mind: she reproves Sender for acting "like a coarse peasant" which "does not behoove a person in the military" and proceeds to give him the cold shoulder. On the other hand, Sender's father, in an uncharacteristic display of derision toward the womenfolk, dismisses her plaint with a smile: "She is nothing but a fool [...] This is truly the military way." In an attempt to make peace between the two lovebirds, the old man acts like a benevolent but stern commander, issuing well-earned reprimands to his subordinates. Finally, Sender's avowal that, when Masha is angry with him, the performance of his duty also suffers erases the line between untrammeled eroticism and military bearing: "I feel so terrible when you are angry with me [...] Even when I am on duty, I get confused, keep losing my head. Yesterday, I almost got it [...] for not removing my service cap during the admiral's inspection."[75] This entire scene of sexual confrontation and blissful reconciliation, which culminates in a promise of marriage, conveys Rabinovich's highly politicized view of the potency of enlightened virtue, associated explicitly with the Nicholaevan disciplinary state and the military-inspired values of personal decorum. Marriage plays the crucial mitigating —Jewish—role, gracing a Russian soldier's display of physical force with the blessings of love and affection; Jewish marriage domesticates Sender's passions without rendering him effeminate or weak.[76]

If "Family Candlestick" is to be read as a political fable, then the carefully calibrated delineation of the interaction between Sender and Masha may be interpreted to refer to Rabinovich's contemporary subtext which goes something like this: under Nicholas I, Jews were pressed into state service, both under the conscription law and under the auspices of "official enlightenment." Their readiness to embrace the autocracy and the empire was compromised by the element of compulsion that attended the Nicolaevan experiment in Jewish reform. Nevertheless, their love for their sovereign remained earnest and deeply felt, awaiting only the consummating act of legal union, that is, emancipation, in order to blossom and produce a new generation of Russian Jews. Sender's passionate nature attests to the "family romance" between tsar and people, linking the hot-blooded spirit of the Russian-Jewish South to the image of enlightened, restrained, but still eminently vigorous masculinity.[77] As in his earlier work, here Rabinovich turned on its head the conventional elevation of the scholarly North of the Lithuanian Jerusalem above the ignorant and boorish South of New Russia. His Sender is, of all things, an enlightened Jewish southerner, a faithful reflection of the image of the autocrat as the "good father" (Rus. *tsar'-batiushka*) in his modern incarnation as tsar-liberator, the embodiment of the transition between Nicholas, the stern patriarch — Sender literally belongs to Nikolaev, the genitive form of Nicholas — and Alexander, his loving son.

THE HOLY COMMUNITY THAT WASN'T

The *fictional* self-sacrifice of the Malkins, junior and senior, inspired a return to the idea of Jewish memory. For Rabinovich and his fellow maskilim in New Russia — new in time and in space — the assertion of regional identity answered the desire for community at a time when the ties of traditional collective ties began to compete with alternative allegiances to class, estate, family, profession, and self. Modeling Russian Jewry on the image of the conscript as a Jewish martyr, Rabinovich translated the conception of "holy community" (Heb. *kehillah kedoshah*) into a contemporary political idiom and endowed the notion with renewed ideological force at a time when increasing numbers of Jews grew more and more distant from their pious origins in the Pale of Settlement. Sanctifying the memory of Nicholaevan conscripts, Rabinovich turned Russia's new south into Jewish sacred ground.

In the wake of his literary success, Rabinovich embarked on a project to carve out a native Jewish space in a place without Jewish roots, to colonize the Russian south by enshrining the memory of Jewish recruits who had fallen in the defense of Sevastopol. The initiative came from a reader of *Dawn*. In a letter to the editor, a Jewish resident of Sevastopol complained that the local Jewish cemetery had fallen into disrepair.[78] Both the old synagogue, destroyed in the siege, and the cemetery of the town had been under the care of the Jewish servicemen stationed in Sevastopol; most of them, however, had died defending the port. In 1859 seventy-five Jewish veterans of the campaign successfully petitioned the local authorities to rebuild the synagogue. The call for the restoration of the cemetery was part of the public effort to resurrect Jewish Sevastopol, a "holy community" with a short and decidedly modern history.

Rabinovich and the Jewish *obshchestvo* of Odessa responded with a civic campaign that took four years. A flurry of articles first appeared in *Zion* (Rus. *Sion*), the journal that immediately succeeded *Dawn* (closed by the government for its "radical" emancipationist agenda), announcing plans not only to rebuild Sevastopol's Jewish cemetery but to erect on the site a memorial to its fallen Jewish heroes.[79] In 1865 a committee was finally formed composed of Odessa's most prominent Jewish residents, headed by Rabinovich himself, and including the rabbi of the liberal Choral Synagogue, Dr. Shimon Schwabacher, as well as the editors of *Zion*. The project engaged the incipient Russian civic consciousness of enlightened southern Jews committed to the idea of emancipation. At the same time the patriotic attempt to memorialize Nicholas's Jewish soldiers as a community constituted by the experience of heroic self-sacrifice reflected the contemporary Jewish interest in unearthing and celebrating historical sites of martyrdom.

Initially inspired by local efforts at historic preservation, this sort of search often took its secular proponents to cemeteries, preeminent destinations on the collective memory tour where the beautiful death of the righteous could be contemplated with all due reverence by their less-than-orthodox descendants.[80] Sometimes, to the disappointment of the travelers, there was nothing to find: "One visits both cemeteries in Berdichev," wrote the indefatigable Odessa publisher Alexander Tsederbaum (1816–1893) of his pilgrimage to the center of old Jewish Ukraine: "The ancient cemetery is surrounded by a heavy brick wall. Very few headstones remain [. . .] We tried hard to find the oldest headstones, especially those from the 1648 [Chmielnicki] massacres but it proved impossible."[81] The absence of ready markers of Jewish memory lent itself to creative efforts at constructing new traditions and erecting new devotional sites. The Sevastopol memorial, conceived in the spirit of urban renewal, enshrined the persistence of maskilic piety in immediate proximity to Odessa, home to the most radically secular, culturally emancipated Jewry of the Russian Empire.

The erection of the monument, publicized in the 1866 literary anthology that celebrated the achievements of the recently formed Society for the Promotion of Enlightenment among the Jews of Russia (Rus. *Obshchestvo dlia rasprostraneniia prosveshcheniia mezhdu evreiiami v Rossii*, or OPE), first and foremost celebrated the respectable philanthropic instincts of Odessa's Jewish society.[82] The reflexive gesture not only promoted the fetishization of place as a signifier of Jewishness but contributed to the displacement of observance (doing Jewish things) by observation (looking at Jewish things) as a competing expression of religious self-consciousness. Reading edifying

71

literature and contemplating inspirational sites—both a form of voyeur-ism—now emerged as model acts of enlightened Jewish devotion. In the vicarious identification with Rabinovich's recruits, the ones he created in "Family Candlestick" and the ones he helped to memorialize in Sevastopol, the maskilim of Odessa asserted their personal piety against the contempo-rary charge that "seven fires of hell" burned around the pit of vice and godlessness that they proudly called home.[83]

The holy congregation of Nicholaevan recruits, martyred for the "the land of their birth and their king, his majesty the emperor" provided a foil for a Russian Jewry fractured by decidedly unholy pursuits. At the same time the biblical inscription on the monument offered an oblique testament to the political faith of Russian Jews and to their abiding investment in the possibility of making Russian Jewry through an act of messianic imperial grace. On one side the marble obelisk bore an inscription from Isaiah 26:19 (JPS): "O dwellers in the dust, awake and sing for joy. For your dew is radiant and the earth will revive those long dead!" While the passage is a fairly conventional memorial invocation, heralding the promise of resurrec-tion, its scriptural context gave the verse a contemporary edge. Verse 19 brings to a rhetorical end a section of text that compares Israel awaiting the Messiah to a woman in labor. Promising collective restoration from a divine source, the prophet claims that his people have "won no victories on earth." Informed by the heightened mood of political expectation that attended the post-Crimean period, this claim spoke directly to the situation of Russian Jews poised to be transformed by an act of collective emancipation. Rabino-vich asserted in his fiction that the Crimean War was important for Jews precisely because Nicholas's Russia had "won no victories" on the battle-field; its political salvation in the guise of the Great Reforms came out of Russia's ignominious defeat. Nicholaevan oppression had been, perhaps, the labor pains of the Messiah. Endowed with unlimited autocratic power and a will to reform, a new king could raise an enlightened Russian Jewry from the dust of Nicholaevan martyrs, a feat no less miraculous than turning Odessa into a "holy community."

3

THE ROMANCE OF ENLIGHTENMENT: GENDER AND THE CRITIQUE OF EMBOURGEOISEMENT IN THE RECRUITMENT NOVELS OF I. M. DIK, GRIGORII BOGROV, AND J. L. GORDON

THE DOMESTICATION OF ENLIGHTENMENT
IN THE AGE OF EMANCIPATION

During the 1870s Russian Jewry's conscription past emerged as a key theme in the expanding repertoire of maskilic literature, written in Russian, Hebrew, and Yiddish, and aimed at an increasing number of Russian Jews eager to claim the fruits of economic and educational opportunities afforded by the policy of "selective integration" in order to move beyond the Pale. One of the characteristic features of this literature, cutting across generic and linguistic differences, was a self-conscious commitment to the defense of the Haskalah at a time when it grew increasingly clear to its proponents that the historic effects of emancipation did not necessarily coincide with the triumph of Jewish enlightenment. To be sure, emancipation led to the emergence of Russian-Jewish educated society and to the exponential growth of Russian-Jewish publishing. At the same time, however, principled adherents to the Haskalah now found themselves competing for authority in the expanding literary marketplace rather than in the halls of Russian administrative power or in the courtyard of study houses and synagogues. With the decline of official support for Jewish enlightenment and the growth of an increasingly self-conscious Jewish orthodoxy, maskilic values emerged in new forms in order to hold the attention of its discerning and fractious Russian-Jewish public.

The rapid expansion of Jewish belles lettres, a phenomenon generally associated with the ostensible "zenith" of the Haskalah in the 1860s to the 1870s, came into its own precisely at the moment when it first became possible to conceive of Jewish educated or semi-educated society and when it became increasingly difficult to monopolize its attention and control its tastes.[1] The contradictory effects of the political turn toward the "unserfment" of Russian society accounts for the impressive growth of imaginative prose and historical narrative. As Jewish enlightenment discourse spilled over into new literary modes, conscription became a compelling source of interest to three writers—Isaac-Meir Dik (1807–1893), Grigorii Bogrov (1825–1885), and Judah-Leib Gordon (1830–1892)—whose work exemplified the aspirations and anxieties of maskilim struggling for cultural capital in the age of emancipation.

In the work of Dik, Bogrov, and Gordon, the conscription story speaks directly to the tension between the virtues of enlightenment and the aims of emancipation, a conflict that transformed both the content and prevailing style of maskilic literary production. The ties that bound these three writers to the same dilemmas of conscience and creativity are not immediately obvious, given the kinds of works each of them produced and the languages in which they expressed themselves. Dik wrote primarily Yiddish romances, Bogrov melodramatic Russian stories about contemporary Jewish life, and Gordon scores of publicistic pieces and essays in cultural criticism but was best known for Hebrew narrative poetry. The voice of Jewish liberalism in nineteenth-century Russia, Gordon devoted himself to burning contemporary causes like the state of the rabbinate, the plight of Jewish women, religious reform, and the improvement of Jewish education.[2] Dik and Bogrov are, by contrast, less well known. Scholarship segregates them by language and ideological orientation. Dik, who wrote in Hebrew and Yiddish, remained throughout his life a pious and observant Jew; thus he is characterized as a "moderate maskil," the "guardian of enlightened faith."[3] Bogrov, the Russian "assimilationist," remained completely secular, referred to himself as an "emancipated cosmopolitan," and converted to Orthodoxy on his deathbed.[4] Gordon, the staunch Hebraist, occupies a special place at the crossroads of the Haskalah and Zionism, a "national poet" before his time.[5] Yet, such qualifications notwithstanding, Bogrov, Dik, and Gordon all shared an unprecedented degree of popular acclaim as Jewish writers, specifically as authors of Jewish fiction explicitly informed by the ideals of the Haskalah. All three were equally troubled and inspired by the often conflicting demands of commercial authorship and intellectual authority. Despite differences in lifestyle and linguistic choice, all three were driven by similar concerns about the consequences of emancipation to elevate Jewish domesticity and to attempt the domestication of Jewish reading habits.

Dik, Bogrov, and Gordon each marshaled the conscription story as a moral lesson, aimed explicitly at an upwardly mobile readership vulnerable to the risks of bourgeois ambition at the expense of maskilic principle. The turn toward conscription in their work highlights the tension between the ideological embrace of modernity and persistent anxiety about its disruptive social and cultural effects; maskilic self-criticism, in turn, found an outlet in the gendering of enlightenment discourse.[6] The uses of conscription in the maskilic reconstruction of the Jewish domestic order pointed to the limits of the rhetorical commitment to personal liberation which Jewish enlighteners prized. Eager to halt the secularization of desire, the maskil as novelist sought to inspire his reader with exemplars of enlightened Jewish virtue. The cost of such heroic restraint against the temptations of modernity was, both in fact and in fiction, borne primarily by Jewish women; Rabinovich's silent outcasts from the city of Nicholas — maskilic paradise — would eventually be recast by his successors as the bad conscience of enlightenment.

Rabinovich marshaled the conscription story as a Jewish subtext for a decidedly secular story of embourgeoisement; the archetypal city of Nikolaev, the imaginary "maskilic utopia" where Jewish soldiers suffered and died, served as a foil for real Odessa where Jews lived and prospered. The defenders of enlightenment similarly turned to conscription in order to turn the recent history of Russian Jews into a morally compelling and urgently contemporary Jewish fiction. While the narrative logic of Rabinovich's transparent call for Jewish emancipation spoke to the mood of nearly messianic expectation that had attended the ascendance of the tsar-liberator, Dik, Bogrov, and Gordon all took for granted the ambiguities of "selective integration" as a permanent feature of the Jewish social landscape, resistant to sweeping political solutions. Indeed, unlike Rabinovich, Dik, Bogrov, and Gordon shared the conviction that emancipation constituted the answer to the dilemmas of Jewish economic, social, and cultural marginality *as well as* an urgent problem with grave consequences for the future of Jewish collective life. This is why, throughout the 1870s, the conscription theme moved into the conservative register of the family romance. No longer a polemical symbol of collective Russian-Jewish origins, the herald of a people waiting to be initiated into the imperial family of nations, the figure of the recruit as a paragon of enlightened Judaism became associated with the domestic cure for the alienation of an up-and-coming generation of Jewish sons from the maskilic roots of their fathers.

The transition from Rabinovich's exemplary "scenes" to the extended family romance accorded with the moral investment in the vernacularization of Jewish literature, the new source of Jewish values for an audience more accustomed to reading (Yid. *leynen*) books than to studying (Yid. *lernen*) sacred texts. The cultural embourgeoisement of Jewish imaginative

75

writing, a process with its roots in the "genre revolution" of the eighteenth century, provided an impetus for the nineteenth-century turn toward self-consciously contemporary forms like the family romance, the historical novel and the narrative poem.[7] Jewish history, one could argue, was born not in an academic context but in this essentially literary one, the line between fact and fiction notoriously blurry, subject to the demands of moral and aesthetic judgment rather than to the critical imperative.[8] At the end of his *Popular History of the Jews* (Ger. *Volkstümliche Geschichte der Juden*), published in 1888, Heinrich Graetz celebrated his own narrative talents as one of German Jewry's best-loved authors in the hope that the writing of Jewish history would help to "reconcile children with the hearts of their parents."[9] As a faithful follower of *Wissenschaft des Judentums*, Graetz attached this kind of affective value specifically to history writing; but, in fact, his work as a historian was supremely literary, in marked contrast to the "microscopic" philological treatises of his fellow *Wissenschaftlers*, Geiger, Steinschneider, and Zunz.[10] Ludwig Phillipson, instrumental throughout the 1850s to 1870s, in the effort to create a German-Jewish reading public, designated literature as a source of private religious instruction, providing an ethical defense against materialism and "secular life."[11]

Russian-Jewish enlighteners similarly embraced the spiritual potential of literary retellings of the Jewish past. In 1875 Abraham Friedberg (1838–1902) began to translate Grace Aguilar's historical novel *Vale of Cedars* (1850) into Hebrew.[12] Writing to his editor, Peretz Smolenskin, about the psychological effect this book produced — "I was stirred by this wonderful story which warmed my heart and aroused all my senses," he said — Friedberg adopted the maskilic convention of attributing a morally elevating role to literature to a populist critique of enlightenment:

> This entire story is composed in the spirit of the people, rendered keenly with the pure holiness of sentimental feeling, in accordance with the tastes of our readers who are just beginning to appreciate romantic literature; in accordance with the needs of the present time, [the story will] fasten the bond of strong faith and unite our hearts as in the days of yore. Even the most cold-hearted reader will not be able to refrain from weeping; his tears will fall like pouring rain to soften his heart and awaken in him love and great affection for his people and for his place of birth [Heb. *moladeto*],[13] that love of one's people which is growing weaker in our midst among this generation as a result of the spirit of cosmopolitanism which has ensnared us all in its clutches.[14]

Expressing long-standing maskilic concerns about the secularization of enlightenment values and the erosion of piety under the impact of embourgeoisement and professionalization, Friedberg raised the ideological stakes attendant on the creation of an edifying and inspiring Jewish literature meant for an upwardly mobile, culturally ambitious readership. In fact, Friedberg hammered the morally instructive point home by changing the love interest in Aguilar's story from "a Christian nobleman" into a Marrano, an "ardent" Jewish aristocrat from the illustrious Abarbanel family.

Graetz's point about "reconciling the hearts of parents and children" encapsulates perfectly the way that such efforts at Jewish literary "improvement" served to relocate the inculcation of Jewish loyalty from the institutional venues of school and synagogue into the private domain of the Jewish home. Only there, and only through the cultivation of modern literary sensibility, would the otherwise estranged fathers and sons—alienated primarily by the increasingly different public worlds they inhabited and the public roles they assumed—find common Jewish ground. Model Jewish paternity, enshrined in the fiction of Dik, Bogrov, and Gordon, would, these authors claimed, preserve the maskilic ideal both from the unbridled ambition of Jewish upstarts, whose force threatened to dissolve the confessional ties of Judaism altogether, and from the vocal defenders of the Jewish communal discipline who threatened to drag the beleaguered enlightener back behind the Pale.

ISAAC-MEIR DIK AND THE SEARCH FOR
ENLIGHTENED PATERNITY

In 1856 an imperial decree effected the return home of thousands of Jewish sons who remained in the now defunct cantonist regiments. By the 1870s this miraculous reconciliation would serve as a foil for the far more ambiguous legacy of the Great Reforms—the large-scale departure of Jewish children for Russian student culture and the expanding ranks of the revolutionary movement.[15] The promise of personal liberation through education also made accessible the threat of temptation away from Judaism; in the era of "unserfment" the results of experiments in enlightenment could no longer be controlled, not by the state nor by the new maskilic elite. For the latter, the tension grew increasingly acute.

In the 1860s through the 1870s Vilna, where, thanks to their social status and their piety, the first generation of Russian maskilim had attained a measurable degree of local prominence and respectability, had become the seat of Polish insurrectionism and revolutionary radicalism, and the target of an aggressive Russification campaign.[16] In 1873 the government closed down the rabbinical seminary, putting the final nail in the coffin of "official enlightenment." In addition, neighboring Kovno saw the rise of a rival neo-traditionalist camp, dead set against the kinds of compromise between faith and reason that the Vilna enlighteners advocated as a cure for what ailed Jewish society.[17] In response to the challenges facing the maskilic utopia of the Lithuanian Jerusalem, Vilna enlighteners began to cultivate an explicitly regional pedigree, rooted in the formation of a maskilic canon.[18] Interest shifted from promoting institution building and wrangling with local rabbinic rivals to fighting over the consciousness of the Jewish reader.[19]

Isaac-Meir Dik, Vilna enlightener par excellence, parlayed such concerns into an unprecedented career as a popular Jewish writer. Translating the distinguished cultural genealogy of the Vilna study house into the idiom of the Jewish kitchen, Dik adopted into his Yiddish fiction the persona of the female reader in order to discipline male Jewish desire. Through the cultivation of natural, affective, domestic (read, feminine) ties to Judaism, Dik hoped precisely to reconcile the hearts of children and parents. Male-marked language of rationality and autonomy, characteristic of the Jewish enlighteners' rhetorical debt to Kant's injunction "Dare to know!" gave way to a marked stress on sentiment and a predilection for tearful scenes of family reunion.[20] Nicholaevan maskilim had embraced the martial spirit of "official enlightenment" as a harsh verdict of reason upon the pathology of traditional Jewish life; Alexandrine efforts at emancipation, by contrast, were interpreted by Dik and others as acts of paternal mercy, an image of liberation fully consistent with Alexander's own highly sentimental perception of autocratic rule.[21] For Jewish enlighteners, the abolition of the Nicholaevan conscription decree became the most evocative symbol of Alexander's desire to restore the hearts of Jewish children to their parents, the grace of providence acting *against* the implacable dictate of history. Of course, as Dik saw all around him, the Great Reforms had precisely the opposite effect; emancipation sharpened generational difference, exacerbated social conflict, and undermined Jewish family discipline.[22]

Turning to the conscription story in his quest for affective Jewish paternity, modeled on Alexander's triumph of feeling over reason, Dik sought to resolve the tension between the paternal expectation of enlightenment with the filial experience of emancipation. During the late 1860s–early 1870s Dik composed a series of contemporary chronicles in which the Nicholaevan period provided the historical backdrop for a parodic assault on Jewish communal corruption, social vice, and cultural backwardness. The series, keyed to specific instances of Jewish resistance to government-initiated reform, included *The Panic of 1835* (1867–1868) and *The Change in Jewish Clothing That Was Instituted in 1844* (1870); in 1871 Dik published *The First Levy of Recruits in the Year 1828*, certainly intended as another installment in the comic cycle. In *The First Levy of Recruits*, Dik introduced his own autobiographical persona to his female reader for the first time and identified himself directly with the narrator who, as a child, witnessed the events Dik described and evaluated as an adult.

In *First Levy of Recruits*, Dik fused the historical drama of conscription with the story of his own coming-of-age; in fact, he fudged his date of birth (contrary to the literary testimony on which most scholars uncritically rely, Dik was probably born in 1807)[23] so that he could appear to be at the liminal age of thirteen in 1828, when the decree was instituted.[24] Dik equated the historic maturation of Russian Jewry, symbolized by Nicholaevan reform legislation, with the personal coming-of-age of the Jewish enlightener. Conscription implicated the government in this process, collapsing the difference between the political sign of male adulthood and the Jewish ritual of initiation into the age of religious responsibility and rational judgment. By contrast, Dik associated the nonage of Russian Jewry with unenlightened, shrieking motherhood, and the newly acquired maturity of the maskil with perfect paternity, both eminently reasonable and emotionally satisfying. Locating the absurdity of the popular reaction to the conscription decree in the behavior of Jewish mothers who go to the cemetery to pray that their sons may die before the age of seventeen so that they might avoid conscription, Dik intimated that the problem with Jewish society—which the conscription decree supposedly cured—lay in the irrational power of women over men, kept in childlike bondage to the regime of superstition and self-destruction. Highlighting the gendered reading of family pathology, Dik described women, who already lost their children, blessing their fate "that they have been rendered worthy of having brought a Jew into the world destined for a Jewish grave [Heb./Yid. *kever yisroel*]" (16–18). Motherly love here led only to Jewish death; a father's love, by contrast, promoted heroic Jewish life in a world governed by beneficent providence.

Dik depicted the narrator's richly allusive recollection of his moment of spiritual fusion with his father on Yom Kippur as a cathartic rebirth:

> I spent the entire time [in the synagogue] under the watchful eye of my blessed father. He blessed me, wrapping me close in his surplice [Heb./Yid. *kittel*] and in his prayer shawl. He prayed, bathing me in the tears streaming from his wise eyes [. . .] His blessing for me consisted of only one thing: he bade me to remain a faithful Jew, not to depart from the proper path no matter what fate God had in store for me. My young heart could hardly stand it; I felt like our forefather Isaac at his own [averted] sacrifice [. . .] I cried until I had no more strength. And the streets, too, were filled with crying. Tears such as this have not been shed since the destruction of Jerusalem. (22–23)

This scene of symbolic conscription echoed the sermon of the Prague sage Ezekiel Landau, recalled by Dik as paradigmatic of the enlightened view of conscription, in which the rabbi enjoined departing Jewish recruits to serve both their God and their emperor with equal loyalty and zeal (8–9).[25] Landau's faithful acceptance of conscription in turn highlighted the narrator's father's fitting skepticism in response to the last-minute rumor that the decree has been annulled. The tsar's law had the force of history on its side; how, then, could it be abrogated? (26). The adult narrator, a perfect reflection of his father, delivered a similarly measured assessment of the social effects of the conscription decree (31–36).

The "critical overview of Jewish recruitment" largely consists of conventional maskilic pieties about all the ways in which the evils of conscription were entirely the result of communal corruption.[26] One remark stands out, however: Dik avows that many among the Jewish recruits were lucky to have been conscripted. Jewish soldiers, Dik asserts, were able to remain pious and even grew rich. They formed their own communities in Moscow and St. Petersburg, founded study houses and even raised better Jewish children then their "free" counterparts in the Pale.[27] This idealization of the parenting talents of Jewish soldiers — learned, wealthy, and living outside the Pale — anticipates Dik's homo-social maskilic utopia without Jewish women, featured in *The Runaway Recruit* (1872) and developed more fully in the 1876 conscription romance *The Soldier's Son*. In *The First Levy of Recruits*, the image of recruitment as a fantasy of integral Jewish paternity highlights the immediate consequences of the critical difference between Jewish mothering and Jewish fathering which Dik positioned at the center of an otherwise rambling and disjointed work. The unhinged wailing mothers of Dik's "first" recruits will finally be silenced into submission by the "soldier's son."

In the 1872 novella *The Runaway Recruit* (more precisely, *The Little Runaway Recruit*) Dik elaborates in the form of a maskilic history-cum-parable the proposition that Jewish soldiers made the best parents. In fact, the contrived and schematic plot of Dik's little nugget illustrates beautifully Graetz's proposition that an artful representation of the Jewish past may serve to "reconcile children with the hearts of their parents"; Dik's anti-Oedipal comedy revolves around the shared fate of father and son recruits. At the end, the narrator virtually collapses the two into each other; the son gains his autonomy not at the expense of his father but directly through his superior moral and military authority, and the father, in reclaiming his son, effectively fulfills his public duty so that he, too, can become free.

Just as in *First Levy of Recruits*, fatherhood here served as the supreme embodiment of both public reason and private sentiment, perfectly joined in the image of enlightened benevolent autocracy. Indeed, in the final scene of affective reunion, the emotional connection of father to son recapitulates the theme of paternal benevolence that Dik attributed to the "noble heart" of Alexander II, who, in complete empathy with Jewish suffering, abolished the conscription of Jewish minors and thus, in his "gentle fatherly" way, sought to restore Jewish children, "illegally" conscripted by their own communities, to their grieving parents.[28] Dik's conflation of Jewish paternity with autocratic mercy echoes Rabinovich's depiction of the Malkin household. But whereas Rabinovich attributed the tragic fate of the Malkins Sr. and Jr. to an unjust law, Dik located lawfulness and justice exclusively on the side of Jewish authority. The problem, in Dik's view, lay instead in the inequitable implementation of the decree; because "God is high above and the tsar is far away," arbitrariness and corruption reigned unimpeded (10–11). When the father of the little recruit attempts to secure the release of his only son, drafted against the letter of the law, he, too, falls victim to the vengeance of the "lawless world," characterized by the venal abuse of enlightened tsarist legislation and depicted in Dik's Nicholaevan chronicles.

In contrast to the father's energetic, if futile, resistance to injustice, the hero's mother completely falls apart in the absence of husband and son. Capable of little more than crying her eyes out and endlessly rehearsing her sad story (more pointless, maudlin chatter), she leaves her tavern and her hometown to wander, "a second Naomi," into the town of Dubno. Together with her daughter, she ekes out a living selling milk and bread, a modest feminine occupation singularly appropriate to her retirement from the world of men. The narrator duly rewards his heroines' embrace of feminine passivity by providing the daughter with an enlightened husband in the person of Itzik, an established young householder settled on one of the government-sponsored Jewish agricultural colonies, a Nicholaevan institution in which maskilim placed great hopes for future Jewish productivity (16–17).[29] The figure of the Jewish farmer forms the masculine counterpart of the feminine idyll of pastoral innocence associated here with the provision of milk and bread. Meanwhile, the story of the runaway recruit turned into an object lesson in the evils of smuggling, another staple of maskilic social criticism aimed at the Jewish commercial economy. The hero unwittingly finds himself across the border in the bustling Galician town of Brody, where he eventually gains the protection of a newly acquired foster father, a Jewish horse trader, who, although generous and kind, involves him in shady dealings with contraband goods. The hero, now a deserter and a smuggler, thus remains both morally and legally indefensible. His rehabilitation and return to his homeland occur under the providential rule of Alexander II — the tsar who restored children to their parents — through an auspicious meeting with the man who turns out to be his father, serving, not coincidentally, as a border guard, literally the embodiment of Russian justice in a geographically and ethically liminal space. Thus enlightened Jewish masculinity surfaces by negotiating an open frontier, guided by the well-timed intervention of father, tsar, and God himself; proper Jewish femininity, in contrast, locates its métier in the closed spaces of home, garden, and barn, "in a little house in the corner of the city" where Jewish maidens are required dutifully to sit and spin until the arrival of their maskilic suitors (17).[30]

Unlike the Oedipal tragedy in which the son suffers from a surfeit of responsibility for his fate, the recruit bears no guilt; his moral failings are the result entirely of comical circumstances beyond his control. In marked contrast to this unqualified rehabilitation of the runaway recruit, Dik expressed far more ambivalence about the parallel figure of the "runaway daughter" even when she presumed to follow the maskilic script toward the attainment of romantic love.[31] Indeed, as a projection of maskilic anxieties about the risky consequences of promoting the active pursuit of individual want, the provocative presence of the "runaway daughter" effectively inspired the therapeutic counter-image of the "runaway recruit." In his embrace of the latter at the expense of the former, Dik adopted the conscription theme to the needs of an enlightened self-consciousness acutely sensitive to the socially destabilizing promise of emancipation projected onto "unruly" Jewish daughters which served not the progressive improvement of Jewish life but the increasing secularization of Jewish desire. Framed as a necessary fulfillment of historical destiny, a perfect teleological union between past and present, Dik's fantasy of ideal paternity spoke directly to contemporary anxieties about the increasingly unmanageable effects of the struggle for individual autonomy waged by refractory children on both sides of the gender divide.

The bourgeois protagonist of *The Soldier's Son* embodies the struggle for self-discipline that was now required of any Jew who aspired to enlightenment in the age of emancipation. Internalizing the ethos of enlightened Jewish masculinity, the maskil as recruit grew up to become his own father. The "soldier's son" is Dik's middle-brow paragon in the making, seeking an ideal marriage, a felicitous quest that results in the happy union of economic security and romantic love. He experiences a steady rise in fortunes, owing largely to the serendipitous intervention of paternal figures such as the Russian count who takes him under his wing and educates him along with his own children. The initial disaster of his father's recruitment becomes the first step in the son's ascent. For the father, service in the imperial hinterland provides an opportunity to get rich and to broaden his social and cultural horizons in the company of enterprising Jewish merchants who have, on their own initiative, left behind the stagnant backwater of the Pale. Quickly promoted to officer's rank by a wise and open-minded Russian commander, the father embodies the rewards of "official enlightenment" in the age of emancipation, a lesson about the benefits of duty that he effectively imparts to his son, who no longer had to be conscripted by force.

The "soldier's son" joins the Russian army voluntarily to escape a life of oppressive and demeaning drudgery in service to a willful, idle, Polish aristocrat. The effect of the paterfamilias on the son represents the internalization of legal and rational — adult — authority of the Russian state, an aspect of perfect paternity thematized both in *First Levy* and in the *Runaway Recruit*. Mirroring the path taken by his father, the son also serves in a region barred to Jewish residence. He becomes a regimental scribe and, like his father, advances rapidly with the support of benevolent military authorities. Significantly, he achieves success not as a result of commercial ingenuity but because of his command of Russian, culled from extensive reading of literature, a language more polished and genteel than the "official style" of his fellow scribes. In fact, because of his "refinement," his superiors vouchsafe his discharge from the military and promise to support his promotion into the civil service. He begins to frequent the houses of local military gentry and becomes a particular friend of a young, pretty, and appropriately cultivated wife of a local colonel.[32] Of course, he resists her gentile charms and eventually weds a proper Jewish bride, the daughter of a wealthy army supplier who, through his good offices to the state, has acquired the right to reside anywhere in Russia. This self-made Jewish "humanist," who bears the same name as his father, embraces the young hero and paves the way for a triumphant public return to Judaism and a reunion with his own family.[33]

The plot, although thick with incident and descriptive detail, is woefully thin in historical plausibility, despite Dik's avowal that his first-person narrator is eminently "trustworthy."[34] So far-fetched is this story of Jewish success in the pre-reform Russian military that it virtually parodies itself.[35] This raises the awkward question as to why, if Dik wanted simply to write a Jewish *Bildungsroman*, he felt the need to fit it into the procrustean bed of conscription history. As I have argued elsewhere, Dik appropriated the conscription theme as a framework for an enlightened *midrash* on the biblical story of Joseph, stressing particularly the "martial" virtues of Jewish self-discipline, both sexual and economic.[36] Here I would go further to suggest that the invocation of Joseph as a paragon of male empowerment and self-control provides a key to the conspicuous silencing of Jewish women in *The Soldier's Son* and in other, less ungainly versions of the conscription romance.

As David Roskies amply demonstrates, Dik's contemporary "bourgeois exempla" relied on the radical distinction between two types of women, "those who rule and those who obey."[37] "A woman who wishes to have the upper hand and rule over her husband," Dik wrote in *The Stepmother,* a popular early romance reprinted for the second time in the same year as *The Soldier's Son,* "is neither a man nor a woman. She has no feelings of tenderness or mercy as a real woman ought to have."[38] More than merely obnoxious and hypocritical, Dik's "female typology" spoke to the general problem of desire in the rhetoric of upward mobility expounded by the proponents of Jewish enlightenment, a problem that demanded both an ethical and political solution. Grafting the story of Jewish embourgeoisement onto the conscription theme allowed Dik to indulge in a fantasy of Jewish modernity without Jewish women, to embrace enlightenment, and, at the same time, to evade the secular risks of emancipation associated with a feminine lack of self-discipline.

The conscription story, by locating the telos of emancipation in duty, service, and filial/civic responsibility, provided a disciplinary confessional model of self-improvement, a cure for the ostensibly pathological instability of class and gender categories produced by the "unserfment" of Jewish society in the aftermath of emancipation. This instability, in fact, was not so much historical as ideological insofar as it emerged out of the radical disparity between enlightenment expectations and the realities of economic, social, and cultural change, a rupture that the enlighteners experienced personally.[39] Thus "AMaD" — an anagram of "Adam," which also means "human being" in Hebrew — Dik's maskilic authorial persona claimed to command a docile feminine audience, ready to be inspired, enlightened, and transformed. In reality, Dik's ability to write depended on the income his wife earned in the singularly unregenerate business of pawn broking.[40] Moreover, the expansion of the literary marketplace, ostensibly a boon for the creation of a model Jewish audience, left Dik at the mercy of commercial publishing and the tastes of an audience that stubbornly preferred satire and sensational romances to elevating historical parables. All three of Dik's conscription tales date from a late period when his work had become overtly didactic in tone and content, and his popularity had declined.[41] Hence the urgency of his call for literary/domestic discipline and the ambivalence, starkly evident in the conscription stories, toward the female reader as the clamoring voice of unreason.

In the shadow of emancipation, conscription appealed to Dik as a metaphor for the yearned for but elusive convergence of individual and historical progress. But back in 1846, when conscription was a reality, Dik had coauthored and signed a report submitted to Sir Moses Montefiore, then visiting Vilna, which argued that *rekrutchina* spelled the ruin of the Jewish community and led to mass conversions of Jewish children.[42] Dik consistently used conscription to show that the Haskalah was a product of cooperation between the middle class and enlightened Russian officials. But, in fact, his own position as a teacher in a government-sponsored school fell victim to the same process of state retrenchment from "official enlightenment" that eventually claimed the rabbinical seminaries and led countless Jewish students into Russian institutions of higher learning.[43] Dik adopted the conscription theme to the defense of an enlightenment utopia set in the well-appointed parlors of the rising middle class; yet his own family life remained thoroughly traditional, and his own initiation into enlightenment occurred not at home but in the Vilna town square.[44] An active supporter of radical causes throughout the 1840s, Dik acquired his maskilic pedigree by signing a petition to the deputy minister of education mandating government intervention in the institution of clothing reform; yet throughout his life he never abandoned his traditional beard and gabardine.[45]

The paradoxes that divided the fictional persona of "AMaD" from his real creator, Isaac-Meir Dik reveal all the ways in which the maskilic turn to literature in the 1860s, and especially in the 1870s, was *not,* as per the historians of the modern Jewish canon, the telos of Jewish enlightenment but instead an ironic sign of the Haskalah in retrenchment.[46] During its formative period in the reign of Nicholas I, Jewish publishing had been severely restricted not only by established monopolies and state censorship but through the active intervention of the maskilim themselves, always concerned with the cultural promiscuity of Jewish reading habits.[47] Jewish enlighteners remained highly suspicious of literature even when they invoked its potential social "usefulness" as a vehicle of reform.[48] The development of modern Jewish belles lettres in the age of the Great Reforms took shape against maskilic resistance to literature as well as against the state's retreat from the active institutionalization of the Jewish enlightenment in Russia. Without the support of the government, heroic feats of social engineering such as the creation of a German-style rabbinate, the founding of a reformed school system, and the shift from commerce to agriculture grew increasingly beyond the reach of maskilic ambition.[49] The counter-intuitive discovery of literature as a vocation, and as a paradigmatic feature of maskilic activity rather than a sideline, became more urgent precisely when other avenues of entry into Jewish public life became more contested or simply unavailable. Indeed, the embrace of moral influence over the private sphere, claimed by Jewish writers in the name of Jewish enlightenment, reflected a net loss of maskilic social power.[50]

BOGROV'S CAPTIVE RECRUITS:
ENLIGHTENED MISOGYNY AND JEWISH EMPOWERMENT

Grigorii Bogrov began his career as the nineteenth century's most prolific author of Jewish fiction in the Russian language with two stories about conscription. The first of these, "The Adventures of Yerukhim," constituted the penultimate chapter of Bogrov's vast confessional novel, *Notes of a Jew,* serialized between 1871 and 1873 in *Notes of the Fatherland* (Rus. *Otechestvennye zapiski*), a progressive literary journal edited by the poet N. A. Nekrasov (1821–1877) and published separately in 1874. The second, a novella entitled "Captive Recruit," graced the first one hundred pages of the fourth volume of St. Petersburg's first Russian-Jewish literary annual, *The Jewish Library* (Rus. *Evreiskaia biblioteka*) in 1873. Despite the marked difference in mood — "Yerukhim" was a lugubrious tale of suffering innocence whereas "Captive Recruit" recounted in a comic vein the triumph of the trickster-hero over folly and corruption — the two stories fit neatly together as twin aspects of Bogrov's attempt to forge a normative image of enlightened Jewish masculinity liberated from domestic tyranny. While "Captive Recruit" marshaled the conscription theme in the name of a misogynous critique of embourgeoisement, "Yerukhim" raised the figure of the conscript to the level of tragedy in order to affirm a radically new possibility for Jewish fraternity, untainted by the debilitating presence of Jewish women and the material temptations they embodied.

Putatively inspired by the contrast between "then," characterized by Nicholaevan oppression, and "now," informed by a fundamental shift in the "spirit of military and civil laws,"[51] "Captive Recruit" was less preoccupied with the search for a usable Russian-Jewish past and more with undermining a complacent faith in the present. Bogrov's Nicholaevan fable referenced the contemporary concerns of his audience, the upwardly mobile Jewish householders of St. Petersburg, distinguished particularly by the ways in which their fortunes remained solidly connected to the commercial and residential privileges first gained under Nicholas I. Even as they attempted to raise a new generation of Jewish children in the liberal spirit of the Great Reforms, the fathers of Jewish St. Petersburg, in their social conservatism, their profound commitment to Jewish piety and European civility, as well as their economic ties to the state, represented the visible link between the "hardships" of Nicholaevan militarism and the achievement, under the benevolent rule of Alexander II, of "freedom [. . .] equality [. . .] openness [. . .] [and] education."[52] The ambiguous triumph of the "captive recruit" signified precisely the problematic nature of this connection; cutting into the comic logic of his own plot, Bogrov foregrounded the achievements of emancipation not in the messianic passing of Nicholaevan despotism but in the effective displacement of autocratic discipline by domestic tyranny and the corruption of enlightenment by the trappings of embourgeoisement.

The conflict at the heart of "Captive Recruit" pits an upwardly mobile young stranger against an old-timer whose conspicuous show of piety masks a greedy and conniving nature. Following the conventions of maskilic geography, Bogrov plotted the contrast between virtue and vice along the line that divided the enlightened North, dominated by Vilna, the Jerusalem of Lithuania, from the benighted southern borderland, overrun by Jewish smugglers beholden to venal and fanatical Hasidic *rebbes*. The story, set typically on the frontier, opens with a roadside encounter between two traveling natives and a mysterious visitor. The southerners, old Reb Genekh and his son, Shmul', offer their companion a ride and a room at their inn. Over the course of the ensuing conversation, the stranger reveals that he has come "from afar, from the land of hunger and poverty," a "foreigner," a "pilgrim [. . .] an alien."[53] Eventually he introduces himself as Aaron Listig, "from the region of K. where our brothers have for these past two years been dying of hunger and need" (22). Listig is an enlightened *litvak* (Lithuanian Jew) on a journey "in search of work in the blessed provinces" of the South, known as a place of opportunity for the enterprising (24).

Just like Dik, here Bogrov projected the economic situation of his own time back into the Nicholaevan period, seamlessly tying enlightenment aspirations with the promises of emancipation. For Bogrov's readers, the reference to the impoverished "region of K." surely brought to mind the contemporary devastation of Kovno Province, hard hit by famine in 1869.[54] Likewise, the contrasting image of the "blessed" South evoked the prodigious economic growth of that region in the post-Crimean period.[55] Bogrov set Listig apart from his hosts by his "short side-locks and trimmed beard," signs that reveal he is not "from among the Hasidim"; he is, furthermore, learned in the Talmud and also has a command of Russian. While Listig carries himself like a civilized "European," Reb Genekh looks like "a cunning old fox with a fluffy tail [. . .] a tame, well-heeled, faithful, sly dog" licking the boots of his master, the Polish nobleman. More grotesquely, Shmul' combines the wide chest and thick neck of an ox, the paws of a bear, the eyes of a cat, and a mouth like the maw of a wild animal.[56]

The distinction between North and South, colorfully rendered in the difference between Listig and his hosts, finds direct expression in a discussion of "captive recruitment," rampant in the South but, according to Listig, unheard of in the North. In the last four years of the Nicholaevan reign, a new provision of the conscription decree allowed any individual to "capture," as a substitute for himself or another person chosen for the draft, any person caught without written permission to leave his community. Bogrov relied on the narrative possibilities implicit in the abuse of this provision to fuel his melodramatic plot. Genekh and Shmul' conspire to lure Listig into their inn, steal his passport, denounce him as a vagrant, and present him to the local authorities as a "captive recruit" in exchange for a precious "receipt" they will use to extort a tidy sum from some unfortunate family in line for the draft.

The eventual triumph of the "captive recruit" over his enemies culminates in a marriage contracted for love and profit. The comic resolution here parallels Dik's conscription romance. Listig's marriage to Sarah, Genekh's ward intended for marriage to Shmul', felicitously combines properly tempered romantic urges with economic advantage, highlighted in the contrast between Aaron's self-control and the unbridled lust of his southern rival. The purity of Aaron's intentions toward Sarah likewise finds expression in his unblemished standing in the eyes of Russian law, attested by a set of papers "so correct" that, in the words of the local police chief, "he is free to travel all the way to the tsar himself" (100). In the end, Listig becomes Sarah's lawful husband and the representative of justice in the corrupt South, exposing to the imperial authorities the shady activities of Genekh', Shmul', and their Russian cronies. As her protector from both her guardian and her intended, Aaron earns Sarah's love and, replacing the crooked Genekh as head of the household, claims the latter's fortune into the bargain.

All is not well in this bourgeois paradise, however, for the scene of family happiness at the end of the story is built on a foundation of lies. Not only is Aaron's betrothal the product of a ruse, but his success in discrediting Genekh and Shmul' depends on his own ability to dissemble. When Aaron spins out a false tale of desertion, smuggling, and murder in order to extort money from Genekh and Shmul', even the police prefect is taken in, despite his knowing full well that Aaron is lying:

> The policeman was taken with the romance of the talk and listened on the edge of his seat. But remembering suddenly that a very clever farce was being performed right before his very eyes, [he] abruptly broke out in irrepressible laughter. [And] he grew rather uncomfortable with his own misplaced weakness. (92)

Aaron's fake denunciation is not only completely convincing but places him in an extraordinary position, vis-à-vis his enemies. The polarities of good and evil have been radically reversed, the "authentic" Jew transformed into

CONSCRIPTION AND THE SEARCH FOR MODERN RUSSIAN JEWRY

"a demon in human form" (93). An accomplished liar who at last has revealed himself, Aaron is now ready to displace his hosts. In the final scene the Russian policeman, himself about to be duped, pays his "accomplice" a prophetic compliment: "You will be the first among all the *berdichevers*" — that is, the southern crooks and swindlers (96).[57]

Aaron's enlightened household replaces Genekh's shady tavern; his erotic and economic conquest of the underdeveloped southern wilderness, primed for cultivation, reflects the historical passage from Nicholaevan "then" to Alexandrine "now." But, in fact, Aaron's victory betrays his latent similarity to the likes of Genekh and Shmul' — every *litvak* is, at heart, a *berdichever,* a maskil ready to succumb to the material rewards of sex and money, implicit in the image of women as the bad conscience of Jewish enlightenment.

At the very end of the story Aaron calls Sarah his "happiness" (Rus. *shchastie*); she responds by referring to him as "my captive [recruit]" (Rus. *poimannik*). This ironic exchange of endearments speaks to contemporary anxieties about the fate of Jewish enlightenment in the age of emancipation. Sarah and her money are indeed the source of Aaron's "happiness" or, better still, "fortune," the other meaning of the word *shchastie.* Her presence reminds the reader that Aaron's authority as husband and paterfamilias remains connected to the world of deceit and manipulation inhabited by the likes of Genekh and Shmul'. At the same time Aaron's new identity as his wife's "captive" binds him to a lifetime of service no less then conscription; trapped by his own desires within the company of women — the household consists of his wife, his own mother, and hers — Aaron's fate embodies the feminization of enlightenment that transformed the official bondage of Nicholaevan decree into the soft tyranny of Jewish marriage.

For Bogrov's "captive recruit" who symbolized the seemingly smooth transition from the dark winter of Nicholaevan discontent to the springtime of "freedom [. . .] equality [. . .] openness [. . .] [and] education," the escape from the hell of conscription into a bourgeois paradise was no escape at all, an idea Bogrov elaborated more fully in *Notes of a Jew.* Here Bogrov effectively reclaimed maskilic virtue in the name of Jewish manhood by elevating to heroic stature a recruit who, in pointed contrast to the wily Aaron Listig, does *not* evade his fate. The fantasy of masculine self-generation that informed Dik's romance with conscription lost little in Bogrov's Russian-language treatment of the same theme.

Despite the title's obvious reference to the open-ended, first-person form that linked *Notes of a Jew* (Rus. *Zapiski evreia*) with Turgenev's *Sportsman's Sketches* (Rus. *Zapiski okhotnika*) and Dostoevsky's *Notes from the House of the Dead* (Rus. *Zapiski iz mertvogo doma*), Bogrov's attempt to filter social criticism through the discriminating consciousness of an acutely sensitive narrative persona remains solidly rooted in maskilic teleology.[58] There are few surprises of the kind that emerge from the striking juxtaposition of dispassionate observation of sordid detail with moral or aesthetic illumination, a technique that, in the hands of Dostoevsky and Turgenev, elevated the incidental to the level of art. There are, in fact, no incidents in Bogrov's rambling story that are not fully subordinate to the melodramatic rendering of psychological and social progress central to the plot. The narrator's inflated voice never actually rises above his own imaginary navel. Everything and everyone around him serves only to provide an object lesson for his developing ego, a sign in a system where he is the only signified. Thus its filiation with the realism of Turgenev's and Dostoevsky's use of "notes" notwithstanding, *Notes of a Jew* bears a stronger family resemblance to Dik's maskilic romance, an elaborate defense of enlightened Jewish self-consciousness against the fear of being unmanned and imprisoned by Rabinovich's "revolting, fat-bellied specter" of bourgeois success.[59]

Like Dik, Bogrov turned to conscription in his depiction of an idealized form of Jewish fraternity, an alternative to the dystopian view of modern Jewish life, subject to the sexual economy of desire. Introducing the pathetic description of "entire regiments of Jewish children — boys dragging behind them inordinately long government-issue greatcoats and drowning in their cavernous army service caps,"[60] Bogrov digressed into a scene that exploits the comic potential of the homology between the recruitment of Jewish children into the Russian army (as opposed to Russian *men*) and the recruitment of Jewish boys into marriage:

"The boy? [says a matchmaker to a customer] — this is a future star of the Jewish people. He is only ten years old, but he already knows by heart two whole volumes of the Talmud with their commentaries. His Hebrew writing is simply a marvel, he is smart, quiet, doesn't say a word and would not hurt a fly. In a word, a treasure."
"Well, and what about his health?"
[The matchmaker] lost his composure for a moment but managed quickly to regain it.
"A very beautiful boy, very beautiful, almost a girl, in fact."
"I am not asking you about his looks. What is beauty, after all? About his health I am asking. They say he suffers from epileptic fits, God spare us!"
"God have mercy and preserve us! What are you saying, Reb Shmul'! The boy is completely healthy. Maybe a little pale. But what is that, if not a sign of a delicate complexion? Health is for water carriers and wagon drivers. He who occupies himself with Torah cannot have red cheeks like some bricklayer."
"Well, you see, my dear matchmaker (Yid. *shadkhen*): learning is learning, so far as it goes, but health, too, is a blessing from God. My daughter is going on sixteen. She is a strapping, filled-out young thing in the bloom of health. What kind of a husband will a ten-year-old make, especially one who is weak, pale, and sickly? You know that the stupid womenfolk cannot be satisfied with learning alone — that is the thing! Isn't that so, my dear *shadkhen*? Ha-ha-ha!"

"Reb Shmul'," replied the [matchmaker], in an aggrieved tone of voice, "I must admit, I did not expect to hear such improprieties from you. Can it be that you are seeking a husband for your daughter who is like a Russian soldier?"[61]

The distinctly nontraditional view of marriage, associated here with the satisfaction of adult sexual urges, is marked as feminine and linked explicitly with the potential emasculation and embarrassment of the hapless Jewish bridegroom. The precociously bourgeois paterfamilias speaks not in the name of Torah — in contrast to the matchmaker, the indignant voice of Jewish propriety — but in the name of female desire, the single most dynamic and dangerous force in the novel that continually threatens the narrator and at the same time spurs him to action. Embodied in the familiar demons of the Jewish wife and mother-in-law, female desire represents secular bourgeois ambition as the quest for economic and social power for its own sake, without the mitigation of cultivation or culture. These, in turn, are associated with the noble virtues of pride, honor, generosity, and love, all model qualities of enlightened Jewish masculinity that emerge in the narrator's relationship with the gentile woman Ol'ga and Yerukhim, the Jewish recruit. Instruments of the narrator's spiritual development, the gentile woman and the Jewish recruit fulfill their imaginary destiny in helping to direct the protagonist toward the proper expression of manhood, and then conveniently exit the story by dying tragically.

As iconic projections of the narrator's ethical posturing, the twinned characters of Ol'ga and Yerukhim emblematize the angelic qualities notably absent in the representation of Bogrov's Jewish women — the former are weak, and the latter are strong; the former victims, the latter bullies; the former uninterested in material aspects of life to the point of self-destruction, the latter greedy and acquisitive; the former childlike and naïve, the latter cynical and preternaturally calculating; the former static, the latter brimming over with a kind of irrepressible, fiendish sprite. In the novel, modern Jewish masculinity depends precisely on the elective affinity with Ol'ga and Yerukhim at the expense of a kind of genetic tendency toward the unnamed wife and mother-in-law, a contrast Bogrov associated with the programmatic distinction between cosmopolitan Jewish selfhood, distinctively male, and tribal loyalty, based on maternal blood ties. Bogrov's enlightened misogyny reflected a politicized — that is, to say, cultural — construction of gender categories, not an equation of biology with destiny. Writing after Marx's equally controversial "On the Jewish Question" (1844), Bogrov might well have said that the emancipation of Jewish women required, first and foremost, the emancipation of the Jews from the bourgeois straitjacket of modern Judaism.[62]

How did the idealized relationships of the narrator with the gentile woman and the Jewish recruit represent the social utopia Bogrov imagined as the alternative to contemporary Russian-Jewish society, governed, he claimed, by the degenerative struggle for embourgeoisement? In his depiction of the narrator's social life, Bogrov distinguished secular relationships —both with Jews and non-Jews—borne of ceaseless conflict and enervating struggle, leading to alienation and loneliness, from special spiritual bonds that result in perfect identification and moments of epiphanic rebirth. While the former characterize the everyday life of Bogrov's archetypal modern Jew, the latter, embodied in the complementary bonds with Ol'ga and Yerukhim, punctuate the narrator's development with a well-appointed literary significance. Here, for example, is Bogrov's overwrought depiction of the climactic scene between the protagonist and his gentile paramour. Note the self-conscious slippage between the ethical value of literature and "real life," as well as the calibrated stress on the singularly transformative quality of Ol'ga's feelings for her Jewish lover:

> "You have nice eyes, warm even. Notice, I did not say *beautiful*. Don't give yourself airs, if you please," she added, pressing my hand.
> "I have no right to any such thing."
> "Right? Man is power, there is your right."
> "As far as you are concerned . . . I am not a man," I said with some venom.
> "What? Ha-ha-ha! Let me look at you; perhaps you are a schoolgirl in man's garb?"
> "Don't make jokes. I repeat in all seriousness: as far as you are concerned, I am not a man."
> "So what are you, pray tell? Ha-ha-ha!"
> "I am a Jew."
> She was silent and looked sternly at me.
> "I know you are a Jew. So what of it?"
> "Jews don't have the right to give themselves airs."
> "Listen to me. If you have the slightest respect for me, if you want to be in my . . . acquaintance, don't even try to lump me with the others. I was brought up from childhood to see a person as a human being rather than a Russian, Frenchman, or Turk, a human being, not a Christian, a Mohammedan, or a pagan, a human being, not a general, a merchant, or a townsman. When I was a young girl, I was even in love with one of Cooper's characters! An Indian, can you imagine? If you persist in speaking to me in this manner, I will form a very poor impression of you; I will think that you are posing. And I like poses only on canvas, not in real life."
> My God, with what bliss did these words fill my heart, worn out with suffering! I was raised up in my own eyes.[63]

The similarly life-altering meeting between the narrator and the recruit follows immediately in the wake of Ol'ga's death from consumption. Here, too, Bogrov ran literary interference in the creation of enlightened Jewish sensibility, introducing the "adventures" of the recruit with the well-worn assertion of authenticity used in the creation of a stylized folktale:

> Yerukhim, or, as he was known later, Yerofei, spoke rather well in the sol-
> dier's dialect, but his conversation was jerky, incoherent, inconsistent. Nev-
> ertheless, little by little, I discovered all his adventures (Rus. *pokhozhdeniia*)
> from the time of his being drafted into military service. These adventures
> throw such a bright light onto the life of the Jewish soldier of that time that
> I consider it fitting to share the story of Yerofei with my readers. Of course, I
> will transmit this story not in the disconnected form and with those expres-
> sions that I heard directly from the lips of the soldier-martyr.[64]

The narrator, acting as Yerukhim's literary executor, finally becomes his
double, a role for which Bogrov has been preparing his protagonist since
the initial incident of mistaken identity that nearly results in the conscription of the hero instead. Their fraternity implicates conscription in the
project of parthenogenesis of enlightened Jewish masculinity that Dik associated with the image of Jewish soldiers as ideal fathers.

Appropriately, once the narrator internalizes the lessons of Yerukhim's
fate, the recruit disappears as a character in his own right. Forever frozen as
a projection of the protagonist's Jewish consciousness, he goes on to become an icon of Jewish suffering, rehearsed in the ritual retelling of his tale.
His story now elevated above a mere subplot to the status of a tale within a
tale, Yerukhim appeared so fully enclosed in his own mythology that later
readers, not surprisingly, divorced him from the rest of the novel. In 1915
"The Adventures of Yerukhim" was translated into Yiddish and published in
New York with the title *The Child-Snatchers of Russia: A Novel of Jewish Life in
Russia in the Time of Nicholas I*.[65]

In his choice of the word *pokhozhdeniia*, which can also mean "trials," to
refer to the "adventures" of Yerukhim, Bogrov elevated the literary import
of this story to a new level of significance; in Russian, the word carries
connotations of martyrdom undertaken in imitation of Jesus' *via dolorosa*.
Bogrov, the enlightened Jewish writer, here flirted with the religious affect of
the Christian story in order to inspire in his readers a reverence for the
literary depiction of Jewish suffering that was nothing short of devotional.
Indeed, Bogrov dwelled with ritual intensity on Yerukhim's particular talent
for bearing the physical blows of fate that the narrator himself successfully
avoids. Destined to be the victim, Yerukhim induces in the narrator a
vaguely masochistic sense of guilt, appropriately assuaged by one whose
carefully contrived name is synonymous with the vicarious self-consoling
pleasures of pity (Heb. *rahamim*).

Yerukhim's emotional communion with the narrator transcends all forms
of Jewish institutional and collective life, social expressions of maternal
kinship; in the seamless identification — brotherhood — of the narrator
(named Srul' a nickname of Yisroel, literally Israel, the Jewish everyman)
Bogrov elevates the discipline of community to the theater of communion,
the achievement of catharsis in response to the representation of pain:

"My God! The rod, always the rod [Yerukhim says]. But I am not guilty of anything. God only knows [. . .] for what." The sick man wept like a child. I myself could hardly keep back the tears. "Forgive me, my friend. Perhaps I was the cause of your suffering. I didn't know [. . .]" I began to justify myself, not knowing how to do it. "How are you at fault?" he came to my aid, in a strangely embittered voice. "This is my fate. God wills it to be so. But when will they finish me off? Oh, but that it should be soon! As soon as I get well — there will be the lash, the rod, again and again. When will it all end, my God?"[66]

As a result of this conversation, the narrator suddenly feels "lighter, as if [he] had seen [his] own brother" (3:155). So affecting is the debut performance that he returns to see Yerukhim in the military hospital with the regularity of a loyal fan. Now the virtuoso of pain, the recruit quickly acquires a much larger audience; he is allowed to leave the hospital to attend the synagogue where he prays with such fervor and such a moving display of tears over words he hardly understands that he "inspired the collective empathy and attention of all the Jews" (3:158). For the narrator, the travails of the recruit constitute a personal revelation of the fraternal bond between Jewish men which transcends the narrow familial ties that imprison Israel, the Jewish everyman, within the oppressive female "guardianship" of Jewish society (3:274). Significantly, in the aftermath of his formative encounter with the recruit, the narrator finally obtains the long sought-after divorce from his Jewish wife, gains sole custody of his children, and brings his story to a close. Thus the recruit, like the gentile woman, serves as an agent of the narrator's spiritual release from the bourgeois prison of emancipation. Ironically the same promise of liberty and fraternity that enabled the public self-expression of modern Jewish masculinity limited the aspirations of Jewish women to the nursery and the drawing room, places where even the most enlightened women were best seen and not heard. In the case of Judah-Leib Gordon the fantasy of masculine empowerment underlying the conscription story clashed with the reality of learned and ambitious women trying to breach the walls of this domestic utopia.

FATHERS, BROTHERS, AND (M)OTHERS: J. L. GORDON'S "DRY BONES"

No maskil defended the cause of Jewish enlightenment in the age of partial emancipation with greater vigor and imagination than Judah-Leib Gordon. Gordon sought throughout his career to widen the audience of maskilic literature in the name of aesthetic cultivation and moral improvement. In his unwavering commitment to the Hebrew language as the medium of modern Jewish self-expression, Gordon sought both a new Jewish style and a new Jewish ethics. The creed that emerged out of Gordon's enlightened Hebraism found dramatic expression in a single line of his 1862–1863 poem, "Awake, My People!" — a line destined to become "the most memorable phrase he ever wrote": "Be a man in the streets and a Jew at home."[67] Celebrated and vilified as the motto of maskilic integrationism, Gordon's dictum epitomized the "bifurcation of Jewish identity," associated with the split between the "realms of the sacred and the secular" that potentially divided the modern Jew against himself.[68]

The "Jewish version, as it were, of separation between church and state,"[69] Gordon's line has become the "slogan" of Jewish modernity.[70] In retrospect, it is too easy to miss just how radical it was, given the durability of maskilic belief in the benefits of using the resources of the Russian "state" to reform the Jewish "church." Indeed, the determination to "relegate Judaism to the private sphere of life" did not arise spontaneously out of what the conventional reading of the poem ascribes to the "naïve taxonomy of the Haskalah."[71] Rather, the inward turn Gordon advocated in his poem spoke to the way that the historical realities of emancipation exacerbated long-standing maskilic concerns regarding the formation of "fully perfected and fully Jewish manhood."[72]

Gordon viewed the private and public divide from the vantage point of emancipation, the success of which threatened to make Judaism and the Haskalah equally irrelevant. He cast, in the form of an urgent ethical imperative, the conventional bourgeois distinction between cosmopolitan masculinity and domestic piety in order to safeguard enlightened Judaism from erosion in the *public* sphere, dominated on all sides by enemies of Jewish enlightenment. In his own hardly "naïve taxonomy" of gender, ideal women, modeled on the heroines of Jewish antiquity, replaced rabbis as guardians of Jewish virtue. At the same time the experience of real women, drawn from the small tragedies of nineteenth-century Russian-Jewish life, signified rabbinic trespass into the newly hallowed private domain of Jewish conscience.[73]

On the basis of the sympathetic depiction of women, informed largely by his antipathy toward rabbinic prerogatives, as well as for his efforts on behalf of women's education, Gordon has justifiably acquired a reputation as an enlightened feminist.[74] In fact, his literary treatment of conscription demonstrates that, for Gordon, women were both the problem and the solution, at once instrumental to the preservation of Judaism and yet the single greatest threat to maskilic self-possession. Like Dik and Bogrov, Gordon turned to the conscription theme to highlight the hidden dangers of desire awakened by the secular possibilities of emancipation without the moral testing ground of enlightenment. With greater subtlety but with no less conviction, Gordon projected onto the image of the conscript the maskilic yearning for a world without Jewish women.

Gordon addressed himself to conscription on two separate literary occasions. The first of these constituted his Yiddish debut. The stylized folk-lament entitled, "The Mother's Farewell to Her Child Who Was Recruited in 1845," was published in 1866, in the *Herald* (Yid. *Kol mevasser*), the Yiddish supplement to *The Advocate* (Heb. *Ha-melits*), the Odessa Hebrew weekly. The second, a Hebrew short story titled "Dry Bones," was serialized in *Ha-melits* between 1 September and 29 September 1881. The poem locates the tragedy of conscription not in political oppression but exclusively in the sphere of private anguish, embodied in the figure of the mother grieving for her son who is about to be recruited. The female voice here identifies recruitment itself with "horrid fate," betraying a limited understanding of tsar's law: "Go whither the wind takes you / What God wills, shall obtain."[75] The poem depicts Jewish allegiance to God as a displacement of military duty, and contracts the heroic posture of the warrior to the confines of the Jewish home. The mother, the commanding voice of the poem, naturally takes over the public authority of rabbis and teachers, and assumes the role of collective disciplinarian. The "wedding clothes" which she had hoped to sew for her son are but another version of the uniform he now wears as a soldier of the tsar. Most telling is her injunction, "Give me your hand and *swear to me* / That you will remain a Jew," loaded language which evokes the act of taking the induction oath, the first step in initiating recruits into the service.[76] The poem thus deploys the familial agony of conscription in order to enlist the domestic power of women where, according to Gordon, rabbis as bearers of public Jewish authority have failed — failed, that is, in the maintenance of Judaism against the dangerous attractions of secular public life. In 1866, ten years after the recruitment of Jewish children had become obsolete, Gordon was talking not to mothers of recruits but to mothers of Jewish students who were flocking to universities in the hope of serving the reforming state.

Faced with an urgent need for effective Jewish leadership in the aftermath of "southern tempests," the first shock wave of pogroms that swept through the southwestern borderlands in the spring and summer of 1881, Gordon went on to use conscription to invest new hope for the continuing reform of Judaism in the lost children of enlightenment.[77] The recruit, who first appeared in the Yiddish poem as the object of Jewish motherly love, returned as the hero of "Dry Bones" to father a new generation of modern Jews.[78] Gordon's unease with women cast as the bearers of Jewish tradition, which marked the language of the poem, now manifested itself more openly in the Hebrew conscription story.

In "The Mother's Lament," Gordon confined Jewish women to the private sphere of moral influence. Tellingly his Yiddish-speaking mother uses emotionally manipulative language that reduces the recruit to perpetual infancy. In effect, she makes him Jewish by attaching him permanently to her nurturing breasts. With the image of "wedding clothes," she practically insinuates herself into his marriage bed so that army service looks like an escape into adulthood. The recruit remains entirely silent in the poem;

Gordon casts him exclusively as the object of his mother's strident and emotionally charged exhortation. Even the patriarch Isaac, the paradigmatic victim of Jewish parental authority, when he is about to be sacrificed by his *father*, finds a way to speak up (Gen 7:22); Jewish *mothers*, it seems, brook no interruptions.

The measured male voice of the Hebrew conscription story provides an antidote to the relentless shrieking female tone of "A Mother's Lament." The plot of "Dry Bones" details the asexual reproduction of the Jewish republic of letters as a way of avoiding the domestic entrapment of Jewish biology, silencing the cloying cacophony of the Jewish mother-tongue (Yid. *mame-loshn*), the object of potent maskilic ambivalence.[79] With the move to Hebrew, Gordon symbolically evades the emasculating attractions of the Jewish womb/tomb. Like Dik and Bogrov, Gordon imagined his enlightened Jewish utopia devoid of the presence of Jewish women; his returning recruit fathers a nuclear Jewish family by adoption. The story takes place in a world of benevolent uncles, foster fathers, and brothers, heroic and self-sufficient agents of Jewish continuity, undaunted by violence and communal fractiousness.

Dominated by the over-determined phallicism of its central image, an oak tree sprouting atop a steep hill, "Dry Bones" glosses the prophet Ezekiel's eschatological vision of God breathing life into the "dry bones" of Israel (Ezek 37:1–14).[80] The image of "lost Jewish children" — returning cantonists — as the "dry bones" of an "afflicted and assailed" Russian Jewry emblematized, for Gordon, the possibility that "the hoped-for synthesis of Russian humanism and Jewish reform could, and indeed, would triumph," despite the shock of pogroms and official indifference.[81] Read within the context of maskilic sexual politics, however, Gordon's allusion to Ezekiel made a profound point about the contemporary relevance of the conscription motif. The convoluted plot fully exploited the literary possibilities implicit in a reading of miraculous resurrection as a fantasy of Jewish reproduction without the need for conception, that is, without the need for women.

The protagonist, a returning cantonist baptized in the ranks, aids a fellow cantonist seeking a teaching position in a government-sponsored Jewish school. In the process, the two discover that they were childhood friends and that the latter is engaged to the niece of the former. In a remarkable series of coincidences, substituting authorial for divine intervention, the former Jew and now Russian military officer becomes the ideal patriarch of an enlightened Jewish family, without the travails of real fatherhood. Gesturing toward continuity, the couple name their son after him. Here, essentially, is Gordon's version of Dik's anti-Oedipal comedy, in which the future of enlightenment is guaranteed without the angst of sexual desire and the uncertainty of generational conflict. Given the radical challenge to maskilic self-understanding that occasioned the writing of "Dry Bones," and the

continuing worry about the fate of enlightened Jewish manhood, threatened now by violence from without as well as continually tempted by its own
desires from within, the realization of the hopes animating the story required nothing short of a miracle.

Like the work of Dik and Bogrov, Gordon's "Dry Bones" exemplified the
way in which the conscription motif emerged as central to the Jewish revision of the realities of emancipation, a testament to maskilic faith cutting
across the grain of maskilic experience. For one thing, Gordon invoked the
Nicholaevan merger between the reformist ambitions of Jewish enlighteners and the social power of the state at a time when the radically secular
heirs to the legacy of the Haskalah were no longer interested in Jewish
reform while the traditionalists gained ground. This was a generational
tension which Gordon himself felt most acutely as a crisis of his vocation, a
dilemma that animates the poetic credo, "For Whom Do I Toil?" (1871).[82]
In the poem, the despairing Gordon addresses himself to Jewish women, the
last hope of enlightened Judaism in the age of "nihilism" and "orthodoxy":

> Daughters of Zion! Perhaps you
> Will turn your hearts to my plaintive cry?
> God has planted in you the spirit of mercy
> As well as grace, taste, and warmth —
> But alas you have been raised as captives
> "He who teaches his daughter Torah teaches her folly!"[83]

The last line in the stanza is a Talmudic citation (TB Sotah 21b). The
innocuous English word "folly" misses the resonance of the original Hebrew
word *tiflut* which carries connotations of lechery and lewdness. The sexual
sins of immodesty allude to the problems attendant on women's violation of
the precincts of the household in search of public, religious authority. Medieval rabbinic commentary made this link explicit in a story of a woman
"expert in Scripture and Talmud" teaching "Bible to young men [while
being] enclosed within a building, in a room with one window [so that] the
students . . . do not see her."[84] Gordon's poem, in turn, resolves the issue of
sexual and intellectual decorum by associating women's "learning" with the
quiet domestic virtues of "grace, taste, and warmth." The latter, presumably,
comprise the fitting objects of a woman's modern Jewish education, her
private Torah.

As Gordon had reason to know personally, however, the experience of
Jewish women in the age of emancipation did not necessarily conform to
maskilic design. On the contrary, the promise of individual liberation from
parental and communal authority implicit in enlightenment discourse
proved no less compelling to Jewish daughters than to Jewish sons. Gordon's
epistolary relationship with Miriam Markel-Mosessohn (1839–1920), an
aspiring author and translator, provides evidence of female resistance to the
gendered logic of Jewish enlightenment, so powerfully expressed in "Dry

Bones" and in the works of Dik and Bogrov. Like her biblical namesake, Markel-Mosessohn insisted on speaking to men as something other than mother, daughter, or wife. Her irrepressible literary voice offers a fitting historical gloss on the pregnant silence of Jewish women in the literature of the Haskalah, written by enlightened — and deeply anxious — Jewish men.

"AND MIRIAM BADE THEM SING" (EX 15:20–21)

In her quest to "enter the sanctuary" of Hebrew letters, Miriam Markel-Mosessohn appears to have been almost entirely on her own.[85] While Jewish women were enthusiastic consumers of enlightenment literature, production remained almost exclusively a male preserve.[86] Markel-Mosessohn enjoyed a long-standing correspondence with Gordon; she also exchanged letters with two other prominent Jewish enlighteners turned Hebrew writers, Abraham Mapu (1808–1867) and Moses-Leib Lilienblum (1843–1910). Like all three of her male correspondents, Markel-Mosessohn acquired her intellectual pedigree in Lithuania. Unlike them, however, she took up the study of Hebrew not in opposition to the prevalent system of Jewish learning, which focused on the Talmud, but instead as an antidote to the temptations of secular Polish culture. She was, like most of the women who knew Hebrew and read maskilic fiction at the encouragement of their fathers, never defensive or even self-conscious about such visibly nontraditional but essentially private pursuits.[87] Markel-Mosessohn exemplified the domestication of enlightenment that Gordon understood as the true calling of modern Jewish womanhood:

> Receiving a letter in the holy tongue from the Jewish woman [a female correspondent he wrote to in 1881] is to me like receiving manna from heaven. [. . .] All the writings in the holy tongue composed by women that I chance to read are better in style and purer in language than many of those by men. The woman writes with the pen of a bird and the man with the pen of iron and lead. [. . .] The reason for this, in my opinion, is that the minds of women were not ruined in their youth in the death chambers of *hadarim* [Jewish primary schools] and their common sense was not distorted with sermons and petty [Talmudic] arguments.[88]

Women's Hebrew "letters" (composed for the benefit of the correspondent and not for display to an audience) nurture the Hebrew poet. The image of "manna from heaven" suggests mother's milk, similar in its mysteriously protean taste and in the way that its supply always miraculously meets demand. Note, too, the contrast between the natural literary grace of women who write as birds sing and men who wield language defensively, artificially, as if it were, made of "iron and lead." In fact, Gordon's language is highly fraught here; he damns women with faint praise, turning writing into an attribute of female *biology*, on the one hand, and masculine *power*, on the other, the latter a product of heroic struggle in the "death chamber" of traditional Jewish schooling. This subtle rhetorical move actually handicaps women precisely where it presumes to champion them at the expense of men. The moment that women are elevated by the ostensible virtues of their nature over culture, they may also be diminished and confined by them.[89]

Indeed, for all of Markel-Mosessohn's insistence on leading the life of the mind, Gordon recalled her to the life (or lack thereof) in her uterus. In 1869, the same year that saw the publication of her masterful Hebrew translation-adaptation of the first part of Eugen Rispart's *The Jews and the Crusaders under Richard the Lionhearted*, Gordon greeted her with his hope that "God will bless you in the forthcoming [Jewish] New Year and remember you as He remembered Sarah [the matriarch, with the child Isaac]."[90] Introducing the second part of the translation, published in 1895, Markel-Mosessohn finally responded to Gordon, so to speak, in kind:

> Since the time that the first part of the translation was published, a new generation has come of age. I brought my first born near only to my brothers [but] then the love of our language grew among our people [. . .] and it found a way into my sisters' hearts. [. . .] Many daughters of Zion have come to enjoy reading and writing Hebrew [. . .] I heard great fear in my own heart, I praised the Lord who had not forsaken the language of Moses and the prophets, the language of Miriam, Deborah, and Hannah. So now I bring my baby near as well to my sisters for their delight. And I will be well rewarded if they lift up their faces toward me [. . .] and I will bless them in the name of the Lord.[91]

Markel-Mosessohn's language of figurative maternity-sorority at once appropriated and defied the exclusionary ideal of maskilic fraternity. Her invocation of female poets-prophets who give voice without first giving birth establishes an alternative genealogy for female Jewish authorship. Miriam and Deborah remained childless, and Hannah sang her song to God while she was barren; as soon as she gave birth to her son, the prophet Samuel, she passes her gift to him and never speaks again.

So much for Jewish mothers; Markel-Mosessohn likewise challenged the domestication of female sexuality, the locus of maskilic concern about the emancipation of Jewish desire. In an unpublished letter to Gordon, written at the start of 1869, at a time when Markel-Mosessohn was contemplating with trepidation her imminent literary exposure, she flouted rhetorically the posture of due modesty appropriate to women who "may read good books but [. . .] not write and publish them."[92] This, from Markel-Mosessohn's description of a visit to Warsaw:

> I walked in the streets accompanied by my brother, meandering from one site to another [. . .] mingling with the crowd that is so varied in language and dress. I would be all the more pleased if I were to happen upon a Hasid,

> dressed in rags, emerging from the ritual bath, dripping with water [. . .]
> and upon encountering a woman, his face would become distorted, con-
> vulsing into a spasm.[93]

Contrast Markel-Mosessohn's teasing evocation of "varied dress" with the following characterization, in the same letter, of her own looming entry into the literary fold: "I have violated the law [that a woman shall not wear that which pertains to a man, neither shall a man put on a woman's garment] by dressing like a man. Who knows whether a crowd of people will gather and strip this garment from me? And then what will be the fate of my work?"[94] Markel-Mosessohn conflates the biblical prohibition against cross-dressing with the maskilic gender taxonomy that insisted on a rigid, constitutive divide between the sexes, in direct opposition to the functional split be-tween the sexes — men learn, women earn — central to traditional Juda-ism.[95] In fact, Jewish enlighteners wanted nothing so much as to reform what they understood as the most fundamental pathology of Jewish social life by restoring to nature what rabbinic culture had allegedly put asunder.

Markel-Mosessohn's anxiety about being exposed seems to be playing true to the maskilic feminine type; but in the Warsaw passage, fear of being left open and vulnerable to male eyes adds to the frisson of courting such danger. Neatly substituting "a Hasid *dressed in rags*" for the implicit presence of a well-appointed maskilic critic, Markel-Mosessohn shatters the illusion of difference from the former which underlies the latter's claim to social power. Desire reduces maskilim and hasidim alike to "convulsions." Both devise elaborate disciplinary systems — in the first instance, symbolized by the "law" against cross-dressing; in the second, by the rite of the "ritual bath" — to avoid confronting expressions of their own corporeality that they cannot control. Markel-Mosessohn radically reverses here the maskilic po-larity of nature (read, feminine) versus culture (read, male) by depicting *men* as enslaved to the "convulsions" of their bodily selves. Her own freedom as a woman lies "in the streets" among the "crowd, so varied in language and dress," that is, in her ability to manipulate cultural and social codes at will, to hide and expose herself at will, to assume the mask of feminine modesty and put it aside in order to flaunt her sexuality.

In this kind of public play lay the historical meaning of emancipation. The creation of a richer metropolitan public sphere allowed Russian Jews to blend easily into the "crowd" even as Russian Jewry remained a thing apart. The fear of social and cultural promiscuity haunted the dreams of those who were wont to assume responsibility for Jewish collective survival — rabbis and maskilim alike — as well as the nightmares of Russian officials, striving for an ever-elusive administrative transparency, and, indeed, of an increasing num-ber of Russian intellectuals who preferred their Jews Jewish and their Rus-sians Orthodox. Thus the official retrenchment from "unserfment" in the age of counter-reform actually spoke to a far more general conservative turn of Russian educated society. In Russian-Jewish circles, the rising tide of cultural pessimism was the result not of the failure of "selective integration" but of its unprecedented and unexpected success, highly provoking to defenders of the Haskalah who turned with increasing nostalgia to the memory of conscription and to the age of "official enlightenment."

The processes of socioeconomic differentiation, professionalization, loss of piety, family breakdown, generational conflict, all unleashed or exacerbated by emancipation, could not be so easily checked. Despite the imposition of quotas on Jewish enrollment in Russian institutions of higher learning, Jewish men, and an ever-increasing number of Jewish women, continued to follow well-trodden paths beyond the Pale, driven by ambition, talent, economic necessity, intellectual curiosity, passion, and a host of other personal reasons that seemed to have little to do with the collective vision of Russian-Jewish enlighteners. The reality of Russian-Jewish life proved truer to Markel-Mosessohn's view from Warsaw than to the cultural expectations that Gordon inscribed into his own vision of "dry bones." In the last quarter of the nineteenth century, Miriam, poet and prophet, would lead her sisters and brothers "singing" through the streets, while Judah-Leib brooded alone at home, surrounded by his books.

4

RETURN OF THE NATIVE: THE NICHOLAEVAN UNIVERSE OF SH. J. ABRAMOVICH AND THE ENLIGHTENMENT ORIGINS OF RUSSIAN-JEWISH POPULISM

THE HEBREW RENAISSANCE THAT WASN'T

The conscription theme formed a cornerstone of the maskilic narrative of resistance to the historical realities of emancipation. While the "selective integration" policy stalled in the last years of the reign of Alexander II and into the reign of his son, Alexander III, the process of fracture along social, economic, and cultural lines continued unabated. As a result, maskilic skepticism about the imminent reform of Judaism and Jewish life grew apace. The malaise in enlightened Jewish circles was of a piece with the general sense of diminished political expectations. By the late 1870s Russian public opinion had taken a decidedly conservative turn, a consequence, at least in part, of the widespread disappointment — both on the left *and* on the right of the emerging political spectrum — with the results of the Great Reforms project.[1] The consensus of the 1860s to the early 1870s that had united enlightened tsarist officials with liberal publicists, and even radical populists broke down, as each of these segments of educated society became more and more alienated from one another.[2] The buoyant public mood which had informed the era of good feelings and Great Reforms gave way to increasingly vocal tensions over foreign policy, especially during the Russo-Turkish War (1877–1878), as well as a host of domestic issues, the Jewish question prominent among them.[3] On the Jewish street, these tensions expressed themselves in the growing gulf between a new generation of "radical" enlighteners and the Russian-Jewish university-educated intelligentsia.[4] The voices of the former, united by their disappointment in providence and in the possibility of a meeting of the minds with an enlightened autocracy, resonated in a self-lacerating critique of the maskilic project. Increasingly they saw the destabilizing effects of emancipation and, paradoxically, enlightenment itself as a threat to Jewish continuity and Jewish ethics.[5] The latter dominated Jewish philanthropy and the defense of Jewish causes in the Russian press but became less and less engaged in the attempt to reform Jewish religious practice and the standing communal order, issues that still animated maskilic minds.

Out of the split between the radical maskilim and the Jewish beneficiaries of emancipation emerged a new stream of conservative social criticism in the Russian-Jewish press, chiefly in a new Jewish thick journal called *The Dawn* (Heb. *Ha-shahar*), published in Vienna by the Russian expatriate Peretz Smolenskin (1842–1885).[6] In the aftermath of the assassination of Alexander II and the pogroms of 1881–1882, Smolenskin's "prophetic" rhetoric, already available in the late 1870s, would be mobilized in the name of the Hebrew "renaissance" (Heb. *tehiyah*).[7] The emergent politics of national revival developed in tandem with the idea of the so-called linguistic and literary rebirth of the Jewish people.[8] Within this cultural context, the conscription story served the rewriting of the contemporary secular history of the Russian Jew into the collective mythology of an ever-dying, ever-living Russian Jewry, the biological repository of the nation and, at the same time, the preeminent signifier of collective Jewish death-in-exile. The dual image found expression in the twinned representations of the Nicholaevan veteran and the child-recruit, icons of Jewish peoplehood (Rus. *narodnost'*).

This chapter examines the conscription story as a literary-autobiographical subtext in the self-creation of a writer whose personal mythology is inextricably bound to the shift toward nationalist self-critique within the discourse of the Jewish enlightenment. Known as the father of modern Hebrew prose and the grandfather of modern Yiddish literature, Shalom Jacob Abramovich (1835–1917) exemplified both for his contemporaries and for virtually every subsequent reader of Russian-Jewish literature, the genesis of national consciousness in the Jewish hothouse of the shtetl.[9] His literary persona, Mendele the book-peddler (Heb./Yid. *Mendele mokher-seforim*) speaks to the teleological significance of Jewish Eastern Europe in nationalist historiography as the "museum of ghetto misery."[10] Mendele's Eastern European Jewish medievalism, comparable in cultural stature to "Cervantes' *Don Quixote* [. . .] the epitomization of a degenerate Spanish chivalry or Gogol's *Dead Souls*, the immortal representation of decadent Russian feudalism" dialectically informs the "brave new world" of the national revival, a world made inconceivable without the "truly gigantic" presence of Abramovich as its patriarch.[11]

How and why Abramovich emerged as the creator of a "degenerate" and "decadent" Eastern European Jewish past against which the hopes for a national future would be cast are central questions in the discussion of his particular affinity for the conscription theme, a motif that, as we shall see, pervades his body of work. Every narrative that Abramovich devised—including his unfinished autobiographical novel (Heb. *Hayei shlomo,* 1903/ Yid. *Shloyme reb hayims,* 1899–1917)—depends, in some measure, on conscription as a plot device and, more generally, on the eternal recurrence of the pre-reform shtetl past in the collective life of Russian Jewry.[12] Of course, the literary subtext here must be distinguished from historical context. Abramovich lived and worked in post-reform Odessa, not in the Nicholaevan shtetl of his own imagination.[13] The confusion between the former and the latter expresses itself in the critical view of his ostensible transformation from enlightenment "ideologue" into the epic voice of the national "artist"—as if his work were the product of "two completely separate personalities operating within one literary consciousness."[14] The divorce of Abramovich the maskil from Mendele, his allegedly populist alter ego serves only to underscore the difference between the idealized, post-pogrom image of the Hebrew Renaissance and the actual course of cultural developments that were, in fact, neither exclusively "Hebrew" nor much of a "renaissance."

The conventional view of Abramovich's career locates in his person a perfect reflection of the nationalist paradigm of Russian-Jewish history, neatly split between reform-era optimism and the post-1881 "return" of disappointed maskilim to the bosom of their people.[15] Before 1881, critics point out, Abramovich had worked in the conventional maskilic idiom: he wrote programmatic tracts in Hebrew as well as popular Yiddish novellas, satirizing the prevailing intellectual and social stagnation of the Pale of Settlement. After a five-year absence from the literary scene, attributed to some form of the contemporary crisis of conscience afflicting his fellow maskilim, Abramovich reemerged in the mid-1880s as a highly original Hebrew author, committed to the cultural revival of the Jewish people, if not wholly in tune with Zionist politics.[16] As translator of his own early Yiddish books into Hebrew, he was disposed to inject a vernacular sensibility into the language of learning and liturgy, as it were, sneaking Yiddish into Hebrew. Initiating his audience into the unique speech-world of Mendele, Abramovich, critics maintain, secularized the maskilic style and laid the foundation for modern Hebrew literature.[17] Readers, in his day and in ours, see in the work of Abramovich, the father figure of the Hebrew Renaissance, an enduring memorial to the imminent death of the shtetl:

> Abramovich [wrote the critic David Frishman, in his introduction to the
> anniversary edition of Abramovich's collected Hebrew works] encom-

passed the full spectrum of Jewish life in the alleys of the small towns of Russia in the first half of the preceding century, developing it into an enormous, fully detailed picture [. . .] If, let us suppose, a deluge came, washing from the face of the earth the Jewish ghetto and the Jewish life it contains, not leaving behind so much as a sign, a vestige except by sheer chance, Mendele's four major works, *Fishke the Lame, The Travels of Benjamin the Third, The Magic Ring,* and *Shloyme, the Son of Hayim,* as well as two or three shorter works—I do not doubt that with these spared, some future scholar would then be able to reconstruct the entirety of Jewish shtetl life in Russia of the first half of the nineteenth century in such a way that not even a single detail would be missing.[18]

The redemptive potential of the apocalypse that Frishman here imagined overtaking the *galut* resided in Abramovich's singular mastery of the Hebrew language, a source of inspiration for his literary progeny, charged with converting the enlightener's negation of the present into the positive future-oriented values of national revival.

For both contemporaries and subsequent generations, the persona of Abramovich thus emerged providentially out of the post-pogrom crisis that allegedly divided the Jewish intelligentsia from the Jewish people and the Haskalah against itself. To his readers, Mendele, the Tiresias of the Pale, became the paternal Jewish conscience for whom the previous generation of enlighteners had yearned. This teleological view of Abramovich's career first emerged in the author's own attempt to devise an original conception of modern Jewish authorship, a project that was actively informed by the persistence of Jewish enlightenment within the Hebrew Renaissance.

For all the insistence on the centrality of Hebrew both for Abramovich's post-pogrom "return" to fiction and for the work of his younger followers, his own career and theirs cannot be separated from the legacy of maskilic polyglotism. Just as before 1881, Russian-Jewish writers continued thereafter to express themselves in a variety of languages. The so-called revival of Hebrew at the turn of the century cannot be set apart from the contemporary flowering of modern Jewish literature in Yiddish, not to mention Russian, Polish, and German.[19] The well-ordered literary genealogies canonized in subsequent assessments of the Hebrew revival do not do justice to the climate of ideological and cultural "confusion" that faced aspiring Jewish writers and readers in this period.[20]

Moreover, the dramatic image of modern Hebrew culture rising like a phoenix out of the ashes of pogrom violence—a fin-de-siècle conceit of Zionist iconography that continues to inform the idea of a modern Jewish renaissance—does not stand up to historical scrutiny.[21] The ideology of the Hebrew renaissance has its roots in the maskilic reaction to the no less dramatic social consequences of emancipation, particularly in the growing apprehension on the part of Jewish enlighteners that the costs of personal freedom for Russian Jews would be the continued collective survival of Russian Jewry. It should not be surprising, in this context, that the pogroms of

1881–1882 so quickly became a milestone in the teleology of the Jewish enlightenment. The sudden and, it ought to be underscored, unprecedented outbreak of popular violence fed directly into maskilic pessimism regarding the socially disruptive effects of personal freedom—for the perpetrators, peasants radically dislocated from the village economy, no less than for their Jewish victims, associated with conspicuous consumption and the secular economic consequences of urban capitalism.[22] The subsequent lack of official empathy for the Jewish plight served to confirm the concert of maskilic opinion, growing louder at least since the 1870s, that the government had withdrawn from Jewish life, now with catastrophic results.[23] Initial consternation about the state's indifference, particularly among the most energetic proponents of Jewish enlightenment in St. Petersburg, explains the immediate and widespread appeal of the highly improbable theory of tsarist complicity in anti-Jewish violence, a conspiracy theory that had its roots in maskilic faith in the unbounded power of the autocracy to steer the course of social change.[24]

Increasingly bereft of faith both in the power of the state and in God's promise of Jewish continuity, radical maskilim like Peretz Smolenskin, Moshe-Leib Lilienblum—and Shalom-Jacob Abramovich—sought throughout the 1870s and 1880s to reclaim the promise of enlightenment in the name of Jewish peoplehood. Theirs was a conservative revolution dedicated not to the political and cultural autonomy of the modern Jew but to a new form of Jewish self-discipline. The very idea of a Hebrew Renaissance proved to be the most compelling ideological legacy of the Haskalah; its only effective rival for custody of the Jewish mind proved to be the original master story of exodus and divine revelation at Sinai. The all-important turn in the discourse of the Jewish Enlightenment that led to the invention of the Hebrew Renaissance, in fact, originated not in the "crisis" of Russian Jewry but in a new literature dedicated to the epic of an ever-dying people, a nationalist text with a distinctly maskilic subtext. Indeed, as some of the proponents of the revival claimed, the way to Zion lay primarily through the formation of modern Jewish culture.[25]

This paradoxical triumph of Russian-Jewish enlightenment in the age of Zionism lurked behind the persistent nationalist claim that the collective métier of Russian Jewry was to suffer, to die, and to be reborn in a modern colonial paradise. In the Zionist utopia of Theodor Herzl, for example, the old-new Jews of Eastern Europe, aliens marked for humiliation and destruction on their own native ground, were always already at home in *Altneuland,* the only place where a maskil might crown himself king.[26] Herzl's vision of national Eden had a direct counterpart in the world of Mendele, where the ever-living dead of Jewish Eastern Europe awaited national redemption. Unlike Herzl, Mendele's creator was never so carried away by the power of his own imagination. Abramovich, who had every reason to know the reality of Russian-Jewish life better than Herzl, remained singularly attuned to the ironies implicit in the ideological embrace of Russian-Jewish decline in an age marked by nothing so much as Russian-Jewish vitality, both cultural and demographic.

The dead children of the Hebrew Renaissance, Jewish recruits created by Abramovich and his self-appointed literary progeny, signified very precisely the tension between Russian Jewry as an undifferentiated object of maskilic fantasy—benighted, impoverished provincials trapped in Yiddishland and mired in a perpetual state of cultural and economic decline, caught, in short, in an irremediable state of crisis—and Russian Jews as subjects of their own modern history—an expanding population, increasingly sophisticated in its reading habits, socially and linguistically labile, precociously entrepreneurial, mobile, and, on the whole, highly adaptable to the economic rigors and legal challenges of everyday life in the Russian Empire.[27] Abramovich's own career exemplified the complex relationship between the former and the latter. Even as he remade his authorial persona in the image of his suffering people, he remained at a critical remove from the nationalist aspirations which he helped to inspire not because he saw them as unrealistic or delusional but because he saw modern Zion as a whiter shade of Pale, a projection of familiar maskilic designs onto a foreign landscape. His own mission lay closer to home, in the romantic apotheosis of Russian-Jewish life, with himself cast in the role of creator, seer, and moral conscience of his modern Russian-Jewish reader. Displacing Judah-Leib Gordon and his fellow enlightener-*auteurs*, Abramovich elevated secular literature to the stature of a modern confessional text. In this regard, his work is inexorably linked—as both cause and effect—to the mythology of the Hebrew Renaissance. Fully master of his own fiction, Abramovich spoke as God the Father of the Haskalah in its new nationalist incarnation.

PORTRAIT OF THE ARTIST AS A YOUNG MASKIL

At the beginning of his career Abramovich's goals as a writer of fiction served conventional maskilic ends. The plot of his first Hebrew novel, *Learn to Do Well* (Heb. *Limdu hetev*), published in 1862, and then enlarged and retitled *The Fathers and the Sons, A Love Story* (Heb. *Ha-avot ve-ha-banim, sipur ahavim*), and reprinted in 1868, elaborates within the setting of the transition from Nicholaevan "winter" to the Alexandrine "springtime" of reform, the imminent triumph of reason over folly, modern bourgeois virtue over traditional venality, education over ignorance, productivity over idleness, and love over money. Conceived in the early years of the Great Reforms, *The Fathers and the Sons* was the first Hebrew novel to treat the problems of Russian-Jewish life historically rather than as an example of the metaphysical conflict between good and evil.[28] The teleological victory of the sons over the fathers coincided with the momentous passage from collective oppression and obscurantism to the deliverance of Jewish talent and ambition from internal and external constraints. The Crimean War plays a pivotal role in the private lives of the characters, providing the backdrop for the downfall of the older generation and the rise of the new; it makes the fortune of David, the poor maskil teacher, and bankrupts his nemesis and reluctant father-in-law, Ephraim. Set in the dynamic setting of the Russian-Jewish South, the story thus links the process of political and economic reform of the Russian state with the embourgeoisement of its enlightened Jewish heroes, David and his cousin Shimon.

The recurrence of the seasonal metaphor symbolizes the ineluctable, as it were, natural, progress of historical time, a conceit that was basic to the form of the novel in its earliest stages of development. The shift from winter to spring punctuates the development of the bourgeois love story. A winter landscape, a transparent signifier of the Nicholaevan period, mirrors the hero's despair and at the same time contains the seeds of the future underneath, so that "even at that time, when everything lay sleeping and appeared to be dead, the spirit of God lived inside and continued to work its countless miracles [. . .] A cradle filled with new life would take the place of the grave, the resting place of dry bones would become the source of new life."[29] The providential coming of enlightenment is embedded in the hero's own experience of time; his psychological state is pregnant with historical significance. " 'Ours is a struggle between ignorance and enlightenment,' " says David, despairing, " 'in a moment, oh! it seems that the hand of ignorance will triumph.' In a moment, the candle went out. In a moment, the heavenly eastern gates opened and the dawn emerged in its robes of royal purple and the dark clouds disappeared" (12). The heavy-handed iteration of the phrase "in a moment" points to the fact that time is on the side of the man who walks in step with history, whose "dress and manners conform to contemporary ways of the land" and who acts in accordance with "objective" circumstances (7–8). The merger between history and nature fulfills itself in the fathers' ultimate recognition that they themselves are subject to the same inexorable laws of time that work to ensure the victory of the sons; in a self-serving deathbed confession, Elkanah-Arieh, David's long-lost father, articulates the maskilic rejection of historical and individual contingency in favor of an all-embracing teleology that flattens human agency: "A generation goes down and a generation comes up in its stead. People do evil because of their circumstances and from the oppression of the times" (158).

The felicitous outcome, that is, the removal of the "fathers" and the creation of a bourgeois domestic utopia—what the critic Dan Miron calls the Jewish novel's *locus amoenus*[30]—spoke to the mood of messianic expectation that attended the enactment of peasant emancipation, a model in the maskilic imagination, for a similar resolution of the Jewish question.[31] Abramovich devised the structure of the plot in the early 1860s; its basic outline already appeared in *Learn to Do Well*.[32] By the time the second version of the novel was written, however, he had moved closer to the kind of ambivalence toward the relationship between enlightenment and the secular effects of emancipation that informed the work of Dik, Bogrov, and Gordon. In fact, the new, much more explicitly historical treatment of the conflict between the fathers and the sons, now positioned at the foreground of the novel, intimated the extent to which the realities of emancipation challenged maskilic faith in history.

Here, as in the slightly later work of Dik, Bogrov, and Gordon, the evocation of conscription served the critique of emancipation; the heroes of *The Fathers and the Sons,* David and Shimon, escape conscription to the Crimean front lines, in the name of attaining the material and romantic success due them as aspiring enlighteners. The flight from conscription into the bourgeois *locus amoenus* reified the highly contingent aspect of enlightenment in the name of emancipation and manifested Abramovich's skepticism about the meaning of personal freedom divorced from a sense of collective responsibility. He doubted, in other words, that the emancipation of Jewish individuals was anything other than a secular process, divested of the imprimatur of both God and Reason. Eventually this skepticism would inspire an incisive critique of the arbitrary and capricious nature of autocracy itself, a jaundiced view of the reforming state born, paradoxically, of freedom; the regime of "official enlightenment," by contrast, both inspired and assured maskilic belief in the providential significance of the Russian-Jewish encounter for the imminent coming-of-age of both modern Jewry and modern Russia.[33]

The evasion of conscription in *The Fathers and the Sons* signifies the absence of effective fathering of the novel's three sons — David, Shimon, and a minor character named Levi, the agent of a local Hasidic seer. David has not seen his father since the latter sent him away to study in Germany for fear that David would be conscripted. Shimon, the son of the merchant Ephraim, flees his wealthy and superstitious father, unable to stand the relentless pressure to conform to his rigid observances; Shimon prepares for entrance examinations to the medical faculty of the university in secret because he runs the danger of being caught without a valid passport and drafted as a captive recruit. Meanwhile, Ephraim is led to believe that his son has, in fact, been drafted and either died at the battle of Sevastopol or was taken prisoner. Levi, who has also had a narrow escape from the draft, acquires his pedigree as a trickster masquerading as the "grandson" of a nonexistent Hasidic luminary. All three figures are again linked up at the end of the novel, in the setting of David's bourgeois household, the holy grail that serves as the prize of enlightenment. Thus, in all three lives, the escape from conscription enables, and at the same time renders ambiguous, the process of emancipation from the ostensibly dark legacy of the Nicholaevan past, embodied in the figures of absent, estranged, or fictive fathers. In fact, the agent of escape from the duties of Nicholaevan service into the privileges of Alexandrine freedom represents contingency in its most radical form; he is a criminal, that is, a specialist in evading the decree of tsarist law and, it would seem, of history itself. Elkanah-Arieh, David's father and Shimon's uncle on his mother's side who harbors the young fugitive and aids him with his medical studies, is the chieftain of a gang of Jewish highwaymen. His pivotal function in the lives of Abramovich's heroes points to a counterintuitive reading of emancipation that proved crucial to the radicalization of the Haskalah in the 1870s. The depiction of Elkanah-Arieh marks Abramovich's shift toward a new rhetoric of suspicion of the state. His precocious political pessimism came, increasingly, to bear not only on his own work but on the post-pogrom literature of the Hebrew Renaissance.

The central question, tied to the socially marginal identity of Elkanah-Arieh, is this: why did Abramovich see fit to associate the attainment of the fruits of enlightenment with the evasion of conscription, a fiction that actually ran against the grain of contemporary Jewish experience? Beginning in the reign of Nicholas I and throughout the tsarist period, Jews continued to enter the Russian ranks in numbers disproportionate to the size of the Jewish population within the empire.[34] But, like his predecessors who mobilized the conscription motif in the service of Jewish enlightenment, Abramovich was not actually interested in the realities of Jewish military service.[35] The mysterious figure of Elkanah-Arieh makes sense within the context of Abramovich's ambivalence toward emancipation as the telos of enlightenment. The significance of this ideological breach emerged powerfully in the image of enclosure attached to the bourgeois idyll at the end of the novel. Life in this manicured hothouse built by secular Jewish ambitions had become "as beautiful as Jerusalem" and as distant, it seems, from Russian-Jewish reality.[36] Abramovich limited the effect of emancipation to an ironic commentary on the continuing need for enlightenment, perhaps even more acute in an age that privileged the one at the expense of the many. This is the import of Levi's remark at the end of the novel that he has been reduced to collecting money for the poor of Jerusalem because "from day to day, the number of fools and ignoramuses is shrinking" and there is no audience for his trickery.[37] Of course, Levi, the fool, means the opposite of what he says; the Jewish bourgeoisie makes a perfect dupe for his new confidence game in which it discharges its public responsibility to Jewish society and to the state by dispensing money for an imaginary charity without ever leaving the comforts of home. The two Jerusalems — *both* fake, as far as Abramovich is concerned — refract the distance between Jewish enlightenment and the emancipation of the Jews.

Darkly hinting at the possibility that enjoying the fruits of emancipation could be construed as an act of political evasion and a denial of the historical import of the Haskalah, Abramovich created in the anti-hero of Elkanah-Arieh a foil for the august author of the policy of "selective integration," Alexander II, a father figure endowed with the authority of Nicholas I to direct the course of history but without the requisite ethical and political resolve. Like many of his conservative Russian contemporaries, Abramovich increasingly saw in the "unserfment" of late imperial society, the diminishment of the reforming tsar's ability to steer the ship of state.[38] In *The Fathers and the Sons*, the tsar-liberator appears in the guise of a Jewish crook who has tricked aspiring enlighteners into exchanging public power for private freedom. Devised by the head of a gang of thieves, "selective integration" appears as a money-driven plot, the product of combined interests of Jewish capitalists and a state increasingly committed more to its own commercial and political expansion and less to the improvement of its subjects, both Russian and Jewish. In the course of this process, the bourgeois notables of St. Petersburg — Jewish robber-barons — have effectively hijacked both the state and Jewish society from Jewish enlighteners.

Herein lies the elusive connection between Abramovich's novel and Ivan Turgenev's vastly more famous novel of the same title. In Turgenev's *Fathers and Sons* (1862), the "new men" of the 1860s, embodied by the anti-hero Bazarov, have likewise stolen the special self-appointed mission of Russia's intellectual aristocracy. The result, for all the good intentions of the younger generation, Turgenev seemed to be saying, was the triumph of personal egotism, social anarchy, and the displacement of high-minded philosophical ideals by vulgar materialism.[39] It is no coincidence that the chosen professions of Abramovich's heroes — Shimon is a doctor and David ends up a capitalist even though he starts out as a teacher — are all about the body, contributing to the development of the material rather than the moral improvement of society.[40] David's occupation, hearkening back to his father's career as a thief, seems particularly suspect, marking his degeneration on the maskilic scale of social value.

Abramovich embraced, if reluctantly, the Jewish new men who seemed to walk in step with history; despite the accusations of contemporary readers, Turgenev was no less taken by the "intelligence and heroism" of his own creation, the "nihilist" Bazarov.[41] Despite his reservations about the historical process that resulted in the generational shift, Abramovich similarly sought to endow his "sons" with energy, confidence, and strength of will.[42] By the time his novel appeared, the new generation — Jewish university students, professionals, and capitalists — claimed to represent the future of modern Russian Jewry. Where did this leave the maskil, namely, Abramovich himself? At the end of the novel he appears in the guise of the Hebrew poet, Nahum Kimhi, living under the patronage of the newly established bourgeois paterfamilias and composing odes to the passing seasons. As we have seen, the image of the natural cycle informed a conventional maskilic view of the historical relationship between the Nicholaevan "winter" and the Alexandrine "spring." At the same time Nahum Kimhi's paean, placed at the conclusion which potentially reversed the avowedly secular trajectory of the novel, pointed to a more complex, even paradoxical, reading of the seasonal metaphor.

In the Jewish rendition of Kimhi, winter gives way to spring every year and winter comes back again. Kimhi here alludes to an alternative conception of time that operates more subtly in the novel than its apparently teleological plot. Set against the background of Jewish ritual time, the story moves along the track of regular recurrence of the holidays that fix and order the chaos of contemporary life and undermine the reality of the changes the plot chronicles; in view of the Jewish cycle of time, history appears as a self-serving illusion, an epiphenomenon.

Abramovich encapsulates the power of Jewish recurrence, referenced by Kimhi, to militate against historical change in the image of the holiday dumpling (Heb. *levivah*) "rolling" eternally through time. The dumpling mocks the historicist faith of Abramovich's new men:

> In truth, can you, who thirst after the new and pine after antiquity, show me a better and more lasting monument than the dumpling? For pillars of stone will fall and their heights will be no more, but the little dumpling, made of dough, will stand from generation to generation and will not stir from our lips and from the lips of our children from now until eternity.[43]

The "eternity" of the dumpling relies precisely on its impermanence, on the fact that it is destined to be consumed. The dumpling signifies the sustaining paradox of Jewish time, bound up with ritual and food, everlasting in their constant disappearance and reappearance, the whole of Judaism a systematic reenactment of absence, longing, and fulfillment entirely antithetical to the idea of progress and to the durability of historical transformation. Nahum Kimhi, with his odes to the continual *passing* of the seasons, personifies the competing significance of Jewish time in the novel. Insinuating himself into David's bourgeois stronghold, he uses Jewish time to carve out a Jewish space in the heart of modern life. Like David's two sons, named after their Nicholaevan grandfathers, Kimhi reminds his patron of the connection between the patriarchal authority of the bourgeois paterfamilias and the claims of Jewish loyalty upon which it rests. The maskil thus becomes the conscience of modern Judaism. David internalizes Jewish self-discipline, consuming modern Jewish culture for spiritual nourishment, as one would eat a Jewish dumpling. The producer-consumer relationship between the maskil and the modern Jew effectively ensures Jewish continuity, endlessly re-creating the symbolic time-space of exile within the historical time-space of diaspora.

Abramovich himself may not have been entirely at ease with the role of maskil as the court jester of the new Jewish bourgeoisie who conspires with his patron to turn Judaism into a commodity; his alter ego, Kimhi, is both old-fashioned and undignified. At the same time as he was composing *The Fathers and the Sons*, Abramovich actively sought new ways to tap into the Jewish public sphere, ways that would not leave him at the mercy of the Jewish nouveaux riches. Thus, even as he was beginning to question the social effects of the Great Reforms, Abramovich was taking full advantage of the intellectual freedom and commercial opportunities that Alexander's policies provided.

Prodigiously interested in the possibilities of the new Jewish periodical press, Abramovich initially acquired his reputation as a writer not for the maskilic Hebrew of *The Fathers and the Sons* but for the vernacular stories he published between 1864 and 1869 in Alexander Tsederbaum's *Herald* (Yid. *Kol mevasser*), a weekly Yiddish supplement to the Hebrew *Advocate* (Heb. *Ha-melits*) that was the first of its kind in the Russian Empire.[44] At the same time Abramovich undertook a translation project that anticipated his later efforts to turn himself into the creator-god of a mythological Russian-Jewish universe. Usually understood as an example of maskilic interest in the pedagogic function of popular science, Abramovich's Hebrew version of H. O. Lenz's *Popular Natural History* (Ger. *Gemeinnützige Naturgeschichte*, 1835–1839) actually served a romantic interest in the connection between the artistic aspect of nature and the natural genius of art.[45] Recapitulating the foundational act of Adam, similarly charged with naming the animals, Abramovich sought to fashion in maskilic Hebrew a discursive landscape, complete with flora and fauna, to rival the garden of Eden and, implicitly, to underline his literary autonomy, his originary, godlike power as the creator of worlds. In this regard, the tasks of the writer of popular Yiddish stories complemented the work of the maskil naturalist. In both instances, Abramovich effectively sought dramatic ways to unite a fractured Russian Jewry on literary common ground, to create a modern Russian-Jewish readership, rooted in a single imaginary landscape that transcended geographic, economic, class, and cultural differences dividing Russian Jews from one another. The two authorial personae would merge in the figure of Mendele guiding the reader through the strange yet familiar terrain of *Benjamin III,* Abramovich's best-known tale of near-recruitment.

THE RETURN OF THE NATIVE

The writing of the Yiddish novella, known as *An Abridgement of the Travels of Benjamin III,* foregrounds the critical transition in the self-image of the maskil from propagator of knowledge among the unenlightened to moral conscience of modern Jewry too enlightened for its own good.[46] In *Benjamin III,* Abramovich dialectically juxtaposed the image of Russian Jewry as a new creation with the idea of a return to an archaic world outside history. The conception of Russian Jewishness as living death, which Abramovich first attached specifically to his literary project, would take on an ideological significance of its own in the post-pogrom mythology of the Hebrew Renaissance.[47]

Effectively setting the historical clock back to the Nicholaevan period, Abramovich propounded the benefits of eternal Jewish backwardness, a view in which every return to the Pale was understood also to be a trip back in time to the pre-reform era, perpetually on the threshold of the apocalyptic arrival of modernity.[48] Radical disenchantment with the results of Alexander's policy of "selective integration" led to a rereading of "official enlightenment" not as a precursor of progress but as a stalled experiment, aborted by the contingency of history and the caprice of autocratic will. Unlike his contemporaries, Dik, Bogrov, and Gordon, Abramovich did not associate Nicholaevan conscription with the quest for maskilic empowerment, the recruit an icon of disciplined, restrained, enlightened Jewish masculinity. In the shadow of the military reform of 1874, he saw in Nicholaevan conscription an omen only of more conscription to come, more Jewish lives to be fruitlessly wasted in the name of imperial aggrandizement.

Looking wistfully back to the political martyrdom of the Crimean defeat from the immediate vantage of the Russo-Turkish War and its embarrassing victories — *Benjamin III* was written between 1876 and 1878 — Abramovich now associated the adventurism of enlightenment with Russia's saber-rattling in the east, a stab at civilizing the natives that represented, in terms of both internal reform and geopolitics, a form of colonial sport.[49] Abramovich's sense of disjuncture between the goals of enlightenment and the ends of reform developed against the background of his personal failure to thrive in the post-emancipation economy.[50] The experience of self-improvement had failed to provide him with sufficient scope for his ambition and yielded a meager return on his commitment to the cultural vocation of a maskil. Although he had successfully completed a course of study at the Zhitomir Rabbinical Seminary and received official certification as a crown rabbi, he could not secure a position. Nor was he able to support his growing family on the meager income he earned from literature. Between 1874 and 1882 he earned more money from publishing marketable nonliterary items like calendars, a guide to the new military statute of 1874, a merchants' almanac, and a tariff table, as well as a number of Yiddish translations of liturgical songs and psalms. Despite his attempts at a variety of occupations from journalism to teaching to editorial work, the Abramovich of the 1870s remained an obscure provincial Jewish intellectual, socially and financially stuck.

Professional and cultural marginalization threatened the last cohort of Nicholaevan auto-didacts, faced with increasing competition from the ideological commitment to emancipation on the part of both the new Jewish intelligentsia and, in a more radical form, of Jewish revolutionaries. Abramovich's paradigm of return, first articulated in *Benjamin III*, paved the way for the enlightenment ethos back into the center of modern Russian-Jewish culture. Embracing the elective affinity between the Haskalah and the Nicholaevan state, Abramovich exposed the embrace of emancipation as a form of living death; it was the unreconstructed mass of Russian Jewry in the Pale, seemingly dead to the world, that contained the seeds for Jewish regeneration. In the guise of Mendele, Abramovich wandered in circles through the ever-dying shtetl on a perpetual rescue mission of Russian Jewry from its well-intentioned reforming benefactors—the emancipating state and its self-appointed Jewish delegates armed with nothing but their diplomas. Mendele's task, as maskilim-turned-nationalists would soon insist, was their own vocation.

The so-called Mendele introduction to *Benjamin III* models and subverts a *midrash* on the creation story.[51] At the same time Mendele's initial self-presentation foregrounded the idea of the journey, a theme that controls the structure of the work as a whole.

> A word from Mendele the book-peddler: Praise be to the Creator, Who guides His heavenly orbs in their paths and His earthly creatures in their ways! Surely, if our holy books relate that not even the tiniest blade of grass can stick its head above ground unless an angel taps it and says, "Grow, little grass, get thee up and about," surely, I say, a man must have his angel, too, tapping and crying: "Up and about with thee!" And even more so must this be the case with our fine Jews, each of whom most certainly has at least one hundred legions of angels tapping and rapping and telling him: "Heikele, dear soul, borrow whatsoever money thou canst, and get thee west of the border to Germany, and buy there all the goods that thou art able to. Sprout, Heikele, wax, Heikele, up from thy bog, thou villain! Filch the selfsame goods from thine own store and flinch not when thou claimest the insurance!"[52]

The reader is immediately propelled into a universe that continually moves but never goes anywhere, a universe pulsating with life and yet doomed to remain forever still; the paradigmatic Jewish businessman increases profits by destroying his own goods. This paradoxical image of the Pale, seen through the eyes of the Jewish hero, Benjamin, and his sidekick, Senderl, parodies purposeful movement. Mendele compares Benjamin's flight from home with an ethnographic expedition undertaken in the illustrious name of the "Royal Geographic Society of London," the travel agency, as it were, of Europe's greatest empire (303). The ironic homology between the ever-expanding horizontal landscape of the state and the "prodigious discoveries" of the Jewish traveler (302)—they are, of course, nothing of the kind—displays the essential folly of any journey undertaken in the name of human mastery of nature, a journey associated with purposeful mapping of the world and with civilizing its natives.

In counterpoint to the imperial presumption of linear movement, Abramovich offers a model of circularity, peculiar to the unknown, unmapped, untutored, unproductive world of the Pale. Benjamin's universe is not uncivilized but pre-civilized, both degenerate and generative, like Eden on the eve of the Fall, where human beings perversely choose death in the midst of naturally abundant life and are thereby expelled. In Benjamin's hometown, appropriately named Tuneyadevka (variously translated as Idlersville or Moochville), all movement is circular, pointless, and self-contained. No one works, and no one leaves. Rumors circulate, Talmudic debates continue indefinitely, their resolution eternally deferred until the arrival of the Messiah, which no one seems to crave very much. The town responds in alarm at Benjamin's attempt to depart from the enchanted circle of collective inertia and mutual responsibility, a system based on the much-deplored fact of life in pre-reform Russia known suggestively as "circular guilt" (Rus. *krugovaia poruka*). The solution to the crisis, inspired by Benjamin's temptation to journey forth, characteristically absurd and solipsistic, involves a walk around all the houses to check the status of all the mezuzahs "a flaw in any one of which could have easily let the Evil One into the town," and culminates, inevitably, in an increase in the tax on kosher meat, the "expenses of the delegation [being] public responsibility" (312). At all times Tuneyadevka bustles with pointless movement but remains unchanged, all "public" activity confined to the endless loop of home–synagogue–bathhouse, topoi that circumscribes the fantastic Jewish universe of the shtetl.[53] This is the world that Benjamin desires to escape, his imagination fired by the unexpected temptation of a fig from the Holy Land, another allusion to the creation story and to the problematic quest for enlightenment leading to expulsion from Eden and the coming of death into the world.

Placed at the juncture between the end of the Nicholaevan period and the "messianic" arrival of Alexander II, Benjamin's journey recasts the historical teleology of the Haskalah which sees, in the departure from the Pale, the ultimate signifier of enlightenment, as a falling away from (cyclical, eternal) nature into the trap of (linear, mortal) history. In fact, the presence of Alexander II, the false Messiah of the Jewish intelligentsia, hovers over the entire story, particularly in the ironic invocation of Benjamin's personal idol, Alexander the Great, as well as, more tellingly, in the figure of Senderl, Benjamin's slow-witted but preternaturally resourceful companion — the name Senderl is a Yiddish diminutive of Alexander. The two Alexanders merge in a devastating allusion to the tsar as "bloodsucking" vermin thirsting for Jewish blood. In chapter 12 Benjamin and Senderl find themselves in "Dnieperovitsh," a southern port town known for its voracious bedbugs. Senderl immediately senses trouble and wants to leave, but Benjamin overrules him. That same night Benjamin has a dream in which he is promised a meeting with Alexander the Great who turns into a stinking "crushed bedbug,"[54] a transparent allusion to Russia's diplomatic humiliation in the aftermath of the Russo-Turkish War. Senderl, meanwhile, has a dream in which he is kidnapped by robbers who drag him off to be slaughtered. In the course of events that immediately follow these prescient nightmares, *khappers* — the evocative Yiddish word for hired kidnappers of potential recruits — trick Benjamin and Senderl into joining the army.

From the beginning of the novel to its conclusion, the plot forms a complete circle; the story cannot end until Benjamin not only subconsciously revises the image of Alexander but actively renounces his warrior-hero, abandons his partnership with Senderl, and returns home to his wife and to the pre-reform shtetl where he belongs. The journey spirals Benjamin and Senderl from the illusion of the "fortunate sin" (Lat. *felix culpa*) — liberation from Eden — to denigration and confinement, twin symbols of Jewish life outside the preserving framework of the Pale. In the shtetl Benjamin and Senderl, paradoxically, enjoy more freedom than on the outside. The Jewish authorities of Tuneyadevka, as ineffective at maintaining social discipline as they are at any other attempt to control their environment, cannot keep Benjamin from leaving home. The army, on the other hand, puts him in prison. Tuneyadevka thus proves a receptive environment for the cultivation of desire and for the nourishment of the maskilic dream of Jewish freedom. The outside world proves to be less hospitable to the conspicuously free but now rootless, self-made, modern Jew.

Conscription, the last stop on Benjamin's trip, represents the ultimate test of maskilic optimism about the link between enlightenment and emancipation. Benjamin starts out by founding with Senderl a fellowship of liberated Jewish spirits — a tiny republic of letters — and ends up in the Nicholaevan army, revealed here as a mockery of the homosocial ethos that informed the ideal of Jewish masculinity propounded in the conscription stories of Dik, Bogrov, and Gordon. In Senderl, Benjamin, the enlightener aspiring toward emancipation, finds his ideal companion. Their intellectual partnership presents a form of escape from the domestic tyranny of traditional Jewish marriage, labeled by the maskilim as a pathological reversal of natural gender roles. But the joint enterprise of Benjamin and Senderl dramatizes the displacement of sex by romance; the first is a product of nature, the second distinctly of culture.

Abramovich appropriates maskilic categories of social analysis in the name of a conservative critique of enlightenment from within its own system of values; Benjamin and Senderl are overgrown children, effete intellectuals afraid to claim the "natural" fruits of adult masculinity. The maskilic dream of modern Judaism is the product of the nightmare of impotence; the so-called pathology of Jewish marriage, Abramovich asserts, is not the result of traditional Jewish social mores, based on the biblical imperative to "be fruitful and multiply," but precisely the reverse, the elevation of modern Jewish culture above the biological imperatives of Jewish life. Even as they aspire to be men of the world, Benjamin and Senderl are afraid to confront their wives, uncomfortable, even brutal, reminders of their own inadequacy; Benjamin, the "great coward," has "no idea how to part from his wife" (310, 319). And, of course, the seemingly happy union with Senderl is no solution to the chronic weakness of the enlightener.

Senderl is a passive, submissive, emasculated creature, subordinate to Benjamin's false pride in his own intellectual accomplishments and presumably superior judgment, which, in the end, lands the pair smack into the hands of *khappers*. This, for Abramovich, is the most ironic result of the shortfall of culture — the literal subjection of the bodies of Benjamin and Senderl to the inhumanity of an institution devised exclusively by civilized man for the defense of his all-too-human political interests and vaunted cultural institutions. The military, dedicated to making men out of boys, is in Abramovich's view, the height of childish self-delusion. Benjamin, re-capitulating Mendele's ironic voice, derides military discipline as bitter mockery of circular, self-contained movement characterizing Tuneyadevka:

> "I swear, Senderl," [he says], "what a baby you are, playing soldier like a schoolboy! What are you accomplishing? How can a married man, and a Jew to boot, spend all his time making right-faces and left-faces? What is the point of all this? What difference does it make whether you start with the left foot or the right when you go, what-do-you-call-it, about face [Rus. *krugom*, lit. "in a circle"]?" (384; translation slightly altered)

Jewish masculinity, so obviously lacking in the qualities that make a good soldier the ideal of adult manhood, Abramovich asserts, is most gifted, pre-cocious, hyper-masculine, where it most counts, in the reproduction of hu-man life. This is why the redemption of Benjamin and Senderl lies in their return to their wives:

> "We wish to make an official statement" [Benjamin says to the military tribunal at their court-martial for desertion]. "Go ahead, Senderl, speak up! Why are you standing there like a clod? Don't be afraid to tell them the truth, by God! We hereby declare, the two of us, that we are, have been, and always will be ignorant of all military matters; that we are, God be praised, married men with other things on our minds than your affairs, which are totally alien to us. and that we cannot possibly be of any use to you, who have every reason to discharge us!" (389)

As Russian soldiers, Benjamin and Senderl play (badly) at being men; as Jewish husbands, they do (best) the "other things" that men are designed to do. The conclusion of the story neatly merges the image of collective degen-eration with the promise of regeneration; Abramovich sends Benjamin and Senderl back to the Pale to fulfill the imperative of God and Nature, to engage in the only kind of creative act that is possible in the primordial stillness of Eden, the one act, as it were, that turned the vegetation of Russian Jewry into the fruits of paradise. And, given the unprecedented and still unaccounted for demographic explosion of Russian Jewry in the nine-teenth century, Abramovich's provocative defense of Jewish vitality may not have been so far-fetched.

Benjamin's last word, his "divorce" from state authority — the final chap-ter is called "A Bride No More, Once More a Maid" (Yid. *oys kale un vider a moyd*)[55] — revises the meaning of emancipation in accordance with Abra-movich's pessimistic outlook on Jewish modernity, devoid of faith in the historical triumph of reason and providence. Benjamin falsely imagines freedom as the liberty to leave home; by the end, he comes to understand emancipation as the freedom to return home. Here the journey of enlightenment serves not the emancipation of the Jewish person but the effort to become a better Jew, to move, as it were, from a state of innocence to a state of grace. Indeed, the paradigm of return only makes sense as a post-emancipation phenomenon; its self-conscious conservatism is distinctly a product of Abramovich's engagement with the promise of enlightenment, not its out-of-hand rejection in the name of Jewish piety. Abramovich addressed himself not to the traditional vernacular reader but to aspiring Russian-Jewish moderns like himself, faced with a set of complex choices between personal ambition and collective loyalty, choices that arguably informed every Jewish life in post-emancipation Russia and that define Jewish life still. Both repelled and enchanted by the Pale, Abramovich's readers, then as now, found in his vernacular mythology the literary refraction of the undeniable pull beyond the Russian-Jewish Eden as well as a trenchant analysis of its risks and limitations, the latter symbolically linked to the miseries of Benjamin's short-lived military career — alienation, indignity, institutional anti-Semitism, a barren life bereft of family, community, and all the comforting, generative pleasures of Jewish food, Jewish children, Jewish sex.

Mendele, in his prophetic wisdom, pronounces the final verdict on the dangers lurking in the temptations of modernity, apparently found not just beyond the Pale — Benjamin thinks he is going out but ends up only traveling around — but in the Jewish backyard itself:

> Alas, Benjamin and Senderl had had no inkling that the greatest
> dangers are not those posed in the wilderness by snakes,
> scorpions, and other wild creatures, but those that are in our
> own backyards. For the time during which our heroes embarked
> upon their wanderings was a most difficult, darkest, most bitter
> time — a time when Jew would hunt after Jew
>> Stalking with his eyes poor men,
>> Like a lion in its den,
> and impressing helpless souls into the tsar's army so that others
> should not have to serve. Too late did our heroes realize that *they*
> *were in the wilderness already*, with beasts of prey all around them,
> none more cruel than the two ogres who had sold them into
> military service.[56]

In the life of every Jew making the intellectual, social, economic, or geographic transition from a life within the confines of the Pale — geographic and cultural — to a life beyond its borders, it is always already the critical moment of passage from Nicholaevan enlightenment to Alexandrine emancipation, the "most difficult, darkest, most bitter time" of separation from everything known, familiar, safe. The Nicholaevan time-space transfers the collective teleology of the Haskalah from Russian-Jewish history into the individual psychology of the modern Jew. The *khappers* here represent the internal bad conscience of Jewish desire for freedom. These conspicuously pious Jews are the hired guns of collective vengeance against the "modern Jewish intellectuals, blast them all" (378). Their job is to punish Benjamin by making his wishes come true, that is, by thrusting him into a world which seems to be the opposite of everything he wants to leave behind. But without the mediation of the *khappers*, Abramovich seems to suggest, there can be no opportunity for emancipation, no chance, that is, for the Jew to experience the consequences of the dangerous quest for enlightenment.

Without the historical risks of emancipation, there can be no return, no effective ending to the story, no opportunity for Benjamin to attain self-consciousness and to grow into the responsibilities of Jewish manhood — no *Jewish* enlightenment. The *khappers* here represent the violent force of contingency that unexpectedly inverts the causal relationship between enlightenment and emancipation. In Abramovich's modern drama of the Fall, they are the dark angels of Benjamin's better — read, Jewish — nature. Thrusting him into the secular world of knowledge, work, and death, they unwittingly release the fly of human freedom into the divine ointment of history, dialectically serving the cause of Benjamin's return.

The image of Benjamin's abortive journey toward emancipation, "abridged," as the title asserts, by the unanticipated act of return, acquired paradigmatic status in nationalist discourse. In its Hebrew translation — which appeared within a year of the First Zionist Congress (1897) — *The Travels of Benjamin III* recast the vernacular mythology of modern alienation into a mock epic of the Jewish exodus from European history.[57] Benjamin's discharge from the Russian army on the grounds of insanity might, in this context, be interpreted as an empowering gesture of auto-emancipation, the ironic signifier of the essential "insanity" of the modern gentile state.[58] In the aftermath of Jewish statehood, it became possible, again, to reread the canonic *Benjamin III* as a "counternarrative to the translation of messianic dreams into the language of nineteenth-century nationalism and of return to an 'original' space," in other words, as a critique of the essential "insanity" of Zionist politics.[59]

Both readings get it right — and wrong — mainly because they treat the Hebrew version of the book as autonomous. But the Hebrew text was born of the Yiddish original; the former never lost its genealogical connection to the latter. Benjamin's successive existence first as a vernacular jester — the Jewish "schlemiel" par excellence — and then as the universal hero in Jewish guise — a Hebrew Odysseus "embattled with his own society"[60] — serves as Abramovich's answer to the central question of the national revival: how Europe's oldest, most backward Jewry could bring forth the fruits of modern Jewish culture. Enshrined in the twinned images of the recruit as child and old man, this productive tension emerged in Abramovich's pressing creative concerns, as he himself completed the magic circle of return and embraced the self-styled vocation of the national (Rus. *narodnyi*) writer in the years immediately following the initial publication of *Benjamin III.*

LITTLE MEN

In the wake of Benjamin's imaginary return to his own Jewish nature, Abramovich produced two other works that addressed directly the implications of his hero's radical act of disengagement from modernity. In all three works — *Benjamin III;* the revised and expanded version of Abramovich's first Yiddish novel, *The Little Man* (Yid. *Dos kleyne mentshele*); and the Yiddish play, *The Call-Up* (Yid. *Der prizyv*) — the conscription theme presented Abramovich the opportunity to assess the wages of freedom as experienced by his own contemporaries. Once again, the conscription story served the creation of a therapeutic mythology that argued for Jewish sameness against the reality of deepening Jewish difference. At the center stood the image of the collective Russian-Jewish body, at once completely vulnerable and totally invincible, both the perennial victim of history and the eternal conqueror of time, always forsaken and still entirely self-sufficient, dead in the cradle but alive to an eternally ripe old age.

The 1879 version of *The Little Man,* in which the conscript appears in the guise of a missing child, and *The Call-Up,* where he turns up as a Nicholaevan veteran, form two parts of a single project that set the stage for Abramovich's abandonment of his enlightenment persona and his return to the Pale. Defying the limits of a thoroughly conventional maskilic autobiography, Abramovich turned the clock back two generations to become his own grandfather, permanently blurring the line between himself and his fictional Nicholaevan double, Mendele the book-peddler. True to his commercial calling, Mendele effectively sold Abramovich and his distinctly modern Jewish books to a generation of readers reared not on the dream of enlightenment but on the realities of emancipation. Mendele's ironic Nicholaevan voice endowed Abramovich with unprecedented cultural authority at a time when a series of seductive secular alternatives undermined the practical, theological, and political relevance of Jewish piety, Jewish community, and Jewish practice. Through Mendele, Abramovich entered into the conscience of a new cohort of returning sons. In fact, the moment of public recognition of Abramovich's new persona coincided with the signal failure of the project of enlightened Jewish fatherhood, the last best hope for modern Judaism nurtured by maskilim like Dik, Bogrov, and Gordon. Abramovich had reason to take this failure very personally; in the late 1870s his only son, along with many other young Russian radicals of Jewish extraction, was arrested for revolutionary activity and subsequently converted to Russian Orthodoxy. The shock contributed to Abramovich's departure from the literary scene for a period of five years (1879–1884).[61] The crisis—and here the line between public and private becomes blurry—in turn occasioned a professional return to the business of literature, the only possible means of saving the sons that the maskilim were losing to the revolution.

Himself having tried and failed in a variety of respectable enlightened occupations, including those of crown rabbi, teacher, and Hebrew publicist, Abramovich attempted, in 1879, to consolidate his achievements as a writer of fiction by publishing his collected works. The first volume of the projected series comprised a new version of *The Little Man*, Abramovich's first literary success, originally serialized in *Kol mevasser* in 1864–1865.[62] While the collected works project did not materialize, the revision of the novel, expressly designed to introduce the reader into the expanded world of Mendele, already reflected the critical shift from Abramovich's maskilic identity, available in a series of prior works that went beyond the mediation of the book-peddler to a more profound identification with the colloquial voice of his own editorial persona.[63] In its early incarnation, *The Little Man* assumed the form of a simple maskilic parable, cast in the familiar style of a Yiddish chapbook (Yid. *bikhl*) that now promoted not conventional collective pieties but the modern personal virtues of proper upbringing and practical education. The eponymous motif of the "little man" symbolized the inherent potential for moral degeneration and conveyed the urgency of the enlightenment project: the child was a blank slate, easily corruptible—reduced in moral stature—by bad influences, and therefore in need of systematic social and intellectual training. Appropriating the structure of a traditional genre—the ethical will—Abramovich produced an engaging confessional tale of greed and egoism, a chronicle passed down to Mendele by a repentant communal "strongman" (Heb. *takif*) to be published and circulated for common edification.

Abramovich's addition of a romantic subplot to the 1879 edition of *The Little Man* substantially changed both the tone and content of the original version.[64] The new story of the protagonist's seduction and abandonment of the virtuous and aptly named Golde became the vehicle for the introduction of the conscription theme into the story. The unhappy union between Takif and Golde takes place as a result of Takif's manipulation of the law to get his rival drafted. Takif and Golde produce a child together, whom Takif abandons and who eventually grows up to fight, fall, and go missing in the defense of Sevastopol. Takif initiates the process of repentance by seeking the services of Mendele in the name of reclaiming and saving his long-lost son. In addition, the second version significantly amplified the voice of Mendele, who was no longer responsible for the dissemination of enlightenment and, instead, was assigned the task of rescuing "the children of Israel" (Yid. *di yudishe kinder*) — literally, Jewish children, and figuratively, the Jewish people — deserted by their fathers.

In a world where the primary task of Jewish manhood is reproductive, child abandonment becomes the ultimate transgression against the prerogatives of Jewish masculinity and against the biological imperative of Jewish continuity; beginning with *Fishke the Lame* (Yid. *Fishke der krumer,* 1869), this theme recurs in virtually every single one of Abramovich's works.[65] In *The Little Man,* Takif's private sin signifies the abandonment of the people to their historical fate by Jewish "strongmen" who serve only their own ambitions. The conscription and almost certain death of Takif's son mirrors the collective fate of an orphaned Jewry, left to the designs of the state which only wants Jewish bodies for cannon fodder; conscription here symbolizes Abramovich's disillusionment with *raison d'état,* a sensibility already in evidence in *Benjamin III.* Conscription no longer functions as a sign of maskilic empowerment by the state on behalf of reform; instead, it provides the state with an opportunity to divide and conquer, that is, to use the desires of the Jewish individual against the needs of the Jewish collective. Let us recall that Takif, in order to get rid of his rival, has him drafted, initiating the process that will culminate in the loss of his own son to the army. The modern state thus effectively fosters the moral corruption of the Jew, never more so than when it makes possible the "unserfment" of his desires and his liberation from the Jewish community.

Set in 1855, at the critical juncture between official enlightenment and emancipation, Takif's story recapitulates the psychological tension implicit in the Jewish experience of personal freedom. In the later version of *The Little Man,* the project of individual repentance, Takif's ultimate recognition of his responsibility to his son overshadows the project of enlightenment that informed the original. Just as he did in *Benjamin III,* Abramovich here displaced enlightenment faith in the happy marriage between the political history of the Russian state and the moral life of its subjects with the act of "divorce" of the emancipated Russian Jew from the tsar-liberator.

Takif's repentance — like Mendele's mission of rescue — seeks to turn time back to the critical moment just before the act of abandonment, before, that is, Takif's son has had a chance to grow up and become master of his own fate rather than the empty cipher of his father's morally indifferent, blind ambition and his mother's blinding, numbing, automatic rage. In Takif's conscription nightmare, his son is reduced nearly to the point of absence by the irresistible power of his parents' private desires:

> Golde tormented me more than anything [Takif writes]. It seemed as if I could see her lonely and sad, hunched over her sewing. The needle pricks her fingers but she feels nothing, does not even cringe in pain but continues to sew like a machine while all the time rocking, rocking the heavy squeaking cradle and singing quietly, "Rock-a-bye, rock-a-bye [. . .] " And her voice is inexpressibly sad. And the cradle is empty, there is no one in it. "Golde!" I scream, "Where is he? Where is the child?" But Golde just keeps rocking and singing, not speaking a single word to me: "Rock-a-bye my little son . . . my poor little white lamb."

> And with these words, Golde rises; bloody tears stream from her eyes. She looks around, stretches forth her hands, and wails: "Oh, my little white lamb is no more!" In horror, I run from the house; all around me I see wolves and bears! And I hear the crunching of their fangs on the tender bones, and from afar I hear the bitter cries of the poor, unfortunate little lamb.[66]

Takif's imagination radically diminishes his twice-lost son — once to his father and then again on the battlefield — to the absent cradle and to the echo of being eaten, bones and all, by wild beasts; as pure projection of his father's neglected Jewish consciousness, the child cannot ever be allowed to escape the family drama into which he is cast. Defined by his absolute powerlessness over both his parents — Golde, the grieving mother, Medea-like, implicates herself in his destruction in order to avenge herself on her former husband — Takif's son represents the aborted liberation of the many at the expense of the relentless private ambitions of the one.

Emancipation is the temptation that leads to the fall of the maskil and to the split between Russian Jewry and the Russian Jew; the post-emancipation act of return requires that Russian Jewry be collectively cast in the role of objectified Nicholaevan innocence, just before the Fall. In Mendele's world it is always 1855 — just before the promise of emancipation enabled every Jewish child to defy parental and communal authority, and to come into his own as a historical subject. Takif, on the other hand, is the Nicholaevan "strongman," the *übermensch* who masters history first in his precocious self-liberation from collective discipline and ethical constraints, and then by leaping back in time to reclaim his moral responsibility, an act of freely chosen and therefore heroic self-abasement that bears all the marks of performance; hence the dramatic monologue that marks the high point of Takif's inner drama of confession and repentance.

The post-emancipation return of the native, the self-conscious transcendence of modernity, involved a theatrical gesture in *The Little Man* no less then in *Benjamin III* or, for that matter, in Abramovich's own creative life. Abramovich actually cast another Nicholaevan *übermensch* — the old soldier Shmuelik — in an important supporting role in a play that provided the script for his well-orchestrated return onto the stage of Russian-Jewish culture. Published in 1884 but written in the late 1870s, directly under the impact of the Russo-Turkish War, *The Call-Up* concerns the drafting of a Jewish recruit into the newly reformed Russian army.[67] In the process, the play took up directly the question of Jewish generation that the plot of *The Little Man* left ominously unresolved. In *The Call-Up*, Abramovich depicts the corrosive effects of modernity on the future of Russian Jews; the robust longevity of the Nicholaevan superman contrasts with the fruitlessness of the young bourgeois hero, aptly named Alexander, placed at the center of the family drama. The eternal soldier Shmuelik effectively rehabilitates the image of Russian Jewry as a dead child, stillborn in the empty cradle which is also the grave of Takif's son.

The Call-Up focuses on the relationship between a wealthy and devout patriarch and a young couple whose efforts to unite in marriage are threatened by the persistence of antiquated customs, narrow-minded prejudice, and the imperious authority of a corrupt communal order, dominated by old-fashioned, self-serving hypocrites. So far so good. It turns out, however, that the failure of the romantic plot has less to do with resistance from without and more with the dispiriting lack of will within. In fact, the ancients, represented chiefly by the gullible tax farmer, father of young Reyzele, are just as passive as the moderns, embodied in the person of Reyzele's beloved "misfortune" (Yid. *shlimazl*) Alexander. Neither can resist the manipulation of the matchmaker and the rebbe who use the principals in carefully orchestrated plots that move the action of the play forward.

The matchmaker initially persuades the tax farmer of the suitability of the match with Alexander. Later, when a letter arrives claiming that Alexander has died from wounds sustained in battle, the matchmaker swiftly changes sides and talks a depressed and pliable Reyzele into showing some interest in the despicable Haskel, the recently widowed son of the local rebbe. The rebbe also uses the tax farmer to his own advantage. First he bribes an official to get Alexander conscripted instead of his own son; this goes against the letter of the law, since Alexander, being an only son, is not eligible for the draft. Then he approaches the tax farmer and successfully plies his own son's suit. Reyzele ends up married to Haskel; Alexander returns home from the front to find himself betrayed not so much by a rival as by the force of circumstances. The news that he had fallen in battle turns out to be an unfortunate case of mistaken identity; Alexander, the modern Jew as eternal adolescent, cannot rise to the stature of heroic manhood even through death.

The abortive bourgeois romance commands little sympathy in *The Call-Up;* Abramovich views Alexander's pointless conscription — tellingly, into the recently reformed military of the protagonist's royal namesake — from the ironic position of the pre-reform veteran. The old soldier Shmuelik, Abramovich's Nicholaevan alter ego, outlives every specimen of young Jewish manhood in the play including his own grandson-in-law, another "newfangled" conscript. Shmuelik first appears on the scene at the start of the second act, set in front of the local military office, where induction of the new recruits takes place. His first comic tirade contrasts with the wailing of a Jewish woman, lamenting the conscription of her "little Berel." The name of this new recruit — Ber means bear in Yiddish — sets up perfectly the sarcasm of Shmuelik's drunken harangue against the hysterical gushing of an overprotective Jewish mama who keeps her grown-up son tied to her skirt even though "little Berel" is really a great big bear of a man.

> My Berele, my Berele [Shmuelik teases]! Pah! Oh, these new-fangled inductions! Berele, shmerele, if you please, walk yourself over there on your own little feet. Oh, what would you know of those years, you "who walk on

your own feet"? Try being fettered with the "bracelets," a whole musical band of chains going zumm, zumm, so everyone can hear. That's what used to be called an induction.[68]

When Hershele, Shmuelik's grandson-in-law, a soldier himself, tries to quiet the old man, Shmuelik reverts to his soldier's stance. He even tries to cut a dashing figure of a fifer in the old Nicholaevan army, proudly twirling his mustache, the symbol of gallant masculinity, modeled after the tsar himself:

> Say the memorial prayer [Heb. *yizkor*] and stand at attention! Pah, a little soldier, a new-fangled little soldier. A puppy with little whiskers. Yesterday he started his service, and the day after tomorrow he's had enough, he's all served out, oh merciful Father [Heb. *av ha-rahamim*]! Twenty-five years we served God and the tsar, and took plenty of whippings. "Soldier Shmuel!" my commander would call out to me when I was wanted. And just like that, all in good fun, slap! slap! right across my mug. And I would answer, "Happy to oblige, Your Excellency!" and spit out a tooth. (act 2, scene 1)

According to Shmuelik, the new army—the product of the Great Reforms with its shortened term of service—makes inferior men and substandard Jews. The irony here is that Shmuelik, completely at ease in his subordinate position, actually achieves a greater degree of freedom than do his younger presumably emancipated counterparts, subject entirely to the modern economy of desire that takes the place of traditional hierarchies. He successfully evades fate and survives while they succumb to it, falling, as he describes them, like helpless "doves," "poor little orphans," "calves" and "sheep" fattened expressly for slaughter. Fed on the personal rewards of emancipation, the new generation is fit only to be plucked by the predatory state. Despite his good intentions, Alexander remains incapable of any autonomous productive—or reproductive—act; for all his modern ways, he remains in humiliating financial and sexual bondage, relying for support [Yid. *kest*] on his father-in-law. This comes out in Shmuelik's sly indictment of the chronic impotence of Jewish manhood, binding the generations together in irreversible decline:

> Up a little tree, in a nest
> Sit two happy doves
> Sitting, pecking, eating *kest*
> Undertaking to multiply.
> .　.　.　.　.　.　.　.　.
> But the doves in the nest are no more
> And there is no more happiness there
> Only the father-in-law lives
> All alone, without his offspring. (act 2, scene 3)

Emancipation is hardly liberating. The rhyme between "nest" (the Yiddish word is the same as the English) and *kest* underscores that the definition and pursuit of personal desire depends on the political commodification of the individual. The comforts of the bourgeois love "nest," purchased by the wealthy tax farmer — himself beholden to the state's appetite for capital — emasculate Alexander and enervate Reyzele to render them fit for nothing. Contrast this with Abramovich's depiction of the highly charged and fruitful union between the two servants, Mendel and Dvosye, whose pursuit of each other lies beyond the purview of bourgeois domestic economy.

Like Shmuelik, Mendel and Dvosye find an unexpected measure of freedom from tradition within existing social hierarchies. Dvosye's ability to articulate and satisfy her own sexual appetites provides an especially striking contrast with the listless sentimentality of her former mistress, the tender flower, Reyzele (her name means "little rose" in Yiddish). Here is Dvosye bragging to Reyzele about her recently attained marital happiness. As in *Benjamin III*, sex trumps romance:

> I wish all lovers enjoyed good fortune such as mine! My Mendel loves me, pampers me. It's all "precious Dvosye," "my little Dvosye." And in my heart, I have such a love for him, such a love . . . I have, thank God, nothing to complain about. You may think Mendel is a nobody. And truly he is a simple man, nothing at all like those pampered overgrown boys. But none of them are worth even as much as his little finger. (act 5, scene 4)

Here Dvosye explicitly echoes Shmuelik's dismissal of "Berele" in her own disdain toward "pampered overgrown [modern] boys." Mendel, on the other hand, commands her complete devotion; suggestively Dvosye's declaration trails off in ellipses, intimating that Mendel offers his wife more to love than vulgar, conventional endearments. Little Mendel, the "nobody," is a big man; just as in the case of Benjamin who becomes a man by reclaiming his sexual responsibility, here the measure of a man has everything to do with the "worth" of Mendel's "little finger."

The hyper-masculine servant Mendel is a foil for the old soldier Shmuelik; they, like Takif, represent the generative potential of Russian Jewry, the collective durability of which defies the apparently linear logic of history and contrasts with the fruitlessness of modern Russian Jews. Shmuelik reappears in the final act, when it is revealed that his own grandson-in law, Hershele, not Alexander, was the soldier who died in battle. While Shmuelik is himself eternal, overcoming the oppressive weight of time, even his offspring is doomed to bear its continual "knocks." The old man's final words dispel the illusion that the freedom granted to Jews by Alexander II in exchange for service supersedes Nicholas's demand for service in exchange for freedom: "Lament your troubles, your knocks, your lashes all you want as long as you say the law is just — glad to be of service your Excellency!" (act 5, scene 7).

In the play Shmuelik alone understands that the law of the tsar, like the law of God, is an arbitrary, inscrutable decree (Heb. *gzerah*) that sometimes saves and sometimes kills, both without "justice" and without teleological significance, without logic at all, in fact; history must be survived, like an accident, rather than understood like a book. Hardly an intellectual, Shmuelik is preeminently a survivor whose strength of will is itself a counter-historical force of nature, similarly beyond reason or understanding. His infinite capacity for resisting death is the inverted likeness of the aborted life of Takif's son. The twinned images of the two Nicholaevan recruits complete a single circle in which Russian Jewry is simultaneously cast in the role of the dead child pressing its moral claims upon estranged fathers and of the grandfather outliving his own barren children. Abramovich's own drama of return, occasioned by the publication of *The Call-Up,* derived its inspiration from long-standing maskilic anxieties about the effects of emancipation on the future of Jewish enlightenment, concerns linked by the complementary images of Nicholaevan conscripts to the absence of effective Jewish paternity.

PORTRAIT OF THE ARTIST AS AN OLD MAN

Following the publication of the second version of *The Little Man* in 1879, Abramovich departed the literary scene for five years. Critics attribute this self-imposed silence to a personal crisis, the effects of which Abramovich himself described both in a private letter to his friend, Lev Binshtok,[69] and in the dedicatory epistle appended to *The Call-Up:* "The troubles of the recent past have turned my heart to stone so that my tongue could not be moved to speak and my hand could not be moved to write even a single word."[70] The literary scholar Joseph Klausner stresses the immediate economic causes of Abramovich's collapse: between 1879 and 1881 Abramovich had virtually no income and was forced to apply personally to Baron Horace Guenzburg; the two knew each other in Kamenetz-Podolsk, where Abramovich started his career. Although Guenzburg granted him a small monthly pension, the writer's professional and financial problems were not settled until 1881, when, through the intercession of friends, he was appointed principal of the progressive Talmud Torah, a charity school, in Odessa. Klausner's economic explanation elaborates the psychological reasons invoked to explain Abramovich's silence: the death of his younger daughter and the imprisonment, and subsequent conversion, of his son.[71]

In fact, the shift in enlightenment discourse, which Abramovich himself inaugurated in his work, endowed his particular "troubles" with historical significance. In taking a job at the Talmud Torah, Abramovich did not simply secure a position; he performed the act of rescuing poor Jewish children, a task he had assigned to Mendele in *The Little Man.* The conversion of his son and the loss of his daughter similarly enacted the central theme of *The Call-Up:* the failure of modern Jewish fatherhood to ensure

Jewish continuity. What is important is not whether these events moved Abramovich to silence but that he interpreted his life in literary terms that inspired him to return to speech. Psychology and economics alone, without the mediation of discourse, do not explain why Abramovich persisted, particularly after 1884, in blurring the distance between life and art.

The 1884 publication of *The Call-Up,* five years after it was finished, marked the twenty-fifth anniversary of Abramovich's initial entry onto the literary scene. Significantly the play was published by the son of Alexander Tsederbaum; Tsederbaum senior had been responsible for publishing Abramovich's first work of fiction, *The Little Man,* in *Kol mevasser.* The occasion was greeted by the appearance of a spate of review articles in the Russian-Jewish press which, for the first time, celebrated Abramovich for his achievements as a writer. The first of these journalistic panegyrics appeared in July 1884 in the short-lived St. Petersburg "scientific-literary" monthly *The Jewish Review* (Rus. *Evreiskoe obozrenie*). Authored by the editor, Judah-Leib (Lev Osipovich) Kantor, the article emphasized that Abramovich taught his contemporaries "how to write simply, to express their thoughts clearly, without the recourse to poetic imagery and metaphoric expressions, in a word to write in the same style that is used by all enlightened people."[72] However, claimed Kantor, this enlightener was drawn to his true calling, the composition of "sketches, humorous silhouettes, and satirical studies based on the life of the folk."[73] Kantor underlined the dual aspect of Abramovich's craft which qualified him as a literary genius; Abramovich was an enlightener, in command of the most sophisticated modes of self-expression, who, nevertheless, drew his inspiration from popular experience. This quality distinguished Abramovich from the previous generation of maskilim, like Abraham Mapu, whose style Kantor described as "naïve imitation of the prophetic voice."[74]

In another congratulatory essay published in the weekly supplement to St. Petersburg's *Dawn* (Rus. *Voskhod*), Abramovich's friend and fellow graduate from the Zhitomir Rabbinical Seminary, the Odessa publicist Menashe Morgulis, characterized him as a member of " our homegrown (Rus. *narodnaia*) intelligentsia," whose creative life had "merged organically with the life of the people."[75] Morgulis was the first to refer to Abramovich as a "national writer"; he claimed that Abramovich deserved this "honorable title" more than any of his contemporaries, including even Judah-Leib Gordon, the most distinguished Hebrew poet of his generation, whose own "literary anniversary" had been celebrated in St. Petersburg almost exactly three years earlier.[76] Morgulis argued that while Gordon's most recent efforts also bore the stamp of "nationality" (Rus. *narodnost'*), only Abramovich's work could both withstand the scrutiny of "scholarly, scientific criticism" and command "popular interest."[77]

In his article in the weekly *Russian Jew* (Rus. *Russkii evrei*), the literary critic Akim L'vovich Flekser (better known under his pseudonym, A. Volynskii) picked up on Morgulis's designation and praised Abramovich as a "true national writer who abandoned the language of Scripture to become a talented master of satire in the vernacular" and, above all, a defender of the "weak and aggrieved." In Abramovich's "laughter" Flekser heard the echo of a "deep love for the Jewish people." Flekser's Abramovich "studied" the people not for the sake of a "false objectivity" but in order to show the "blamelessly blamed" the way to a better life and toward moral self-fulfillment. A master of the "diction of folk thought, the structure of the folk imagination, and the character of folk humor," Abramovich, claimed Flekser, "merges" (Rus. *slivaetsia,* from *sliianie*) with the people in order to fulfill an "inner" need to participate in the process of their spiritual and cultural rebirth.[78] Flekser was one of the first critics of Jewish literature to abandon the radical realist program charted by Chernyshevskii and Dobroliubov; in his description of Abramovich's interest in the "blamelessly blamed," he alluded to Dostoevsky's parallel concern with the fate of "the insulted and the injured" as a source of inspiration for artistic creativity and for moral awakening.[79] The pointed reference to the writer "merging" with the people polemically invoked a term which had singular importance in the contemporary debate over Jewish emancipation. Russian and Jewish publicists alike contrasted "merging" with "drawing closer" (Rus. *sblizhenie*) to mark the desirable degree of Jewish integration into *Russian* society.[80] Flekser's appropriation of "merging" and his insinuation that, like Dostoevsky's, Abramovich's moral imagination had its roots in the life of the people, served a new understanding of the creative impulse of the "national writer," one that provided its own social impetus for the creation of modern Jewish literature. In fact, Morgulis's reference to Judah-Leib Gordon, as well as Kantor's comparison of Abramovich with Mapu, indicates that the making of a "national writer" was a contested process; the critics who elevated Abramovich above Gordon and Mapu remained vague about his "unique" claim to the title. Thus the first biographical sketch about Abramovich had to take on the difficult task of explaining how an author whose cultural pedigree was no different from other maskilim transformed himself into "a microcosm" of his own "unfortunate tribe."[81]

Written by the author's closest friend, Lev Binshtok, the article reveals the traces of Abramovich's own subtle hand. The writer collaborated in the making of his own myth to produce a life filled with enough "chance happenings" and "miraculous" coincidences to rival his fiction. In Binshtok's account, Abramovich's most important quality as a writer was his sterling character, tempered by suffering. For the first time Binshtok elevated Abramovich's so-called crisis to the position of a test of the writer's "selfless" commitment to literature.

The story of Abramovich's development, as told by Binshtok, turned the "national writer" into a new kind of hero, given to extraordinary feats of moral strength under "pressures which could have felled even a giant."

Born into humble circumstances, his gifts were gradually revealed and providentially nurtured until he was "anointed" by fate. Recounting how Abramovich "missed" an important opportunity, which would have advanced his career but would have necessitated his leaving Russia to study at the rabbinical seminary in Padua, Binshtok concluded that Abramovich was destined to attend a different kind of "school":

> But it can be said with great certainty that [had Abramovich gone to Padua] Russian Jewry would have lost its very own national writer, a writer who together with his long-suffering people passed through the bitter school of survival, enduring misfortune, disappointment, and all kinds of privations. Studying in this practical school the spiritual life of his people enabled him to transmit with inimitable artistry the most delicate nuances of the national soul and to feel for himself the slightest beat of the national pulse.[82]

Consistent with Binshtok's description of the "national writer" as a new kind of folk-hero (Rus. *bogatyr'*), a popular moral champion steeled by affliction, the celebration of his literary anniversary focused on his twenty-five years of "selfless service for the good of [his] long-suffering people."[83]

For all this critical attention, the celebration was at least a year off the mark. Abramovich's first publication, "A Letter concerning Education," appeared in 1857. His first book, a collection of articles and various literary miscellany called *The Judgment of Peace* (Heb. *Mishpat shalom*), was published in 1860. His first work of fiction, *Learn to Do Well*, came out in 1862. In 1859 — the year emblazoned both on the inside cover of the special anniversary edition of *The Call-Up* and on the special address sent to Abramovich in Odessa by his friends from St. Petersburg — Abramovich published only a short and unexceptional Hebrew piece in David Gordon's conservative weekly *The Preacher* (Heb. *Ha-magid*). Moreover, the literary quality of the play which putatively celebrated Abramovich's talents as a writer could hardly be said to represent his best work. It was not mentioned by any of the reviewers, who concentrated their praise on *Fishke the Lame, Benjamin III,* and especially *The Nag* (Yid. *Di kliatshe*, 1873). In light of this strange discrepancy, the connection between the content of *The Call-Up* and the year 1859 acquires a new resonance.

The year 1884 coincided with the twenty-fifth anniversary of the appearance of Rabinovich's "Penal Recruit." In choosing to publish *The Call-Up*, a play that juxtaposes a Nicholaevan veteran who is a veritable paragon of legendary strength with an effete and passive Jewish soldier of the new generation, Abramovich's admirers may have been seeking to draw a parallel between Rabinovich's image of the "penal recruit" — who similarly bore the literary brunt of collective responsibility — and the self-image of the "national poet" as well as to endow the recently arrived Abramovich with a creditable literary lineage, a link with Odessa's enlightened Jewish elite. Abramovich returned to literature as a modern writer in the guise of a

Nicholaevan hero, a maskil who transcended the material inducements of emancipation in order to suffer alongside his own impoverished people.

The persona of the book-peddler redeemed Abramovich from his own success. The return demanded the self-conscious suppression of the difference between the epic voice of the popular bard — Mendele — and the gentlemanly bearing of his creator who, in the last quarter of the nineteenth century, grew into an eminent litterateur and notable member of educated Jewish society in Odessa.[84] Abramovich's carefully contrived literary anniversary served the creation of his public persona, not the revelation of a slumbering national imagination.[85] In elevating him to the status of a "national writer," the celebration simultaneously transformed an obscure maskil into a modern author. Before nationalist critics could discover in Abramovich a founder of the Hebrew Renaissance, Russian-Jewish educated society had to claim him as its own native son. It was Jewish critics writing in Russian, for a Russian-Jewish audience, well read in contemporary Russian literature, who first made Abramovich's reputation as a vernacular sage.[86] Ironically the newly minted "national writer" met an initially cool reception among the Hebrew "congregation." Similarly, despite the intellectual appeal of Yiddish works like *The Nag* and *Benjamin III,* both translated into Polish by enthusiastic Polish *writers,* readers of the *Jewish People's Post* (Yid. *Dos yidishes folksblatt*), St. Petersburg's only Yiddish weekly, greeted Abramovich's anniversary with total indifference.[87]

FULL CIRCLE — IN PLACE OF AN EPILOGUE

In the years following the anniversary celebration, Abramovich began to cultivate a new Hebrew style, increasingly less reliant on biblical paradigms and ever more self-consciously rabbinic, both closer to the vernacular and more authoritative.[88] The original Hebrew stories he wrote between 1886 and 1896 clothed in fictional form the debates that animated Abramovich's own Odessa circle.[89] Yet, even as he was drawn toward the present, Abramovich engaged in a sustained attempt to rewrite and canonize the past. Continually revising the story of his life, Abramovich also set upon a project of self-translation from Yiddish into Hebrew. In the introduction to his much reworked and ultimately unfinished autobiography, *In Those Days* (Heb. *Ba-yamim ha-hem,* 1900–1911), Abramovich emphasized the creative tension between the immediate "temptations" of the present and the eternal "enchantments" of the past.[90]

> God save us from these new-fangled goods, the trinkets and baubles of Jewish modernity [says one voice]! Everything that you see before you is a fiction, a mirage, gilded clay, empty, swollen air [. . .] leave these noisy toys and embrace the pleasures of the past, the deeds of the fathers! And yet,

the other voice calls: Come to me! Look at my merchandise, abandon that which is useless and gone from the world, why engage in sorcery, attempting to speak to the dead? Let the mourners mourn the past. Is it not this constant turning back that makes Jews stumble along their path, causing them to fall blindly as the world spreads dark before them? In all their ways, in their homes and in their synagogues, in their books, they are the living dead.[91]

This ambivalence toward the "living dead" who continually inspired Abramovich to engage in literary "sorcery" deepened as the author morphed into his own Nicholaevan persona during the uncertain years following the revolution of 1905. By the time that the "Jubilee" edition of his collected works was published in 1909–1913, there was no longer any need for Mendele since the author and his creation had become interchangeable. In fact, in the few new works Abramovich produced after 1905, he no longer spoke through Mendele but *as* Mendele. So recognizable was this voice that Abramovich could dispense with his persona altogether and return to writing under his own name.[92] In 1913 he completed another circle in the process of self-fashioning that over the years transformed him into the personification of the Russian-Jewish folk. In the 1860s the enlightened author of *Toledot ha-teva'* had produced a new discursive universe modeled directly on contemporary "natural history," a modern Hebrew landscape meant to rival the Bible. Fifty years later the vernacular bard began work on a modern Yiddish translation of Scripture, collapsing the distinction between sacred word and secular literature altogether.[93] In this process of creative revolution, the conscription theme emerged as central to the process of revising *The Wishing Ring* (Yid. *Dos vintshfingerl,* 1866, 1888–1889), a work that, together with *The Little Man, Fishke the Lame,* and *Benjamin III,* made up the Mendele universe.

The first version of *The Wishing Ring* was published in Warsaw probably in 1866, in the conventional form of a chapbook, ostensibly translated from the German but authored by "ISH," both an acronym of Sh. Abramovich spelled backward and a Hebrew word meaning "man."[94] The first two parts of the expanded second version in Yiddish came out serially in 1888–1889 in the first Yiddish literary journal, *The Jewish People's Library* (Yid. *Di yudishe folks-bibliotek*), edited and published by Sholem-aleichem. Continued in St. Petersburg's Yiddish daily, *The Friend* (Yid. *Der fraynd*), in 1905 (*The Jewish People's Library* ceased publication after the first two issues) up until the second chapter of book 6, this version finally appeared in its complete form as the seventh and eighth volumes of the 1909–1913 "Jubilee" edition. Meanwhile, Abramovich also produced a Hebrew version of the novel under the title *In the Valley of Baka* (Heb. *Be'emek ha-bakha*), first serialized, in 1897, in Ahad ha'am's Odessa journal, *The Spring* (Heb. *Ha-shiloah*).[95]

In Hebrew, the novel has acquired the canonic status of a "Jewish epos" (Heb. *shirat yisrael*), a definitive retelling of Russian-Jewish peoplehood that anticipates the modern creation of the Jewish nation.[96] Conscription occupies a prominent place in this retelling; however, as the various peregrinations of the work attest, this critical element was an afterthought, a later addition, first assimilated into the revisions of 1888–1889 and then growing to increasing prominence in the Hebrew text. The complicated inter-text between the three versions of the novel exemplifies the growing importance of the conscription motif in the emergence of Abramovich's personal mythology. In fact, more than any other work of the post-1884 period, *The Wishing Ring* dramatizes the gradual disappearance of Abramovich into Mendele and the consequent displacement of a degenerating Russian-Jewish present by a compelling mythology of a regenerative Russian-Jewish past.

Like the first version of *The Little Man*, the initial version of *The Wishing Ring* revolves around a literary conceit and focuses on the education of the naïf. The story distinguishes between popular superstition, signified by faith in the power of the talisman, a magic ring, and science, the "real" magic ring, the science found in books, the "goods" peddled by Mendele, as the source of authentic unimpeachable wisdom.[97] The main character, Hershele, inherits the story of the supernatural powers of the "magic ring," a tale that rolls from tongue to tongue, sustaining the life cycle of Kabtsansk (Beggarsville), the shtetl where Hershele lives.[98] A chance meeting with an outsider—the stock character of an enlightened "Northener," a *litvak*—reveals to Hershele the moral folly of magic. The stranger adopts Hershele, removes him from Kaptsansk, and teaches him that real magic, the power to transform and improve Hershele's life, resides exclusively in education, which turns the little credulous Jewish boy into a respectable man named Hirsh Rotman.

The memory of the magic ring lingers in the form of a literary device, linking the world of childhood yearnings with the world of adulthood, where undisciplined desires are sublimated into productive activities. Like the image of the rolling dumpling in *The Fathers and the Sons*, the recurring memory of the magic ring that Hershele "inherits" figures as a trace of Jewishness in an otherwise secular process of historical change.[99] Mendele, who deals in books, commodifies the process of Jewish enlightenment, selling maskilic virtue in the guise of a diverting wonder tale (Yid. *mayse*), seemingly pandering to the wishes of an eager, ignorant public but edifying them instead. The commercialization of literature—a potentially risky and morally dubious effect of post-reform cultural "unserfment," an unsavory task which, in his autobiography, Abramovich expressly "assigned" to Mendele—figures as a kind of white magic, a foil for the trick Hershele's enlightened patron employs to lure his charge to the fount of knowledge.[100] Here Abramovich uses Mendele as a bridge between enlightened Jewish ethics, located firmly in the Nicholaevan past, and the realities of modern Russian-Jewish culture, increasingly subject to the demands of the marketplace rather than to the moral imprimatur of the tsar and his Jewish experts.

On the whole, then, the first version of *The Wishing Ring* looks forward more than backward, constituting a vigorous defense of emancipation in the spirit of enlightenment. In the second version, Abramovich reconfigured the teleological relationship between the former and the latter so that *The Wishing Ring* became a novel of return, its hero a repentant Jewish Odysseus revisiting his place of origins. It was only in this version, the second in a series of revisions of earlier works that began with the 1879 rewrite of *The Little Man*, that the conscription theme came to the fore as integral to Hershele's pre-reform shtetl childhood. The child-recruit became completely identified with the Jewish conscience — the inner child, as it were — of every adult who, like Hershele, aspired to get beyond the poverty of Kabtsansk and the stagnation of Tuneyadevka, the trace of Nicholaevan discipline in every experiment with freedom inspired and produced by the process of emancipation.

The second version of *The Wishing Ring* tells the story of Hershele's childhood in Kaptsansk from the perspective of an adult Hirsh Rotman returning to his place of birth to alleviate Jewish suffering wreaked by the pogroms of 1881–1882. The return, described by Mendele in his prologue as "a story about a story," marks an event of messianic proportions, "good news" for the ailing holy communities of Kabtsansk and neighboring Tuneyadevka.[101] The gospel itself comprised the new version of *The Wishing Ring*, Rotman's story of his life, based, he claims, on his earlier book published in Leipzig in "simple German," which he now offered to Mendele for translation into Yiddish and publication. Abramovich here evoked the original *Wishing Ring* as a paradigmatic maskilic text, shifting the place of publication from Warsaw to Leipzig, the center of maskilic publishing, and referring to the enlightenment view of Yiddish as a minor Germanic dialect, a popular jargon rather than a proper language; in fact, there is no substantive difference between the Yiddish of the first version and that of the second. Rather, the characterization of the first *Wishing Ring* carried polemical weight; it is not an accurate description of the former but an implicit characterization of the latter as a self-conscious detour from the Haskalah. As in the revised version of *The Little Man*, Mendele took up the task of publication not in the name of dispensing enlightenment for a price but freely for the sake of rescuing "Jewish children" from their troubles. No longer a commercial transaction, the literary relationship between the writer and his editor was recast as an act of love and compassion. The subtitle characterizes the new *Wishing Ring* as a "gift for beloved Jewish children / children of Israel [Yid. *di liebe yudishe kinder*]."[102] The story of a single Jewish boy, Hershele, served the collective redemption of the children of Israel. At the same time the wishing ring itself no longer signifies knowledge but self-knowledge, the newly gained sense of identification — itself a magical effect of return and recognition — between Hirsh Rotman, the modern Jew who has learned to act and talk like a "German," and Hershele, the little boy still in the thrall of his pre-reform childhood.

Hershele's own story is set in Nicholaevan Kaptsansk, another version of the Jewish Eden, the chief virtue of which is the multiplication of Jewish poverty. The economic dysfunction of the town, newly exposed to capitalism, cuts across the biological imperatives of Jewish generativity, derived from the primary biblical commandment "to be fertile and increase" (Gen 1:28 JPS):

> Say what you want about the Jews of Kaptsansk: they're *not* such big self-starters, they *don't* pull any major coups in their humdrum little lives or set the outside world reeling with anything at all. Go ahead and say that they live from hand to mouth. Say all this, and plenty more. But when it comes to increasing and multiplying, don't, God forbid, say a word against them; they're as punctilious as other Jews. Not even their enemies can deny that every Jew in Kaptsansk is weighed down, touch wood, with a parcel of children.[103]

The ambiguous rendering of Kaptsansk as a town teeming with nothing but Jewish life captures precisely the necessary tension between stagnation and continuity that informs Abramovich's image of the Pale as both paradise and burial ground of Russian Jewry.

The duality comes out even stronger in the Hebrew title of the novel, *'Emek ha-bakha,* commonly mistranslated as *In the Vale of Tears.*[104] The phrase actually refers to Psalms 84:7 where the word *bakha,* spelled with an *aleph,* refers to a place rather than to the Hebrew word for tears or weeping which would be spelled with a *heh*—thus *bakhah.* This is an easy mistake to make since the two words are homonyms, and *bakha* is very obscure. In light of its biblical source, it seems that Abramovich used the phrase specifically to mislead. The confusion between the biblical text and its literary context is an elaborate word play that registers the ambivalence attached to his conception of the Pale. The entire verse reads: "They pass through the Valley of Baca, regarding it as a place of springs, as if the early rain had covered it with blessing" (Ps 84:7 JPS). While the same-sounding *bakhah* suggests mourning, weeping, as it were, in the valley of the shadow of death, the actual word *bakha* leads to a reading of the title that suggests the opposite—rain leading to fecundity and "blessings." Abramovich here required both the word and the trace of its opposite in order to capture the paradox of Russian Jewry's ever-living death, a theme which grew in importance within the plot of the novel in its transition from the Yiddish *Vintshfingerl* to the Hebrew *Be'emek ha-bakha.*

The tension echoes in the dual image of the wishing ring as a magical device that enables the secularization of desire. The hero, Hershele, spends his childhood in idyllic, undisturbed idleness; his imagination is given free play, but he has nothing to eat. The story of the magic ring nourishes the boy's fantasy life and awakens feelings for his "princess [. . .] in the guise of Beyle, a short brick backhouse of a girl with full red cheeks, a turned-up nose, and burning black eyes."[105] This enchantress, herself a kind of wishing ring, tells stories "about bandits, sorceresses, witches, and rabbis with their wives" so well that Hershele ends up "staring into her mouth with pleasure — and nothing more"(32). Beyle reflects both profusion and emptiness; Hershele's longing for her mirrors the collective desires of Kaptsansk (no wonder — her father is a glazier):

> As a means of entertainment and a way to pass the time, wishing was one of the commonest occupations in Kaptsansk. It was an occupation that arose from the constant shortage of the most vital necessities [. . .] The simplest conversation immediately turns into a wish. So, to take a random example, if they're talking about the ocean, one will indulge himself and wish, "May I have as much money as there is sand on all its shores." "Eh," says a second, "Let the whole ocean be ink, and give me as many thousand-ruble bank drafts as that ink would be able to sign." "As for me," wishes a third, sighing and raising his eyes skyward, "Both of you should die, and let me be your sole heir." (33)

The residents of Kaptsansk turn the absence of things into the abundance of images which seduce and, finally, corrupt: the grand "oceanic" vision of plenty ends on a nasty note. Beyle, the princess, awakens in Hershele the first stirrings of sin, the recognition of a private "embarrassment" that puts him at a distance from the community. As in *Benjamin III*, the problematic separation of the individual from the Jewish collective, even when it is cast in the form of a mordant joke (as above), always come from inside, from the sheer force of Jewish fantasy, the source of all longing. Thus, in the latter version of the novel, the device of the wishing ring works ironically, that is, precisely in the way it is intended — against the radical disenchantment of the universe. Ensuring the triumph of imagination over reason, the magic ring makes Hershele see a princess in the girl next door just as it will enable the returning Hirsh to envision a Jewish paradise in his own unkempt provincial backyard.

In *Benjamin III*, the conscription story forms an epic motif of separation from Eden, an enabling violation that ensures the hero's eventual return; in *The Wishing Ring*, a near-conscription of the hero's double plays a similar literary role. At the same moment that Hershele encounters the "hidden maskil" Rafael, destined to become the young orphan's surrogate father, Hershele's best friend, the angelic young genius Moishele, meets a darker fate (bk. 3, chap. 8). Kidnapped by the *khapper* Shneur-Wolf — who is providentially staying at the same inn as the benevolent Rafael — Moishele becomes an unwitting pawn in Shneur-Wolf's scheme to kidnap Hershele. As an only son, Moishele is legally ineligible for the draft; but Hershele is an orphan without protection, a perfect sacrificial lamb for the community. While Hershele evades his fate, Moishele ends up in the clutches of Shneur-Wolf, his distraught father running behind the wagon. The narrator delivers the verdict — "for this was the time of the *khappers*" — in terms that crystallize the meaning of the Nicholaevan period for Abramovich as the terminus of Russian Jewry's collective past, the place-time where the *Heilgeschichte* of Jewish history passes into the secular history of the Jews:

> "Brothers," lament the dirges from that time, "all your hundreds of thousands slaughtered by the wicked Titus at the time of the Temple's destruction; who were killed, burned at the stake in Spain; all other such murder victims combined do not embitter our lives so much as the Jewish noses which the Jews themselves have torn from one another's faces. There at least was still consolation: Heroes! They died for their country . . . Martyrs! They were killed in Sanctification of the Name. But, *gevalt*, what can you stick under a Jewish nose when it is being ripped off by Jews themselves? We weep over blows from others and say, "That's all right. The good and the weak often suffer in this world, perhaps the strong will yet have occasion for regrets." But when the beaten beat, the bleeding spill blood, we weep and say, "Oy vey." For there is nothing to say. When we recall the tormented ones whom you yourselves "caught," our heart breaks, it weeps and cries out, "How, oy, how horribly degraded, how sickeningly fallen are the people of Israel." (109; translation slightly altered)

In a single stroke Abramovich discredits the power of the martyrological paradigm — its limits as rationalization for murder compromised as something "stuck" under a Jewish nose — and exposes the potentially pathological consequences implicit in the emancipation of the one from his responsibility to the many. The dispensation of conscription that pits the predatory Shneur-Wolf against Jewish parents ironically anticipates the enlightened surrogacy of Rafael over Hershele as well as that of Moishele's own rescuer, the rich tax farmer Mikhoel Sapir who ends up taking Moishele away from his weak, loving, pious father, the ragman Shmulik.

The 1889 revision of *The Wishing Ring* ended dramatically with Moishele's kidnapping; Abramovich brought the story to completion in the Hebrew version, fully rewritten for publication in *Ha-shiloah*. Only here was the significance of Moishele's near-conscription fully revealed for the first time. In book 7 (the novel ended with book 8), Moishele, rescued by Mikhoel Sapir, tastes the "new Torah" of enlightenment (242). Sapir sends him to the Rabbinical Seminary in Zhitomir, which paves the way toward medical studies at the university. Official enlightenment and conscription are thus twin sides of Nicholaevan experiments in making modern Russian Jews. That Moishele starts out as a recruit only to end up as a doctor points to the derailment of Jewish reform on the wheels of Jewish emancipation; even Shmulik comes around to the "smiling" image of his son, the doctor. As the narrator cynically concludes, emancipation creates the unlikeliest maskilim:

> This smile deserves to be placed in our archives, so that future historians and researchers can use it to prove how far the Haskalah had penetrated by then. I mean, a little while ago we saw a Jew crying and moaning over the

rejection of the study of Torah; there was nothing better or greater to him than a rabbi, an authorized instructor of the Jewish people. Yet the same Jew later turns away from the rabbi; he's pleased by the doctor, delights in him with a sweet smile — and it took no more than four years to go from the weeping to the smiling, from the rabbi to the doctor. And who might this Jew be? Shmulik, who, from being a ragman, became a taxman! (265)

In fact, Moishele's entire life is a series of derailments, accidents and mistakes. He is *not* the true hero of the Jewish epos. Moishele exits the story as a foil for Hirsh's efforts to transcend the contingencies of the historical process that have so successfully claimed them both. Evading *rekrutchina*, Abramovich effectively claims, Moishele nevertheless becomes a metaphorical "conscript," tethered to the autocratic vagaries of the project of state-sponsored social engineering that first made Jews into Russian soldiers and then promised to turn them into Jewish doctors. Such secular contingencies of the historical process, Abramovich argues here with greater emphasis than in any previous work, must be transcended by an effort of individual will. Embracing the promise of emancipation, Moishele runs headlong into the arms of the reforming Romanovs.

At the same time, in claiming the risky fruits of freedom for his own, Moishele the near-recruit also escapes the imaginative hold of the wishing ring which has Hershele in its grip and induces the return to Kaptsansk. Moishele's continuing story, Abramovich intimates, would constitute an altogether different kind of book, a book singularly bereft of Jewish magic, a secular, still-to-be-written, "emancipated" history of Russian Jews. Hinting at the possibility of another story, Abramovich gives the reader news of Moishele in a letter delivered to his parents; Moishele, it would seem, writes his own book, whereas Hershele's return requires the moral and aesthetic mediation of Mendele the book-peddler. Abramovich's nationalist readers picked up on the risks to collective Jewish survival implicit in the choice between Hershele's messianic return to Kaptsansk and Moishele's conspicuous detour from the promised land; like his biblical namesake, Moishele the letter writer remains eternally a wanderer. The child-recruits in the fictions of Mendele's heirs all died without ever leaving the Pale for the "wilderness" of the diaspora, taking the secular aspirations of Russian Jews into their graves.

5

DEAD CHILDREN OF THE HEBREW RENAISSANCE: THE CONSCRIPTION STORY AS NATIONALIST MYTH

AN ARCHAIC AVANT-GARDE

Written between the mid-1880s and the revolution of 1905, the conscription stories that appeared in the work of authors associated with the Hebrew Renaissance anticipated the moment of national rebirth. The contemporary mood of apocalyptic expectation projected back onto the Nicholaevan period raised the coming of the Jewish nation to the level of prophetic certainty. This, at a time when the historical future of Zionism was by no means assured; the movement achieved its greatest political and social victories only during the interwar period.[1] The paradigm shift inaugurated in the writing of the national revival was, in fact, greater than the sum of its Zionist parts.[2]

Abramovich's younger followers embraced his Jewish populism, rooted in a sustained and compelling critique of emancipation, as the rationale for the creation of modern Jewish culture. Long before the Zionist leadership officially expressed its begrudging commitment to cultural "work in the diaspora" (Ger. *Gegenwartsarbeit*, lit. "work in the present"), Russian Jews had been reaping the literary fruits of their own imminent revival.[3] Translating the imaginary return to the pre-reform shtetl into the ideological register of collective mythology, the wayward sons of the Haskalah produced a parable of miraculous resistance to the secularization of Jewish experience and expression. The apocalyptic drama of national rebirth offered a "mythopoetic" resolution to the tensions that beset the maskilic attitude toward emancipation.[4] While urging the necessary death of the nation-in-exile, the literature of the Hebrew Renaissance effectively ensured the survival of *galut* as the repository of Jewish consciousness.[5]

Continued imaginative investment in the Jewish topology of the Pale of Settlement, even as its social and cultural boundaries steadily eroded from within, partook of the same ambivalence about the "unserfment" of collective Jewish life that shaped Abramovich's identity as a writer. Social, economic, and legal pressures unmoored increasing numbers of Jews from their places of origin; the secular effects of this process, nowhere more evident than in the fractured lives of Jewish enlighteners-turned-nationalists themselves, made the task of literary ingathering that much more urgent. To the chagrin of Russian reactionaries who everywhere sought evidence of pernicious Jewish solidarity, Russian-Jewish life at the turn of the century was subject both to the continuing effacement of formal divisions of estate and confession ostensibly dividing Jews from non-Jews, and to the sharpening of the same differences from everyone else that allegedly united Jews with one another.[6]

The railroad and the spread of Jewish print culture (thanks both to increasing literacy and the loosening of censorship restrictions) in Hebrew, Russian, and Yiddish helped to bridge the distance between the Pale and the rest of the empire.[7] A growing population of Jewish travelers — migrants, commercial agents, students, and revolutionary activists — undermined the sense of provincial isolation.[8] Steady urbanization and the uneven impact of capitalism on Jewish occupational structure radically stratified Jewish society.[9] While there were greater opportunities for personal enrichment through investment, there was no protection against the vagaries of the market. Along with the exponential growth of the Jewish mercantile and professional population came, for the first time, the development of a Jewish proletariat as well as the expansion of a visible underclass without steady means of support and only occasional employment. Internal social cohesion continued to decline, as an assertive orthodox leadership, buoyed by the support of a conservative regime, closed ranks against impiety.[10] The generally low ebb of religious observance and the erosion of confessional discipline provided additional impetus for the development of secular ideas about collective life; these took root not only among Jewish students and Russian radicals but also within the expanding network of middle-class philanthropic, civic, and cultural organizations.[11] A vibrant secular institutional life presented an alternative to the synagogue and to the more established forms of Jewish association, even as the world of the traditional learned elite came to comprise its own special subculture self-consciously elevated above what its leadership disdained as religious philistinism and popular superstition.[12]

The centripetal effects of socioeconomic and cultural change exacerbated long-standing anxieties in enlightened Jewish circles about the future of Jewish life in Russia. Widespread disagreement as to the nature of community came to the fore during the first decade of the twentieth century in the heated public debate about possible ways to counteract the glaring absence of Jewish solidarity.[13] G. B. Sliozberg (1863–1937), a St. Petersburg-trained lawyer, Jewish public activist, and the most outspoken defender of Jewish individual rights against legal discrimination, lamented that the "traditional unity of the Jews has been in the realm of myth for a long time. The history of the disintegration of this unity," he added, "is exceedingly depressing."[14] Sliozberg's doleful reference to the "mythological" origins of Jewish unanimity evoked the contemporary tension between the interest in the cultural preservation of the Pale and the commitment on the part of Jewish educated society to the emancipation of the Jews from all forms of legal oppression, including the infamous university quotas and the economically devastating residential confinement. The Jewish liberalism of Sliozberg — immune, it would seem, to the "adventurist" politics of Zionism — was, ironically, heir to the same maskilic anxieties that implicitly informed the polemical uses of literature in the nationalist reconstruction of Jewish native ground.[15]

The voice of Mendele left an indelible impression on the character of nationalist writing in Hebrew, Yiddish, and Russian. Self-consciously adopted to the mode of the folk tale, conscription stories written in the apocalyptic register of the Hebrew Renaissance moved toward the unifying structure of an authentic Jewish tradition. Actually their similarities derived from a series of motifs that Abramovich first employed in the construction of his Nicholaevan universe — specifically, the representation of the recruit as both child and old man; the depiction of the shtetl as an epic place-time, a stagnant Eden in which the Jewish people degenerates and regenerates itself; and the stress on the absence or impotence of Jewish paternity, a marker of maskilic suspicion toward the disruptive effects of modernity. The consistent recourse to these narrative elements makes it possible to speak of the emergence, at the turn of the century, of an apocalyptic morphology which effected the "return" to the Nicholaevan past not merely in content but also in style.[16] This narrative move, characteristic of the fin-de-siècle strategies of the "archaic avant-garde," involved the self-conscious striving on the part of Jewish modernists to ground radically new forms of literary expression in the revelation of popular genius.[17] Indeed, nationalist fiction boldly invested the distinctive authorial vision of Mendele's symbolic world with the authority of Jewish memory. The stylized idiom of the recruit as witness or naïve native informant now replaced the ironic mediation of Abramovich's fictional Nicholaevan persona.

The textual transformation of the conscription story stood for the messianic secret — the imminent rebirth of the Jewish people — while the context that informed this latest reverberation of the recruitment theme in Russian-Jewish literature testified to the enabling persistence of Jewish enlightenment as both an ideology and a set of cultural practices. The conscription tale of the Hebrew Renaissance may be read against itself, both, that is, as a polemic against the Haskalah and as evidence of the continuing importance of Jewish enlightenment to the historical fortunes of the Jewish revival. Abramovich's self-appointed progeny, driven by their particular "anxiety of influence," defined their sense of literary discipline and their hieratic literary style in direct opposition both to the tight-lipped ironies of maskilic social conscience and to the sentimental affect of Jewish melodrama. Adopting Mendele's skepticism to their own radical politics of misreading, the "strong poets" of the Hebrew Renaissance killed him off entirely.[18] Acts of literary subversion bore unexpected historical fruit; nationalist writing did nothing so much as invigorate the conservative critique of emancipation that Abramovich championed in the name of the radical Haskalah. Under the banner of the Hebrew Renaissance, the returning sons of the nation produced a cosmopolitan and multilingual, self-consciously Jewish literature, singularly attuned to contemporary aesthetic values. In the creation of a flourishing periodical press, and in the promotion of Hebrew, Yiddish, and Russian publishing, they ensured that this literature would become the vehicle of the maskilic ethos and a powerful ideological tool in the domestication of Judaism. Finally, in the course of recovering the nation, they endowed the modern writer with an unprecedented degree of social and intellectual prestige. Insofar as the commitment to integral Jewish peoplehood motivated the creation of modern Jewish culture and the formation of a secular Jewish intellectual class, nationalism thus served the ends of Jewish enlightenment. The turn-of-the-century revision of the conscription tale represents a spectacular example of this nexus.

APOCALYPSE NOW

The apocalyptic reading of conscription, exemplified in the Nicholaevan fictions of P. Ia. Levenson (1837–1894), I. L. Peretz (1851[?]–1915), Ben-Ami (pseud. M. Ya. Rabinovich (1854–1932), Judah Steinberg (1863–1908), and M. Z. Feierberg (1874–1899), presents a case study in the development of nationalist mythopoesis.[19] In the last two decades of the nineteenth century, the ideological response to Jewish modernity acquired an increasingly urgent tone. Pessimism about the future of the maskilic ethos, already manifest in the ironic characterization of Jewish embourgeoisement as "pseudo-enlightenment," found its most eloquent expression in the decadent strain of the Hebrew revival.[20] Driven by the enabling conceit of

143

"crisis," the creative explosion of Jewish writing at the turn of the century rendered explicit the ambiguities involved in the cosmopolitan poetics of the national renaissance.[21] In fact, the act of translating the dark vision of Jewish exile into the creation of a vibrant and sophisticated modern Jewish culture, subversive though it was, can hardly be characterized as secular.[22] Like earlier forms of apocalyptic writing, the imaginative recasting of Russian Jewry's collective pre-reform past by the authors of the Jewish revival both exposed the historically irremediable pathologies of *galut* and signified their miraculous mythopoetic remedy.[23] Revisiting the commonplaces of Abramovich's fictional universe, the recalcitrant heirs of the Jewish enlightenment sought out a new messianic topography of the shtetl. The dialectical space in which Russian Jewry died in order to be reborn appeared under the sign of three eschatological tropes.

The nationalist variant of the conscription tale depicts the recruit as either a child or an old veteran who has a tutelary affective relationship with a child; sometimes the author encases the narrator in the role of the latter, and at other times the two figures merge through the use of a flashback, in which an old man relates his experience as a child-recruit. This conflation of youth and old age recapitulates Abramovich's dual image of the recruit as Takif's missing infant, on the one hand, and as Shmuelik, the heroic survivor of the pre-reform army, on the other. For Abramovich, the contrast embodied the shortcomings of Jewish adulthood; nevertheless, the representation of these characters remained securely tied to the secular rules of verisimilitude. Abramovich's ironic recourse to the extreme ends of the human life cycle never violated the conventions of representing the orderly passage of biological time. In the nationalist conscription tale, however, the symbolic collapse of the difference between youth and old age explicitly served the utter rejection of all linear teleologies and the embrace of apocalyptic recurrence.

A transparent gloss on the biblical story of the near-sacrifice of Isaac (Heb. *'akedah,* see Genesis 22), Ben-ami's "Ben yukhid" (1884) relates the tragic tale of an angelic "only son" (Yid. *ben-yukhid*). The scriptural allusion in the title anticipates the secret spiritual mission of the title character to act as a scapegoat for the sins of his community by dying in expectation of being conscripted. Ben-Ami's Shraga — the boy's name means "candle" in Aramaic — is the Nicholaevan recruit as a prematurely aged child, precocious in his religious observance, a closed circle of fragility and eternity, a cipher for the androgynous face of folk piety, the strength of weakness: Shraga, named after a dead *tzaddik,* "grew up quiet, mild, soft as mother-love [. . .] of weak physical build," admired even by passing gentiles as a "beautiful, blackbrowed, black-eyed little Jew-boy." Yet little Shraga is, from the beginning, almost a corpse: "And truly how beautiful was this child, pale to the point of transparency, with his large, quiet, thoughtful, sad eyes, sitting motionlessly, supporting his long chin with a hand so thin one could count all its bones."

His Jewish garb emphasizes "his prominent, marble-white forehead, surrounded by black shiny curls. The older he grew, the more serious his face, the softer and more tender his heart."[24] At the same time, Shraga is possessed of an other-worldly strength of character, signified by his willingness to abstain from food on the minor fast of the seventeenth of Tammuz. In contrast to his perpetually hungry sisters, this ghostly child feeds exclusively on faith, "pure as a mountain stream and hard as mountain granite."[25]

In Levenson's "Enchanted One" (1884), a well-heeled merchant, initially mistaken for a Frenchman by the narrator who encounters him on a train, turns out to be a Jewish ex-cantonist, an "enchanted" child of incredible faith who successfully, miraculously, resists all efforts to convert him.[26] Conscripted at the pivotal age of thirteen, he is instructed by his pious grandfather "to remain a Jew no matter how much they may torment you. You will suffer much," his grandfather promises prophetically, "but you will bear it all and be happy. Very happy. Remember that!" (24). Levenson dwells in excruciating detail on the suffering of the boy; like Shraga, he is a martyr who experiences conscription as a form of death, here represented symbolically by "steaming" in the bathhouse, a kind of passage through hell after which the hero is reborn (39). When the narrator picks up the story, the child is already a "veteran," a distinguished, venerable, wealthy patriarch with a moral conscience awakened by his martyrdom. The transformation from the former to the latter seems to be instantaneous, itself a form of "enchantment" which here displaces the contingencies of emancipation.

M. Z. Feierberg's "Yankev the Watchman" (1896) similarly represents the experience of conscription as a form of living death, in which the spiritually gifted child is "offered up on the hellish altar by the high priests of his people."[27] Like Ben-Ami, Feierberg invokes the Jewish martyrological tradition in his ironic allusion both to the motif of the 'akedah and the story of Hannah and her seven sons; the hero of this story, "this only son, this mother's sole worldly support, was fraudulently impressed into the army of the tsar to ransom the seven sleek sons of some wealthy Jew" (44). Similar to the young heroes of Ben-Ami and Levenson, Feierberg's Yankev endures conscription with a preternatural strength, even though he is "a weak helpless boy" (45): "Like a hero without flinching, he fought the good, the difficult battle for his own soul" (49). Here, too, the story comes full circle when the young boy returns to his native village as Yankev, the old watchman, the guardian, as it were, of Jewish conscience who awakens the narrator, "a small boy at the time," with the cry, "Woe that the Shekhinah [Divine Presence] is in exile!" (49). Like Levenson, Feierberg elides the stretch of historical time between Yankev's youth and his old age. His hero fulfills his special task through a form of living death, the significance of his compressed existence revealed only to the narrator's heightened literary conscience.

I. L. Peretz's "Good!" (in Yiddish, 1907; in Hebrew, 1911) places the conscription motif into the context of a neo-Hasidic tale, a genre linked to the "stories in the folk vein" (Yid. *folkstimlekhe geshikhtn*) which enacted the "drama of faith against reason."[28] But the very short story—almost a parable—also bears the traces of its kinship with other conscription tales of the period. The title alludes to Feierberg's description of the "good, difficult battle" that takes place in the cantonist's soul. Peretz positions his child-recruit in relation to the Old Man of Shpola, a legendary Hasidic seer. In their first fateful meeting, the Old Man of Shpola—then still the young man of Shpola—predicts a "long journey" for the narrator and bids him only "not to forget his name!—Yudele" (lit. "little Jew") before he mysteriously disappears.[29] Immediately abducted by *khappers*, the narrator undergoes near-martyrdom in the ranks and returns as an old watchman with his Jewish selfhood preserved intact. Finding strength in the symbolic reenactment of his meeting with the seer of Shpola, the "little Jew" finds his own perfect reflection in the "old man"; Peretz complicates the child–old man homology, but its ideological import stands. The prophetic figure of the Old Man of Shpola intervenes in the life of the hero to bring the dead hand of the Jewish past to bear on the miraculous rebirth of Jewish conscience, always already at hand. In an earlier conscription story titled "The Messenger" (1894), Peretz similarly depicted the old Nicholaevan veteran as the repository of pious memory.[30] Without the ethical urgency that inspired the introduction of the Old Man of Shpola into the later story, "The Messenger" dissolves into pure sentimentality, a form of populist kitsch. In both stories, however, the recruit's "good difficult battle" against forgetting represents the post-emancipation experience as the constant crisis of the adult soul in search of its inner Jewish child, a process of recovery projected here onto modern Jewish literature, the "watchman" of Jewish conscience.

Peretz's pregnant emphasis on the essential symbolic quality of the hero's Jewishness, his childlike purity contained entirely in his name, relates this story to Yehudah Steinberg's "In Those Days" (1906), where the Jewish identity of cantonists prefigures the nationalization of Judaism. Steinberg's protagonist is an old Nicholaevan veteran named Shmuel who tells the story of his childhood to the narrator. In the way that the story merges childhood with old age, the role of the hero in this story bears a strong resemblance to the monitory role of Feierberg's Yankev and Peretz's Hasidic seer. Shmuel, as his name intimates, is also a child-prophet with a special mission, although here he is sacrificed by his parents to the seemingly greater spiritual potential of his older brother. In fact, Shmuel turns out to be the true hero who internalizes the martyrological tradition thrust upon him by the rabbi at his parting.[31] He embodies this tradition as the adopted son of Anna/Hannah, the repentant Jewish daughter and Christian wife at whose home Shmuel lodges as a cantonist. Through the intervention of Shmuel, Anna recovers her Jewishness and bonds with the boy. Returning to her people, she becomes his true mother, in contrast to his real Jewish mother who abandoned him to recruitment in the first place, betraying him to the clever and more learned older son. The overly determined literary kinship between Anna and Shmuel — not only is Hannah the mother of the martyred seven sons but Hannah is also the name of the prophet Samuel's mother — forms the basis for a new model of collective Jewish life, a sharp rebuke to existing Jewish society based on debased religious ideals and the corruption of family ties.

Steinberg depicts Jewish cantonists, mothered by the prodigal Anna, as a community of martyrs who collectively represent the expression of Judaism as an integral aspect of personality (238–240). The issue here is not their transgressions but their identity, conceived as a form of Jewish self-awareness, a heightened state of consciousness, a heroic posture not dissimilar from military bearing; the point is to remain inwardly whole, to "return to our fathers as Jews" even while eating *tref.* The fathers, of course, see it differently; when Shmuel returns home, his own father gingerly inquires as to the "matter of [his] *religion,*" that is, his observance (254; emphasis added). In the figure of Shmuel, Steinberg presents an alternative to the "religion" of the fathers. The secret meaning of pure cantonist faith — pure, as both innocent and essentially evacuated of ritual and textual mastery — is that it presents a form of nationalism *avant la lettre,* natural, as it were, to the childlike folk, untouched by the ambiguities of Jewish creed, Jewish learning, and Jewish law. Ben-Ami's Shraga similarly exemplifies the heroic absence of proportion that characterizes absolute Jewishness stripped entirely of "religion." His self-conscious choice of a minor fast as an opportunity to showcase his inner resolve manifests not his strict orthodoxy but the purity of his convictions which lifts him above confessional discipline and rabbinic authority (he may as well, under such circumstances, eat *tref*). The antinomian idea that conscience is all, an inversion of the Talmudic insistence on the primacy of praxis above intent, represents the source of the singular spiritual genius of all the recruits in nationalist fiction. "For them," Shmuel says, "there is a different Judaism," one that anticipates the messianic revival of the nation in the post-emancipation age (140).

The nationalist retelling of the conscription tale derived from Abramovich its representation of the shtetl as a place and a time. In this reading, the Nicholaevan moment merged a mythological prehistory pregnant with apocalyptic expectation destined to be fulfilled in the post-emancipation period with the image of a specific location, defined by its ambiguous status as both the cradle and grave of Russian Jewry. Here, for example, is Ben-Ami's description of Shraga's hometown, an "epic" (Rus. *byl'*) set back in "the time of the '*lovchiki*' [Rus. recruit-catchers or *khappers*]":

> The tavern of reb Nukhim [Shraga's father] stood at the very end of a village, almost on the road that led to a none-too-big local town [Rus. *nebol'shoi uezdnyi gorodok*] of the Podolia district. The entire village was

located in a none-too-deep valley [Rus. *neglubokoi doliny*], on the two sides of a none-too-big stream [Rus. *nebol'shoi rechki*] which, incidentally, could only be called that in the spring, since during the rest of the year, no matter the season, it became either a swamp or simply a ravine, covered with entirely dried up, cracked silt.

The two banks were then connected entirely by garbage, that is, piles of manure thrown into the river; but in the spring, with the powerful pressure of the streams, not a sign of this garbage remained. Only in the fall, when the stream became nothing but a swamp, the manure served its purpose. Beyond the village stretched fields and meadows, encircled at the edge by enormous timber forests, and beyond the forests, far, far away, merging with the azure of the sky, stretched chains of hills, spread over the wide horizon almost as if they constituted a special world of their own, beyond the clouds.[32]

Ben-Ami's initial proliferation of negatives heightens the disjunction between the earthly mire of the shtetl—the town is knit together, literally, by a river of shit which is also a swamp—and its location on the edge of eternity. The shtetl is a non-place, always tottering on the edge of time and space, beyond the big towns and big rivers, beyond history. At the same time the shtetl is a utopia, like no place on earth; its muckiness is a sign of its transcendence, because it is a hell that stretches directly toward heaven. The signs of decay symbolize their opposite; the image of a stream of garbage giving way under the pressure of water in the spring points to the apocalyptic function of the pre-reform shtetl as both the site and the moment of regeneration.

Feierberg similarly merges space and time in an apocalyptic scenario. The narrator's moral epiphany immediately takes him back to the Nicholaevan shtetl and to his own childhood:

I was just a small boy at the time.

It was autumn. The mud and mire were neck-high. The sky was covered with thick, dark clouds. Up before the crack of dawn, I set out for the *heder* [school] with lantern in hand.

It was utterly still in the streets. The town was shrouded in silence. Now and then the watchmen making their rounds called to each other out of the night. And among them I heard a not unfamiliar voice as it cried:

"Woe that the Shekhinah is in exile!"[33]

Here again is a scene marked by radical contrast between impenetrable darkness, death, stagnation, stillness—note the neck-high mud of the town, an echo of the motif of burial which resounds throughout this story—and the imminent awakening, signified by the presence of the lantern and the nearness of dawn. The scene, which merges space and time, instantly projects the narrator from his own post-emancipation moment of reflection back to the liminal Nicholaevan world of Yankev, where he, as a child, experiences the apocalyptic revelation of exile in the person of the old soldier.

The image of death and rebirth which blurs the distinction between space and time informs the apocalyptic function of the Nicholaevan topos. In "Good!" Peretz completely effaces this difference by transplanting the shtetl into the person of the Old Man of Shpola, the creator of a preternatural, generative Jewish space in a place literally frozen in time. The seer both articulates and enacts the secret of the Nicholaevan moment.

> And there he stood, in the shade of a tree, moving back and forth and reciting the Song of Songs. I didn't want to disturb him. I remained a few steps back, and I waited till he was finished . . . And meanwhile I looked at the tree in the shade of which the young man stood.
>
> And suddenly the tree was different from all the other trees in the wood . . . All the others were still in their mourning clothes, still not awake from the sleep of winter, and this one — it was all green, all in bloom, shiny and glowing, its leaves spreading, sheltering the head of the young man . . . and among the leaves was a flock of birds, hopping and skipping, and singing and echoing the words of the Song of Songs in happiness and joy!
>
> And I stand there still and excited, my mouth gaping and my eyes wide open and I am amazed!
>
> And then the Song of Songs was finished — and the birds disappeared and the tree withered, and he turns toward me and commands me:
>
> "What you have seen here shall remain a secret."
>
> "Yes, yes," I answer, shaking a little.
>
> And he laughs lightly, and says,
>
> "And now I have a favor to ask of you . . ."[34]

The momentary flowering amid the Nicholaevan winter, concentrated in one spot around the Hasidic master, precedes the narrator's awakening to his own special destiny. The arcadia that instantly surrounds the Old Man of Shpola reconstitutes Jewish Eden in the midst of the Russian woods, prefiguring the remarkable bloom of Jewish conscience in the heart of the boy who will shortly leave the magic circle for the Nicholaevan army. The "sleep of winter" and the bare trees "still in their mourning clothes" suddenly signify not the passing of the natural cycle but the fullness of Jewish time; in this Jewish paradise, even the birds do not have their own songs but sing, instead, the Song of Songs, the poem of love between God and the people of Israel. Thus the obscure ground of Shpola under the Old Man's feet — who cares where Shpola really is? — is the humble "mud and mire" of the pre-reform shtetl from which the nation is poised miraculously to rise.

The Nicholaevan time-space distinguishes all the conscription stories informed by the idea of national awakening; this is no less true of Steinberg and Levenson than of Peretz, Feierberg, and Ben-Ami, even though the former use more naturalistic means to achieve parallel symbolic effects. In both "The Enchanted" and "In Those Days," a mode of conveyance — in the first instance a train, in the second a cart — serves to collapse the difference between memory of the pre-reform period and movement through space. The symbolic function of the train and the cart, in fact, undercuts the conventional usage of such devices in realistic fiction, namely, to create the effect of forward movement.[35] Neither Levenson nor Steinberg employs the metaphor of the journey, the setting for the telling of the conscription stories, to serve the elaboration and eventual resolution of the plot, that is, the teleological progress toward denouement. In both instances, the movement is circular; the narrator ends up where he started, nothing has changed, except that the Nicholaevan period has been transposed from the past directly to the present, as a competing reality, a Jewish counter-text set against the postemancipation moment in which the *telling* of the story is set.

In Levenson's case, the forward journey of the St. Petersburg train "rushing the eminently respectable public beyond the borders" of the Russian Empire takes second place to the circular movement of memory back to the Nicholaevan period.[36] The recollection of the cantonist past of the protagonist, the narrator's interlocutor, actually recalls the two back to St. Petersburg, where they started, to the discussion of a legal case brought against a converted cantonist who abjured his Orthodox faith upon being discharged from the military. The immediate recollection of the case, a foil for the story of the protagonist, brings the reality of the Nicholaevan past directly into post-reform Russia where the rule of law has displaced the rule of military discipline; everything has changed, and yet, for the Jews, nothing has. The specter of the cantonist hovering over post-reform Jewish life implies that all Russian Jewry inhabits the same zone of enchantment, no matter how much Jewish individuals may pretend to enjoy the benefits of emancipation. This is, in fact, precisely the case of the protagonist, a typical Russian bourgeois in every respect whose daily habits are those of a "Frenchman" — except, that is, for his memories which serve to distinguish him morally from the social privileges of his estate. For example, he is an industrialist who acts as a virtual paterfamilias to his workers. His own suffering as a Jew has rendered him especially sensitive to the suffering of others in a more jaded secular age. His Jewish conscience, his private "enchantment," has spared him the soul-deadening effects of embourgeoisement which afflict his Russian — and this would presumably include his secular Jewish — counterparts. For the narrator, the resolution of his own private Jewish question — Where, if not in the Pale, does post-emancipation Jewishness reside? What, in other words, is a modern Russian Jew, bereft of confessional discipline? — finally reveals itself in the significance of the Nicholaevan identity of the protagonist.

> With feeling, I shook the hand of this man, who had so impressed [Rus. *podkupil*, lit. "bought" or "bribed," which carries an obviously ironic connotation] me with the absence of those negative traits that characterize those upstarts constantly trying to hide their past. No, this was no upstart but a good person, a useful citizen, worthy of the highest respect and greatest sympathy.[37]

"Useful citizenship" here inheres not in the juridical leveling of the difference between Russians and Jews but in the collective Russian-Jewish particular. "Useful" citizens are, first of all, good Jews, people who do not stoop to "trying to hide their past." The road to Jewish consciousness in post-emancipation St. Petersburg leads straight back to the ethics of Jewish memory which resides in the recall of the pre-reform collective past, always already dead and yet very much alive in the little provincial towns on the edge of empire. Levenson's nameless protagonist introduces himself as a Jew by reference exclusively to place; he is "born (Rus. *rodom,* lit. "of the tribe") in the town of Zhmud', not far from the Prussian border," a metonym for the marginal place—note the qualifier "not far" and the reference to the liminal status vis-à-vis the West, characteristic of the Western borderlands, the Pale as a whole—where Russian Jewry is born in the Nicholaevan crucible, where it dies in the age of emancipation, and where it is destined to be reborn as a "tribe" (Rus. *rodom*) in the imminent post-emancipation *now.*[38]

Steinberg's protagonist, the cantonist Shmuel, recovers his Jewish roots through the cemetery, an ambiguous metaphor for the Nicholaevan past, both dead and palpably present in the midst of Jewish life; in Hebrew, a cemetery is called the "house of life" (Heb. *beit-hayyim*). To convey the apocalyptic effect of Shmuel's Jewish rebirth, the critical moment in the story, its description requires quoting in full:

> I dreamt of the end of service. I imagined to myself my parents meeting me, the tears, the kisses, the embraces, the faints, neighbors coming around. I believed, like a foolish child, that I would find all of them still alive, that the Angel of Death would lengthen their days until my return, that he would recompense them for all their suffering on my account. For if not, surely this would be a great sin to hold against God, good people rending the heavens with their cries of longing for me, should they die in the end without being comforted?
>
> But as I approached my hometown by and by, my yearning grew cold, from the unfamiliar wind that blew from all those places. No, perhaps this was not unfamiliarity but the recognition of the old that brought on such pain. I don't know how to describe this feeling, it is a like a bad dream of an old man from the days of his youth.
>
> The weather was very much like it is now. The roads were bad, there was a lot of muck. You sit in the cart, look over at the mud, a mute witness to the mess in your soul and count the steps of the horses, one two, three. You're better off getting down off the cart and walking rather than riding in this kind of weather.
>
> So that's what I did. I was already close to the town of my birth, only one hill and one valley to go and there was the town's cemetery, this is what you always see when you enter a shtetl.
>
> The horses breathed with difficulty. I led them through the only path

between the farmers' fields. I thought I had a special right to pass through Jewish property even though I still wore my soldier's uniform, its buttons glittering off me.

When I began to descend into the valley, I had an idea to take a shortcut through the cemetery.

The cart remained far behind me, and I walked in small steps in the direction of the gate so I would not have to wait for the cart when it met me on the way out.

Among the tombstones I saw a few darkened ones, bent low to the ground, as if poised to listen in on the conversations of the underworld, and a few others white and pointing straight up to the sky. I had entered a mute world. The silence of the cemetery is harsh, a silence that speaks. It is not for nothing that they say the dead chatter in their graves. It seemed to me that the tombstones looked at me in reproach, because I had defiled the place with my shiny buttons.[39]

Here Steinberg calls up the image of a Jewish community poised in a state of suspended animation, awaiting the return of the Nicholaevan recruit. Shmuel has his reunion with the dead in the cemetery; their "reproach" is an echo of the talk that will, in a moment, attend the actual reception of the Nicholaevan hero with his shiny buttons. The shtetl is itself a cemetery, located in the indeterminate far away "valley" beyond the hills, a place of mediation between heaven and earth. The recruit's passing through this enchanted space represents the unaccountable intrusion of the present into the past. The cemetery, like his own memory, constitutes a "short cut" both in time and in space that closes the gap between the past and the future. The glitter of Shmuel's buttons both defiles the sacred stillness of Nicholaevan ground and at the same time allows for an instant connection between then and now. This form of magical intercourse — no less magical than the conversation between the Old Man of Shpola and his young charge that results in the instantaneous "flowering" — has an immediate bearing on the narrator, virtually dragged into Shmuel's memories, in the insistence that everything that exists today remains as it was, even the mud. This critical passage in the description foregrounds the title of the story, "In Those Days," a pointed reference to the mythological state of the pre-reform period.

Shmuel's exit line points to the epic reality of the Nicholaevan moment: "Those were the days. Those were soldiers. Now everything is changed, new times, new people, new soldiers. Now everything is only 'as if.' "[40] The "as if" here points to the rhetoric of authenticity surrounding Shmuel's reconstruction of the Nicholaevan period; in fact, the blurring of the difference between Shmuel's journey home, his movement through the cemetery, and the recollection of the journey on the present trip with the narrator recapitulates the ethical quest for a post-emancipation Jewish identity involved in the recovery of the cantonist past that collides with — "defiles" —

the hallowed world of the dead to which Shmuel returns. Shmuel finds a cure for his lost childhood in the heroic community of his cantonist youth, recalled when he is an old man in order to hasten the new Jewish society's coming into being. The Jewish nation springs miraculously forth from the cemetery like the bloom around the Old Man of Shpola which also constitutes an "unnatural" growth, a Russian-Jewish miracle. Shmuel's parents, the old pious Jews lying among the tombstones or living out their last days, dialectically contribute to the moment of rebirth by sending Shmuel away. They, in the end, are like the *khappers* to whom they sell their son, the agents of national awakening who do not recognize the epic significance of their act as a catalyst for collective regeneration.

National history does not proceed in a coherent, linear fashion, the logical outcome of a transparent order dictated from above by an eminently rational Divine and perfectly accessible to human reason. The road to the Jewish renaissance, rather, takes place in the "short cut" through the Jewish cemetery of the Nicholaevan shtetl, triggered by an unaccountable act of human will. Shmuel's desire to get down off the cart and walk is neither rational nor irrational but rooted in the inescapably oppressive, deadening reality of Russian mud. The radical abridgement of history that connects Shmuel directly to his ancestors, bypassing the mediation of his parents, brings up the question of "fatherlessness," another persistent motif in these stories.

The Nicholaevan universe that forms the setting for the nationalist conscription tale typically connects the drama of the story with the critical deficiency of Jewish parents, particularly fathers. Levenson's hero is the sole pride and joy of his widowed mother and his supremely pious maternal grandfather. Peretz and Feierberg explore more fully the narrative possibilities of fatherlessness. Peretz's protagonist pursues his fate when his father is away, working in the fields. The Old Man of Shpola, even though he is still a youth, first manifests his capacity "to bring souls back to life" in connection with the same critical moment, effectively becoming the Old Man he is destined to be; grandson and grandfather are miraculously born in the same instance of paternal absence. Feierberg's Yankev loses his father early to tuberculosis; the boy's identity as the "watchman" of exile forms in the shadow of his father's spectral—absent—presence. Depicted as a living corpse, the latter hovers apocalyptically, like the Nicholaevan setting in which he is embedded, between heaven and hell:

> His cough was dreadful. It seemed to come from some rock bottom of the soul. And the shadows rocked, rocked back and forth, like harbingers of death.
>
> He crooned melodically, his voice rising and falling. Sometimes it seemed pregnant with longing, his soul a tender young thing that poured itself forth in a fury of fancy for the precious object of its love, toward which it strove boldly with all the vigor of youth, for which it waited trustingly with the

innocence of youth. Then the shadow swayed calmly and his cadaverous face shone by the candle's dim light.

But sometimes his voice trembled badly, and he let out a horrible groan of self-denying, life-denying despair. How hopeless! His black shadow darted swiftly about the room and the storm inside him erupted in a cough.

It blew itself out with a bitter sigh, and he cried from the depths of his heart:

"Woe that the Shekhinah is in exile!"[41]

The orphan had figured prominently in Abramovich's critique of the domestication of Judaism; in his work the plight of the abandoned child spoke to the ethical failure of embourgeoisement. The lost son of Takif emblematized the absence of Jewish enlightenment in the promise of emancipation. Even the good father of the recruit and future doctor in *The Wishing Ring* is morally suspect. In nationalist stories the motif of fatherlessness highlights the coming of the nation. Adopting the victims of communal and familial disorder, "orphans" of the chronic decline of Russian-Jewish society, the nation became the new source of lost Jewish patriarchy, replacing the father whose lack, in every sense of the word, highlighted the dissipation of Jewish collective potency. Steinberg's hero, betrayed by his parents, finds in his new adopted family composed of unconventional Jews fellow recruits and their renegade mother, Anna, a model for national fraternity that is meant to transcend entrenched but thoroughly corrupted ties of blood, kin, and confession. The conscription tale, which in its apocalyptic foreshortening of history skips over enlightenment entirely in its movement from the epic Nicholaevan past to the assumption of a national future, elevates the embrace of fatherlessness to the status of a cultural ideal, an ironic symbol of Jewish continuity in the post-emancipation age. The apocalyptic leap accounts for the importance of the grandfather or grandfather figure as a paragon of unimpeachable integrity, the moral imperative of Jewish politics that now serves to endow the nation with the full extent of social power formerly the preserve of family and community. This displacement finds its most striking expression in the relationship between the hero and the author of Ben-Ami's "Ben-yukhid."

Reb Nukhim, the father of Shraga, his "only son" — this is the meaning of the title, an allusion to Isaac, the son of Abraham — appears entirely unworthy of the treasure that providence has bestowed upon him; hence the miracle. Possessed of "not a single attractive feature," despite his obvious intelligence, Reb Nukhim literally pales into insignificance. He exhibits signs of "some sort of effort to hide even from himself evidence of his own appearance."[42] He is, in short, a sympathetic nonentity, perpetually surprised at the spiritual greatness of his own offspring. Before Shraga, he had succeeded in fathering only daughters, all thoroughly corporeal, without a shred of their brothers' unearthly gift for dying. Ben-Ami insinuates a greater spiritual kinship between his title character and his own authorial persona; this is the first story in which Mark Yakovlevich Rabinovich premiered the pseudonym, Ben-Ami, which he went on to use throughout the rest of his literary career. Ben-Ami means "son (Heb. *ben*) of my people"; there is an obvious homology with the "son" in the title of the story. Prior to the writing of this story, Mark Rabinovich had written "Dispatches" from Paris to the Russian-Jewish monthly *Dawn* (Rus. *Voskhod*) under the provocative pen name "Resh galuta," the Aramaic word for "exilarch," a reference to the titled head of the Jewish community in Babylonia, ca. 500 CE).[43]

The turn from "Resh galuta" to "Ben-Ami" involved the domestication — the imagined return — of the correspondent-as-exile; in fact, Ben-Ami wrote most of his stories about the "inner spiritual world of [pre-reform] patriarchal Judaism," including "Ben-yukhid," in Switzerland where he lived until 1887.[44] "Resh galuta" turned into "Ben-Ami" through the mediation of his own creation, his literary "ben-yukhid." Staking his literary future on an imagined Nicholaevan prehistory, Ben-Ami severed the ties between his former persona and his present self. The modern "son of his people," as it were, abjured the cosmopolitan claims implicit in the ironic title of "Resh galuta" in order to become a worthy heir / creator of *his* adopted patriarch, the "only son" of an undeserving father; like Shraga's miraculous birth, this transformation defied the natural course of things. In the figure of Shraga, estranged from his father as his father is estranged from himself, Ben-Ami effectively created the most fitting ancestor for his own nationalist alter ego. Here we have another version of the apocalyptic elision of Jewish fatherhood in the construction of an epic past that was immediately anterior to the post-emancipation ideal of national revival.

The folk-tale typology transformed conscription into a quintessentially Jewish experience, a model for the post-emancipation return to nationalism in which turn-of-the-century Jewish writers located their own sense of mission. This, however, was not the only way to write about Jews in the Russian army. The extreme — and highly polemical — stylization of Nicholaevan conscription as a paradigm of exile arose within the context of the historical naturalization of this experience between the military reform of 1874 and the Russo-Japanese War of 1904–1905. By the turn of the twentieth century military conscription of the Jews ceased to be extraordinary; Russian Jews now served in the army as a matter of course, supplying a disproportionate number of recruits and volunteers.[45] Integrated into the fabric of everyday life, military service (and its avoidance) could and did enter literature as an aspect of Jewish modernization as various in its effects as any other aspect of Russian life, neither more nor less Jewish in consequence than the vagaries of education, ambition, love, money, and class. The contrast between contemporary writing about the post-reform Jewish experience of the draft — the subject of the next section of this chapter — and the apocalyptic telling of Nicholaevan *rekrutchina* provides a way of thinking about the difference between secular literature about Jews and Jewish literature as a form of cultural resistance against secularization. While the second is, perhaps, more obviously tendentious, the first is no less ideologically charged; in the first instance, the figure of the Jew as Russian soldier effectively unsettles the "givenness" of Jewish conscience, an axial premise of the Hebrew revival. The move toward the radical secularization of Jewishness in the conscription stories of Sholem-aleichem, Joseph Hayyim Brenner, and L. A. Arieli (Orlov) led either to a compelling Jewish argument for emancipation or to the controversial politics of "sheer Zionism," (Heb. *tsiyonut 'artilait*), a "cosmopolitan ultra-nationalism" stripped of its connections to "Jewish intellectual and cultural history" and premised on the "immutable [. . .] genetic and biological dispositions" of collective will.[46]

BEYOND THE TALE

The poetics of modern Jewish literature arose out of the Jewish politics of the Hebrew Renaissance; Jewish literature was less a response to the "apocalypse" of persecution than to the potential cultural devastation of modernity. The fin-de-siècle image of "apocalypse," itself a literary event of the first order, mobilized the reserves of Jewish conscience for the preservation of collective discipline in a world where Jewish social institutions ceased to have a commanding presence over the conduct of Jewish men and women.[47] But the persistent ideological investment in the social and moral authority of modern Jewish literature that nationalism took over from the Haskalah generated its own polemic. Conscription tales inspired by the idea of the Hebrew Renaissance present a striking example of literature as mythopoesis. Conscription stories that reached beyond the ideological confines of the Jewish revival made the claim, engendered by the powerful counterexample of Abramovich and his literary progeny, that a different way of writing about conscription constituted a different way of *writing*. Acts of radical departure from the typology of the nationalist conscription tale subverted the marriage between Jewish literature and Jewish enlightenment as a cure for what ailed the modern Jew. In fact, the secular reading of conscription offered a trenchant critique of maskilic social conservatism from both a liberal and radical perspective. These alternatives to the reforming ethos of the Haskalah testify to the dramatic politicization of Jewish life that followed in the wake of the 1905 Revolution.[48]

Stories in which conscription present overshadowed conscription past implicitly, and sometimes explicitly, engaged the nationalist mythology of the Nicholaevan draft. Abandoning the defining premise of the conscription tale — that the recovery of the travails associated with the era of Nicholas I provided an opportunity for the instantiation of Jewish conscience in the post-emancipation reign of Nicholas II — Sholem-aleichem, Brenner, and Arieli challenged both the contemporary relevance of the pre-reform period and the ideological coherence of nationalist discourse. Abandoning the ethical-prophetic prerogatives that the writers of the Jewish nationalism inherited from Abramovich, they insisted on the irremediable force of historical contingency as the basis of secular Jewish literature and secular Jewish politics. This claim found expression both in the style and content of the conscription stories they wrote.

The conscription tale, as written by Peretz, Feierberg, Levenson, Ben-Ami, and Steinberg, derives its rhetorical force from its structure; the messianic resolution of the tension between absent fathers and orphaned sons recapitulates the connection between the Nicholaevan *galut* and the post-emancipation rebirth of Jewish conscience. Rigorous patterns of repetition characterize the conscription tale as modern Jewish apocalyptic. Rooted in the idea of literature as revelation, the conscription tale is always already the same *story*. By contrast, the conscription stories of Sholem-aleichem, Brenner, and Arieli share nothing so much as their embrace of difference, reflected in their aesthetic of studied incoherence. All three writers abandon the promise of moral awakening that endows the conscription tale with both its excess of form and its historical function. All three privilege a sense of the essentially fragmentary and unfinished nature of the present—before its objectification as a common Jewish past—at the expense of an ending. All three, in line with their post-enlightenment politics, struggle with finding a means of Jewish expression consistent with the evacuation of Jewish tradition from Jewish experience.

Obscured by his image as the "first and last true folk writer the Jews have ever had," the Russian-Jewish writer S. N. Rabinovich (1859–1916) has been entirely eclipsed by the timeless "presence" of his literary "persona," Sholem-aleichem.[49] Few critical studies consider the connection between the poetics of "Sholem-aleichem" and the (local) politics of S. N. Rabinovich; fewer still consider the complex relationship between text and context.[50] For his popular audience, Sholem-aleichem is a phenomenon in his own right, even a country unto himself,[51] Jewish critics celebrate Sholem-aleichem as a peerless virtuoso of vernacular realism, a normative characterization seemingly impervious to the ideological differences between various readings of his work.[52] For all the tensions between Soviet, Israeli, and American scholarship on the subject of Sholem-aleichem, universal consensus reifies his art as unimpeachably Jewish. But the successful performance of Jewish authenticity that went into the making of Sholem-aleichem was precisely that—a highly idiosyncratic representation of Jewishness. Reading Sholem-aleichem's conscription stories with an eye toward their contemporary frame of reference offers an opportunity to examine the ways that his one-man show constituted a public act of resistance to the contemporary ethos of Jewish literature. Committed to the emancipation of the Jewish individual, Sholem-aleichem depicted the drama of recruitment in a way that undermined the cultural apotheosis of Jewish peoplehood. In the aftermath of 1905 the conscription story served to expose the problematic relationship between liberal politics and a conservative social order, a contradiction that, as far as he was concerned, blighted the private lives of Russian Jews.

Sholem-aleichem wrote two stories about conscription: "The Automatic Exemption" (Yid. *Funem prizyv*), originally published in 1902 in the Warsaw Yiddish weekly *Der yud* and subsequently included in the *Railroad Stories* collection, which was first published in the anniversary edition of collected works in 1909–1914; and "Goody 'Purishkevich' " (Yid. *Gitl purishkevich*), a monologue first published in the Warsaw Yiddish daily *Der haynt* in 1911.[53] In both stories the author assailed every element of the nationalist morphology of the conscription tale. First, the stories are set in a free-flowing, unresolved post-reform conscription present rather than in the petrified prereform conscription past; the narrative time line, moreover, does not follow a predetermined course in which the beginning of Russian-Jewish history neatly folds into its apocalyptic end. Plot and character alike reflect a disorienting sense of contingency. Much like the other railroad stories in the series, "The Automatic Exemption" never resolves the question at the heart of the plot; the reader knows only obliquely whether the potential recruit escapes his fate, and that, for all the insistence of the speaker-father, does not seem, in any case, to be the point of the telling. In "Goody 'Purishkevich,' " the escape from the draft, ex post facto, occurs not as a result of anything the narrator does but through the unaccountability of the system. As in "The Automatic Exemption," the means undertaken ostensibly in the name of escaping the draft constitute their own ends; the most important of these for the author lies in the unintended self-revelation of the pathological similarity between the authority of Jewish parents and Russian bureaucrats.

Second, the stories invert the typology of unworthy, impotent, or absent fathers overshadowed by their heroic sons. Here there are no elders, no pious grandfathers, no "old men" recalling modern Jewish orphans to their collective destiny. The protagonists are not the recruits themselves but their overbearing, all-too-present and overly potent parents; in the case of "Goody 'Purishkevich,' " the conventional poor widow who figures prominently in the melodrama of the Nicholaevan conscription scenario is, in fact, a force unto herself, a highly competent woman who is both father and mother to Moishe, her ne'er-do-well son.[54] Paradoxically the fear of conscription of her son, whom she claims as her sole means of support, motivates her to take up some very profitable business ventures so that she ends up supporting him. Gitl-Goody "Purishkevich," as her nickname intimates, is not only a commercial entrepreneur but a political one as well, whose motives, vis-à-vis the son in whose name she is moved to act and speak, are entirely self-serving and contradictory. V. M. Purishkevich was a figure on the right side of Russian politics post-1905, associated with the strikingly illiberal usage of Russia's new parliamentary forum to further an anti-

Semitic reactionary agenda.[55] In relation to the Jews, Gitl is no less reactionary than her namesake; both, for different reasons, see the conscription of Jews into the Russian army, a signifier of emancipation, as fundamentally antithetical to the established principles of filial obedience and to the preservation, indeed the reinforcement, of social boundaries.[56] Just as Purishkevich was making his exclusionary arguments against Jewish civic integration in an auditorium that included Jewish deputies, Gitl makes her public case as a poor widow in the process of proving that although she may be a widow, she is hardly poor. The forces of reaction, paradoxically enabled by the liberal order, reduced Russian Jews to perpetually troubled and troubling adolescents in need of strict control. "Goody" and the Russian right wing are similarly invested in this outcome, even though they themselves are direct beneficiaries of the process that leads exactly to the reverse. Their own newly gained freedom to participate in the political and socioeconomic order results in a more strident insistence on the necessity for greater conformity and more stringent patriarchal — in Gitl's case, matriarchal — discipline. The ironic exposure of Gitl as a Jewish Purishkevich indicts the complicity between Jewish mothers and Russian reactionaries, an alliance fostered by common anxieties about the social consequence of individual liberation.[57]

The conspicuously vacant sons in Sholem-aleichem's conscription stories bear the brunt of history, contained in their parents' entirely secular desire for control and transparent self-interest. The boundless energy of Jewish mothers and fathers seems to have a paralyzing effect on their children. Neither Gitl's Moishe nor his counterpart, the hapless Avrum-Yitskhok, also known as Itsik, also known as Alter of "The Automatic Exemption," possesses any extraordinary gifts, spiritual or otherwise, and barely any personality except perhaps a kind of dull resentment of parental ambition on their behalf. They are both hardly present except as foils for the self-actualizing speeches of their parents, and they hardly speak at all.

The near-absence of the sons — Avrum–Yitskhok–Itsik–Alter sleeps through the whole story as, presumably, he has slept through the events that his father recounts — brings up the third point of difference between the conscription tale and Sholem-aleichem's stories. In the latter, the conscripts are not children, preternaturally precocious and prematurely aged, but perpetual adolescents who never quite make it as adults, prevented from doing so largely by their parents' obsessive efforts. The struggle to keep near-adult sons out of the army actually presents an opportunity for keeping them bound to the patriarchal order in perpetuity. There is no higher purpose in evidence, no invocation of religious discipline or love or any other redemptive explanation offered to excuse the oppressive nature of parental power. In "The Automatic Exemption," Sholem-aleichem exposes, to the increasing horror of the reader, nothing but the naked awfulness of Jewish familial dysfunction, an ironic moment of disclosure which conscription happens to bring to light. Here Sholem-aleichem plays with the idea that conscription constitutes an ethical trial and occasions the awakening of Jewish conscience; this conceit, central to the creation of the nationalist conscription tale, actually foregrounds the governing principle of the nationalist revival that modern Jewish literature of the "Old World" serves the revelation of collective memory. The stream of Jewish talk in "The Automatic Exemption" reveals nothing except the presence of a moral vacuum at the heart of Jewish life. Let us look more closely at how this process of psychological unraveling works on the level of Sholem-aleichem's literary practice.

Reread as a text that demolishes the mode of "creative betrayal" implicit in the recovery of the "language(s) of tradition" as the basis for national culture, "The Automatic Exemption" demonstrates the function of Jewish literature in the disenchantment of Jewish language.[58] We move here from deliberate acts of appropriation inherent in the pious heresy of Jewish modernism to the radical secularism of Jewish modernity. In his story of the beloved only son, Ben-Ami had alluded to the *'akedah* in order to endow Shraga's sacrificial death with trans-historical significance, a sign of Russian Jewry's imminent national awakening. The obviously ironic invocation of the connection between conscription and the *'akedah* in "The Automatic Exemption" makes it difficult not to read Sholem-aleichem's story as a parody of Ben-Ami, in particular, and, more generally, of the apocalyptic significance that Jewish nationalists invested in the literary sacralization of the pre-reform past. The connection rests on two singularly important details. First, the recruit is named Avrum-Yitskhok, or Abraham-Isaac. He is both the sacrificing father and the sacrificed son, doomed to repeat the same scenario of parents subconsciously willing the death of their children. The drama is set in motion by parental neglect; the younger son, also named Isaac, is scalded to death when he is accidentally on purpose left without adult supervision. The death of the second son, Isaac, puts the identity of the older brother into formal question and leads to his being recruited by mistake. The father, now "blessed" with an only son, proceeds to obliterate his remaining offspring into insignificance as he maneuvers through various bureaucracies to prove that his "only son" is not only not who the state says he is but a poor specimen in any case and therefore ought to be exempt from service. In fact, this father can barely admit that his son, sleeping and as it were dead to the world when his father relates the story, is alive at all; "I've seen them lay better-looking corpses into the grave," his father says.[59] "Unfit" for military service, he is potentially unfit for anything else: "I know myself that he's no good (not that he's no good, just no good for soldiering)."[60] The latter proposition is granted only reluctantly in parentheses, for the benefit, it seems, of the father's interlocutor.

Second, the father punctuates his tale with a refrain that goes directly to the biblical text: "An only son, a real only son, a proper only son, a pure candidate for a first-class, automatic exemption."[61] Notice the absence of the "beloved" here, a self-conscious misreading of the original verse which reads: "your son, your favored son Isaac, whom you love" (Gen 22: 2 JPS). More subtly, Sholem-aleichem subverts Ben-Ami's modern 'akedah which draws a direct homology between the special fate of the only beloved son and the affective bond which makes the Jews into a community of beloved sons, bonded to the nation rather than to their fathers. The invocation of the 'akedah by way of its rereading as a conscription tale undoes the idea that Jews — even when they are fathers and sons, especially then, in fact, — have any sort of affective bond that allows them to transcend the promiscuous effects of history. A nation, even if it were comprised of spiritually gifted beloved sons, is destined to engage in the same process of killing its own children as any other, Sholem-aleichem implies. Here the apocalypse is mere death, without the redemptive promise of rebirth. The real link between conscription and national awakening for Sholem-aleichem is that both are based on the fundamentally misleading association between the exercise of power and the expression of love; what the father in "The Automatic Exemption" represents as acts of love, the reader knows to be acts of power. The parental bond is part of the same secular system of coercion based in social and psychological discipline that produces community, that produces nations which in the end demand the killing of their beloved sons for nothing other than the display of aggression signified here by the father's desire for triumph in an endless war of verbal attrition.

The near-sacrifice of the "only son" in "The Automatic Exemption" fails to bring about national awakening and rebirth; rather, it is a sleeping death, a state of self-imposed stupor that represents the only possible posture of resistance to the constant harassment of conscience which is the proper métier of Jewish authority, a relentless clatter that begins at home. The defeat of this kind of ideological assault comes from a quarter rendered immune, it would seem, to the exhortative demands of Jewish special pleading by the cooler realities of the law which, it must be remembered, made conscription universal and therefore less of a Jewish problem. The father — echoing Ben-Ami and company — wants precisely the reverse: for someone to recognize the singularity of his situation, the distinctive quality of his Jewish love. Obsessed with the righteousness of his exemption crusade, he cannot simply pay a fine and walk away. He persists in his self-justifying "concern" for the fate of his son who, on the whole, would not really mind being conscripted. Finally, in the office of his seasoned Jewish attorney, the father meets his match: "Get out of here," the exasperated lawyer says in Russian, dismissing the alarmist vernacular rhetoric for the Jewish self-absorption it really is, "you are an annoying, irritating Jew." "What do you think of that?" exclaims the father as he draws his tale to a conclusion on the train. "He was talking about me, me! Me, annoying?! Have you ever heard of such a thing? He calls me annoying! ME!!!"[62] The St. Petersburg lawyer delivers the definitive verdict on the father's personality which, given the parodic context of Sholem-aleichem's story, may be read as a reflection of contemporary impatience with the parochial moralizing of the Jewish intelligentsia, recast into the infinite expression of concern for "beloved Jewish children" — Mendele's *liebe yudishe kinder*— always already in need of rescue from the risks of emancipation. The stunning effect of the father's discomposure, in fact, brings the story to an end without resolution, without closure, and without comfort.

Brenner and Arieli, no less than Sholem-aleichem, confounded the nationalist typology of conscription by privileging the incidental quality of conscription-present over the epic significance of conscription-past. Whereas Steinberg had used the recruitment of Shmuel's son in the present as a frame for relating the story of the "old man" himself, Joseph Hayyim Brenner, in his 1908 novella "One Year" (Heb. *Shanah ahat*), does precisely the opposite.[63] The story, allegedly based on Brenner's own service in the Russian military between 1901 and 1904, recounts the contemporary military experience of Haninah Mintz, whose father had, according to Haninah's grandmother, almost been snatched by *khappers* himself.[64] But even Mintz senior does not accept this version of events; the pre-reform past here frames the present only to be dismissed as an elaborate old wives' tale, literally a *bubbe-mayse*:

> Their grandmother, their mother's mother, was a talented storyteller, and from her they [Haninah and his siblings] knew all about what those *khappers* were like in those days [Heb. *bayamim ha-hem*]. "What *khappers*?" their father would mock them. "How old do you think I am? I am only forty. In my day, the hour of the *khappers* had passed. It was only some Russian official and his government-appointed underlings in charge of conscription. Do you hear me?"[65]

The polemical allusion to Steinberg's title "In Those Days" (Heb. *bayamim ha-hem*) as appropriate only to the credulous minds of children sets the tone for the radical disjuncture between the cultural mythology of nationalism and the realities of Zionism evident in both Brenner's "One Year" and in L. A. Arieli's 1910 conscription story, "In the Light of Venus" (Heb. *Le- or ha-venus*).

Brenner and Arieli rewrote the conscription story in light of the Zionist revolution, an event they understood entirely in secular terms, within the immediate context of 1905. The politicization of the widow "Purishkevich" under the impact of the possible conscription of her son parallels the process of political education that the heroes of Brenner and Arieli undergo while serving in the Russian army.[66] The revolution provides the immediate impetus for the plot and sets the tone of Brenner's "One Year," written while Brenner was en route to Palestine, and Arieli's "In the Light of Venus," written in 1910, when its author had already landed in Jaffa.[67] In some sense, these are stories about getting to Zion. They evoke the ideological formation of the so-called Second Aliyah (1904–1914), the wave of migration to Palestine that comprised the political elite of the New Yishuv.[68] Understood not merely as a "sociological phenomenon" but as a "revolutionary political value-concept," this cohort "molded the basic social and political thought patterns of most of the Jewish community in Palestine during its struggle to achieve socioeconomic strength and political independence."[69] The experience of revolution and collective mobilization against the anti-Jewish violence that followed in the wake of the Kishinev pogrom of 1903 shaped the "anti-utopian and often out-and-out Marxist attitudes" of the members of the Second Aliyah.[70] The radicalization of nationalism found expression in the secular ideology of "land and labor," centered on the importance of economic autonomy and self-defense.[71] The images of Haninah Mintz and Yaacov Pergold, the protagonist of "In the Light of Venus" — secular heroes of the Zionist "conquest" — displaced the dead children of the Hebrew Renaissance.

Brenner and Arieli focus their conscription stories upon a single conceit of the Zionist as an alienated Russian-Jewish intellectual who experiences his Jewishness as a pathological absence of power, a malady that Zionism is meant to cure. Prefiguring Isaac Babel's bespectacled Jewish soldier in *Red Cavalry*, they, too, are men "with autumn in the heart" who seek their emancipation from Judaism through the imaginative — and highly fraught — identification with the masculine élan of the Russian barracks.[72] The imperial army on the eve of 1905 provides the setting in which both the problem and its solution appear self-evident. Russian *intelligenty* cast in the awkward role of Jewish soldiers, Haninah Mintz and Yaakov Perlgold experience Jewishness as nothing other than absence and impotence. In the act of reclaiming their masculinity, they shed not only their second-class confessional status which emasculates them politically but also their Jewish identity, a perfect reflection of state-imposed disability; Perlgold's fascination with mirrors amplifies this echoing effect.[73] Significantly, Haninah refuses to be hobbled, made impotent, by a Jewish agent in order to escape army service.[74] In Brenner's ambiguous rendering, the Russian Jewishness of Haninah represents the dialectical relationship to power, embodied in the hierarchical discipline of the barracks that must be internalized (rather than avoided) in order to be transcended.[75]

The Russian army works as the training ground for the Zionist revolution, because it is both the place that destroys the illusion that Jewishness is anything other than a matter of politics and the only place, therefore, where Jewish men can remodel themselves in the image of Russian soldiers. Only in Palestine can Jewish men become Russian Cossacks.[76] The Nietzschean current in this insistence on the secularization of Jewish masculinity emerges explicitly in the romantic depiction of Perlgold as a Zionist superman, arriving in Palestine as an outlaw, a political assassin who successfully eludes the Russian military authorities. Perlgold the dangerous criminal, the Jewish soldier who experiences his moment of personal awakening in the supreme "act" of will involved in the murder of his commanding general, is the antithesis of all those compliant children and old men who dominated the conscription literature of the Hebrew Renaissance. The "act" of murder inspires a political, not a moral, awakening.[77]

For Brenner and Arieli, the depiction of military service elaborates a fantasy of Jewish masculinity; in this sort of projection they returned to the maskilic vision of enlightened self-discipline that had informed the conscription stories of Gordon, Dik, and Bogrov. This is why their soldiers are, first and foremost, cosmopolitan-minded intellectuals with universal ambitions. Unlike their enlightened predecessors, however, Brenner and Arieli abandoned any sort of Jewish providentialism, enlightened or nationalist, that attempts to impose meaning on history, to turn the history of the Jews into Jewish history. Both stories present the Zionist revolution not as a revolt against secular time but the willed acceptance of its verdict, as an embrace of historical accident, not the moral turn from contingency to the redemptive embrace of apocalypse. This is most strikingly evident in the matter of narrative style, premised on the notion of incompleteness.

Brenner and Arieli explicitly reject the view of the Jewish present from inside the nationalist circle in which past and future merge. Brenner's story is in the form of a diary that relates only to a piece of time, "one year" consciously set apart from what came before and what follows afterward. Within this context, Haninah's conscription and its consequences—his coming of age within the fraternity of soldiers—are not at all a given. Connections between everything that happens to him are justified only by the fact that he chooses to relate his life in this particular order; these are mere "notes," after all. The story suffers from the chronic absence of plot, as Haninah himself suffers from a dispiriting lack of character which, apparently, afflicts him to the end.

In the case of Perlgold, the arrival in Palestine as a form of escape appears equally arbitrary. How his fall from grace as a Russian revolutionary leads to his becoming a new Palestinian Jew, a member of the exclusive male fraternity in which he finds himself a storyteller "speaking the language of the prophets without feeling any connection to those great souls," remains entirely mysterious even to himself.[78] Secular Zionism seems here to be a matter of opportunity, fortuitous rather than foreordained. The wayward spirit of Perlgold undermines the foundational teleology of the Hebrew Renaissance.

By far the most radical departure of Brenner and Arieli from the originary conscription mythology of Jewish nationalism involves their representation of fatherhood. The failure of Jewish parenting here serves more generally to indict all authority, Jewish and Russian, as fundamentally corrupt. Brenner and Arieli write not about missing fathers but about killing fathers.

The secular indifference of Mintz senior to the fate of his son is actually worse for the ambivalence he allows himself to express; Haninah's father reflects on the possibility that it might be a good idea for his son to serve, because it might somehow make him more amenable to parental control.[79] Of course, the disciplinary system in the army is thoroughly oppressive. Haninah's only potential relief from Jewish fatherhood lies in the notion of military fraternity, but here his Jewishness, conflated with his intellect, gets in the way. In Steinberg's tale, the society of cantonists had served as the ideal for the post-emancipation recuperation of Judaism. In Brenner's story, which deals with the integrated army, there is no separate society for Jewish soldiers, just conventional and persistent anti-Semitism, a result of Jewish disempowerment.

Brenner, like Arieli, identifies with the notion of an alternative social order for Jews based on the political ideal of a masculine fraternity that, on its own terms, will not admit Haninah because he is a Jew. Perlgold expresses universal ambition through his longing for brotherhood, viscerally rejected by military society because, like Haninah, he is a Jew and (therefore) an intellectual. He has to kill the ultimate father figure, the commanding general Yergunov, in order to avenge his bruised filial ego. For these "corrupt" personal motives, Perlgold's revolutionary credentials are ultimately discredited by his fellow Russian radicals; he is like a man who "glories in wearing the revolutionary mantle that is not rightfully his."[80]

Arieli's secular notion of Jewish brotherhood has nothing to do with affective or tribal ties — going, presumably, back to the idea of shared parentage — only in the common politics of resentment that inform the radical rejection of fatherhood on principle.[81] The revelation of Perlgold's crime, the secret that makes the Zionist revolution possible, induces in Perlgold's Jewish compatriots — the "divine youths" laboring in the "orchard" of the new Zionist Eden who listen to his story — the sense that they are bound together in an unremitting heroic struggle for integral Jewish manhood.[82] The difference could not be more striking between Arieli's patently homoerotic elitism, embedded in the open-ended vision of permanent Zionist revolution, and the populism of the Hebrew Renaissance, premised on Abramovich's conservative ideal of the moral awakening of the intelligentsia to the social and biological responsibilities of Russian-Jewish paternity.[83]

The misalignment between the cultural ambitions of the Hebrew Renaissance and the "symbolic codes" of the Second Aliyah, evident in the possibility of writing differently about conscription, highlights the extent to which the search for modern Russian Jewry remained bound up with the creation of modern Russian-Jewish literature.[84] Ahad ha'am, the editor of the most important publishing venue of the Hebrew Renaissance, *Hashiloah*, and the father of "spiritual nationalism" — the idea that Jewish nationalism involves the cultural, not to say moral, regeneration of Eastern European Jewry — understood that the drama of Russian Jewry's death and rebirth played itself out, first and foremost, in the search for a sense of narrative coherence.[85] Debating the disposition of the main character of Feierberg's 1899 confessional novel, *Whither?* (Heb. *Le-an?*), Ahad ha'am suggested suicide as an effective way to control the fate of the protagonist, a character whose inchoate yearnings for self-transcendence symbolized the acute tension between the person of the Russian Jew and the destiny of Russian Jewry. Admitting the teleological element of "necessity" into the hero's death, he felt, would be less contrived than the "capricious" — read, secular — accident of a cold, a device Feierberg had used in the first version of the novel.[86]

Ahad ha'am's interest in the willful foreshortening of Russian-Jewish history demonstrates the extent to which the romance of modern Jewish nationhood depended on the constant literary reinforcement of the tension between the epic heroism of the imagined pre-reform past and the unexpected hazards and opportunities that defined Russian-Jewish lives in the post-reform present. The collective resumé of the authors who, in their conscription stories, reified the apocalypse exhibits in all the ways that history shaped the Hebrew Renaissance *not* in accordance with the terms of its own hypnotic rhetoric but as a work in progress which — irony of ironies — served the cause of the Haskalah.

THE JEWISH REFORMATION AT THE HEART OF
THE HEBREW RENAISSANCE

The literature of the Hebrew Renaissance bears the traces of its active connection to the Jewish Enlightenment. Contrary to the rhetoric of perpetual crisis propounded by the nationalists themselves, the steady advance of Russian-Jewish culture which nurtured the *tehiyah* did not develop in spite of the failure of the Haskalah to take root in Russia but, instead, as a direct result of its astonishing success in the era of counterreform and revolution. The ideology of return mobilized a new cohort of Russian-Jewish intellectuals to invest in the idea of modern Russian-Jewish culture as well as a new class of Russian-Jewish consumers and patrons, not to mention a host of public institutions, journals, and newspapers where ideas might be aired and exchanged. In fact, the Hebrew Renaissance represented the historical expansion of the enlightenment project far beyond what the first generation of maskilim had envisioned. The purveyors of the Jewish revival, seeking to tap into the collective unconscious of the Jewish folk, actually exemplified the creation of modern Russian Jewry, a process evidenced not in the morphology of nationalist conscription tales but in the sociological profile of their authors.[87]

Take, for example, the question of occupational identity of Russian-Jewish writers, clearly linked to the larger post-reform pattern of Russian

Jews entering the liberal professions: Ben-Ami made his living as a freelance journalist, and Levenson and Peretz were both practicing lawyers (although Peretz was disbarred in 1888 on suspicion of Polish insurrectionary activity). Steinberg sought consistently to acquire the kind of professional independence that would allow him to write full-time. In the last two years of a life cut short by lung cancer, he finally abandoned the difficult and time-consuming labor of teaching for the long-coveted steady job in journalism. Between 1906 and 1908 he served as the Russian correspondent to the New York socialist Yiddish daily, *Di varheyt.* The only author in the group who did not exhibit signs of the professionalization of the Russian-Jewish intelligentsia was Feierberg; he died from tuberculosis at the age of twenty-five.

Then there is the matter of the urban, cosmopolitan, and increasingly transnational character of Russian-Jewish culture, no less evident in the lives of authors who devoted their talents to memorializing the most peripheral of all imperial spaces. Ben-Ami may have been born in tiny Verkhovka in the Ukrainian province of Podolia, but he attended the New Russian University in Odessa, a city where he made a home of sorts. He spent most of his life traveling in Europe and for a number of years resided in Geneva. Levenson, also born in Podolia, received his legal training in St. Petersburg, where he lived the rest of his life. Steinberg was born in a small town in Bessarabia, traveled to Warsaw in search of literary contacts, and finally moved to Odessa. Peretz was born in Zamosc and lived most of his life in Warsaw. Even Feierberg, too ill to travel very much and requiring the constant care of his family in the small town of Novogrod-Volynsk in northwestern Ukraine, spent some time in a big city; in the winter of 1895–1896 he went to Warsaw for medical and literary consultations.

Finally, and most tellingly, the publication record of this small group testifies to the fact that, first, the Jewish nation was made, not born, and, second, that its creation proved impossible without the facilitating role of a far-flung, multilingual periodical press and the spread of Russian-Jewish publishing, the visible results of technological advancement, increasing mass literacy, market forces, and greater freedom from censorship. Ben-Ami, for instance, published mostly in the eminently respectable Russian-language *Voskhod,* but many of his stories were also translated into Hebrew and Yiddish; he is known today primarily as a Hebrew writer.[88] "Ben-yukhid" was written in Russian and originally published in *Voskhod.* Levenson contributed to all three of the major Russian-language Jewish periodicals published in St. Petersburg — *Razsvet, Voskhod,* and *Russkii evrei.* He also wrote articles on Jewish topics for Russian legal journals. Like Ben-Ami, Levenson wrote "The Enchanted One" in Russian and published it in *Voskhod.* Feierberg published in Warsaw's Hebrew daily *Ha-tsfirah* as well as under the tutelage of Ahad ha'am, in the latter's *Ha-shiloah;* "Yankev the Watchman" was published in *Ha-tsfirah.* And, even though this wunderkind wrote exclusively in Hebrew, he was *read* in Russian as well; his collected works were published in St. Petersburg in Russian in 1902, two years before they were published in Warsaw, in the original Hebrew.[89] Peretz continually shuttled back and forth between Hebrew and Yiddish.[90] His work was likewise well known in Polish and Russian translation.[91] He contributed to a variety of Hebrew and Yiddish weeklies and dailies in Russia, Poland, and the United States, and to a number of outstanding anthologies. "Good!" appeared in both Yiddish and Hebrew as part of the bilingual collection of *Stories in the Folk Style.*

The most outstanding example of the way that the invention of the national revival was bound up with the making of modern Russian-Jewish literature is the phenomenal twentieth-century publication history of Steinberg's "In Those Days." Published in its original Hebrew in Krakow in 1906, the novella had gone through ten *separate* editions by 1961, reprinted in New York, Berlin Chicago, Jerusalem, and Tel Aviv; there were numerous editions of Steinberg's collected and selected works in Hebrew and in Yiddish translation, which also contained "In Those Days." The number of separate editions does not include the three Yiddish translations, two in Warsaw (1909–1910 and 1922) and one in Montreal (1971), as well as two English translations, the first published by the Jewish Publication Society in Philadelphia in 1915 and the second in 1967 by the Board of Jewish Education of Greater New York. It is difficult to think of any other single work by any modern Jewish author—with the possible exception of Sholem-aleichem's *Tevye the Dairyman*—that achieved such prominence so quickly in so many of the outposts of the Russian-Jewish diaspora.

The Russian-Jewish publishing boom ensured the passage of ideas across state borders and ideological frontiers. The maskilim who, in the 1870s, had turned to literature in despair of their loss of public stature were more right than they knew; literature proved to be a highly effective tool in fostering the evolution of modern Jewish consciousness. The literary turn of the Haskalah in the 1860s and 1870s had manifested the signs of a vocational crisis. Following the apotheosis of Abramovich in 1884, nationalists fully embraced literature as both the medium and the message of the Jewish renaissance.[92] In fact, the literary revival placed the revolution in conscience —the reformation of Russian Jewry—into a much larger public domain. Driving the local free thinkers out of town or denouncing them to the authorities no longer sufficed to suppress the creep of enlightenment. The extensive socialization of modern Jewish authorship in the period of national revival effectively transcended the public-private divide that had bedeviled maskilim in the course of the shift from the era of "official enlightenment" to emancipation.

Jewishness was, by the turn of the century, firmly entrenched in the private sphere, associated with the modern experience of reading and iconically associated with the Jewish bookshelf.[93] The shift from confession to nation resulted in the creation of a new Jewish public culture in which nationalist writers likewise figured prominently. To be sure, the Hebrew Renaissance produced the literature of domestic Judaism, oriented to the celebration of the family as the seedbed of Jewish regeneration. But this imaginative withdrawal into kitchen, bedroom, and nursery—what one might call literary embourgeoisement—went hand in hand with the irruption of Jewish politics. Nationalist writers were radical conservatives, at once engaged in the marketing of Jewish domestic nostalgia and in uprooting the existing social, civic, and economic order of Jewish life. The literary-political commitments of Levenson, Ben-Ami, and Peretz may be taken as exemplary of this symbiosis, evidence of ongoing enlightenment-inspired investment on the part of the Russian-Jewish intelligentsia in the reformation of Judaism and the reform of the Jews.

The careers of Levenson, Ben-Ami, and Peretz exemplify the way that ideological differences among those who embraced nationalist discourse may ultimately be less historically significant than the way that nationalism served to empower a cohort of Russian-Jewish enlighteners-despite-themselves. Levenson was a Russian liberal; Ben-Ami, a Zionist; and Peretz, a wayward socialist. All three, however, embraced the cultural and social possibilities implicit in the idea of national regeneration as a source of authority over the mind of the Russian Jew and over the collective body of Russian Jewry; all three writers held in common the imminence of Jewish moral awakening of the former, and each, in his own way, worked toward the social, economic, and political regeneration of the latter.

Ben-Ami and Peretz, for instance, contributed heavily to the development of a new Jewish children's literature, that is, to literature aimed explicitly at Jewish children and to literature for Jewish adults that depicted Jewish tradition as a form of collective childhood. Conscription stories, of course, played a key role in this development. More generally, the talents of Ben-Ami and Peretz—not to mention a host of their contemporaries—were eventually canonized in a modern devotional book that focused on the Jewish life cycle and the "calendrical morality" associated with the Jewish holidays.[94] This kind of writing was geared to the explicit displacement of ritual and liturgy by literature. Special compilations of tales, lavishly illustrated, elevated the bar mitzvah and the domestic celebration of holidays which had a special meaning for the Hebrew Renaissance, particularly Hanukkah and Passover.[95] Literary anthologies—themselves a kind of portable Jewish "bookshelf"—containing stories and poems in the original Russian or translated from Hebrew and Yiddish, served to introduce nationalist discourse and the talents of Russia's Jewish writers directly into the modern Russian-Jewish home, located not in the shtetl but in Odessa, St. Petersburg, Moscow, and other urban centers of the empire.

The memory of pious Jewish childhood, still associated with the traditionalism of Eastern European Jewish life was, for all intents and purposes, invented by the likes of Ben-Ami and Peretz, seeking to effect the regeneration of Jewish conscience among their contemporary cosmopolitan audiences. But even as they infantilized the past of Russian Jewry, Peretz, Ben-Ami, and Levenson all worked tirelessly for the grown-up secular causes that increasingly shaped the twentieth-century future of the Russian Jew. Levenson, like many of his Jewish contemporaries in the Russian legal establishment, campaigned tirelessly for Jewish civil rights and sought to bring public attention to Jewish legal disabilities. He was also a member of the Committee for the Dissemination of Enlightenment, Handicrafts, and Agriculture, a section of the Jewish Colonization Association, and an active supporter of the nationalist-philanthropic organization which was the focal point for the political activities of Russian Zionists, the Society for Aid to Jewish Agriculturalists in Syria and Palestine. Contrary to current expectations that journalists remain dispassionate observers, Ben-Ami participated directly in the international lobbying efforts of Russian Zionists. He joined in the call for the establishment of Jewish self-defense against urban violence, a staple of the Zionist program in the aftermath of the pogroms of 1903–1905. In 1881, anticipating the diplomatic work of the Zionist Congress, Ben-Ami went to Paris as a Russian delegate to the Alliance Israélite Universelle in order to lobby for Western European aid for Russian emigrants who had fled across the Galician border in the wake of the "southern tempests" of 1881. Peretz's political track record is well known. Disbarred in 1888, he held, beginning in 1891, an administrative position on the Warsaw Jewish Community Council which for twenty-five years provided him with a stable income. At the same time he became active in the socialist movement. His radical Yiddish pamphlets, ironically titled *Holyday Leaflets,* brought him to the attention of the police. In 1899 he was arrested and briefly imprisoned. By 1901, in part thanks to his romantic image as a revolutionary and to his popularity within the Jewish Workers' Movement, Peretz had become a public figure. In fact, the establishment of his literary fame remained linked with his radicalism. And, despite the informal quality of his affiliation in the aftermath of his arrest, Peretz never abandoned his radicalism; in 1912 he campaigned actively for the socialist candidate to the Fourth Duma.

Ben-Ami, Levenson, and Peretz exemplify the gamut of possibilities for the political expression of a commonly held belief in the national regeneration of Russian Jewry. The collective task of literary excavation of the pre-reform Jewish past in the name of a post-emancipation Jewish future brought Nicholaevan conscription to the forefront of the work of the cultural ingathering of Russian Jewry, central also to the development of Russian-Jewish autobiography and history. By the First World War it was increasingly difficult to tell where the writing of the Jewish conscription tales ended and the Jewish historical record began. And by the end of the twentieth century the image of Russia's first Jewish soldiers as the epitome of modern Jewish self-consciousness had become a commonplace in the normative reading of the Russian-Jewish past.

6

THE WRITING OF CONSCRIPTION HISTORY AND THE MAKING OF THE RUSSIAN-JEWISH DIASPORA

RUSSIAN JEWRY WITHOUT FRONTIERS

Between the last quarter of the nineteenth century and the end of the First World War, roughly 1.6 million Russian Jews (a little more than a quarter of the total population of 5 million) emancipated themselves — with their feet.[1] Viewed within the context of the rapid and unprecedented urbanization and concentration (by the turn of the century eight hundred thousand Jews constituted at least one-third of the local population of twelve of the largest cities in the empire), emigration to the United States might be said to represent the last leg of the journey beyond the social and geographic confines of the shtetl and eventually beyond the Pale.[2] The causes for this demographic upheaval remain a subject of contention among historians; the pious truism that Jewish mass migration to America and elsewhere was the result of tsarist persecution and popular violence has been challenged by a more secular economic account.[3] In fact, the pressures of overcrowding in the Pale — itself a pernicious type of legal discrimination — exacerbated the persistent economic problems that drove the currents of internal and external migration. The waves of pogroms that shook the southwestern borderlands in 1881–1882 and in 1903–1905 and induced a kind of immigration fever likewise had their roots in the uneven and destabilizing impact of capitalism in the region, again a product of government policy but not one that was aimed specifically at Jews or meant, intentionally, to produce anti-Semitic violence.[4]

Given the indissoluble connection between the impact of economics and politics on the uprooting of Russian Jewry, it makes sense to see the "selective integration" of Russian Jews into the imperial social structure and their mass migration overseas along the same historical continuum. Following Hasia Diner's pointed remark about the earlier wave of German-Jewish migration to the United States, one could argue that the story of the Jews' bilateral movement both into the Russian middle class and into the proletariat cannot be told apart from the story of their movement to America.[5] Emigration effectively intensified the processes initially set in motion by the "unserfment" of Russian-Jewish society in the age of the Great Reforms. It did not make Americans or Europeans out of Russian Jews, at least not all at once. For as long as migration remained a possibility, the emancipation frontier remained open. Geographic concentration in New York City and other urban centers, combined with the impact of successive waves of new immigrants, actually fostered the assertion of modern Russian-Jewish consciousness — political, religious, and cultural — across the Atlantic and elsewhere. At the same time ties of language, kinship, and regional loyalty helped to preserve the connections between Eastern European Jews at home and abroad. Migration resulted in the creation of a Russian-Jewish diaspora, linked not only to the Jewish populations ensconced in the urban centers of the empire but also to Jewish immigrant and émigré communities in Western European cities, particularly London and Berlin and across the Atlantic, in the Americas.[6]

By the end of the First World War, as a result of the migration trend, accelerated by a refugee crisis, famine, violence, and the political restructuring of Eastern Europe, *Russian* Jewry was no longer a geographic reality. With the formation of the USSR in 1923 and the creation of independent states in several of the territories formerly incorporated into the Pale of Settlement (which ceased to exist in 1915), the Jewish population of the Romanov Empire was scattered among the various sovereign peoples of Poland, Lithuania, Latvia, Estonia, and Romania, as well as the Soviet Socialist Republics of Ukraine and Belorussia. A smaller outpost of Russian Jewry could also be found in Palestine, now under the British mandate.[7] Like its counterpart in the United States, the New Yishuv was distinctly a product of migration as a radical act of Jewish self-emancipation from the imperial fetters of estate and confession.

The expansion of the Russian-Jewish diaspora culminated in the creation of an imagined community without frontiers, a process that began with the literary reconstitution of Russian Jewry.[8] In 1891–1892, the years that Jewish immigration to the U.S. peaked at nearly 250,000 (this total was subsequently surpassed only once, in 1906–1907), the historian Simon Dubnow issued a public call for the founding of Russian-Jewish archives and the formation of a society expressly dedicated to the "holy work" of re-creating the Russian-Jewish people.[9] Alluding to the connection between the upsurge of immigration and the famine of 1891, Dubnow saw in the promise of reviving the collective Russian-Jewish past on its own "spiritual soil," a cure to the present-day crisis of physical survival that forced Jewish "masses across the sea in search of bread."[10]

> The trajectory of the historical work that lies before us is roughly as follows: (1) the collection and systematization of raw materials; (2) the writing of monographs and individual studies of particular moments of Russian-Jewish history [. . .]; (3) the systematic outline of Russian-Jewish history in its entirety on the basis of the collected materials [. . .] From the mass of dusty charters, edited, compiled and contextualized, gradually a living figure will arise, a full-grown figure of the Past, exactly like in the "valley of bones" in the words of the prophet Ezekiel [. . .]
>
> Yes, gentlemen, we, too, are destined to witness and even to participate in the great act of resurrection. Before us lies a valley filled with the "dry bones" of archived charters, mute documents, memorials of a former, extinguished life. Doubts arise: will these dead remains of the past live again? Yes! You shall see it — and believe. Collect them diligently, move them closer together, "bone to bone," connect them, give them flesh and bone, and finally *breathe life into them* — and this dead mass shall live. And in its place shall stand before you a row of living generations from the past, living images of people dressed in the bright costumes of yesteryear. And you shall be certain that these "bones" are the "entire house of Israel" and in them is buried the life of our past. With the strength of our spirit we will again compel this life to resurrection, we will force the dead mass of ancient charters to speak [. . .] But in order to achieve this, we must be blessed with the strength of giving life, with the strength of the *imagination*.[11]

Note the contrast between the "mass" of documents with the "masses" of people leaving Russia in the quotation above; the former takes the place of the latter. Note, too, Dubnow's emphasis on the "imaginative" intervention required for the recollection of a common Russian-Jewish past. Finally, there is the prophetic persona of the historian (and of the historian to be), the bearer of the collective consciousness of the Russian-Jewish people.

Dubnow's exhortation bore fruit in the aftermath of the 1905 Revolution — which did not necessarily make him a prophet. Deeply involved in realizing the agenda outlined above, Dubnow collected, edited, and published "documents," participated in the founding of the Jewish Historical-Ethnographic Society (Rus. *Evreiskoe istoriko-etnograficheskoe obshchestvo*) in 1908, and wrote one of the first comprehensive histories of the Jews in Russia and Poland.[12] Dubnow's activities on behalf of transforming Russian Jewry into a historical object exemplified the crucial importance of Jewish history writing as a form of "spiritual" inoculation against the secular forces of history itself. The medical language of "crisis" that pervaded Dubnow's essay echoed the anxious rhetoric of Jewish enlighteners who were similarly worried about the destabilizing effects of emancipation; Dubnow, in fact, envisioned the Russian-Jewish historical society as an active partner of the "overburdened" Society for the Promotion of Enlightenment among the Jews (OPE), first established in the early years of the Great Reforms.[13]

Diligent readers of Graetz, the preeminent proponent of Jewish history as Jewish literature and sacred writ, Dubnow and his followers substantially revised the categories that informed the emancipationist agenda of the "juridical" school of Russian-Jewish historiography represented chiefly in the work of I. G. Orshanskii.[14] Working on the basis of literary—rather than legal—precedents, the new historians, many of them lawyers like Orshanskii, produced a riveting and enduring history of tsarist oppression in which the argument for Jewish emancipation appeared in constant tension with the monitory narrative of spiritual resistance against its potential effects on Jewish conscience. The earliest explicitly historical treatments of conscription—Dubnow's among them—relied on the secular "collection" and dispassionate collation of "documents" dealing with the pre-reform past. But the imaginative revival of "dead" sources implicitly drew on normative precedents within the sacred history of exile and redemption, primarily, as we shall see, on the legacy of the Iberian expulsion of 1492. In this retelling, Russia's first Jewish recruits became modern *marranos* and the Russian-Jewish diaspora, the new Sefarad.

The Russian-Jewish diaspora, forged in both voluntary and involuntary acts of departure from the Pale, produced a historical literature aimed at the imaginative recuperation of Russian Jewry and at the integration of the Russian-Jewish experience of migration into the normative script of Jewish exile. To the first memoirists of the pre-reform past, conscription signified the ambiguities involved in experiencing and interpreting emancipation as a form of personal *galut*. Thematically and ideologically linked to the maskilic telos of conscription fiction in the work of Jewish writers, the first attempts to write conscription history, by contrast, emerged out of the effort to reclaim the Russian-Jewish diaspora in the name of the "entire house of Israel."

FEAR OF FLEEING

The treatment of the conscription theme in Russian-Jewish autobiographical writing vividly illustrates the creative tension between personality and history to which attempts at "Jewish self-fashioning" proved especially liable.[15] Ideologically linked to the maskilic program of Jewish renewal,

Eastern European Jewish autobiographies oscillate between the confessional impulse (after Rousseau) and the no less potent desire to endow the personal and the idiosyncratic with all the weight of a cultural paradigm.[16] Put another way, the autobiographies of Jewish enlighteners enact the conflict between a book about a Jew and a Jewish book. The problem arises with particular urgency in the case of autobiographies written in the Eastern European Jewish vernacular — Yiddish — or in Hebrew, the language of Scripture and rabbinic literature. Here Jewish discourse militates against the possibility of a secular autobiographical narrative; for this reason, perhaps, the first modern Hebrew autobiographies focused so intently on the psychology of apostasy.[17]

The preoccupation with the paradox of *Jewish* autobiography — how can autobiography aspire to go beyond the particularity of its human subject? — and its implications for modern Jewish culture inspired a self-consciously autobiographical turn in Hebrew and Yiddish literature at the end of the century. Hebrew and Yiddish literary scholarship simultaneously shaped its own "critical and theoretical discourse of autobiography" that was "extraordinarily prescient in [its] anticipation of later theoretical developments in the study of the genre."[18] The singular importance of literary form in shaping the meaning of historical content is well in evidence in the translation of conscription into a Jewish story. Autobiographical reflections on conscription highlight the power of such imaginative intervention in the conversion of private Jewish memories into the idiom of Jewish tradition. Their historical value lies not so much in what they tell us about conscription — which, I would argue, is not all that much — but in the way that their authors' personal identification with the figure of the departing recruit serves the negotiation of the conflict between Jewish experience and Jewish expression.

All four of the autobiographical sources on conscription, Mark Antokol'skii's letter to the critic V. V. Stasov, Yekhezkel Kotik's *Memories* (Yid. *Mayne zikhroynes*), Eliakum Zunser's *Biography,* and Judah-Leib Katsnelson's *What My Eyes Have Seen and What My Ears Have Heard* (Heb. *Mah she-rau 'einai ve-sham'u 'oznai*) were written in various urban outposts of the Russian-Jewish diaspora, under the pressure of geographic removal from the Pale. Antokol'skii left his native Vilna in 1862, at the age of nineteen, alighting first in St. Petersburg, then in Rome in 1871, and settling, finally, in Paris where he lived from 1877 until his death in 1902; he wrote his conscription letter in Rome.[19] Kotik, born in 1847, moved to Warsaw in 1881 and began to write his *Zikhroynes* in 1912; the second revised edition was published in Berlin in 1921, just after he died.[20] Zunser (1840–1913) emigrated to America and published his *Biography,* in the original Yiddish and in English translation, in New York in 1905.[21] Katsnelson (also known under the pseudonym Buki ben yagli), born in the same year as Kotik, started working on his autobiography in 1916, shortly before his death in wartime Petrograd and in the shadow of the physical disintegration of the Pale.[22] Originally serialized in St. Petersburg's last Hebrew weekly, *Ha'am*—according to Kats-nelson's friend and biographer, Ben-Zion Katz, four chapters simultane-ously appeared in the short-lived Yiddish newspaper, *Petrograder tageblatt*—the autobiography eventually was published in a single volume in 1947, in Israel.

Focused on conscription as a signifier of departure, Russian-Jewish auto-biographies attached to the figure of the recruit the anxieties attendant on leaving home. The departing recruit provided a foil for the author's own exit from the Pale. The memory of conscription registered the psychologi-cal costs of geographic detachment in the same ambiguous terms that in conscription literature defined the social and cultural consequences of emancipation.[23] Autobiography lent itself readily to the articulation of such personal ambivalence about leaving the confines of Russia's Jewish world.

With the physical disappearance of the Pale, the compulsion to flee now prevalent among Jews in the collective resulted in the radical reconfigura-tion of departure as an autobiographical trope. Once there was no longer a home to leave behind, conscription was integrated into the redemptive fiction of exile, inscribed onto the life history of the modern Russian Jew. Now the parting of recruits no longer stood for the actual peregrinations of the autobiographical person but symbolized, instead, the enduring faith of the generalized persona of the Jewish people. As autobiography shifted into the higher gear of sacred history, its author dropped the confessional pose and assumed the public role of travel guide through the newly hallowed terrain of his own Russian-Jewish past. The evolution in the autobiographi-cal treatment of conscription from the reminiscences of the Russian sculp-tor Mark Antokol'skii—the first such treatment—to the oracular *Zikhroynes* of Yekhezkel Kotik neatly encapsulates this transformation.

Antokol'skii was the first Jewish provincial to enter into the world of modern Russian art. His personal emancipation from the confessional, so-cial, and economic strictures that governed Jewish life in the Russian Em-pire dovetailed with the emancipation of his art from the aesthetic con-straints of classicism. Antokol'skii's embrace of realism in sculpture became a landmark in the integration of Russian painters and sculptors into the artistic life of Western Europe. Until the 1863 "revolt" (Rus. *bunt*) of the Wanderers' Group (Rus. *peredvizhniki*) from the Russian Academy of Arts, Russian artists were themselves cultural provincials.[24] The depiction of con-temporary Russian subjects, enlivened by innovative and radical techniques, brought I. E. Repin, I. N. Kramskoi, N. N. Ge, and other Russians in An-tokol'skii's immediate circle closer to Europe.[25] Antokol'skii's self-creation as an artist, his professional and personal liberation from his Jewish origins, similarly derived from the imaginative recovery of his own native ground.

Antokol'skii's journey from Vilna to Paris epitomizes the formative rela-tionship between the physical remove from Russia and the emancipation of Russian-Jewish consciousness. Antokol'skii began his career as an apprentice to a German woodcarver. His earliest independent work involved the restoration of the cathedral of Mohilev. Thanks to the recommendation of the wife of Vilna's governor-general, who had been impressed with some of Antokol'skii's earliest experiments in wooden reliefs, the aspiring artist moved to St. Petersburg and began attending classes at the Academy but only as an auditor. Jews were not permitted to live in the capitol without a special permit; it took Antokol'skii nine years as well as a major artistic triumph — the tsar commissioned a bronze copy of *Ivan the Terrible* (1871) for his personal collection — to gain official residence and a full-fledged membership in the Academy (which entitled him to a stipend). Until 1871 he still belonged to the Jewish community (Rus. *obshchestvo*) of Vilna; his legal emancipation, in turn, enabled the departure from Russia. As a student of the Academy, Antokol'skii received official permission to study abroad. He left St. Petersburg for Rome in the fall of 1871. After Antokol'skii moved to Paris, he remained there for the rest of his life, returning to Russia (mostly to St. Petersburg and Moscow to supervise his exhibitions) only for brief visits. He died in Bad-Homburg in 1902 and was buried in Preobrazhenskii Cemetery in St. Petersburg. His work, commissioned by Russian patrons, executed and often exhibited in Europe, ended up in Russian museums. Antokol'skii's artistic legacy illustrates the cultural ties holding the Russian-Jewish diaspora together. In Russian art criticism, his sculpture has become associated with the beginnings of a national canon. At the same time Jewish historians place him at the origin of modern Jewish art.[26]

Antokol'skii's departure from Russia generated a voluminous correspondence, spanning the years between 1869 and 1902, with the Russian critic V. V. Stasov as well as with virtually every other notable figure in the world of nineteenth-century Russian art, including painters and patrons. Collected and published by Stasov in 1905, the one-thousand-page volume provides a running confessional commentary on the sculptor's work.[27] Continually rehearsing the theme of return, the letters written home present a deliberate counter-text to Antokol'skii's professional and artistic emancipation from Russia. In fact, the self-image of the Russian-Jewish artist as homegrown prodigy stands in sharp contrast to the studied cosmopolitanism of his art. The conscription letter, which entered Jewish history denuded of its immediate historical and literary context, actually came out of a turning point in Antokol'skii's career.[28] Its significance lies in the way that Antokol'skii's prescient autobiographical appropriation of the recruitment theme rehearsed the psychology of departure in a Jewish key.

The specific circumstance that gave rise to the conscription letter was Antokol'skii's most daring act of imaginative promiscuity — the creation of his *Ecce Homo* (1876–1878), a free-standing sculpture of Jesus that polemically addressed the conventions of Christian representation.[29] The work, well received at the Paris World Exhibition, established Antokol'skii's European reputation; at the same time it put into question his credentials as an authentic Russian-Jewish artist. What was a Russian-Jewish radical doing with a subject that Stasov dismissed as born of "old-time" Christian myths?[30] Antokol'skii's European success in "filthy [lit. pagan] Rome" placed him in conflict with his Russian compatriots and brought his friendship with Stasov to a crisis point.[31] The conscription letter, written as an autobiographical *profession de foi* insisted on the indelible psychological imprint of Antokol'skii's Russian-Jewish origins on his creative choices. He sought in conscription the "historical" source of his own trauma of departure that, more subtly, motivated and explained current acts of aesthetic transgression against the aesthetic and ideological demands of Russian populism.[32]

In the letter Antokol'skii described a scene of departing Jewish recruits that he claims to have witnessed as an eight-year-old boy in Vilna. He insisted that this "drama-in-fact," here focused particularly on the grieving figure of the Jewish mother, would serve as the subject of an entirely new kind of work which he was planning to begin as soon as he returned to Russia, this time, for an extended stay.[33] He never did, and the work never materialized. On the contrary, the letter testified to the imbrication of Antokol'skii's Jewishness with the Christian idiom of the Western European visual tradition which his sculpture of *Ecce Homo* explicitly engaged. Jewish memory here took on the highly intimate color of a confession to a sympathetic audience. In calling Stasov "uncle," an emphasis on the surrogate familial ties, beyond the boundaries of estate and confession, that connected the artist to his epistolary Russian community, Antokol'skii aspired to explain the local Jewish origins of his romance with the Christian "drama" of representation.

Antokol'skii's investment in the symbolic potential of Christianity emerges in his depiction of the mother of the recruit as a hypostasis of Mary, the mother of a suffering Jewish son:

> There was our neighbor, a young widow, a seamstress — from her entire family, she managed to save only one son [from death], a thin and weak boy with big eyes. How she cared for him, how she trembled over him! But they ripped him from her, while he was alive [. . .] And then she would lay there, crying: he would appear to her, standing guard in a field, on a cold stormy winter's night. "My poor one!" she would whisper, "he's cold." At other times, it would seem to her that they were beating him. One night, she screamed loudly in her sleep, waking everyone and herself rising, barely alive. "Oh, my sweet little dove," she whispered in tears, "they're hitting him with lashes, the blood flows [. . .] oh, and for what?" How he screamed for her, asking for her help! She suffered thus, living with the pain daily, weeping quietly at night. But she did not languish long. She died before her time, alone, without consolation, without hope but with love and faith.[34]

This affecting passage implicitly relies on a Christian frame of reference in its stress on flowing blood and the portrayal of the boy as an innocent "dove." Access to Jesus here comes by way of his Jewish mother, herself an icon of Jewish memory for the lost Jewish son, not only the recruit but Antokol'skii himself. He talks about recruitment as an act of autobiographical displacement; in his own house, another child, a distant relative "of the same age" as Antokol'skii himself, was conscripted while the artist remained "hidden in the house of a Christian," a moment that precipitates Antokol'skii's position as a Jewish stranger "in the house" of Christian art (103–104).

In another striking image of a Jewish mother running after her departing son, Antokol'skii's power of recollection traverses the unbridgeable gap between his adult self and his Russian-Jewish childhood:

> I shall never forget the image of one lone woman, running without rest and almost unconscious onto a field, where she was meant to take her leave from her son. She was about thirty-five or so. Her face was thin and weary, her eyes red and sunken, her lips half-open and almost black. She was covered with an old, faded kerchief, under her arm she carried a small bundle, and in her hands she held a pair of old, worn-out shoes, none of which got in the way of her running. She ran with quick, small steps and with her whole body leaning forward. At times, with a great deal of effort, she drank in air as if she were having difficulty breathing. At times she glanced down at her shaking fingers which seemed frozen. It seemed to me that she would collapse as soon as she reached her destination. (104)

The body straining "forward" toward a rapidly diminishing end is at the core of this depiction. The lively focus on physical details and their accessories actually heightens the contrast with the prospect of deathlike "collapse" that awaits this woman. In fact, the tension between the promise of movement, evoked in carefully placed objects, and the stillness of the human figure, characterized Antokol'skii's contemporary work, particularly *Ecce homo* itself.[35] This passage effectively recapitulates Antokol'skii strategy as a sculptor, which is another way of saying that, for a Jewish artist, access to Christ lay directly through the memory of his Jewish mother. The conscription letter is thus both an exercise in the recovery of Jewishness — "Now you see," Antokol'skii deliberately takes care to point out to Stasov, "I have not yet entirely forgotten my own people" — and a Russian-Jewish apologia for making Western European Christian art.[36]

Antokol'skii's aesthetic emancipation demanded the demise of the Jewish mother. He unburdened himself to his "uncle" — it is worth recalling, in this context, that the older soldiers in charge of cantonists were also called "uncles" — in order to leave her sheltering bosom; the confession is, itself, a form of emancipation from Judaism. She needs to die so that her son may live. Safely relocated to the precincts of memory, she becomes the inspiration for his vocation, his personal Russian-Jewish muse. Transformed into the long-suffering Mary, she is the epitome of unconditional love and devotion, absent the vicarious burdens of Jewish conscience.

Here, on the other hand, is Kotik's treatment of Jewish mothers at the scene of the departing recruits:

Despite the terrible sufferings those soldiers endured, perhaps only one in a hundred eventually converted. The mothers of those boys went to inordinate lengths of self-sacrifice to prepare their sons for such an eventuality. They cautioned the cantonists not to convert at any price, and they provided each child with small phylacteries. Their mothers' grief-stricken faces became so deeply implanted in the hearts of those little soldiers that they stubbornly refused to abandon their Jewish faith.[37]

Of the mother of "little Yosele," supposedly "beaten almost unconscious," Kotik says:

[She] never stopped bewailing her child, lest, God forbid, he be forcefully converted. Even if they burned and roasted him, even if they beat him and tore his body apart, he must remain strong and bear up to the physical torture — until his holy soul rises up to heaven. (235)

In the hands of treacherous Jewish agents, motivated, it seems, by pure malice, the conscription decree is nothing if not an opportunity for martyrdom; the juxtaposition between the demonic *khappers* and the angelic cantonists gives Kotik's account the quality of being set in the remote past, where both the capacity for evil and the heroic struggle for good were beyond ordinary human measure. Kotik thus casts the legendary benevolence of his grandmother in apotropaic contrast to the malignant force of the *khappers* whom he describes as "beasts in human form" (240). Her strength of character highlights the importance of the mothers of recruits warding off their sons' conversion. The phylacteries here function as a kind of Jewish totem rather than an instrument of religious observance. Like in Antokol'skii's account, the women are the true heroines of Kotik's recruitment scene, the eternal keepers of the Jewish soul.

Antokol'skii's dead Jewish mothers are key to his psychological reading of recruitment as an allegory of the trauma involved in the emancipation of the modern Jew. Kotik's wailing mothers of dead Jewish sons highlight a contrary tendency within Jewish autobiography toward the effacement of the Jewish personality by the mythological sweep of Jewish history. Antokol'skii represents memory as cathartic; key images drawn, as it were, directly from the life of the mind appear in associative order. The journey back from the site of recruitment, the scene of the crime, as it were, alludes to the fragmentary nature of memory itself as an imaginative journey of return. Note here the "indifferent" landscape, broken by man-made objects, randomly strewn on the road, traces and bits of a human past:

We began our journey home and again returned to the same spot, where just a moment ago, the drama had played itself out. And there was nothing there anymore. The sun still shone and warmed us. Here is a broken bottle lying on the grass, here is the upturned barrel upon which the rabbi stood to bless the recruit. Here is the tavern keeper clearing the dishes from the table. A few people stop and ask for a cool drink of water, but we go on our silent way.[38]

The account itself does not compose neatly into a narrative sequence; the only resolution appears to be in the stark evocations of the abrupt death of the mothers. Kotik, by contrast, is interested in the recruit as a model of self-integration. The cantonists, armed with phylacteries against the dangers and temptations of the modern world, exemplify the inner struggle toward "perfected Jewish manhood" (Heb. *ish yehudi shalem*), the disciplinary ideal of the Jewish Enlightenment, transposed here onto the composition of the "perfected" pre-reform Russian-Jewish landscape.[39]

Kotik presents his own autobiographical work not as a form of confessional self-analysis but as a mode of cultural synthesis; imaginatively, he gathers a world dispersed, "thinned out" by immigration to America, and "ruined" by the "black lead of anti-Semitism."[40] In fact, the "ruin" begins with the "unserfment" of local economic life in 1861. Deprived of the livelihood that small-town Jews derived "from the lords," Jews are not the beneficiaries but the victims of emancipation:

> Poverty became widespread, and many Jewish families neared starvation. Those families that had some capital in reserve lived off it, and those that didn't became totally impoverished. It seemed at the time that the spring from which the Jews had drawn their livelihood for hundreds of years had completely dried up and the chance of finding new livelihoods was small, perhaps nonexistent. It seemed as if everything was lost forever. (341)

Freedom here resides chiefly in the economy of chance, contrasted with the natural and eternal "spring" that brings forth a "livelihood"; the introduction of free labor is nothing short of a catastrophe. Although Alexander's government provides new opportunities, Kotik carefully circumscribes "one of the best periods experienced by Jews in their Russian diaspora" to the big cities, Moscow and Kiev; here the autobiographer parts company with the historian. The new "city Jews" prosper, while shtetl Jews decline to the status of "rural people" (Yid. *yishuvniks*) (354–355). Kicked out of his "secure nest," by the end of the first volume, Kotik spends the entire second volume of *Zikhroynes* trying to leave the village.[41] Ending up in Warsaw in the critical year of 1881, Kotik effectively registers the entire period of emancipation as a personal disaster that begins with the fatal risks of economic freedom and ends with anti-Jewish violence, enabled by peasant "defiance" toward their masters (and their Jewish agents), already ominously apparent in 1861 (342). The depiction of the total collapse of traditional social relationships in the Polish rebellion of 1863 at the end of the first volume actually anticipates the apocalypse of pogrom violence at the end of the second volume. Kotik's migration to Warsaw results in the post-emancipation rebirth of his maskilic conscience, now the object of autobiographical recovery.

Kotik's memory town represents a conservative pre-reform Jewish "Eden" on Russian soil. A gushing Sholem-aleichem wrote to Kotik that his book was a "treasure, a garden, [a] paradise full of blossoming flowers and singing birds." The radically secular writer, tongue firmly in cheek, described the experience of reading Kotik's *Zikhroynes* as a "real spiritual pleasure." Kotik, taking Sholem-aleichem's ironic and extremely funny "approbation" entirely at face value, proudly printed the letter at the start of the second edition of *Zikhroynes* (105). But, in fact, Kotik's Kamenets is a literary artifact, born of resistance to the autobiographical dystopia of the shtetl that characteristically foregrounded the confession of inner breakdown in maskilic autobiography.[42] Behind the desire for escape from decaying Eastern European Jewish society lurked the fear that liberation actually meant being "banished from [the] father's table."[43]

Antokol'skii looked back at recruitment through the same sharp-edged glass of filial ambivalence; the "drama" of emancipation, implicit in his disturbing recruitment scene, demands and brings about the sacrifice of the *mothers*. Kotik's proleptic—oracular—vindication of the recruits (how on earth does the author know that only one in a hundred abandoned his Jewish faith?) gestures toward the self-sacrifice of the *sons*. Here a Jewish son literally cannot live without his mother, her image "forever implanted in the heart."[44] The insistence on the staunch commitment of the cantonists to Judaism "at any price" foreshadows the catastrophic end of Jewish childhood, a horror at the loss of home as premature death which strikes Kotik himself. He begins his account of conscription with the assertion that "precisely at the time when [he] turned eight [. . .] all eight-year-old boys were to be conscripted into the army with the aim of converting them to Christianity" (233). Significantly, the story of Kotik's domestic Jewish haven comes to a near close with the death of his grandmother. In the aftermath, Kotik says,

> Our large family fell apart. The bonds of unity weakened, relationships cooled off, and nothing remained of the once-famous "Tsar's Regiment." If this "Regiment" had a commander—a quiet and invisible one without whom it could not function—it was Grandmother, who safeguarded her soldiers with her life. (397)

The "recruits" of Grandmother's army behave less well than their Nicholaevan counterparts, Kotik laments. But all this hand-wringing comes to a curious end; just as in Antokol'skii's account, the mother figure must finally be removed so that the narrator may escape her clutches. Kotik, in the very last chapter of the first volume, devoted mostly to a disquisition on the historic role of Hasidism in Eastern European Jewish life, elaborates the reasons why he could not join the movement. First, he was "repelled by the adherence to a rebbe." Second, he wanted to maintain a family life and earn a respectable living. Witnessing husbands leading a "happy, joyful life, eating and drinking their fill, dancing and singing in the company of their fellow Hasidim while their wives and children suffered hunger and cold at home [. . .] spoiled his enthusiasm." Finally, he was "keen on working hard and acquiring knowledge," while "gifted Hasidic boys were discouraged from learning" and spent their days in "idleness" (409–410). Kotik presents this as a defense of his choice to lead the life of a Lithuanian *mitnagged;* but, in fact, his disengagement from the atmosphere of Hasidic merrymaking—a form of perpetual childhood, marked by an absence of responsibility and by perfect obedience to the rebbe—can also be read as the entry into the duties of adulthood. Kotik here becomes father, husband, provider, and independent seeker of knowledge; the ideals of the Lithuanian learned elite merge with the maskilic ideal of an integral Jewish personality. Summarily appended to a story which Kotik himself says "ought to have concluded" with his grandmother's death, the narrator's unexpected coming-of-age is made to occur directly in her shadow (398).

Kotik and Antokol'skii focused their autobiographical accounts of conscription on the figure of the Jewish mother. She represents, in both instances, the holding power of Judaism on the conscience of the recruit/author. The autobiographical turn here marks a dialectical shift in the nature of Jewish writing about conscription. As we have seen, the literary treatment of Nicholaevan recruitment relegates the weeping mother of the recruit to the realm of Jewish melodrama. This tradition actually started with the comic scenes of "inconsolable tears, desperate wailing, and prolonged fainting fits of the mothers bidding farewell to their sons as they were being recruited" that featured in the plays staged in Berdichev by vacationing Jewish seminarians from the Rabbinical Academy in Zhitomir during the heat of the Crimean War.[45] The figure of the hysterical Jewish mother again reappeared in Dik's *First Levy* and in Gordon's "A Mother's Farewell." In Abramovich's *Little Man,* the figure of Golde, the Russian-Jewish Medea, is similarly cast in a dark light; she herself is silent, completely in the shadow of Takif's confessional narrative. Generally conscription literature appeared to be more concerned with either the idealization of Jewish fathers or their social indictment. The autobiographical appropriation of recruitment as a story of departure placed the Jewish mother at the center not only in psychological terms but also symbolically. Appearing in the guise of mother Rachel, weeping for her children as they leave Jerusalem (Jer 31: 15–22), a scriptural precedent relevant to Kotik and Antokol'skii alike, the mother of the conscript embodied the redemptive power of Jewish mourning. The collective Jewish memory of Rachel—the icon of Exile and Redemption—embodied in the biblical text, had particular significance for the personal memory of conscription as a signifier of departure.

The autobiographies of Jewish recruits themselves, published in the first decade of the twentieth century as part of the effort at the "resurrection" of Russian-Jewish history, fail strikingly to conform to this paradigm. They resist any reading through the prism of normative literary precedent; foreclosed to the symbolic power of allusion, they do not work as Jewish texts. As we shall see in the next section, historians who claimed Nicholaevan recruits in the name of the Russian-Jewish diaspora either misread cantonist autobiographies deliberately or ignored them altogether in favor of other, less troubling sources. Jewish recruits wrote autobiographies singularly uninformed by the trope of Exile. This discrepancy is most clearly evident in the autobiographical treatment of the relationship between Jewish parents and their cantonist children, a sobering corrective both to Antokol'skii's mothers, faithful and loving unto death, and to Kotik's eternally faithful sons.

Chaim Merimzon's engaging "Story of an Old Soldier" appeared in 1912–1913, in *The Jewish Heritage* (Rus. *Evreiskaia starina*), the publishing organ of the Jewish Historical-Ethnographic Society.[46] Merimzon's story manifests the gap between the Jewish memory of recruitment—enshrined in Jewish autobiography—and the memories of the recruits themselves. The memoir positions the family and the military as two competing systems of authoritarian discipline, the first associated with Merimzon's Jewish childhood, the second concomitant with his adulthood. The Russian military frees Merimzon from the Jewish family; in turn, his Jewish self-consciousness as an adult represents a form of socialization into the army. The collision between the immoveable object of the Jewish family and the relentless force of the Russian army occurs in the key year of 1856. Drafted in 1854, as a boy of eleven, Merimzon remained in military service as a medic for the full duration of twenty-five years "in accordance with the old recruitment law" (290).[47] The new dispensation of Alexander II frees Merimzon not from the army but from his Jewish parents.

In the first year of service, Merimzon reports, his parents sent him monthly letters, enclosing a ruble in each one. Then suddenly the letters stopped, even though Merimzon continued to write home. Despondent, he followed the kindly advice of the woman at whose house he was quartered, to write to his former *heder* teacher. In return, Chaim claimed to have received the following letter from his father:

> To our former son Chaim, the devil only knows what you're called now, Ivan or whatever! We are sending you a ruble so that you could buy for yourself a rope to hang yourself with or to tie a stone around your neck and drown. From this day and forever, may you be accursed. Never mention our names again. Don't send us any more of your false-sounding letters. We won't even accept them from the postman. Now that you have new parents, let them give you rubles. If we should happen to die before you, we will not remain silent even in the next world but continue to curse you so that you shall not have a peaceful day for the rest of your life, for you have blackened our names and the name of the grandfather that you used to bear. You have shamed our family, you blackguard. Because of you, kids chase after us in the street, screaming: that Chaim of yours is a *meshumed* [apostate], *meshumed! Meshumed!* Should this news that we have been told prove to be untrue, send us a formal letter of confirmation from the rabbi that you have not converted; in this case, you shall remain our beloved son. (414–415)

It is difficult to consider this letter entirely in light of its documentary value; its tone seems to belong to the contrarian fictional universe of Sholem-aleichem. Is Merimzon deliberately being provocative? Would any father, Jewish or otherwise, especially one whom Merimzon earlier described as loving and compassionate, ever send such a letter to a son of thirteen? Does it make sense for a Jewish father writing as late as 1855 to manifest such a blatant lack of awareness or understanding of the enormous conversionary pressure brought to bear on underage Jewish recruits? We have no alternative documentary sources on which to base a conclusion that Merimzon's letter is the product of anything but his own powerful sense of the ironic, not to mention an attitude of ambivalence toward his Jewish parents. The jarring contrast between the final hysterical cry of *"Meshumed!"* and the deadpan request for rabbinic confirmation in the last lines is, I think, deliberately funny, a direct jab at the social investment in the show of piety.

This letter puts an end to Merimzon's short career as a potential child-martyr — he has, despite his parents' fears, duly resisted all efforts at conversion and refused to let pork touch his lips. Merimzon fails to provide any explanation, other than this letter, for the ensuing break between himself and his parents; he says that following his abortive attempt at communication, and until his discharge in 1874, he had no contact with them at all. The letter, in fact, concludes Merimzon's Jewish childhood. Immediately after this incident, the story picks up as Alexander II comes to the throne, the cantonist battalions are disbanded, and Merimzon is enrolled in the regular ranks, as an apprentice to a carpenter.

The shift physically removed him from the Pale — he had been stationed first in Kiev and then in Chernigov, both in western Ukraine — to the capital city of Moscow, where Merimzon acquired all the signs of manhood: a job, and the respect of his master and a potential paramour, the cook Martha. The section of the memoir ends with Merimzon's triumph as a Jew in a dispute with a drunken priest. In response to the latter's exhortations, Merimzon reveals not only his Jewish cleverness but his worldly experience, not a product of his Jewish upbringing but of his Moscow service:

> In conclusion, I must tell you, Father," [Merimzon says] "that you have sold your own faith "too cheaply, pushing it on every Jew like a"ommon grocer pushing his goods. You ought to preach "Love thy neighbor" — like, for example, Ivan Vasilievich (my master) who deals so with me even though I am not baptized or like this good merchant [among the company] who leaves his money to charity. (422)

The rest of the group exclaim "Bravo!" and praise the "Jewish kid" for the way he has vanquished the priest, who, mortified, removes himself. It should be said that the expression of Jewish pride goes hand in hand with Merimzon's complete secularization; by the time he gets to Moscow, his stomach is thoroughly "accustomed" to non-kosher fare (416). Jewish dietary restrictions fall by the wayside as a kind of temporary indigestion, a relic of childhood allergies.

Between 1855 and 1874 Merimzon served proudly and well. In 1862 he was moved from the labor brigade into regular ranks where he was trained as a medic. He never, he claims, lost sight of the fact that he is a Jew nor of his difference from Russian-Jewish society. The potential for conflict, first seen in the final letter from his father, came to a head when Merimzon was discharged and returned home; again, his graduation from the Nicholaevan army coincides with the transformation of the army itself, this time with the introduction of universal conscription. In preparation for reentering Jewish society, he studied with a Jewish butcher, relearning his prayers as well as Yiddish. He bought all the accessories of traditional Jewish masculinity, phylacteries and a prayer shawl. But Merimzon's homecoming proved disappointing. His parents refused at first to acknowledge him; in a performance of the sentiments expressed in the father's letter, they requested rabbinic confirmation that he had not converted. Only then did they beg forgiveness "for sending him that ruble for a rope" (229).

The happy reunion was short-lived. At the behest of his parents, Merimzon married a Jewish woman of their choosing and settled in the town, dispensing medical advice to the locals. Nothing went right for him, despite his best efforts to adjust. Owing, one suspects, to the dim intellect of his new wife, his private life as a married man "did not work out." For three years he remained in the heartland of Jewish Lithuania and then "returned to Russia. Mother Russia understands me," he concludes, "and I know her nature. Somehow she will find a way to sustain me." He ends up in the civil service, in the city hospital of Briansk, a town in Orlov Province in the Russian interior, "alone like a stone" (232).

Merimzon's disillusionment with Jewish family life as narrow, poor, coarse, and repressive contrasts with his individual, even idiosyncratic sense of Jewish dignity gained in the ranks. Other cantonist memoirs replicate this tension on a smaller narrative scale.[48] In every case, the decision to remain Jewish represents just one of the contingencies of army service rather than the confirmation of the existence of a collective penchant for martyrdom. Russian-Jewish histories of conscription, based supposedly on the evidence of documentary sources but actually entirely dedicated to the normative image of the Russian-Jewish diaspora, rehabilitated or ignored the old soldiers who appeared on the pages of *Evreiskaia starina*. Following the historiographic precedent of 1492, the chroniclers of the new Sefarad turned Russian *conversos* (converts) — in all but their names — either into Jewish *marranos* (hidden Jews) or replaced their personal stories with invented tales of fresh victims of another Inquisition. Writing Jewish history in full view of the history of the Jews proved so difficult that (in the words of Erich Auerbach), "historians [were] forced to make concessions to the technique of legend."[49]

WRITING RUSSIAN-JEWISH HISTORY OUT OF 1492

Until the period of mass migrations, the writing of Russian-Jewish history was a scattershot affair. Confined largely to Abraham Harkavi's antiquarian studies of early Jewish settlement on Russian soil — mostly in the Crimea — and to the pioneering legal scholarship of I. G. Orshanskii, Russian-Jewish historiography, prior to the 1905 Revolution, failed to produce anything in the way of narrative synthesis. With the founding of the Jewish-Historical Ethnographic Society in 1908 and the creation of two scholarly journals — *Jewish Heritage* (Rus. *Evreiskaia starina*) and *Past* (Rus. *Perezhitoe*) — dedicated expressly to historical scholarship and the publication of primary sources, Russian-Jewish historiography acquired an "institutional framework" which allowed for the production of more ambitious work with a broader grounding in documentary and ethnographic material.[50]

The first attempts to write the history of Jewish conscription under Nicholas I emerged within this context. Between 1910 and 1915 *Evreiskaia starina* published a variety of documents related to the enactment of the decree and its implementation. These included statistical reports, government memorandums, communal records dealing particularly with local resistance and with the hiring of *khappers* in the last years of *rekrutchina,* the text of recruitment oaths administered to Jews, as well as memoirs either written by cantonists themselves or recorded by amateur Jewish ethnographers.[51] The first scholarly essay devoted exclusively to the Jewish experience of Nicholaevan conscription — to cantonists, actually — appeared in the last volume of the journal, in 1930.[52] S. M. Ginsburg's "Child-martyrs: From the History of Jewish Cantonists," a seminal article based on original archival research, was the author's last publication on Russian soil; Ginsburg emigrated to Paris in 1930 and moved to the United States in 1933. Substantially expanded to include material drawn from *Evreiskaia starina* and from conscription literature, "Child-Martyrs" reappeared in Yiddish in the three-volume collection of Ginsburg's *Historical Works,* published in New York in 1937.[53]

The other three historical treatments of Nicholaevan conscription — none of which was a history of conscription per se — all predated Ginsburg's "Child-Martyrs" and were likewise based on the sources published in *Evreiskaia starina.* All three comprised a section within a sweeping narrative of Russian-Jewish history. These included, in chronological order, Iu. I. Gessen's *History of the Jews in Russia* (1914), Dubnow's three-volume *History of the Jews in Russia and Poland* (1916–1920), and Jacob Lipmann Lipschitz's *Memory of Jacob: The History of the Jews in Russia and Poland, 1760–1896* (1924). Of all these works, only Gessen's remained disconnected from the Russian-Jewish diaspora. It had a complicated publication history that ended with the book's near-oblivion. When the war broke out, Gessen was working on a second edition, expanded and split into two volumes. The first volume, retitled *History of the Jewish People in Russia* and covering the years up to 1825, was published in 1916. After the revolution, publication stalled. A third edition of the first volume, shortened and devoid of all illustrations and maps, came out in Leningrad in 1925; the second volume, also shortened, finally emerged two years later. Gessen's work was never translated into any of the languages spoken and read by Eastern European Jews outside Russia. It remained virtually unknown abroad and most likely at home as well, since the print run of the 1925–1927 edition consisted only of two thousand copies.[54]

That was not so for the other two narrative histories. Each, in its own way, became canonic in the making of an integral Russian-Jewish past, a signal achievement of the Russian-Jewish diaspora. Until very recently Dubnow's *History of the Jews* remained the standard Russian-Jewish history text, its future assured by its publication in English. Dubnow himself left Russia in 1922. He moved to Kovno, then to Berlin, and in 1933 to Riga, Latvia (where he died in 1941, during a Nazi raid on the Riga ghetto). In Berlin he initiated an extensive translation project of his major works into Hebrew and Yiddish. Throughout the last fifteen years of his life, the historian maintained close geographical, cultural, and epistolary ties with the scattered Russian-Jewish intelligentsia. Elevated to the status of a popular "culture-hero," Dubnow — precisely in the years of his wanderings — became the doyen of Russian-Jewish history.[55]

Lipschitz (1838–1921), a prominent Kovno rabbi and one of the most vocal activists in the nineteenth-century revival of Jewish Orthodoxy and Jewish learning, was best known for his biography of Rabbi Isaac-Elhanan Spector (1817–1896), the leading luminary of the Lithuanian Talmudic elite. Lipschitz served as Spector's secretary, but he was more inclined to the role of public gadfly. He wrote extensively for *Ha-kerem* and *Ha-levanon*, periodicals devoted to the defense of traditional Judaism. Kovno, located in close proximity to Vilna, the so-called Lithuanian Jerusalem (which passed to Poland in the course of the Polish-Soviet War in 1919–1920) became part of newly independent Lithuania after the First World War. Thus Lipschitz effectively emigrated from Russia without ever leaving home and, more important, without ever leaving one of the most vibrant Eastern European Jewish communities of the interwar period.

Written in Hebrew, *Memory of Jacob* presented itself as a cross between autobiography and scholarly history. The autobiographical gesture was actually critical to Lipschitz's effort at combating the scholarly authority of secular history in order to restore the pious image of Russian Jewry. Lipschitz's alternative conception of the Russian-Jewish diaspora as a holy community (Heb. *kehillah kedoshah*) achieved unprecedented popularity among its devout heirs. A second edition, supplied with all sorts of respectable rabbinic approbations, was published in 1967, in Bnei Brak, the heartland of Jewish traditionalism in Israel.[56] Lipschitz had the benefit not only of the sources in

Evreiskaia starina—his promiscuous use of this material throws into doubt the claim (apparently propagated by Lipschitz himself as a sign of his piety) that he knew no Russian—but also of Dubnow's *History of the Jews in Russia and Poland,* not to mention a wide variety of literary materials. The irony of *Memory of Jacob,* a book which offered itself solely as an eyewitness account, is that it is, in reality, one of the best-documented works of history to emerge from the debris of Russian Jewry's imperial past. What Lipschitz did with all the sources he collected and read is, however, another matter.

Leaving Gessen aside for the moment, it may be said that the initial attempts to produce a synthetic view of the Russian-Jewish past emerged directly out of the wartime dispersion of Russian Jewry; Ginsburg's studies of conscription, a manifest example of scholarship-in-transit, implicitly relied on the narrative paradigm supplied by Dubnow. The connection between the search for a normative Jewish past and the experience of migration initially entered modern Jewish scholarship as the most serviceable explanation for the turn toward sweeping historical narratives within the literary culture of the Iberian diaspora in the aftermath of 1492.[57] In fact, the sixteenth-century effort aimed at the imaginative reconstitution of Sefarad in Solomon Ibn Verga's *Scepter of Judah* (Heb. *Shevet yehudah,* 1554), Elijah Capsali's *Minor Chronicle* (Heb. *Seder eliyahu zuta,* sixteenth century), and Joseph Ha-Kohen's *Vale of Tears* (Heb. *'Emek ha-bakha,* sixteenth century) presents a striking parallel to the work of Dubnow and Lipschitz. In both instances, the literary reconstruction of a Jewish diaspora produced a vision of Jewish collective existence, an integral Jewish ideal, greater as an imaginary whole than the sum of its historical parts.[58]

The connection between the narrative apotheosis of the Russian-Jewish diaspora and its Iberian predecessor may not reside entirely in the speculative realm of phenomenological likeness. There is historical evidence that Russian Jews were themselves invested in the identification with Sefarad, both on the level of popular culture and, as we shall see, on more scholarly ground. To begin with, one of the most widely reprinted books in the history of Jewish Eastern Europe was none other than Ibn Verga's *Shevet yehudah.* The first "improved" Yiddish translation appeared in Krakow in 1591. Reissued three times (1648, 1700, and 1724), it also served as the basis for two subsequent Yiddish editions (1700 and 1810). An entirely different Yiddish edition appeared in 1818, followed by a variety of others. Between the late nineteenth and early twentieth centuries, in Vilna alone, at least five separate Yiddish "re-workings" of *Shevet yehudah*—some under different titles—appeared. Significantly, these clustered precisely around the years of mass migration: 1898, 1899, 1900, 1910, and 1913. The publishing record of the Hebrew original is less impressive but nonetheless significant: six editions in the eighty years between the Zolkiew edition of 1802 and the Warsaw edition of 1882.[59]

Following the Yiddish translators of *Shevet yehudah,* Russian-Jewish writers and publicists read the history of Iberian Jewry according to their own contemporary lights. At the turn of the century, they produced an impressive body of popular Yiddish and Hebrew writing, which included translations — heavily edited — of German-Jewish historical novels and scholarship on the subject, as well as their own Iberian romances.[60] This kind of work moved easily between various outposts of the Russian-Jewish diaspora. In 1899 the subtitle of a Yiddish "historical-scientific novel" about the Spanish-American War pronounced the American victory the "Jewish revenge for the Spanish Inquisition." This masterpiece was not published in New York but in Warsaw.[61]

Nicholaevan conscription inspired direct and specific references to the Inquisition, primarily in Russian-Jewish autobiographies. Antokol'skii's conscription letter referred to the "heartrending" episodes he witnessed, comparable only to those which struck a person when "reading about the times when the Jews and Moors were being chased from Spain."[62] Zunser, who also compared Nicholas to Titus and Antiochus selling "thousands of Jewish children into slavery" and to Pharoah "tossing Jewish children into the Nile," invoked the "Inquisition burning hundreds in the fires of its *autos-da-fe.*"[63] Dubnow and Lipschitz fully exploited the narrative possibilities implicit in the comparison between Nicholas's cantonist system and the Inquisition, and in the casting of Jewish recruits in the role of modern *marranos*. The correlation offered a useful conceptual framework for understanding the evolution, flowering, and dispersion of Eastern European Jewry. The choice to stress different aspects of the comparison between Iberian and Russian Jewish history depended on the etiology of "expulsion" that informed the writing of comprehensive history.

In the histories of Lipschitz and Dubnow, the Nicholaevan reign formed a liminal point between the "medieval" pre-reform period (which, in Dubnow's case, included the "golden age" of the Polish-Lithuanian Commonwealth) and the problematic creation of modern Russian Jews, a process that culminated in the alienation and "expulsion" of Russian Jewry in 1914–1919. Here the modern "assimilated" Russian Jew played the role of the *converso*, ambivalently placed between the Russian state and Russian Jewry. The figure of the *converso* exemplified the risks and temptations of emancipation from Judaism, a self-evidently secular ideal that Dubnow and Lipschitz rejected in favor of a conservative "Jewish" position.[64]

Echoing the traditional trope that Israel's destroyers lodged within its own bosom, Lipschitz blamed emancipated Jews for the loss of the "holy community" of Russian Jewry. The recruits — *marranos* — preserved what modern Russian Jews — *conversos* — sought to destroy. Dubnow was more ambivalent about emancipation. His *History* was based on a radical variant of the maskilic argument that the goals of Jewish Enlightenment, that is, the collective reconstruction of Russian Jewry, ought to be anterior to the quest for emancipation, a goal which, Dubnow insisted, should be pursued in the name of communal self-rule.[65] Dubnow blamed the Russian government rather than Russia's home-grown *conversos* for the fate of Russian Jewry; the programmatic attack on the Russian state does not, however, make his *History* any more secular than the Orthodox history written by Lipschitz.[66] For Dubnow, deeply sympathetic to the maskilic populism of Abramovich, the solitary conscience of the Russian-Jewish *converso* exemplified the "tragic conflict" of selective (rather than collective) integration.[67] In his *History*, the joint martyrdom of the cantonists — in contrast to conscription literature that focused on the fate of individual recruits — presented a foil for the image of "Russian assimilationists" as political apostates, their "separatism" the inevitable result of misplaced faith in the benevolence of gentiles.

Here is what Dubnow had to say about "cases of demonstrative martyrdom" in cantonist ranks:

> One such incident has survived in popular memory. The story goes that during a military parade in the city of Kazan' the battalion chief drew up all the Jewish cantonists on the banks of the river where the Greek-Orthodox priests were standing in their vestments and all was ready for the baptismal ceremony, At the command to jump into the water, the boys answered in military fashion "Aye, aye!" Whereupon they dived under and disappeared. When they were dragged out they were dead. In most cases, however, the little martyrs suffered and died noiselessly, in the gloom of the guardhouses, barracks, and military hospitals. With their tiny bodies they strewed the roads that led into the outlying regions of the empire and those that managed to get there were fading away slowly in the barracks which had been turned into *inquisitorial dungeons*. This martyrdom of children, set in a military environment, represents a singular phenomenon even in the extensive annals of Jewish martyrology.[68]

The section on "military martyrdom" directly preceded a section devoted to the "policy of expulsion" which dealt with the government's periodic efforts — largely unsuccessful, as it turned out — to align the general estate classification of the Jews as urban dwellers more closely with social reality by making all Jews register as residents of towns. This measure was often accompanied by the administrative "expulsion" of so-called village Jews, that is, those who occupied an interstitial position as middlemen between peasants and the local marketplace. Official acts of expulsion did not necessarily lead to actual expulsion; the government continued to insist that village Jews cease "exploiting" the peasants, because such decrees could not be enforced. In fact, the narrative link between martyrdom and expulsion derived less from history than from the comparison of the Russian-Jewish predicament with the choice between "inquisitorial dungeon" and "expulsion" that Jews presumably faced in 1492. Conscription literature enabled and informed Dubnow's typological model. In "Family Candlestick," Rabinovich had similarly employed the ironic juxtaposition of the "military martyrdom" of the Malkins — Nicholas's Jewish soldiers — with the subsequent expulsion of their wives from Nikolaev, the city of Nicholas.

Indeed, the incident Dubnow himself ascribed to Jewish "popular memory" began and ended as literature. Dubnow here presented an embellished version of a story that circulated in the 1840s, of 800 Jewish recruits chased into the river for conversion, two of whom drowned themselves rather than undergo baptism. First reported in 1845 in the German-Jewish *Allgemeine Zeitung des Judentums,* this single published version of the incident failed to mention what happened to the other 798 recruits. The story took hold in its imaginative retelling by the minor German-Jewish lyric poet, Ludwig Wihl (1807–1882) in his 1847 poem, "The Two Sailors" (Ger. "Die beiden Matrosen"). Dubnow read the entire account, including Wihl's poem, in *Evreiskaia starina* in 1909.[69] Wihl had set the poem in Odessa, where Nicholas I was supposedly inspecting his fleet, and pointedly distinguished the two martyrs for their individual "faith and honor." Dubnow blithely changed the mise-en-scène to Kazan' and included all 800 recruits in the mass drowning. As the remainder of the passage makes clear, Dubnow envisioned the entire cantonist system as a slow death, a general "fading away" into martyrdom. Here the Russian state doubled for the Orthodox Church; the characterization of military barracks as "inquisitorial dungeons" established the durable medievalism of the autocracy just as the image of the martyred recruits mirrored the exemplary medievalism of Russian Jewry. In the age of dispersion, their collective self-sacrifice signified the persistence of the body of Israel.

Thanks to Dubnow, the image of mass conversion in cantonist ranks entered Jewish history as a paradigmatic Jewish "response" to Nicholaevan conscription. David Shimoni (1886–1956) again contributed to the story in 1934, in a narrative poem called *The Gift* (Heb. *Doron*).[70] The "legend" subsequently reappeared, with only the barest of qualifiers as to its literary provenance, in two distinguished scholarly histories of Russian Jewry, Louis Greenberg's *The Jews of Russia* and Salo Baron's *The Russian Jew under Tsars and Soviets.*[71] In fact, both historians, carried away by the symbolic possibilities, further enhanced the story with the detail (possibly borrowed from Shimoni whom they do not cite) that the baptism by death took place in the Volga, that is, in the mother of all Russian rivers, identified with the country in the same way that the Rhine functions as a metonym for the Jewish communities of medieval Germany. Wihl's sailors had, by contrast, drowned in the "unwelcoming Black Sea" (Ger. *unheimlich schwarzem Meere*); Dubnow omitted this detail altogether. In fact, there is more than one body of water in Kazan' and more than one river, so there was no reason, either for Greenberg or Baron, to assume that the story took place on the banks of the Volga; they either made it up (which would be quite a coincidence) or picked it up from Shimoni.

The line between history and literature blurs in a number of ways; the entire story strains credibility and begs the question of continuing, ostensibly secular, interest in enshrining the fate of Russian Jewry by reference to the "extensive annals of Jewish martyrology." The Department of Military

Settlements (DMS) did not record any cases of mass suicide as a form of resistance to conversion. This is striking, given that the DMS demanded and received a strict accounting of the numbers of Jewish recruits, baptized or not, from every battalion. When cantonists—Jewish and non-Jewish—died in the ranks, the loss to state property counted heavily against the local command. Most tellingly, there were not even close to eight hundred Jewish recruits in any single regiment, and conversion numbers were, per unit, very low.[72] Strategies of resistance proved far more complicated and idiosyncratic, and yielded stories of survival rather than epic tales of martyrdom. These appeared in cantonist autobiographies on the pages of *Evreiskaia starina* but nowhere in Dubnow's *History*.

The task of rehabilitating individual recruits as exemplary Jews in the age of impiety— *marranos* in the age of conversion —fell to Lipschitz. Invested in reconstituting the authority of rabbis and religious leaders in the Russian-Jewish diaspora, Lipschitz turned the experience of cantonists in exile to account as a model of traditional Jewish institution building on inhospitable, alien ground. Lipschitz was similarly concerned with combating the maskilic critique of a corrupt Jewish oligarchy engaged in the nefarious practice of hiring *khappers* and recruiting the children of the poor out of turn. These indictments of Jewish leadership, along with the accusation that rabbis stood idly by and did nothing to alleviate the exploitation of the widow and the orphan, appeared regularly both in conscription stories and in maskilic autobiographies. Here is a characteristic example from Katsnelson's *What My Eyes Have Seen*. He puts the damning accusation in the mouth of his grandmother, highlighting the contrast between the virtue of Jewish mothers and the venality of Jewish patriarchy. These *khappers,* she says, were hardly "Amalekites and Philistines."

> To our shame and humiliation, my son, the *khappers* were all Jews, Jews with beards and side locks. And this is our great misfortune. Jews have made their peace with all the troubles and evil decrees the gentiles heap upon us; we are, after all, in exile. And it is written in the holy books that, in earlier days, they would come upon us, holding a cross in one hand and a knife in the other, and say: "Kiss the cross, cursed Jews, or die." And the Jews would stretch forth their necks for slaughter and refuse to convert. All this it is possible to understand, for then, too, we were in exile. But now, Jews come, pious Jews with beards and side locks and kidnap Jewish children and give them over to be converted—and this is a punishment not listed even among the Bible's list of the greatest curses. Jews spilling the blood of their brothers, and God sits silent in heaven and the rabbis sit silent down here.[73]

Katsnelson sees the internal corruption of Jewish unity as a distinctly modern phenomenon, one that resulted in discrediting traditional leadership and opened the door to the institutionalization of the Haskalah. In Lipschitz's revisionist account, the experience of conscription actually bolstered Jewish piety and contributed to what might be called the Jewish colonization of Siberia. There are no *khappers,* here and all rabbis appear as benevolent figures aiding Jewish cantonists in keeping the faith.

Lipschitz explicitly introduced his account of conscription—titled "Sea of Tears"—by reference to Dubnow's work, to the sources in *Evreiskaia starina* and to the image of the Inquisition. Dubnow, he says, correctly asserted that this terrible chapter in the history of Israel, that is, the fate of the cantonists, has yet to find its historian. Everything we know about this "Inquisition" comes from literature (Heb. *helek beletristi*). The time has come to put forth the historical "documents" that would bear out the literary picture, "fact for fact." But then Lipschitz does something very strange: he places the entire section in the mouth of an "eyewitness," supposedly the beadle of the synagogue of Irkutsk, Isaac-Zvi Brodotskii, who "collected" the primary sources at the request of Lipschitz himself.[74] Brodotskii is actually the fictional alter ego of S. Beilin, amateur ethnographer and the crown rabbi of Irkutsk who was known to Lipschitz only as a name appended to some of the articles Beilin submitted to *Evreiskaia starina.* The historian here functions merely as the neutral conduit of information. The technique of self-distancing makes Lipschitz appear impartial and detached, rendering the entire account the product of first-person ethnographic reportage—with footnotes from *Evreiskaia starina.*

Lipschitz's imaginary informant provides a description of his own congregation composed mostly, it seems, of former cantonists, "*marranos* [Heb. *anusim*] who were compelled to abandon the faith of their fathers, but their being registered [as Christians] was surely a fiction, recognized as such even in official circles" (205). Lipschitz refers to a nonexistent "law"—passed by Alexander II—and "special permission" that supposedly allowed cantonists to return to the Jewish fold. This explains how all the various recruits who appeared on the pages of *Evreiskaia starina* gathered openly as rehabilitated Jewish penitents (Heb. *ba'alei teshuvah*) and respectable householders (Heb. *ba'alei batim*) under the roof of Brodotskii's "congregation" in Irkutsk. What follows is a composite communal "biography" lifted directly, sometimes with citations, from materials in the journal. The cantonists as they appear in *Zikhron ya'akov,* particularly Itskovich and Merimzon, are virtually unrecognizable.

Itskovich—who, according to his autobiography, sought to reclaim his Jewishness independently—here journeys to Liady, to visit the local *rebbe,* in 1876, at the request of his aging mother. This meeting makes such a profound impression on him that his "fear of Heaven" completely effaces his fear of the military authorities. Empowered by Alexander's "special law" that granted cantonists the right to return to Judaism (there was, we recall, no such law), Itskovich stands up to the Orthodox priest—a foil for the Liady *tsaddik*—and publicly abjures his conversion. Now, "Brodotskii" reports, Itskovich counts himself "among the most important and the most honored members of the [Jewish] community" (207). This happy ending is pure fiction; there is no sign of it in Itskovich's own story in *Evreiskaia starina*. Tellingly, its "source" is an oral report, ostensibly received directly from the mouth of Itskovich himself; "Brodotski" does not supply page numbers from the journal. A similar transformation occurs in the revision of Merimzon's autobiography. "Brodotskii" cuts off the narrative before its ambivalent ending. All we get is the happy reunion between the newly pious Jew and his loving parents. The letter about the ruble is left out and replaced with a sentimental scene of mutual forgiveness for the initial lack of recognition (213).

"Brodotskii" concludes his report with an "object lesson" (Heb. *musar heskel*) for the young. The cantonists, he says, are a living example of Jewish fortitude in "holding fast" to the Torah and to "our traditional piety" (Heb. *datenu ha-mesorah*), an allusion to Lipschitz's model of Jewish Orthodoxy. This is hardly an ideal, confined to the expression of the spirit of Judaism; rather, the synagogue and Jewish society function in tandem as the clearing houses of Jewish consciousness. Jewish leadership restores the lost sons to their fathers. The mediation of "Brodotskii" is instrumental to the construction of Jewish Irkutsk, filled with former cantonists, now loyal Jews, as a model community for other outposts of the Russian-Jewish diaspora. Some of them, grown rich in the hinterland, even send money back to their birthplace in the former Pale of Settlement (205). This fantasy is strangely reminiscent of the philanthropic activity of American Jews on behalf of dispossessed Russian-Jewish refugees during the First World War. Jewish Irkutsk, Russia's northern frontier, thus provides a model for the outreach of the New World, now charged directly not just with zealous Jewish observance but with the work of rebuilding religious life back home in Eastern Europe. Lipschitz's providential vision of the Russian-Jewish diaspora alludes to 1492, a precedent for depicting the enabling violation of "expulsion" as a vehicle of colonization, of the diffusion and reinforcement of Jewish piety and community abroad.

Whatever the religious virtues of Jewish Irkutsk, it seems that they did not stem from the stalwart faith of Jewish cantonists. It is true that there was a soldiers' synagogue in Irkutsk, but it was built and used by adult Jewish servicemen who were expressly permitted to worship publicly and were never subject to conversionary pressure in the ranks. In fact, as of 1839, the cantonist battalion of Irkutsk did not register any Jews entering regular army service; Nicholas I issued special instructions to the Department of Military Settlements not to send Jewish cantonists there.[75] As for soldiers being part of the local community, the Jewish merchants of Irkutsk, the pious *ba'alei batim*, wanted apparently nothing to do with them and in 1859 petitioned (unsuccessfully) the Russian authorities to build their own house of worship in the city.[76]

In the cases of Lipschitz and Dubnow, the Iberian paradigm inflected the writing of conscription history; it served as a highly suggestive metaphor that shaped the structure of explanation at the level of composition. In the case of Ginsburg, the homology actually determined the research agenda. Ginsburg, unlike Lipschitz and Dubnow, attempted to provide a coherent account of the political history of the cantonist regiments as an institution, based not only on Jewish literary sources and memoirs but on original archival research. After a careful study of the documents of the Holy Synod (the ruling body of the Russian Orthodox Church), Ginsburg concluded that government policy, a "predetermined, strictly thought-out system, dictated from above and implemented in an extremely orderly and methodical fashion" produced its "rapid" successes in converting Jewish recruits thanks to "measures" that went unmentioned in the official documents.[77] The documents, Ginsburg said, expressed only the "poetry" of the parade foreground; the "prose" that appeared behind the scenes apparently could not be discerned in the archives.[78] In fact, archival documents, unlike Jewish sources, were full of the "prose" that bedeviled the bureaucrats of the Nicholaevan military establishment. Intended for internal consumption within the bureaucratic establishment, they testified precisely to what went on behind the scenes. By contrast, Jewish cantonists had been visible onstage, as heroes of Jewish "poetry" throughout the imperial period.

Ginsburg's insistence that the real story lay somewhere between the lines of his own government documents effectively discredited the potential usefulness of any non-Jewish sources because of their Christian "conversionary" agenda. The problem, however, lay not in the bias of the sources but in Ginsburg's own angle of vision. Jewish cantonists belonged to the history of the Russian military; Jewish writing had integrated them into the history of Christian persecution, by way of the Iberian precedent. Ginsburg, looking for the Russian version of the fruitful alliance between the Catholic Church and the Spanish monarchy, went to the Holy Synod rather than the state's own military archive, a trove of documents that has recently yielded a radically different picture of the conversion process than the one Ginsburg painted in his essay.[79]

In Ginsburg's account, the Church appears as a partner with the Orthodox state, dedicated to the sole purpose of converting as many Jews in the ranks as possible, of wiping out "Jewish heresy" entirely. In fact, the Synod played virtually no independent role in Nicholaevan policy vis-à-vis the conversion of Jewish cantonists. Higher church authorities did not interfere on their own initiative, did not set the religious agenda, and did not make the work of conversion any easier. In fact, the theologically informed resistance to forced baptism and the insistence on proper form had the effect of retarding mass conversions and, in specific cases, tempering the zeal of regimental priests. The Synod, furthermore, enjoyed no "inquisitorial" powers over converted recruits; all cases of reversion from Orthodoxy were handled in-house, by the military establishment itself, as breaches of military discipline.

Ginsburg's suspicion of the "poetry" of synodal documents confirmed the Jewish image of cantonists as "child-martyrs." Just as Dubnow vastly overstated the cantonists' collective resistance to the state's efforts to convert them, Ginsburg overestimated the state's capacity to enforce or even clearly articulate its own conversionary agenda. Like Dubnow and Lipschitz, Ginsburg made no room for the possibility that the story of Jewish recruitment under Nicholas I could be placed in a secular context, which arguably might have made the story worse rather than better. The catalogue of horrors and indignities undoubtedly suffered by Jewish children in the Nicholaevan army — as well as by their non-Jewish counterparts and, indeed, by anyone subject to the draconian punishment and mind-numbing regimentation of the Russian military in the pre-reform period — actually defies its medieval Jewish precedent. Nicholas's intense investment in the militarization of everyday life owed a great deal to the Petrine revolution; both monarchs saw themselves as radical and uncompromising modernizers from above. The problem, for both Russians and Jews, was precisely that under the reforming Romanovs the experience of modernity could be simultaneously registered as a social catastrophe and as unprecedented opportunity for self-transformation. This is a point more readily evident in conscription literature than in conscription history, which, at least until recently, has consistently embraced the normative view of Nicholaevan persecution proffered in the diaspora narratives of Dubnow, Ginsburg, and Lipschitz.[80]

The histories of Dubnow, Lipschitz, and Ginsburg rendered normative the image of a confrontation between Russian Jewry, primed for martyrdom, and an all-powerful Russian government bent on its destruction. Just as in 1492, the only alternative to this scenario lay in emigration. Once more, the New World beckoned and became the outpost of a Jewish community in exile. Thus the reliance on a traditional narrative paradigm served to normalize the contemporary dispersion of Russian Jewry in the interwar period. The example of the Sefardic diaspora made it possible to argue that there was such a thing as Russian-Jewish consciousness outside the Russian Empire, now defunct. Hence the appeal of the idea of Russian Jew as *marrano* and the notion that Nicholas's mission to Jewish cantonists was an inquisition, a trial which, in fact, strengthened the attachment of Russian Jews to the collective identity of Russian Jewry. Such controlling fictions proved especially important to émigré historians like Dubnow, Lipschitz, and Ginsburg, who personally experienced the collective dispersion of imperial Russian Jewry.[81]

The normative reading emerged at a time when the line between emigration and expulsion grew blurry, and when the process of leaving became especially wrenching because there was no longer a Pale of Settlement to which one could return. Indeed, the very pious Lipschitz, the cultural diasporist Dubnow, and the Russian-Jewish liberal Ginsburg remained ideologically bound to a past that seemed more disconnected than ever from the political reality of postwar Jewish lives. Characteristically the memory of conscription continued to play a greater cultural role in the Russian-Jewish diaspora, explicitly constituted by its link to the imperial past, than among Russian Jews who increasingly embraced a Soviet future.[82]

THE LAST CANTONIST ON RUSSIAN SOIL

In 1915–1916 the former Social Revolutionary S. An-sky (Shlomo-Zanvil Rapoport, 1863–1920), leading member of the Jewish Historical-Ethnographic Society, folklorist, playwright, author of *The Dybbuk,* and chronicler of the wartime destruction of Galicia, wrote the last original conscription tale to appear in imperial Russia.[83] "Two Martyrs" (Yid. *Tsvey martirer*), a minor masterpiece of the short-story form, winds the entire history of conscription writing into a tight narrative skein.[84] Based on the juxtaposition of two parallel life histories — that of the old Nicholaevan soldier Gershon Falk and that of his great-grandson, the Russian university student Mel'nikov — the story appropriates the normative image of the cantonist as martyr in the service of a radical critique of the modern Russian Jew. A brilliant exercise in intertextual comedy, An-sky's conscription *midrash* misreads every cliché that shaped the lachrymose treatment of Russian Jewry's pre-reform past. In "Two Martyrs," An-sky's irrepressibly ironic imagination finds expression in a hilarious parody of conscription literature as Jewish history. The maskil here returns to have the last laugh.

Gershon Falk, with his overdetermined name and his twenty-three children, is the ultimate cantonist as folk hero. His last name, Falk, indicates that he is a man of the people. His first name which starts with *ger,* the Hebrew word for the resident stranger or convert to Judaism, registers his ambiguous relationship to Jewish society. There could be no better name for a cantonist who survives in the ranks as a Jew. His "Slavic" appearance and his "sharp, loud" way of speaking renders him large in every way; the narrator avers that his "entire life" has been lived "on a grand scale." Even his reproductive capacities are nothing short of heroic. By the age of ninety, when the narrator meets him, not only are Falk's mental and physical faculties entirely intact but he is father to twenty-three children, more than a hundred grandchildren, and a score of great-grandchildren. He is also a Russian pioneer, who journeys to Siberia in search of a Jewish wife and amasses a fortune, which likewise turns on the epic amount of half a million rubles.

At the same time Falk's autobiography rehearses every detail of the typical cantonist life. A sickly, precocious son of a poor schoolteacher, twelve-year-old Falk is taken by *khappers* at night, out of bed and out of his mother's arms. Before being dragged off to be conscripted, he swears to his father that he will remain a Jew, no matter what. While undergoing all the horrors of life in the ranks, he passes every test of faith (Yid. *nisyonos*). In Gershon Falk, the pre-reform Russian army meets its match. Standing before an old general, who inquires whether he is still a Jew, Falk replies that he would not convert under any circumstances. The general admits that he has been bested and praises him, for a "man who remains true to his God will surely remain true to his emperor." The other cantonists, hearing of this "legendary" encounter, imagine that the old general must have been an incarnation of Elijah the prophet himself. Falk emerges from the army a "victor," doubly strengthened in both body and soul.

The "fantastic" times of Gershon Falk take place against the background of conscription history *tout court*. In Gershon's regiment, the cantonists undergo every one of the torments catalogued in conscription literature and on the pages of *Evreiskaia starina;* even the story of the double drowning makes its appearance here. The crowning touch, however, is the reference to Vyatka, where Falk supposedly settles as a "rich man" (Yid. *gvir*). Why Vyatka, as opposed to any other obscure town deep in the Russian interior? I think that this detail is a deliberately provocative allusion to the famous impression of Jewish cantonists that the Russian writer and radical Alexander Herzen recorded in his memoirs while on his way to provincial exile in Vyatka. Ever since it first appeared in Gessen's *History* in 1914, this passage has been regularly cited in virtually every historical treatment of Jewish conscription under Nicholas I:

> They brought the children and formed them into regular ranks; it was one of the most awful sights I have ever seen, those poor, poor children! Boys of twelve or thirteen might somehow have survived it, but little fellows of eight and ten . . . Not even a brush full of black paint could put such horror on canvas.
>
> Pale, exhausted, with frightened faces, they stood in thick, clumsy, soldiers' overcoats, with stand-up collars, fixing helpless, pitiful eyes on the garrison soldiers who were roughly getting them into ranks. The white lips, the blue rings under the eyes, bore witness to fever or chill. And these sick children, without care or kindness, exposed to the raw wind that blows unobstructed from the Arctic Ocean, were going to their graves.[85]

The ghostly image of the near-dead Jewish children that Herzen saw near Vyatka stands in marked contrast to the irrepressible liveliness of An-sky's Falk, a grown-up Jewish cantonist who most emphatically does *not* get blown away by the north wind of the Arctic Ocean. All of Falk's own children and grandchildren are very much alive and have made it as "doctors, lawyers, engineers."

The exaggerated—Bakhtinian—depiction of the cantonist as the comic embodiment of the people's inexhaustible capacity for life mocks the theatrical affect of the "weepy" picture painted by Herzen, who is demonstratively unable to "master his sobbing" at the sight of the Jewish recruits.[86] An-sky's Falk is a robust Rabelaisian hero who turns Jewish history upside down. One of his heirs has recently resurfaced in contemporary Russian literature:

> You know, [writes Dina Rubina in her short story "Our Chinese Affair"] there were a lot of cantonists who arrived among the refugees from Siberia. These were people who had been around the block, coarse, with loud voices. I remember once, on Simhat-torah, they had to carry the Torah around the *bimah* — they gave the job of carrying the scroll to an old cantonist, a great honor, by the way. And someone asked him, won't it be too heavy? And he was so offended, started yelling, "I carried cannon on my back! What — I can't lift this shit?"[87]

The recourse to profanity signifies the cantonist's preternatural "coarseness" and strength. In this context, the reference to the Torah as "shit" transforms it into a symbol of Jewish vitality, an echo of the more traditional description of Scripture, embodied in the phallic object of the scroll, as the "tree of life" (Heb. *'etz hayyim*); the comparison with the similarly phallic "cannon" here underscores the power of Jewish embodiment. The image comes from a verse in Psalms, which, incidentally, appears precisely in that portion of the liturgy collectively intoned at the moment the scroll is lifted and carried around the synagogue. As in An-sky's story, the figure of the cantonist initiates the radical transvaluation of Jewish values; he turns the celebration of scriptural renewal into carnival, a demonstration not of figurative spiritual power of Jewish suffering but of actual physical endurance and masculine might.

A radical contrast to the figure of his great-grandfather, the student Mel'nikov is a typical bespectacled *intelligent* who bears no physical resemblance to his ancestor. His name, which comes from the Russian word *mel'nitsa*, or "windmill," implies that he is full of nothing, a bag of air, and a Jewish *luftmensch*. Unlike his grandfather, he is rooted nowhere and merely blows along; he is, in fact, a version of Herzen's Jewish weakling in danger from the northern Russian wind. His story, appended to the heroic tale of his great-grandfather, is distinctly modern, set in St. Petersburg, the contemporary Russian North, where ambitious young Jews, emancipated from the Jewish community, come to seek their fortune.

Unable to gain admission to the university because of quota restrictions, Mel'nikov, along with a number of other enterprising Jewish students, travels to Finland (this is obviously a parody of his grandfather's northern journey), where, for a sum, he can technically "convert" to Christianity. He escapes his Jewish origins and enrolls at the university, only to be unmasked as a false Christian; the Holy Synod does not recognize his new status, and the authorities expel him and deprive him of his temporary privilege of living in the capital.

Mel'nikov's tale of woe smolders with irony. When the narrator tells him of his earlier acquaintance with Falk, Mel'nikov comments that "suffering from Judaism" (Yid. *fun yidishkeit*) runs in their family. The narrator parries that Falk "suffered for Judaism" (Yid. *far yidishkeit*), but the distinction appears lost on Mel'nikov. What is going on here? Mel'nikov's weak-kneed, ethical failure plainly echoes the theme of the degeneration of emancipated Jewish youth, which is a common trope of the conscription story as a maskilic critique of emancipation. The association between university attendance and residential privileges brings this point home. It is not clear what Mel'nikov is supposed to be studying and whether he has anything but a superficial intellect, a Jewish accessory like his glasses, which, in fact, do not help him see anything at all. As a vehicle of getting ahead and beyond (the Pale), university attendance has been divorced from education. Mel'nikov, missing the great lesson of his great-grandfather's life which the narrator offers him at the end, points to the unbridgeable gap between enlightenment and emancipation; for An-sky, the latter represents both the beginning and the end of modern Jewish history. It is not a coincidence that the other person who misses the point of the narrator's distinction is a Jewish attorney and a staunch defender of Jews' rights before the Duma. An-sky reduces parliamentary advocacy to Jewish special pleading; like Mel'nikov, the lawyer cannot see the forest for the trees. They are both Jewish provincials lodging in St. Petersburg, narrow, petty minds masquerading as modern cosmopolitans. If Falk is larger than life, they are much, much smaller.

Neither of An-sky's "two martyrs" qualifies for the role. The title invokes Wihl's "two sailors," the Jewish pair whose baptism-turned-martyrdom manifests the continuity between modern Russian-Jewish history and the sacred tradition of Jewish death for the sake of the Name (Heb. *kidush ha-shem*). An-sky pulls down the entire typological house of cards. The problem with Mel'nikov is not that he looks nothing like his great-grandfather; this is only the impression he makes on the narrator. In fact, they are exactly alike, because they are, as Jews, entirely self-made in Russian institutions — the military and the university. Their analogical — rather than genealogical — relationship is evident in the structure of the story, which positions them side by side. They are both tricksters, fully at home in what Daniel Boyarin calls the "empire as brothel," where clever "rabbis" successfully dodge temptation rather than face death by persecution.[88] Falk's final test before the old general resolves in a comic bit of rabbinical sophistry that reveals the mysterious presence of the messianic herald Elijah. Falk achieves this feat by dissembling, that is, by acting the part, perfectly, of the obedient Russian soldier:

> "Are you a Jew?"
> "Yes, sir, a Jew, your Excellency!" [Falk] answers in a ringing tone.
> "And you will not convert under any circumstances?"
> "No, your Excellency, not under any circumstances!"[89]

The entire exchange is an act of profound Jewish insubordination masking as submission. Not only does it "fool" the general, it also ushers in the messiah.

Mel'nikov's false conversion is similarly the act of a trickster; he finds a loophole in the law which allows him to dissemble an act of apostasy without actually becoming a Christian. Like his great-grandfather, he puts one over on the Russian authorities, precisely by faking his surrender to the imperial confessional hierarchy. Why, then, does he fail where Falk succeeds? I think that Mel'nikov's conspicuous impotence is a sign of anxiety, the fear that the mock-heroic age of Gershon Falk has come to an end. With emancipation, Jewish trickery is reduced to tax evasion. No longer is Jewish cultural survival at stake but, instead, mere survival of the Jew as citizen of the modern trickster state, itself full of Jewish lawyers. This reading is actually implicit in Mel'nikov's identity: the "windmill" man is none other than a Jewish Don Quixote tilting at the windmills of the Russian bureaucracy. If Falk is a real Jewish champion (Rus. *bogatyr'*) who is fully at home in the pre-reform, epic age of Jewish chivalry, then his heir has to be his ironic double, a deluded modern knight who tragically "misreads" his grandfather's story.

In An-sky's imaginary universe, such trivial acts of misprision have catastrophic consequences.[90] The nonending of the story is, in effect, the ominous sign of apocalypse, an inversion of the messianic conclusion of Falk's own story. The final moment of aporia between great-grandfather and grandson cannot be resolved. In the end, there are not "two" of anything in this story, no meeting of the minds; each of the "martyrs" stands alone. The failure of communication between the generations actually refracts the failure of Jewish literature first conceived, we remember, to bring the hearts of the sons back to their fathers. "Two Martyrs" short-circuits the normative impulse in modern Jewish culture. The only martyrdom in "Two Martyrs" is the death of the narrative paradigm that historian Salo Baron called the "lachrymose" conception of Jewish history, marshaled by anxious nineteenth-century enlighteners in defense of Jewish consciousness against the secular effects of emancipation.[91]

But the potentially messianic finale of Falk's career as a "child-martyr" points to an alternative mode of Jewish writing altogether. Here An-sky offers the possibility of a Jewish counter-narrative under the ironic sign of play. Inherent in his displacement of the martyrological paradigm is a carnivalesque inversion of established social and political categories that govern both sides of the Jewish-Christian dialectic. Martyrdom, whether it involves the public killing of Jews or of Christians, is fundamentally a Christian event, rooted in the formative moment of the new faith; it enters into Jewish discourse precisely as a transformative act of cultural appropriation, a self-conscious critique of Christianity on its own terms.[92] However, even within the tradition that apotheosized the rabbi-martyrs Haninah and Akiva, there are traces of resistance to the rhetorical Christianization of Jewishness, to the erasure of the Jewish body in the name of the Name. These emerge in the Bakhtinian celebration of the rabbis as tricksters, "gargantuan," preternaturally embodied Jewish supermen with enormous appetites, infinitely prolific minds, and endlessly generative phalluses.[93] In the figure of Gershon Falk, An-sky presents the cantonist as rabbinic *homo ludens,* an enlightened Jewish "folk hero."[94] Born of maskilic longing for power and potency, the last cantonist on Russian soil represents a fantastic mirror image of the Jewish writer as explorer, entrepreneur, and escape artist.

CONCLUSION

Driven by the tension between emancipation and enlightenment, history and story offered two distinct ways of integrating the Russian-Jewish present into the longue durée of the Jewish past. While conscription tales radically compressed the gap between the former and the latter in order to bring the future into view, conscription history integrated the fits and starts of modern Russian-Jewish life into the durable mythology of the *galut*. The writing of conscription tales registered the apocalyptic inclination in Jewish history; the writing of conscription history, on the other hand, reflected the more dominant normative strain. The idea of a modern Russian-Jewish apocalypse, the death and imminent rebirth of the Jewish people in the benighted East of Europe, derived its vocabulary expressly from the fictions of Abramovich and its rhetorical force from the almost instant appropriation of the pogrom as a painful sign of collective and personal awakening.

The apocalyptic embrace of anti-Jewish violence, linked dialectically to the political and cultural miracle of the Hebrew Renaissance, emerged against the background of an idealized and objectified — read, dead — epic past, untouched by the vagaries of emancipation. At the heart of the maskilic discovery of nationalism, ambivalence about the dangers of "unserfment" reasserted itself in the analysis of pogroms as the failure of modernity. The specter of Alexandrine freedom dispelled by the conservative logic of nationalism, the ghost of Nicholas I returned to haunt any Jew who might be tempted, as it were, to misread the evidence of pogroms and pursue the promise of emancipation. This is, in fact, what happened; for all the sense of crisis cultivated in the nationalist revival, the pogroms failed to stem the tide of Jewish ambition for education, economic security, professional status, and civic privileges.

In the post-pogrom period, the Nicholaevan recruit rose to become a moral fetish of the nationalist imagination. His suffering represented the posture of heroic resistance against the material blandishments of emancipation, while his death became linked to the post-emancipation revelation of modern Jewish conscience. The Nicholaevan moment, pregnant with the possibility of creating a modern Russian Jewry by autocratic fiat, foregrounded the bloody auto-emancipation of the Jewish nation by a trans-historical act of collective will in the shadow of Nicholas II. Returning to the originary site of Jewish enlightenment, nationalist writers, in fact, anticipated the final completion of a cultural project abandoned by the maskilim in the throes of emancipation. In their appropriation of enlightenment discourse, nationalist critics planted the seeds of a Jewish reformation at the heart of the Hebrew Renaissance, creating the potential for conflict between ethics and politics that flowered into full-scale debate within the Zionist movement.

The ideological investment in literature as a means of quickening the collective cultural pulse of Russian Jewry linked the nationalists directly to the messianic tenor of the Haskalah, a sensibility that emerged directly out of the short-lived but exceedingly fruitful alliance between Jewish reformers and the Russian government. Israel Aksenfeld, one of the first of the maskilim to see untold promise in the cultural mission of the Nicholaevan state, drew a direct parallel between the political power of the autocracy and the moral force of literature, implicated together in the instant transformation of Russian-Jewish consciousness and the triumph of enlightenment: "We must request," says the hero of Aksenfeld's 1842 Yiddish novel, *The Jeweled Kerchief*, "that the tsar issue an ukase requiring every Jew to be able to read and write. Jews will read the remarkable works of the excellent young Russian writers that we have nowadays and *our whole life will be changed.*"[1] Nationalist criticism of the Haskalah assumed the enlighteners' belief in the transformative potential of literature as well as its disciplinary social vision without the attendant political optimism regarding the inevitable convergence between Jewish and universal time.

The post-emancipation generation of enlighteners — the so-called radical maskilim, many of whom became the founding fathers of Jewish nationalism — adopted an ironic attitude toward history insofar as they experienced directly the disconnect between the aims of enlightenment and the effects of emancipation. The pogroms, a sign of the ultimately tragic paradox of modernity as well as the hidden wellspring of Jewish revival, heightened the sense of irony and led to the embrace of symbolism, the aesthetic expression of the tension between events and their true hidden meaning. The utopian embrace of the future that had characterized maskilic messianism turned darkly apocalyptic. The hidden purpose of Jewish history would be realized through the subversion of enlightened universalism, poised to destroy the Jew precisely by freeing him from Judaism, its promise of emancipation, unmasked in nationalist literature as a cover story for residual Christian triumphalism.

The national revival demanded an act of collective resistance to the historical tide that offered the Russian Jew everything and Russian Jewry nothing. The depiction of the latter as stuck in its benighted pre-reform state, crude and foolish but naturally innocent of the grown-up temptations that turned enlightenment into a vulgar defense of personal desire, provided a model for the heroic posture of confrontation with modernity, assiduously cultivated in nationalist texts. In their own version of the conscription tale, nationalists saw an apocalyptic omen of the radical split between Jewish and universal time which they themselves performed. In fact, the stylized literary celebration of pre-reform authenticity became enshrined as the quintessential expression of Russian-Jewish identity, emblematic of the tragic irony that the nationalist imagination ascribed to the meaning of Russian-Jewish experience as a whole. As we have seen, however, the original paragon of tradition that ostensibly inspired the post-reform drama of return existed nowhere except in the literature of revival, itself a product of the clash between the values of enlightenment and the realities of emancipation. The exceptionally compelling dream of a national future moved the writers of conscription stories to a prophetic embrace of an imagined past.

The integration of conscription into the normative history of Russian Jewry, the writing of which initially flowered in the first two decades of the twentieth century, considerably lowered the temperature of nationalist apocalypticism. In the post-1905 period, the Zionist movement came to political terms with the persistence of diaspora in the midst of exile; in addition, a variety of alternative nationalist ideologies made a historical virtue out of necessity and asserted that Jews constituted a community of destiny with claims to cultural and social autonomy in a new multiethnic Europe. World War I brought to an end the geographic reality of Russian Jewry, fueling the postwar reassertion of confessional identity, on the one hand, and the radical secularization of Jewish life, on the other. Comprehensive histories of Russian Jewry appeared against this background of wartime dispersion, both a reflection of Russian's Jewry's historical absence and the assertion of its continuing cultural relevance as a unifying concept. The disjuncture between a highly differentiated Jewish Eastern Europe and its imaginative reconstruction recalled the previous formative moment in the creation of a modern mythology of exile, the post-1492 re-creation of Sefarad precisely at the moment of its dispersion. The comparison emerged explicitly in the writing of conscription history. Nicholas I was thus recast in the role of Ferdinand, his army the site of the Inquisition of Russian Jewry. In this revision, the latent Jewish consciousness of Nicholaevan recruits came to stand in for the *marrano*-like persistence of Russian-Jewish consciousness. A collective hagiography of cantonists contrasted their living martyrdom with the betrayal of Judaism for the sake of material interests by Russian-Jewish *conversos* whose secular descendants in the Soviet Union were, at that very moment, declaring their faith in the revolution by voluntarily entering the ranks of the Red Army in droves.

Normative histories of conscription shared the same fundamental commitment to the idea of Russian Jewry as a category of historically transcendent significance. Recalling 1492, writers of conscription history placed the experience of Russian Jews into an enduring liturgical framework in which narrative served the reenactment of exile as constitutive of the Jewish past. Every year at the Passover meal, Jews affirm their collective consciousness of exile through repetition: "In every generation our enemies rise up to destroy us," says the Haggadah, demanding the performance of this eternal enmity as a condition of Jewish survival. Straining toward the effacement of the particular, Jewish historical writing retains this kind of liturgical trace even when it employs all the tools of secular scholarship to bring out the accumulated horrors of persecution. In fact, the association with 1492 endowed the conscription tale with iterative force all its own, enabling its invocation as a paradigm of exile. In the 1920s the writers of conscription history were drawn to the analogy with 1492; in the 1950s the conscription story attained the status of an archetype, the communal abuse of government decree marked as a forerunner of Jewish complicity in the Holocaust.[2]

The construction of a normative history, still the regnant mode of Jewish engagement with the past, demands the substitution of analogy for analysis; the former rests on the ritual impact of pattern and repetition, the latter stresses the secular import of the local and the particular. As conscription became the subject of Jewish scholarship — precisely when primary sources from the Nicholaevan period were first collected — it gradually became completely untethered from context and contingency, both from its Nicholaevan origins and from the post-Nicholaevan process of narrative signification. The view of the Pale as the repository of Jewish authenticity, a key trope both in the nationalist apocalypse and in the normative mythology of Russian-Jewish exile, persists in postwar Yiddishland. The figure of the recruit, born under the radical sign of maskilic difference now serves as a free-floating signifier of the biological link to the shtetl, a contemporary marker of Jewish belonging that unites the diehard secular Zionist with the vaguely traditional American Jew and with the pious, black-hatted follower of the Lubavicher *rebbe*. Such tenuous family resemblances conflate modern Judaism in all its forms with the legacy of Eastern Europe. No longer tied to the representation of the gap between Russian Jew and Russian Jewry, the Nicholaevan recruit stands in for an obligatory nod to one's Jewish roots (Yid. *yikhes*), an image emptied of its ambiguous cultural meaning but freighted with genealogical significance. This is why the vernacular memory of conscription remains so intensely personal and so abstract; every Nicholaevan recruit is someone's — anyone's — beloved Jewish grandfather.

The interwar period saw both the displacement of Russian Jews and the destruction of the Pale of Settlement, the ground which, for better and for worse, had nourished the dream of creating modern Russian Jewry. In immigration, Russian-Jewish intellectuals continued to emphasize the importance of the Pale as a place in the mind rather than on the map. Jewish memoirists and historians, often immigrants themselves, enshrined the irrevocable act of departure — geographic, social, psychological, cultural — involved in the process of transmigration in the normative history of Jewish exile where physical displacement signified the stability of a durable existential bond. In their integrative vision, the image of the Nicholaevan recruit became the symbol of the paradoxical link between the dispersion of Russian Jews and the collective identity of Russian Jewry. This, in fact, was what the Nicholaevan recruit had always been, insofar as the contradiction he embodied informed the making of Russian-Jewish memory beginning in the age of the Great Reforms. Certainly the war had rendered the tension all the more acute, particularly since the apocalyptic transformation of Russian-Jewish life that Jewish nationalists had anticipated came unexpectedly on the heels of the Bolshevik Revolution, the most radical experiment in Jewish reform that Russia had seen since the days of Nicholaevan conscription and official enlightenment. Armed with a new ideology, the state had returned with full force into Russian-Jewish lives. The uncanny image of the first Jewish soldier in the Russian army now took on new significance in the first attempt to write an originary mythology of the Jew as *homo sovieticus*. Isaac Babel's *Red Cavalry* bears the traces of conscription literature. But the agony of the destruction of the Pale, and the radical emancipation of Soviet Jewry which followed, effectively displaced the process of enlightenment from the Jewish mind to the Jewish body. Babel saw in the genesis of the Soviet Jew, the birth of secular Jewish manhood, fully empowered by the state (Babel's Jewish Cossack also had a cousin in Palestine). The moral autonomy with which Gordon, Dik, and Bogrov had associated the figure of the recruit was now recast in distinctly corporeal form. As the bearer of revolutionary Jewish consciousness, the foot soldier of the Jewish enlightenment reemerged in the guise of a Soviet commissar.

NOTES

INTRODUCTION

1. On Dublin in particular, see Cormac Ò Gráda, *Jewish Ireland, Gaelic Golus: The Economy and Demography of Irish Jewry, 1870s–1930s* (Princeton, N.J.: Princeton University Press, forthcoming), chap. 1; and David Cesarani, "The Myth of Origins: Ethnic Memory and the Experience of Emigration," in *Patterns of Migration, 1850–1914*, ed. A. Newman and S. W. Massil (London: Jewish Historical Society of England, 1996), 247–254.

2. Kaplan, "Sickness," in *The Schocken Book of Contemporary Jewish Fiction*, ed. Ted Solotaroff and Nessa Rapoport (New York: Schocken Books, 1992), 136–156, here, 145–146. The story was originally published in Kaplan's collection, *Other People's Lives* (1975). Compare two recent children's books: Carol Matas, *Sworn Enemies* (Toronto: HarperCollins, 1993); and M. R. Schur, *The Circlemaker* (New York: Dial Books, 1994).

3. See, most recently, Ruth R. Wisse's provocative *Modern Jewish Canon: A Journey through Language and Culture* (New York: Free Press, 2000).

4. June Levine, in Máirín Johnston, *Dublin Belles: Conversations with Dublin Women* (Dublin: Attic, 1988), 104–111. I am grateful to Cormac Ò Gráda for this reference.

5. See Isaac Baer Levinsohn, *Di hefker-velt* [1828–1830] (Warsaw: Shuldberg, 1902), 33.

6. On the disciplinary role of the commune and of the extended patriarchal family in serving up recruits to the pre-reform army, see Elise Kimerling Wirtschafter, *From Serf to Russian Soldier* (Princeton, N.J.: Princeton University Press, 1990).

7. On the rise of academic historiography, see Peter Novick, *That Noble Dream: The "Objectivity" Question and the American Historical Profession* (Cambridge: Cambridge University Press, 1988); and Georg G. Iggers and James M. Powell, eds., *Leopold von Ranke and the Rise of the Historical Discipline* (Syracuse, N.Y.: Syracuse University Press, 1990). On the various kinds of academic and nonacademic modes of engaging the past, see David Lowenthal, *The Past Is a Foreign Country* (Cambridge: Cambridge University Press, 1985). For an example of the friendly competition between scholars and purveyors of popular history, see Mark C. Carnes, ed., *Past Imperfect: History According to the Movies* (New York: Henry Holt, 1996).

8. The Soviet regime remains notorious for manipulating the historical record in accordance with the demands of the regnant political orthodoxy; see David King,

The Falsification of Photographs and Art in Stalin's Russia (New York: Metropolitan Books, 1997); and Frederick C. Corney, *Telling October: Memory and the Making of the Bolshevik Revolution* (Ithaca, N.Y., and London: Cornell University Press, 2004). For another no less contentious example of historical revisionism, see Deborah E. Lipstadt, *Denying the Holocaust: The Growing Assault on Truth and Memory* (New York: Free Press, 1993).

9. For examples of the former tendency, see Marc Bloch, *The Historian's Craft,* trans. Peter Putnam (New York: Knopf, 1953); E. H. Carr, *What Is History?* (New York: Knopf, 1961); R. G. Collingwood, *The Historical Imagination* (London: Oxford University Press, 1935); and Herbert Butterfield, *Man on His Past: The Study of Historical Scholarship* (Cambridge: Cambridge University Press, 1969). Examples of the latter abound. Lowenthal offers the best survey in *The Past Is a Foreign Country;* see also the pioneering work of Hayden White, *Metahistory: The Historical Imagination in Nineteenth-Century Europe* (Baltimore, Md.: Johns Hopkins University Press, 1973). Studies that touch on the general themes I address in this book include Michael Kammen, *The Mystic Chords of Memory: The Transformation of Tradition in American Culture* (New York: Knopf, 1991); David W. Blight, *Race and Reunion: The Civil War in American Memory* (Cambridge, Mass.: Harvard University Press, 2001); Joep Leerssen, *Remembrance and Imagination: Patterns in the Historical and Literary Representations of Ireland in the Nineteenth Century* (Notre Dame: Notre Dame University Press, 1997); and Cormac Ó Gráda, *Black '47 and Beyond: The Great Irish Famine in History, Economy and Memory* (Princeton, N.J.: Princeton University Press, 1999). In the field of Jewish history specifically, see the pioneering work of Jeremy Cohen, *Sanctifying the Name of God: Jewish Martyrs and Jewish Memories of the First Crusade* (Philadelphia: University of Pennsylvania Press, 2004); Susan L. Einbinder, *Beautiful Death: Jewish Poetry and Martyrdom in Medieval France* (Princeton, N.J., and Oxford: Princeton University Press, 2002); and Nils Roemer, *Jewish Scholarship and Culture in Nineteenth-Century Germany: Between History and Faith* (Madison: University of Wisconsin Press, 2005).

10. Halbwachs, *On Collective Memory,* ed. and trans. Lewis Coser (Chicago: University of Chicago Press, 1992).

11. See, especially, Pierre Nora, ed., *Les lieux de mémoire,* 7 vols. (Paris: Gallimard, 1984); and Eric Hobsbawm and Terence Ranger, eds., *The Invention of Tradition* (Cambridge: Cambridge University Press, 1983). Nora's grand collection has been translated into English: Lawrence Kritzman, ed., *Realms of Memory: Rethinking the French Past,* trans. Arthur Goldhammer, 3 vols. (New York: Columbia University Press, 1996–1998). There is also a mounting specialized literature dealing with the "collective memory" of the two world wars; see, for instance, Jay Winter, *Sites of Memory, Sites of Mourning: The Great War in European Cultural History* (Cambridge: Canto, 1995); and Amir Weiner, *Making Sense of War: The Second World War and the Fate of the Bolshevik Revolution* (Princeton, N.J.: Princeton University Press, 2001).

12. On the contemporary persistence of belief in what the historian Salo W. Baron — who was, in fact, Yerushalmi's teacher at Columbia — first called the "lachrymose" conception of Jewish history among American Jews *despite* evidence of declining anti-Jewish sentiment and activity, see Jerome A. Chanes, "Anti-semitism and Jewish Security in America: Why Can't Jews Take Yes for an Answer?" in *Jews in America: A Contemporary Reader,* ed. Roberta Rosenberg Farber and Chaim I. Waxman (Hanover, N.H., and London: University Press of New England / Brandeis University Press, 1999), 124–150; and Novick, *The Holocaust in American Life* (Boston: Houghton Mifflin, 1999), chap. 9. For a comparative perspective, see John Klier, "The Dog That Didn't Bark: Anti-Semitism in Post-Communist Russia," in *Russian Nationalism, Past and Present,* ed. Geoffrey Hosking and Robert Service (Basingstoke, Hampshire: Macmillan, 1998), 129–147.

13. See Michael Stanislawski, *Tsar Nicholas I and the Jews: The Transformation of*

Jewish Society, 1825–1855 (Philadelphia: Jewish Publication Society, 1983), chap. 4.

14. On the policy of "selective integration," see Benjamin Nathans, *Beyond the Pale: The Jewish Encounter with Late Imperial Russia* (Berkeley, Los Angeles, and London: University of California Press, 2002), chap. 2.

15. On the dramatic social impact of internal peasant migration in the post-emancipation period, see, in general, N. I. Ivanova, "Goroda Rossii," in *Rossiia v nachale XX veka*, ed., A. N. Sakharov et al. (Moscow: Novyi khronograf, 2002), 111–136; B. N. Mironov, *Sotsial'naia istoriia Rossii perioda imperii (XVIII–nachalo XX v.)*, vol. 1 (St. Petersburg: Dmitrii Bulanin, 1999), chaps. 5, 7. See, too, Joseph Bradley, *Muzhik and Muscovite: Urbanization in Late Imperial Russia* (Berkeley: University of California Press, 1985); Jeffrey Burds, *Peasant Dreams and Market Politics: Labor Migration and the Russian Village, 1861–1905* (Pittsburgh: University of Pittsburgh Press, 1998); and Stephen P. Frank, *Crime, Culture, Conflict and Justice in Rural Russia, 1856–1914* (Berkeley: University of California Press, 1999).

16. On various aspects of this debate, see Andrzej Walicki, *The Controversy over Capitalism: Studies in the Social Philosophy of the Russian Populists* (Oxford: Oxford University Press, 1969); Laura Engelstein, *The Keys to Happiness: Sex and the Search for Modernity in Fin-de-Siècle Russia* (Ithaca, N.Y.: Cornell University Press, 1992); Joan Neuberger, *Hooliganism: Crime, Culture and Power in St. Petersburg, 1900–1914* (Berkeley: University of California Press, 1993); Jeffrey Brooks, *When Russia Learned to Read: Literacy and Popular Culture, 1861–1917* (Princeton, N.J.: Princeton University Press, 1985); and Yanni Kotsonis, *Making Peasants Backward: Agricultural Cooperatives and the Agrarian Question in Russia, 1861–1914* (Houndmills: Macmillan, 1999).

17. On the representation of "rural people" in late imperial Russian culture, see Cathy Frierson, *Peasant Icons: Representations of Rural People in Late Nineteenth-Century Russia* (New York: Oxford University Press, 1993); and Donald Fanger, "The Peasant in Literature," in *The Peasant in Nineteenth-Century Russia*, ed. Wayne S. Vucinich (Stanford, Calif.: Stanford University Press, 1968), 231–262.

18. This social meliorism characterized the Haskalah further west as well. Staunchly loyal to the imperial model of reform, Jewish enlighteners from Vienna to Prague to Vilna promoted "self-cultivation" (Ger. *Bildung*) rather than political activism in order to gain "improvements" in social and economic status. See Israel Bartal, "'The Heavenly City of Germany' and Absolutism à la Mode d'Autriche: The Rise of the Haskalah in Galicia" and Hillel J. Kieval, "Caution's Progress: The Modernization of Jewish Life in Prague, 1780–1830," in *Toward Modernity: The European Jewish Model*, ed. Jacob Katz (New Brunswick and Oxford: Transaction Books, 1987), 33–42, 71–105.

19. This connection was already intuited by the first and only historian of "conscription literature," the Soviet-Yiddish critic Meir Winer; see the essay "Di rekrutchine in der sheyner literatur fun der haskole," in his *Tsu der geshikhte fun der yidisher literatur in 19tn yorhundert*, vol. 1 (New York: YKUF, 1945), 150–192. Unfortunately Winer confined his investigation to the small number of works—basically two—which were written during the Nicholaevan period itself and remained unpublished until much later. See my "Literary Response to Conscription: Individuality and Authority in the Russian-Jewish Enlightenment," Ph.D. thesis, Columbia University, 1999, chap. 2. For the more naïve approach that treats conscription literature as an unvarnished source of information for conscription history, see Adina Ofek, "Cantonists: Jewish Children as Soldiers in Tsar Nicholas' Army," *Modern Judaism* 13 (1993): 277–308.

20. This so-called crisis theory of Russian-Jewish history figures in virtually every study of Russian-Jewish culture and politics; see the magisterial study by Jonathan Frankel, *Prophecy and Politics: Socialism, Nationalism and the Russian Jews, 1862–1917* (Cambridge: Cambridge University Press, 1981), chap. 2.

21. Recent work has, in fact, considerably complicated our understanding of the

relationship between emancipation and enlightenment as a factor in Jewish social history; see Jonathan Frankel and Steven J. Zipperstein, eds., *Assimilation and Community: The Jews in Nineteenth-Century Europe* (Cambridge: Cambridge University Press, 1992). Regarding the cultural impact of emancipation on the discourse of Jewish Enlightenment, see David Sorkin, *The Transformation of German Jewry, 1780–1840* (Oxford: Oxford University Press, 1987).

22. See the recent attempt to rehabilitate Nicholaean maskilim from the charge of imperial toadyism, in Eli Lederhendler, *The Road to Modern Jewish Politics: Political Tradition and Political Reconstruction in the Jewish Community in Tsarist Russia* (Oxford and New York: Oxford University Press, 1989), chaps. 4–5.

23. Lev Levanda, *Goriachee vremia: roman iz poslednego pol'skogo vosstaniia* (St. Petersburg: A. E. Landau, 1875), 61 (emphasis in the original). The book was first serialized in the journal *Evreiskaia biblioteka* between 1871 and 1873.

1. STEPCHILDREN OF THE TSAR

1. On the social function of the army in the period leading up to the reign of Nicholas I, see John L. H. Keep, *Soldiers of the Tsar: Army and Society in Russia, 1462–1874* (Oxford and New York: Clarendon, 1985); on the Nicholaean military specifically, see Wirtschafter, *From Serf to Russian Soldier.* For a comparative perspective on the disciplinary ideal embodied in the military, see the discussion in Yu. M. Lotman, "Problema 'obucheniia ku'ture' kak tipologicheskaia kharakteristika," in his *Semiosfera* (St. Petersburg: Iskusstvo SPb, 2000), 417–425; and Michel Foucault, *Discipline and Punish: The Birth of the Prison,* trans. Alan Sheridan (New York: Vintage, 1995), 135–169.

2. See the discussion of conscription history in chapter 6. For a revisionist critique of the normative approach, see Michael Stanislawski, "Russian Jewry, the Russian State and the Dynamics of Emancipation," in *Paths of Emancipation: Jews, States and Citizenship,* ed. Pierre Birnbaum and Ira Katnelson (Princeton, N.J.: Princeton University Press, 1995), 262–283.

3. See John Klier, *Russia Gathers Her Jews: The Origins of the "Jewish Question" in Russia, 1772–1825* (DeKalb: Northern Illinois University Press, 1986).

4. Ibid., 6; cf. Gershon Hundert, *Jews in Poland-Lithuania in the Eighteenth Century: A Genealogy of Modernity* (Berkeley: University of California Press, 2004). For the first example of the state's effort to mold Jews in "the land of Russia" into a model of reformed Russian Jewry during the partition period, see David E. Fishman, *Russia's First Modern Jews: The Jews of Shklov* (New York and London: New York University Press, 1995).

5. For a discussion of estate as the dominant constitutive category of the imperial Russian social order, see Gregory L. Freeze, "The Soslovie (Estate) Paradigm and Russian Social History," *American Historical Review* 91, no. 1 (1986): 11–36; on the subordination of confession to estate, see the discussion in Freeze, *The Parish Clergy in Nineteenth-Century Russia: Crisis, Reform and Counter-reform* (Princeton, N.J.: Princeton University Press, 1983). On Catherine's Jewish policy and the origins of the problem of dual jurisdiction, see Richard Pipes, "Catherine II and the Jews: The Origins of the Pale of Settlement," *Soviet-Jewish Affairs* 5, no. 2 (1975): 3–20.

6. On the contradictory implications and effects of the decree of 1804, see Salo W. Baron, *The Russian Jew under Tsars and Soviets* (New York: Macmillan, 1964), 17–21; and Klier, *Russia Gathers Her Jews,* chap. 5. On the persistent lack of resources that limited the attempts to institute effective provincial administration throughout the imperial period, see, for instance, George L. Yaney's discussion of the weak link between the state and rural society, in his *Systematization of Russian Government: Social*

Evolution in the Domestic Administration of Imperial Russia, 1711–1905 (Urbana: Illinois University Press, 1973), 143–168; and Frederick S. Starr, *Decentralization and Self-Government in Russia, 1830–1870* (Princeton, N.J.: Princeton University Press, 1972). For a dramatic illustration of the effects of under-government on the relationship between Jews and non-Jews in the Pale, see I. Michael Aronson, *Troubled Waters: The Origins of the 1881 Anti-Jewish Pogroms in Russia* (Pittsburgh: University of Pittsburgh Press, 1990), 45–47, 131–137.

7. The Hasidic master Rebbe Nahman of Bratslav interpreted the statute of 1804 as an "evil decree"; see Arthur Green, *Tormented Master: A Life of Rabbi Nahman of Bratslav* (Tuscaloosa: University of Alabama Press, 1979), 140–141. Hasidic leaders gathered in Berdichev to discuss the imposition of the statute, perceived as a potential crisis of religious authority; see Israel Halpern, "Rabbi Levi-Yitzhak mi-berdichev ugzerot ha-malkhut be-yamav," in his *Yehudim ve-yahadut be-mizrah eiropa* (Jerusalem: Magnes, 1968), 340–347.

8. Klier, *Russia Gathers Her Jews,* chap. 5, esp. 131–133.

9. For a comparative perspective, see the groundbreaking work of Robert D. Crews, "Allies in God's Command: Muslim Communities and the State in Imperial Russia," Ph.D. dissertation, Princeton University, 1999.

10. On the dynamics of Russian imperial administration, see, for instance, John P. LeDonne, *The Russian Empire and the World, 1700–1917: The Geopolitics of Expansion and Containment* (New York: Oxford University Press, 1997).

11. See the original sources in Mordecai Wilensky, *Hasidim and Mitnaggedim: A Study of the Controversy between Them in the Years 1772–1815* [in Hebrew], 2 vols. (Jerusalem: Mossad Bialik, 1970), 1:210–229.

12. On the importance attached to the imprisonment of R. Shneur Zalman as a factor in the spread of Habad, see Naftali Loewenthal, *Communicating the Infinite: The Emergence of the Habad School* (Chicago and London: University of Chicago Press, 1990), 71–98.

13. Cited in Klier, *Russia Gathers Her Jews,* 181; see the original text, cited more fully here, in V[1], O. Levanda, ed., *Polnyi khronologicheskii sbornik zakonov i polozhenii kasaiushchikhsia evreev ot ulozheniia tsaria Alekseia Mikhailovicha do nastoiashchego vremeni, ot 1649–1873 g.* (St. Petersburg: K. V. Trubnikov, 1874), 359 (emphasis added).

14. The figure of M. M. Speranskii represents the crucial link between post-Napoleonic romanticism and the Nicholaevan turn toward administrative, rather than legislative, reform; see Marc Raeff, "The Political Philosophy of Speranskij," *American Slavic and East European Review* 12, no. 1 (1953): 1–21; as well as, more generally, Nicholas V. Riasanovsky, *A Parting of Ways: Government and the Educated Public in Russia, 1801–1855* (Oxford: Clarendon, 1976).

15. Klier, *Russia Gathers Her Jews,* 164–166.

16. On the cultural significance of 1812, see S. R. Serkov, ed., *Kliatvu vernosti sderzhali: 1812 god v russkoi literature* (Moscow: Moskovskii rabochii, 1987). On the plans to establish military colonies, see Richard Pipes, "The Russian Military Colonies, 1810–1831," *Journal of Modern History* 22, no. 3 (1950): 205–219.

17. Wirtschafter, *From Serf to Russian Soldier.*

18. See Kimerling [Wirtschafter], "Soldiers' Children, 1719–1856: A Study in Social Engineering in Imperial Russia," *Forschungen zur osteuropäischen Geschichte* 30 (1982): 63–136, esp. 109–114.

19. See David L. Ransel, *Mothers of Misery: Child Abandonment in Russia* (Princeton, N.J.: Princeton University Press, 1988).

20. N. I. Il'in, *Velikodushie, ili rekrutskii nabor, drama v trekh deistviiakh* (St. Petersburg: Tip. Imperatorskogo teatra, 1807).

21. Il'in, *Velikodushie,* 72–73.

22. On the expectation that all Jewish cantonists would convert as a matter of

course, see the discussion of the confidential and anonymous Third Section memorandum entitled "A Note on Rendering the Jews More Useful to the Empire Through Their Gradual Conversion to Christianity Leading to Greater Closeness to the Remainder of the Population and Eventual Absorption" (1827), in Saul M. Ginsburg, "Di entshteyung fun der idisher rekrutchine," in his *Historical Works* [in Yiddish], 3 vols. (New York: S. M. Ginsburg Testimonial Committee, 1937), 2:3–12; here, 7–8.

23. Rossiiskii gosudarstvennyi voenno-istoricheskii arkhiv (The Russian State Military-Historical Archive), (hereafter, RGVIA) f. 405, op. 5, d. 13028, l. 1.

24. See Stanislawski, *Tsar Nicholas I and the Jews,* chaps. 5–6.

25. See the discussion in Wirtschafter, *From Serf to Russian Soldier,* 34–35.

26. On the introduction of edifying reading material—including Orthodox primers but also math books and pamphlets dealing with the health risks of masturbation—into cantonist schools beginning in the late 1840s, see RGVIA, f. 405, op. 4, d. 6706; f. 405, op. 5, dd. 16343, 16350, 16418, 16432, 16456. On the significance of education in Russian military culture, see Carl Van Dyke, *Russian Imperial Military Doctrine and Education, 1832–1914* (New York: Greenwood, 1990).

27. RGVIA, f. 405, op. 5, d. 18056.

28. RGVIA, f. 405, op. 5, d. 18056, ll. 16, 18, 53. Unfortunately the reports do not provide the total number of cantonists in the Orenburg and Saratov battalions.

29. RGVIA, f. 405, op. 5, d. 18056, l. 38.

30. On "official enlightenment," see Stanislawski, *Tsar Nicholas I and the Jews,* chaps. 3–4.

31. See S. J. Fuenn's letter to Betzalel Stern, in Shmuel Feiner, ed., *Me-haskalah lohemet le-haskalah mashmeret: mivhar mi-kitvei Sh.Y. Fin* (Jerusalem: Merkaz Dinur, 1993), 173–178.

32. On the bureaucratic connection between Nicholaevan bureaucracy and Alexandrine reform, see Richard S. Wortman, *The Development of a Russian Legal Consciousness* (Chicago: University of Chicago Press, 1976); and Bruce W. Lincoln, *In the Vanguard of Reform: Russia's Enlightened Bureaucrats, 1825–1861* (DeKalb: Northern Illinois University Press, 1982).

33. RGVIA, f. 405, op. 5, d. 8158, ll. 1–2.

34. RGVIA, f. 405, op. 5, d. 8158, l. 7.

35. RGVIA, f. 405, op. 5, d. 7370, l. 104.

36. RGVIA, f. 405, op. 5, d. 9273, l. 2.

37. RGVIA, f. 405, op. 5, d. 11187, l. 5a.

38. RGVIA, f. 405, op. 5, d. 11187, ll. 2–3.

39. RGVIA, f. 405, op. 5, d. 17973, ll. 12–13.

40. RGVIA, f. 405, op. 2, d. 4513, l. 4.

41. RGVIA, f. 405, op. 2, dd. 1662, 1851.

42. RGVIA, f. 405, op. 5, d. 16467, l. 14.

43. RGVIA, f. 405, op. 5, d. 16467, ll. 3, 18.

44. RGVIA, f. 405, op. 2, d. 2153, l. 3.

45. RGVIA, f. 405, op. 2, d. 1662, ll. 42–44.

46. RGVIA, f. 405, op. 2, d. 1662, l. 1.

47. RGVIA, f. 405, op. 2, d. 1662, ll. 17–19.

48. RGVIA, f. 405, op. 5, d. 14271, l. 6.

49. RGVIA, f. 405, op. 2, d. 1662, ll. 39–40.

50. RGVIA, f. 405, op. 5, d. 7370.

51. Compare RGVIA, f. 405, op. 5, dd. 7370, 18401.

52. I base these numbers on six sets of reports (Rus. *vedomosti*) that the DMS submitted to the tsar regarding Jewish conversions in cantonist ranks, for the years 1829 (RGVIA, f. 405, op. 2, d. 1662); 1831 (RGVIA, f. 405, op. 2, dd. 1851, 4513); 1842–1843 (RGVIA, f. 405, op. 5, d. 7370); and 1854 (RGVIA, f. 405, op. 5, dd.

17903, 18041). My estimates — admittedly, hardly comprehensive or conclusive — are somewhat lower than the impressionistic figure of "at least half" cited in Stanislawski, *Tsar Nicholas I and the Jews*, 25. Stanislawski uses twentieth-century Jewish scholarship on conversion to arrive at what essentially amounts to a guess; he admits that the "exact number of Jews who converted in Nicholas' army cannot be determined with any precision" (25). Jewish sources, particularly the studies of early-twentieth-century Russian Jewish historians such as S. M. Ginsburg, manifest a compelling interest in over-reporting conversions in their attempt to magnify the horrors of the Nicholaevan system. The internal record of the DMS — which, given the tsar's interest in Jewish conversion, also had a reason to inflate the numbers — seems to offer a more reasonable base line.

53. RGVIA, f. 405, op. 5, d. 7370, l. 8.

54. RGVIA, f. 405, op. 5, d. 7370, l. 9.

55. RGVIA, f. 405, op. 5, d. 9269.

56. RGVIA, f. 405, op. 5, d. 11218.

57. RGVIA, f. 405, op. 9, d. 3143.

58. RGVIA, f. 405, op. 9, d. 3143, ll. 18–19.

59. The internal reform of the navy anticipated the general military reform of 1874 by a decade, owing in large part to the progressive command of the grand duke Constantine Nikolayevich. See Aurele J. Violette, "The Grand Duke Constantine Nikolayevich and the Reform of Naval Administration, 1855–1870," *Slavonic and East European Review* 52 (1974): 584–601; and Jacob W. Kipp, "Consequences of Defeat: Modernizing the Russian Navy, 1856–1863," *Jahrbücher für Geschichte Osteuropas* 20 (1972): 210–225.

60. See Michael Stanislawski, "Jewish Apostasy in Russia: A Tentative Typology," *Jewish Apostasy in the Modern World*, ed. Todd M. Endelman (New York and London: Holmes & Meier, 1987), 189–205.

61. I. Itskovich, "Vospominaniia arkhangel'skogo kantonista," *Evreiskaia starina* 5 (1912): 54–65.

62. The discussion of Itskovich's age at the time of the draft remains problematic and leaves room for doubt. Even Itskovich himself does not take it for granted, careful to attribute it entirely to his mother's subsequent testimony. As far as the army was concerned, Itskovich was twelve when he was drafted. More generally, it ought to be underscored that, contrary to the common perception that the Russian army turned a blind eye to drafting Jewish recruits as young as six or seven, cantonist regiments could hardly function as if they were some sort of hellish Jewish kindergarten. According to the DMS, the average age of Jewish recruits was closer to fifteen and a half than to twelve; see RGVIA, f. 405, op. 5, d. 18353, ll. 8–12, 20–23, 48, 58, 61, 56, 70–72. By 1853, aware of abuses on the Jewish side, the DMS actually returned to their communities "unfit" Jewish recruits who obviously appeared to be younger than the legal age of twelve. See, for instance, RGVIA, f. 405, op. 5, d. 11972.

63. Itskovich, "Vospominaniia," 62.

64. Ibid., 63.

65. On the transformation of Russian legal culture in the era of the Great Reforms, see Wortman, *Development of Legal Consciousness;* and Friedhelm Berthold Kaiser, *Die russische Justizreform von 1864: zur Geschichte der russischen Justiz von Katharina II. bis 1917* (Leiden: Brill, 1972). On the involvement of Jewish lawyers in this process, see Nathans, *Beyond the Pale*, pt. 4; on Orshanskii, 317–320.

66. I. G. Orshanskii, *Russkoe zakonodatel'stvo o evreiakh: ocherki i issledovaniia* (St. Petersburg: A. E. Landau, 1877), 6.

67. Orshanskii, "Istoriia vykliuchki," *Evreiskaia biblioteka* 6 (1878): 15–36. Among Orshanskii's first works, the story was originally written in 1863–1864 and submitted

to the first Russian-Jewish literary anthology published in 1866 by the St. Petersburg Society for the Promotion of Enlightenment among Jews (Rus. *Obshchestvo dlia rasprostraneniia prosveshcheniia mezhdu evreiiami v Rossii, OPE*), which rejected it because of its "radical and denunciatory character." See Iulii Gessen, "O. A. Rabinovich i I. G. Orshanskii," *Galeria evreiskikh deiatelei, literaturno-biograficheskie ocherki*, vol. 1 (St. Petersburg: A. E. Landau, 1898), 77–155, esp. 84; on the initial fate of "Istoriia vykliuchki," see I. M. Cherikover, *Istoria obshchestva dlia rasprostraneniia prosveshcheniia mezhdu evreiiami v Rossii, kul'turno-obshchestvennye techeni a v russkom evreistve, 1863–1913*, vol. 1 (St. Petersburg: Komitet OPE, 1913), 83.

68. Orshanskii, *Zakonodatel'stvo*, 14.

69. On the prevalence of the charge of Jewish draft dodging and on theories of Jewish conspiracy associated with the *kahal* as key themes in Russian Judaeophobia during the era of the Great Reforms, see John Klier, *Imperial Russia's Jewish Question, 1855–1881* (Cambridge: Cambridge University Press, 1995), chaps. 12, 14.

70. Orshanskii, *Zakonodatel'stvo*, 21–30.

71. RGVIA, f. 405, op. 5, d. 16467, l. 4.

72. RGVIA, f. 405, op. 5, d. 16467, l. 11.

73. The Nicholaevan period still constitutes the primary divide between the history of the Russian state and its Jews and Russian-Jewish history proper; compare Stanislawski's *Tsar Nicholas I and the Jews* with Nathans's *Beyond the Pale*. Jewish periodization here echoes the conventional split between the pre-reform emphasis on the "state" and the post-reform focus on "society," a binary common to Russian historiography, most effectively challenged by Lincoln's *In the Vanguard of Reform* and Wortman's *Development of Russia's Legal Consciousness*, two books that examine the enduring dialectical importance of Nicholaevan etatism in the reforming culture of Alexandrine *obshchestvo*. To be sure, Stanislawski explicitly argues that the "transformation of Jewish society" under Nicholas I effectively set the stage for the "flowering" of the Russian-Jewish intelligentsia in the ensuing period; see *Tsar Nicholas I and the Jews*, esp. 109–122. But neither Stanislawski nor Nathans, writing about the "late imperial period," analyze how and why the Nicholaevan project of "transformation" continued to shape the "Russian-Jewish encounter."

74. On the emergence and political significance of the category of Jewish "utility" in the Nicholaevan period, and especially on the way it informed the ministerial discussion of integrating individual Jews into the "imperial social hierarchy," see Nathans, *Beyond the Pale*, 31–49.

75. See Kiselev's memorandum, reprinted in *Voskhod*, no. 4 (1901): 25–40; no. 5 (1901): 3–21. The Russian word *ustroistvo* is suitably ambiguous; it also means "creation" or "structuring," suggesting the social engineering of Russian Jewry and not just the formal organization of Russian Jews.

76. On the dysfunction of the "crown rabbinate," see ChaeRan Y. Freeze, *Jewish Marriage and Divorce in Imperial Russia* (Hanover, N.H., and London: University Press of New England/Brandeis University Press, 2002), 95–130; here, 98; and, more generally, Azriel Shohet, *Mosad "ha-rabanut mi-ta'am" be-rusyah: parashah be-ma'avak ha-tarbut ben haredim le-ven maskilim* (Haifa: Haifa University, 1975).

77. See Verena Dohrn, "Das Rabbinerseminar in Wilna (1847–1873). Zur Geschichte der ersten staatlichen höheren Schule für Juden in Russischen Reich," *Jahrbücher für Geschichte Osteuropas* 45 (1997): 379–400.

78. Nathans, *Beyond the Pale*, chap. 6; here, 215.

79. Shohet, *Mosad "ha-rabanut mi ta'am,"* 110.

80. On the rising percentages of Jewish students at Russian universities between the mid-1860s and the mid-1880s, see Nathans, *Beyond the Pale*, 217–219.

81. On "selective integration," see ibid., chap. 2.

82. On the *razbor*, see Stanislawski, *Tsar Nicholas I and the Jews*, 155–160.

83. Nathans, *Beyond the Pale,* 50–67, 219–220.
84. See ibid., pt. 2.

2. GREAT EXPECTATIONS

1. To clarify, Rabinovich wrote the earliest stories focusing on Russia's first Jewish soldiers; there was no Nicholaevan precedent for conscription literature per se. In fact, during the period of *rekrutchina* itself, Jewish enlighteners addressed conscription only marginally and always within the context of their critique of Jewish communal administration. There are only two surviving examples of this kind of work, neither published in its own time: Isaac-Baer Levinsohn's Yiddish comic interlude, *The Lawless World* (Yid. *Di hefker-velt*); and Israel Aksenfeld's Yiddish comedy, *The First Jewish Recruit in Russia* (Yid. *Der ershter yidisher rekrut in rusland*). Probably written as early as 1828, Levinsohn's playlet circulated in manuscript until 1888, when it was finally published by Sholem-aleichem in the first issue of his short-lived Yiddish literary anthology, *The Jewish People's Library* (Yid. *Di yudishe folks-bibliotek*). Aksenfeld wrote his play between 1835 and 1837, and published it privately in Leipzig, in 1862. For publication information as well as an analysis of these plays in their original historical context, see my "Literary Response to Conscription: Individuality and Authority in the Russian-Jewish Enlightenment," Ph.D. dissertation, Columbia University, 1999, chap. 2. Memoir literature also mentions the existence of a maskilic Hebrew play about conscription, written in 1828 and entitled *The Sound of Weeping* (Heb. *Kol bokhim*), the text of which has been lost; see Abraham Baer Gottlober, "Ha-gizrah v'ha-beniyah," in his *Memoirs and Travels* [in Hebrew], ed. R. Goldberg, 2 vols. (Jerusalem: Mosad Bialik, 1976), 2:147.
2. The journal published three cantonist memoirs in addition to Itskovich, "Vospominaniia," see M. Merimzon, "Razskaz starago [*sic*] soldata," *Evreiskaia starina* 5 (1912): 290–301, 406–422; 6 (1913): 86–95, 221–232; and M. Shpigel', "Iz zapisok kantonista," *Evreiskaia starina* 4 (1911): 249–259.
3. The era of the Great Reforms gave rise to the political usage of the terms "perestroika" and "glasnost"; the first refers to the idea of reorganizing Russian society in the wake of the abolition of serfdom, and the second to the spirit of public criticism associated with the relaxation of censorship restrictions. For a survey of the current literature on these and other aspects of *raskreposhchenie* in the 1860s–1870s, see Ben Eklof, John Bushnell, and Larissa Zakharova, eds., *Imperial Russia's Great Reforms, 1855–1881* (Bloomington: Indiana University Press, 1994).
4. In the era of the emancipation, increasing anxieties about the visibility of the Jews — particularly in the Russian capitals of Moscow and St. Petersburg — informed urgent, if largely futile, demands for greater transparency of confessional and estate categories; see Nathans, *Beyond the Pale,* 100–107, and also the illuminating discussion of the internal divide between Moscow Jewry and Moscow Jews in Vance F. Serchuk, "Continuity and Crisis: The Development of the Moscow Choral Synagogue, 1869–1906," BA thesis, Princeton University, 2001, chap. 1.
5. For example, see the discussion of the way that the identification with the project of judicial reform shaped the Jewish self-consciousness of Russia's Jewish lawyers, in Nathans, *Beyond the Pale,* chap. 8.
6. See Nikitin, "Mnogostradal'nye: ocherki byta kantonistov," in *Otechestvennye zapiski* 197 (July–August 1871): 351–396; 198 (September–October 1871): 69–120, 407–440; and *Mnogostradal'nye* (St. Petersburg: Otechestvennye zapiski, 1872), the edition cited here. A second edition of the book, entitled *Mnogostradal'nye: ocherki proshlogo,* was published in St. Petersburg in 1895; this one included a second part consisting of a fictional autobiography of a cantonist from among the Old Believers

who, like Nikitin, had converted in the ranks and achieved his "liberation" into the civil service during the era of the Great Reforms.

7. On the literary politics of Russian populism, see N. I. Sokolov, *Russkaia literatura i narodnichestvo: literaturnoe dvizhenie 70-kh gg. XIX v.* (Leningrad: Leningrad University, 1968). On the significance of *Notes of the Fatherland* in the development of populism, see Franco Venturi, *Roots of Revolution: A History of the Populist and Socialist Movements in Nineteenth-Century Russia,* trans. Francis Haskell (London: Weidenfeld and Nicolson, 1960).

8. On the emergence and social significance of the Russian-Jewish press in the era of the Great Reforms, see Yehuda Slutsky, *Ha'itonut ha-yehudit -rusit ba-meah ha-tesha' 'esreh* (Jerusalem: Mosad Bialik, 1970); Alexander Orbach, *New Voices of Russian Jewry: A Study of the Russian-Jewish Press in Odessa in the Era of the Great Reforms, 1860–1871* (Leiden: Brill, 1980); U. G. Ivask, *Evreiskaia periodicheskaia pechat' v Rossii: materialy dlia istorii evreiskoi zhurnalistiki* (Tallinn: Beilinson, 1935); and D. A. Eliashevich, *Pravitel'stvennaia politika i evreiskaia pechat' v Rossii, 1797–1917, ocherki istorii tsenzury* (St. Petersburg: Mosty kul'tury/Jerusalem: Gesharim, 1999).

9. See the editor's introduction to Nikitin's memoirs, in *Russkaia starina* 127, no. 9 (1906): 582.

10. V. N. Nikitin, "Vospominaniia," *Russkaia starina* 127 (1906), no. 9, 585.

11. Ibid., 591.

12. Ibid., 594.

13. On the Nicholaevan cult of Suvorov, see Keep, *Soldiers of the Tsar.*

14. Nikitin, "Vospominaniia," 619.

15. Ibid., 620–621.

16. Ibid., 627.

17. Ibid., 633.

18. Nikitin, "Vospominaniia," *Russkaia starina* 128, no. 10 (1906): 94.

19. Ibid., 128:106.

20. On Miliutin, see Forrestt A. Miller, *Dmitrii Miliutin and the Reform Era in Russia* (Nashville: Vanderbilt University Press, 1968); and John S. Bushnell, "Miliutin and the Balkan War: Military Reform vs. Military Performance," in Eklof, Bushnell, and Zakharova, *Imperial Russia's Great Reforms.* On the military reforms of 1874 more generally, see P. A. Zaionchkovskii, *Voennye reformy 1860–1870 godov v Rossii* (Moscow: Moscow University, 1952).

21. Nikitin, *Zhizn' zakliuchennykh: obzor peterburgskikh tiurem i otnosiashchikhsia do nikh uzakonenii i administrativnykh rasporiazhenii* (St. Petersburg: Izd-vo Kolesova i Mikhina, 1871).

22. In his introductory note to Nikitin's memoirs, the editor of *Russkaia starina* noted that for thirty-five years Nikitin had served as the director of the St. Petersburg committee on prisons, a philanthropic society committed to easing the lot of military, naval, and civilian prisoners; see Nikitin "Vospominaniia," *Russkaia starina* 127, no. 9 (1906): 582. On Russian prison reform, see Bruce F. Adams, *The Politics of Punishment: Prison Reform in Russia, 1863–1917* (DeKalb: Northern Illinois University Press, 1996).

23. "V. N. Nikitin: k yubileyu," *Budushchnost'*, no. 18 (7 May 1904): 341–342.

24. Nikitin wrote the first archival study of Jewish agricultural colonies in Russia; see his *Evrei-zemledel'tsy: istoricheskoe, zakonodatel'noe, administrativnoe i bytovoe polozhenie kolonii so vremeni ikh vozniknoveniia do nashikh dnei, 1807–1887* (St. Petersburg: Novosti, 1887).

25. Nikitin, *Mnogostradal'nye,* 133.

26. Nikitin, "Vek prozhit'—ne pole pereiti (Iz rasskazov otstavnogo soldata)," *Evreiskaia biblioteka* 4 (1873): 301–358; here, 342.

27. On the contemporary debate in Jewish circles about the meaning of emancipation, see Klier, *Imperial Russia's Jewish Question,* esp. chaps. 1–6.

28. On the commitment of St. Petersburg's Jewish notables to the principle of "selective integration," see Nathans, *Beyond the Pale*, 50–59.

29. The quotation is from ibid., 58.

30. On the literary appropriation of the Russian imperial claims to the southern frontier, see Susan Layton, *Russian Literature and Empire: Conquest of the Caucasus from Pushkin to Tolstoy* (Cambridge: Cambridge University Press, 1994); Katya Hokanson, "Empire of the Imagination: Orientalism and the Construction of Russian National Identity in Pushkin, Marlinskii, Lermontov, and Tolstoi," Ph.D. dissertation, Stanford University, 1994, chap. 1.

31. For an illuminating discussion of the best-known case of this phenomenon in Russian-Jewish literature, see Dan Miron, "Sholem Aleichem: Person, Persona, Presence," in his *Image of the Shtetl and Other Studies of Modern Jewish Literary Imagination* (Syracuse, N.Y.: Syracuse University Press, 2000), 128–156.

32. On the paradigmatic status of the enlightened North versus the New "Free" South, compare Mordechai Zalkin's treatment of Vilna in his *A New Dawn: The Jewish Enlightenment in the Russian Empire, Social Aspects* [in Hebrew] (Jerusalem: Hebrew University Magnes Press, 2000), to Steven J. Zipperstein, *The Jews of Odessa, a Cultural History, 1794–1881* (Stanford, Calif.: Stanford University Press, 1986), esp. 1–7.

33. On the official "delineation" of the Pale of Jewish Settlement, see Stanislawski, *Tsar Nicholas I and the Jews*, 36–37. On the settlement of the New South, with particular reference to the Jews of Odessa, see Zipperstein, *Jews of Odessa*, chap. 1. On the Nicholaevan conquest of the Caucasus as a civilizing project, see Willis Brooks, "Nicholas I as Reformer: Russian Attempts to Conquer the Caucasus, 1825–1855," in *Nation and Ideology: Essays in Honor of Wayne S. Vucinich*, ed. Ivo Banac, John Ackerman, and Roman Szporluk (Boulder, Colo.: East European Monographs/Columbia University Press, 1981), 227–263.

34. On Eichenbaum, see the wonderful sketch by his grandson, the Russian formalist critic Boris Eichenbaum, "'Ga-krab,' otryvki iz rodoslovnoi," in his *Moi vremennik* (St. Petersburg: Inapress, 2001 [1929]), 27–33. On the southern connection, see Jacob Shatskii, "Haskalah in Zamosc," *YIVO Bleter* 34 (1952): 24–61.

35. Eichenbaum wrote the poem in 1839; according to the literary historian Jefim (Ephraim) Schirmann, it was first published in London in 1840. See Schirmann, *The History of Hebrew Poetry in Christian Spain and Southern France* [in Hebrew], ed. Ezra Fleischer (Jerusalem: Merkaz Shazar, 1997), 46. Rabinovich completed his translation in 1847 and published it alongside the original. A second printing followed in 1874 and is the one cited here. See J. Eichenbaum, *Ga-krab*, trans. O. Rabinovich, 2nd ed. (Odessa: Beilinson, 1874); the above quotation comes from Rabinovich's introduction, 7.

36. On maskilic medievalism, particularly prominent among Eastern European Jewish enlighteners, see Emanuel Etkes, "Immanent Factors and External Influences in the Development of the Haskalah Movement in Russia," in Katz, *Toward Modernity*, 13–33, esp. 29.

37. For an English translation, see Abraham Ibn Ezra, "The Song of Chess," trans. Nina R. Davis, *Jewish Chronicle*, 22 June 1894, 22. On the history and literary context of the poem, see Schirmann, *History of Hebrew Poetry*, 46–48. On the theme of chess in medieval Hebrew poetry and its connection to the maskilic treatment of the game, see Moritz Steinschneider, "Schach bei der Juden," in *Geschichte und Literatur des Schachspiels*, ed. Antonius van der Linde, vol. 1 (Berlin: J. Springer, 1874), 155–202. Steinschneider cites the poem in the Hebrew original; see the appendix to "Schach bei der Juden," 195–197.

38. See Morris B. Margolies, *Samuel David Luzzatto, Traditionalist Scholar* (New York: KTAV, 1979), 144–153.

39. J. Eichenbaum, *Ga-krab*, 9–11.

40. For a thoughtful discussion of the significance of Pushkin's "southern poems"

in the creation of the imperial myth of Russia's "Eastern" origins, see Hokanson, "Empire of the Imagination," chaps. 2–3; see also Iu. Tynianov, "Pushkin," in *Arkhaisty i novatory* (Leningrad: Priboi, 1929), 228–291; here, 254.

41. J. Eichenbaum, *Ga-krab,* 8. Compare the translation to Pushkin's "Oriental style" (Rus. *vostochnyi stil'*) "connoting sensuality and pleasure" in *The Fountain of Bakhchisarai,* in Hokanson, "Empire of the Imagination," 126.

42. For details of Rabinovich's biography, see Menashe Morgulis's introduction to Rabinovich's *Sochineniia* (St. Petersburg: Izdania odesskogo obshchestva 'Trud,' 1880), 1:i–xx; and Gessen, "O. A. Rabinovich i I. G. Orshanskii," 7–70; as well as the most recent appraisal by the literary critic Simon Markish, "Osip Rabinovic," *Cahiers du monde russe et sovietique* 21 (1980): 5–30, 135–158.

43. On the number of Jewish students in Russian universities during the 1840s, see Iulii Gessen, "Prosveshcheniie evreev v rossii do tsarstvovaniia Aleksandra II," in *Evreiskaia entsiklopediia,* 16 vols. (St. Petersburg: Brokgauz and Efron, 1906–1913), 13:46.

44. Founded in 1805, Kharkov University was the oldest secular institution of higher learning in the Ukraine. Throughout the first half of the nineteenth century, the cultural life around the university consistently overshadowed that of the surrounding towns, including Kiev, the seat of ancient Rus' and the capital of modern Ukraine. In those decades, Kharkov hosted the Epiphany Fair, the largest in the region and the third largest in the empire. See Michael F. Hamm, *Kiev: A Portrait, 1800–1917* (Princeton, N.J.: Princeton University Press, 1993), 23. The quotation about the special character of Kharkov's population belongs to the governor of the Kiev Province during the Nicholaevan period; it is cited in ibid., 106.

45. Ibid., 60. For a description of Kharkov University in the 1840s, see M. P. De-Poulet, "Khar'kovskii universitet i D. I. Kachenovskii: kul'turnyi ocherk i vospominaniia iz 40-kh godov," *Vestnik evropy* 9, no. 1 (1874): 75–115; no. 2 (1874): 565–589.

46. See De-Poulet, "Khar'kovskii universitet," 88–104; and Kostomarov, *Avtobiografiia* (Moscow: Zadruga, 1922), 148–149.

47. I. Aizenshtok, "Ukrains'ki poety-romantyky," in *Ukrains'ki poety-romantyky 20–40kh rokiv XIX st.,* ed. B. A. Derkach (Kiev: Dnipro, 1968), 7–64.

48. David Saunders, *The Ukrainian Impact on Russian Culture, 1750–1850* (Edmonton: Canadian Institute of Ukrainian Studies, 1985), 242–247.

49. On Shcherbina, see the biographical sketch by I. D. Glikman, in the one-volume collection of Shcherbina's poetry, *Izbrannye proizvedeniia* (Leningrad: Sovetskii pisatel', 1970), 5–64; the quotation is from an unpublished letter by Shcherbina, cited in ibid., 15.

50. Rabinovich, "O russkom iazyke," *Razsvet,* 19 August 1860, reprinted in idem, *Sochineniia,* 3:147–151; here, 151. The image of the Russian language as a "mediating" agent of Russianness within a diverse imperial social and cultural order echoed the romantic theory of literary "colonization" which asserted that Russian writers were in a position to "create a veritable empire of *narodnost'*" by treating all of Russia's various peoples as subject to representation; see Hokanson, "Empire of the Imagination," 35–38, citing Orest Somov, "On Romantic Poetry [1823]," in *Select Prose in Russian,* ed. John Mersereau and George Harjan (Ann Arbor: University of Michigan Press, 1974), 173.

51. See, especially, Steven J. Zipperstein, *Imagining Russian Jewry: Memory, History, Identity* (Seattle: University of Washington Press, 1999), chap. 3; on Odessa as the locus of Jewish culture, see also Ezra Spicehandler, "Odessa as a Literary [*sic*!] Center of Hebrew Literature," in *The Great Transition: The Recovery of the Lost Centers of Modern Hebrew Literature,* ed. Glenda Abramson and Tudor Parfitt (Totowa, N.J.: Rowan and Allanheld/Oxford Centre for Postgraduate Hebrew Studies, 1985), 75–

90; as well as recent works on the "Jewishness" of late imperial Odessa that persisted into the Soviet period: Alice Stone Nakhimovsky, "Mikhail Zhvanetskii: The Last Russian-Jewish Joker," in *Forging Modern Jewish Identities: Public Faces and Private Struggles*, ed. Michael Berkowitz, Susan L. Tananbaum, and Sam W. Bloom (London: Vallentine Mitchell, 2003), 156–179; and Rebecca J. Stanton, "Odessan Selves: Identity and Mythopoesis in Works of the 'Odessa School,'" Ph.D. dissertation, Columbia University, 2004, chap. 1, esp. 36–52.

52. The term is Ismar Schorsch's; see the essay, "The Myth of Sephardic Supremacy," in his *From Text to Context: The Turn to History in Modern Judaism* (Hanover, N.H., and London: University Press of New England/Brandeis University Press, 1994), 71–92.

53. Rabinovich, "Moritz Sefardi," in idem, *Sochineniia*, vol. 1, 390–391.

54. Rabinovich's radical critique of Jewish embourgeoisement here anticipates the maskilic discourse on "pseudo-enlightenment," the socioeconomic rewards of which similarly "haunted" the Jewish reforming conscience in the decades of emancipation; see Shmuel Feiner, "The Pseudo-Enlightenment and the Question of Jewish Modernization," *Jewish Social Studies* 3 (1996): 62–88, esp. 72–76.

55. Rabinovich, "Shtrafnoi," in idem, *Sochineniia*, vol. 1, 3–4.

56. For the original text of "Shtrafnoi," see *Russkii vestnik* 21, nos. 5–6 (1859): 501–540. On *Russkii vestnik*, see *Russkaia periodicheskaia pechat', 1702–1894*, ed. A. G. Dement'ev et al. (Moscow: Izd-vo politicheskoi literatury, 1959), 340–343.

57. The story dramatizes the historical consequences of the changes in conscription law, enacted on the eve of the Crimean War (1851), which held members of the *kahal* personally accountable for failing to meet the new higher quotas of recruits even if, like Rabinovich's hero, they were way past draftable age. These regulations also permitted communities to fulfill increasing quotas with vagabonds, runaways, social "undesirables," and anyone else caught without proper residential documents. Hence the infamous institution of "recruit-catchers" (Heb. *khappers*, Yid. *lovchikes*) and their prey, "captive" (Rus. *poimannik*) and "penal" (Rus. *shtrafnoi*) recruits. See Yohanan Petrovsky-Shtern, *Evrei v russkoi armii, 1827–1914* (Moscow: Novoe literaturnoe obozreniie, 2003), 57–59.

58. There are a variety of Russian literary precedents, originating in eighteenth-century enlightenment literature, for casting the figure of the old soldier as a purveyor of moral lessons, a paragon of humility and of devotion both to God and to the tsar. Often cast as a dialogue between the veteran and a young gentleman, the story of the old soldier became a staple in Russian genre fiction in the wake of the Napoleonic wars. See especially, A. P. Sumarokov, "Beznogii soldat," in idem, *Stikhotvoreniia*, ed. A. S. Orlov (Moscow: Sovetskii pisatel', 1935), 229–230. For post-Napoleonic examples, see the anthology, *1812 god v russkoi poezii i vospominaniiakh sovremennikov*, ed. N. I. Akopova and V. V. Berezhkov (Moscow: Pravda, 1987), esp. P. A. Viazemskii, "K staromu gusaru," 97–99; A. A. Del'vig, "Otstavnoi soldat," 114–117; and P. A. Katenin, "Invalid Gorev," 139–142. For a discussion of the image of the retired warrior in other romantic poems like Pushkin's "Gorodok," K. N. Batiushkov's "Moi penaty," and K. F. Ryleev's "Pustynia," see Iu. Mann, *Dinamika russkogo romantizma* (Moscow: Aspekt, 1995), 136–137. During the Nicholaevan period, two immensely popular prose works featured the experience of the humble veteran as a model of self-improvement, courage, patriotic devotion, and sensitivity: The first of these was written by the Moscow publisher, historian, and *litterateur* N. A. Polevoi (1796–1846) in 1833 and reissued in 1852; see "Rasskazy russkogo soldata," in *Russkaia voennaia proza XIX veka*, ed. E. V. Sviiasov (Leningrad: Lenizdat, 1989), 127–185. The second, *Correspondence and Tales of a Russian Veteran*, written by the retired general I. N. Skobelev (1778–1849), a veteran of the Napoleonic campaign, was reprinted every year between 1840 and 1844. See the most recent edition,

reprinted in *1812 god v vospominaniiakh, perepiske i rasskazakh sovremmenikov* (Moscow: Voennoe izd-vo, 2001). Both books were lavishly illustrated and written in a popular, highly affected, didactic idiom.

59. Petrovsky-Shtern, *Evrei v russkoi armii,* 361–363.

60. Rabinovich, "Shtrafnoi," 72–73. Ellipses in the original.

61. Ibid., 17.

62. On the latter, see Fanger, "The Peasant in Literature," 244–249. The best example of a "naturalistic" depiction of peasant life that entered into the public debate on emancipation is Ivan Turgenev's *Sportsman's Sketches* (1852). More significant in this context is the peasant tale "Anton Goremyka" (1847) by D. V. Grigorovich (1822–1899), a writer of the St. Petersburg "physiological school," to whom literary historians explicitly compared Rabinovich; see Markish, "Rabinovic," 137.

63. Letter cited in Markish, "Rabinovic," 136.

64. Gessen, "O. A. Rabinovich i I. G. Orshanskii," 39. For another report of contemporary Jewish reactions to "Shtrafnoi," see Israel Zinberg, *A History of Jewish Literature,* trans. Bernard Martin, vol. 12 (Cincinnati and New York: Hebrew Union College Press/KTAV, 1978), 41.

65. Cf. Roemer, *Jewish Scholarship and Culture.*

66. See I. M. Jost, "Schilderungen aus Rußland von herrn Rabinowitsch," in *Jahrbuch für die Geschichte der Juden und des Judentums* 1 (1860): 9–66. The journal was published under the auspices of Ludwig Philippson's Institute for the Promotion of Jewish Literature (Ger. *Institut zur Förderung der israelitischen Literatur*). Philippson (1811–1889), a champion of the Reform movement and the indefatigable publisher of *Allgemeine Zeitung des Judentums,* was an active proponent of the uses of literature to inspire Jewish loyalties in secular Jews. For a review of his career, see Hans Otto Horch, "'Auf der Zinne der Zeit': Ludwig Philippson (1811–1889) – der 'Journalist' der Reformjudentums aus Anlaß seines 100. Todestages," *Bulletin des Leo Baeck Instituts* 86 (1990): 5–21.

67. Petrovsky-Shtern, *Evrei v russkoi armii,* 361.

68. *Dawn* began to be issued weekly in 1860 and ceased publication after a year; see Orbach, *New Voices of Russian Jewry.*

69. On tsarist policy governing Jewish residence in Nikolaev, see Gessen, "Nikolaev," in *Evreiskaia entsiklopediia,* 11:704–707.

70. See the astute comments in Petrovsky-Shtern, *Evrei v russkoi armii,* 366–367, characterizing the domestic scenario of the Jewish sailors as a "maskilic utopia," combining Russian values of "hospitality complete with tea drinking, popular speech, and a native Russian submission to fate" with the "Jewish character" of their everyday life.

71. The actual "exile" of the Jews from Nikolaev (and Sevastopol) in 1831, like other attempts on the part of the state to "expel" the local Jewish residents (mostly illegals) from a town or border region, was an administrative measure of limited consequence; it was not exactly a disaster of biblical proportions, since the expellees invariably returned. See the article "Izgnanie evreev iz Nikolaeva i Sevastopolia v 1831 g.," in *Morskoi sbornik* 62, no. 2 (1863): 162–168.

72. Rabinovich, "Nasledstvennyi podsvechnik," *Razsvet* 1 (1860): 13–17, 30–33, 43–50, 57–65, 78–81, 91–98, 109–116, 130–134; here, 78.

73. Rabinovich, "Perekhodnoe sostoianie evreev," in idem, *Sochineniia,* vol. 3, 160–165.

74. Rabinovich, "Nasledstvennyi podsvechnik," 31.

75. Ibid., 32.

76. Compare Rabinovich's emancipation "scenario" to Alexander's own "scenario of love" as the ideological basis of "unserfment"; see Richard S. Wortman,

Scenarios of Power: Myth and Ceremony in Russian Monarchy, vol. 2 (Princeton, N.J.: Princeton University Press, 2000), pt. 1.

77. On the "family model of politics," see Lynn Hunt, *The Family Romance of the French Revolution* (Berkeley and Los Angeles: University of California Press, 1992).

78. See "Iz Sevastopolia," *Razsvet* 1 (1861): 748–749.

79. *Zion* came out weekly between 19 May 1861 and 27 April 1862. For the first six months it was edited by two Jewish physicians, both of whom had served in the Crimean War, L. S. Pinsker (1821–1891) and E. B. Soloveichik (d. 1875); for the last six months, N. O. Bernshtein (1836–1891) took over for Pinsker. Bernshtein was also a doctor. See Orbach, *New Voices*. The article on Sevastopol, "Zametka ob ustroistve pamiatnika voinam-evreiam, pavshim pri zashchite Sevastopolia," graced the first page of the inaugural issue of *Zion;* see also "Delo narodnoi chesti," *Sion* 1 (1861): 24. When *Zion* failed a year later, subscribers were urged to contribute the cost of their unfilled subscriptions to the construction of the memorial; see the note in *Sankt-peterburgskie vedomosti* 14 (1863), cited in Klier, *Imperial Russia's Jewish Question,* 487.

80. See, for instance, Nils Roemer, "Provincializing the Past: Worms and the Making of a German-Jewish Cultural Heritage," *Jewish Studies Quarterly* 12 (2005): 80–100, esp. 83–85.

81. See the description in his Yiddish travelogue, *Di geheymnise fun barditchev, eyne karakter-shilderung der dortikn yudishn gemaynde* (Warsaw: n. p., 1870), 40–50.

82. The OPE was founded in 1863 in St. Petersburg; an Odessa branch formed officially in 1867. Its leadership overlapped entirely with both the Sevastopol memorial committee and with the editorial staff of Odessa's Russian-Jewish press. See Cherikover, *Istoriia obshchestva dlia rasprostraneniia prosveshcheniia mezhdu evreiiami v Rossii,* 238–39. The anthology was the first official publication of the OPE; see *Sbornik statei po evreiskoi istorii i literatury* (St. Petersburg: OPE, 1866); see Cherikover, *Istoriia obshchestva dlia rasprostraneniia prosveshcheniia mezhdu evreiiami v Rossii,* 82–87. A woodcut of the recently completed memorial appeared on the inside front cover. A report on the "condition of the Jewish cemetery and the memorial to the Jewish soldiers, fallen in the defense of Sevastopol" served as an appendix to the volume; see "Otchet ob ustroistve evreiskogo kladbishcha i pamiatnika evreiskim soldatam, pavshim pri zashchite Sevastopolia."

83. On the folkloric, possibly literary, roots of such images, see the citations, in Zipperstein, *Jews of Odessa,* 1.

3. THE ROMANCE OF ENLIGHTENMENT

1. For the conventional periodization, see Zinberg, *History of Jewish Literature,* vol. 12.

2. See Stanislawski, *For Whom Do I Toil? Judah Leib Gordon and the Crisis of Russian Jewry* (New York and Oxford: Oxford University Press, 1988).

3. See David G. Roskies, *A Bridge of Longing: The Lost Art of Yiddish Storytelling* (Cambridge, Mass., and London: Harvard University Press, 1995), 70–71.

4. For a discussion of Bogrov's reputation as an "assimilationist," see Gabriella Safran, *Rewriting the Jew: Assimilation Narratives in the Russian Empire* (Stanford, Calif.: Stanford University Press, 2000), 32–33. For his self-styled Jewish "cosmopolitanism," see his letter to Levanda, cited in Zinberg's article on Bogrov in *Evreiskaia entsiklopedia,* 4:733.

5. For an overview of this general tendency in the critical writing on Gordon, see Shmuel Werses, "Shirat YaLaG be-mivhan ha-dorot," in his *Criticism of Criticism: Evaluations in Development* [in Hebrew] (Tel Aviv: Hotsaat "yahdav," 1981–1982), 11–33.

See also, more recently, Judith Bar-El, "The National Poet: The Emergence of a Concept in Hebrew Literary Criticism, (1885–1905)," *Prooftexts* 6 (1986): 205–220.

6. See Feiner, "Ha-isha ha-yehudiyah ha-modernit: mikreh-mivhan be-yahasei ha-haskalah ve-ha-modernah," in *Sexuality and the Family in History: Collected Essays* [in Hebrew], ed. Israel Bartal and Isaiah Gafni (Jerusalem: Zalman Shazar, 1998), 253–303; and, more generally, Tova Cohen, *"One Beloved, the Other Hated": Between Fiction and Reality in Haskalah Depictions of Women* [in Hebrew] (Jerusalem: Magnes, 2002). The problem, of course, is hardly particular to the Haskalah: similar anxieties motivated French republican discourse on women, derived largely from Rousseau's gendered critique of enlightenment. See Carol Blum, *Rousseau and the Republic of Virtue: The Language of Politics in the French Revolution* (Ithaca, N.Y.: Cornell University Press, 1986); and Carla Hesse, *The Other Enlightenment: How French Women Became Modern* (Princeton, N.J.: Princeton University Press, 2001).

7. On the genre repertoire of early maskilic writing as a reflection of its social vision, see Moshe Pelli, *Kinds of Genre in Haskalah Literature: Types and Topics* [in Hebrew] (Tel Aviv: Ha-kibbutz ha-meuchad, 1999). The Jewish enlightenment here partook of a more general trend in European cultural history; see, for example, J. Paul Hunter, *Before Novels: The Cultural Contexts of English Fiction* (New York and London: Norton, 1990). See also Dan Miron, *From Romance to the Novel: Studies in the Emergence of the Hebrew and Yiddish Novel in the Nineteenth Century* [in Hebrew] (Jerusalem: Mossad Bialik, 1979).

8. See, for instance, Nils Roemer, "Turning Defeat into Victory: *Wissenschaft des Judentums* and the Martyrs of 1096," *Jewish History* 13 (1999): 65–80.

9. Heinrich Graetz, *Volkstümliche Geschichte der Juden*, 3 vols. (Leipzig: O. Leiner, 1888), 3:749.

10. The characterization of *Wissenschaft* scholarship as *Geschichtmikroskopie* belongs to Ludwig Phillipson; see his "Der Fortbestand des Judenthums: An einen Freund in F.," *Allgemeine Zeitung des Judentums* 43 (1879): 625–627, 657–659, 673–675, 705–707; here, 706–707.

11. See Phillipson's call for the creation of a German-Jewish literary society, "Aufforderung an alle deutsch-lesenden Israeliten," *Allgemeine Zeitung des Judentums* 19 (1855): 87–89.

12. Grace Aguilar (1816–1847) was a popular Victorian Jewish writer and poet. Of Sephardic extraction, she was best known for sentimental domestic fiction but also wrote on Jewish historical themes. *Vale of Cedars* was widely read in enlightened Jewish circles, in both English and German translation; see Michael Galchinsky, *The Origin of the Modern Jewish Writer: Romance and Reform in Victorian England* (Detroit: Wayne State University Press, 1996). To my knowledge, Friedberg's was the first attempt to translate *Vale of Cedars* into Hebrew.

13. Here Friedberg uses *moladeto* literally to refer to the local Jewish community that one is born into, as opposed to the distant "cosmopolitan" metropolis of St. Petersburg; he does *not* mean the Land of Israel.

14. A. S. Friedberg, *Sefer ha-zikhronot*, 2 vols. (Warsaw: Shuldberg, 1899), 1:127–128.

15. On Jewish participation in Russian student culture, see Nathans, *Beyond the Pale*, chaps. 6–7; on the dramatic scenes of Jewish sons departing for the university, see 238–239. On increasing Jewish student involvement in the revolutionary movement, see Erich E. Haberer, *Jews and Revolution in Nineteenth-Century Russia* (Cambridge: Cambridge University Press, 1995).

16. On the social position of Vilna maskilim during the Nicholaevan period, see Zalkin, *A New Dawn*. On Vilna in the aftermath of the 1863 Polish revolt, see Klier, *Imperial Russia's Jewish Question*, chap. 7.

17. On the traditionalist revival movement in mid-nineteenth-century Lithuania,

see Immanuel Etkes, *Rabbi Israel Salanter and the Mussar Movement: Seeking the Torah of Truth*, trans. Jonathan Chipman (Philadelphia: Jewish Publication Society, 1993); and Shaul Stampfer, *Ha-yeshivah ha-litait be-hithavutah* (Jerusalem: Merkaz Shazar, 1995).

18. See Shmuel Feiner's introduction to *S. J. Fuenn, from Militant to Conservative Maskil*, ed. idem [in Hebrew] (Jerusalem: Merkaz Dinur, 1993).

19. With this shift came a new emphasis on the press as "preacher"; see Lederhendler, *Road to Modern Jewish Politics*, 122–130. On the increasing centrality of literature in the maskilic program, see Tova Cohen, "Ha-tekhnikah ha-lamdanit — tsofen shel sifrut ha-haskalah," *Mehkarei yerushalayim be-sifrut 'ivrit* 13 (1992): 137–169.

20. On the importance of the Kantian imperative linking will with reason in the formation of maskilic self-consciousness during the formative years of the Jewish enlightenment, see Marcus Moseley's discussion of Mordechai Aaron Günzburg (1795–1846), in Moseley's "Jewish Autobiography in Eastern Europe: The Prehistory of a Genre," Ph.D. dissertation, Oxford University, 1990, chap. 4.

21. On Alexander's "scenario of love," see Wortman, *Scenarios of Power*, vol. 2, pt. 1.

22. On the unraveling of the Jewish family during the era of the Great Reforms, see ChaeRan Y. Freeze, *Jewish Marriage and Divorce in Imperial Russia*, chap. 3.

23. The year of Dik's birth has been the subject of controversy among critics: see Sh[muel] Niger, "Ayzik Meir Dik and His Hebrew Works," *He-'avar* 2 (1918): 140–142; and idem, "To the Question of A. M. Dik's Birthday," *Pinkes fun amopteyl fun YIVO* 1 (1927–1928): 380–382. See, too, P[inches] Kon, [When was I. M. Dik Born?], *Filologishe shriftn fun YIVO* 2 (1928): 329–344, where the author, based solely on literary evidence provided by Dik himself, concludes that Dik was born in 1813 or 1814. Contemporary scholarship follows Kon; see David G. Roskies, "Ayzik-Meir Dik and the Rise of Yiddish Popular Literature," Ph.D. thesis, Brandeis University, 1975, 102; and Dan Miron, *A Traveler Disguised: The Rise of Modern Yiddish Fiction in the Nineteenth Century* (New York: Schocken Books, 1973), 3. Zinberg dates Dik's birth to 1807, the year inscribed on his tombstone, probably on the instruction of his family, certainly a more impartial source than the literary "facts" invented to suit Dik's narrative agenda; see his article on Dik, in *Evreiskaia entsiklopedia*, 7:189–191; and also his *History of Yiddish Literature*, 12:78.

24. Isaac-Meir Dik, *Der erster nabor, vos ver in dem yor 1828* (Vilna: Widow and Bros. Romm, 1871), 4.

25. Dik claimed to have heard Landau's speech from a traveling preacher who had himself witnessed this archetypal scene. This is hardly credible, given that almost forty years passed between Landau's sermon and the narrator's Vilna childhood. Most likely Dik read the speech printed in the 1788 issue of *The Gatherer* (Heb. *Hameasef*), the first maskilic Hebrew journal, which began publication in Koenigsberg and Berlin in 1783–1784. On the delivery and publication of Landau's address, see Ruth Kestenberg-Gladstein, *Neuere Geschichte der Juden in den böhmischen Ländern* (Tübingen: Mohr, 1969), 70–72.

26. The maskilic view, contemporary with the imposition of recruitment, attributed all the evils of the Nicholaevan conscription system to the administration of the decree rather than to the law itself. See, for instance, Levinsohn, *Di hefker-velt*.

27. Dik, *Nabor*, 32.

28. Dik, *Der antloyfener rekrutl* (Vilna: Widow and Bros. Romm, 1872), 4–5.

29. On Jewish agriculturalists in Nicholaevan Russia, see S. Y. Borovoi, *Evreiskaia zemledel'cheskaia kolonizatsiia v staroi Rossii* (Moscow: Izd. M. & S. Sabashnikovykh, 1928); and V. N. Nikitin, *Evrei-zemledel'tsy* (St. Petersburg: Novosti, 1887). On the economic ideology of the Haskalah, see Zalkin, *New Dawn*, 155–158; and Derek J. Penslar, *Shylock's Children: Economics and Jewish Identity in Modern Europe* (Berkeley and Los Angeles: California University Press, 2001), 68–84.

30. See also Dik's unpublished "maskilic utopia," in which he imagined the literal disappearance of Jewish women from public places like "tavern and shop"; S. Niger, "A maskils utopie: araynfir tsu Ayzik-Meir Diks a manuscript on a nomen," *YIVO Bleter* 36 (1952): 140; and Dik, *Masekhet 'aniyut* (Vilna: n. p., 1878), 26.

31. Roskies, "Ayzik-Meir Dik," 249–250.

32. Dik, *Der soldatske syn* (Vilna: Widow and Bros. Romm, 1876), 69.

33. Ibid., 74.

34. Ibid., 6–7.

35. Actually the closest thing to a parody of *Soldatske syn* is a much later conscription romance called *The Captive-Recruit, or the Hero-Maid*, by the popular writer N. M. Shaikevich (1849–1905). The story includes all the elements of Dik's providential tale of luck, riches, and marital happiness plus the titillating element of cross-dressing. See N. M. Shaikevich (der Shomer), *Der poimannik, oder dos heldishe maydkhen* (Vilna: Levin-Hofshtein, 1891).

36. Litvak, "The Literary Response to Conscription," 143–146.

37. Roskies, "Ayzik-Meir Dik," 232–239; here, 233.

38. Dik, *Di shtifmuter* (Warsaw: Lebensohn, 1876), 10; cited in Roskies, "Ayzik-Meir Dik," 233.

39. Zalkin captures this tension very well; see his *New Dawn*, esp. chaps. 4–5.

40. Dik, "Two Letters to Kh. Y. Gurland," *Reshumot* 2 (1927): 408–410.

41. By the 1870s, Dik was cultivating a self-consciously learned style, replete with Germanisms, biblical references, and extensive footnotes. On Dik's dealings with publishers and on his use of stylistic conventions, see Roskies, "Ayzik-Meir Dik," 113–116, 263–275.

42. Ginsburg, "Denk-shrift fun di vilner klal-tuer tsu Moshe Montefiore," in idem, *Historical Works*, 2:293–298.

43. Dik taught in a government-sponsored school between 1851 and 1864. See P. Kon, "A. M. Dik as a Teacher in the Government School for Jewish Children in Vilna," *YIVO-Bleter* 3 (1932): 84–85.

44. Characteristically Vilna maskilim expressed their ideological proclivities in public institutional forms including the creation of schools, new congregations, and study houses; in private, they remained solidly and traditionally pious. See Zalkin, *New Dawn*, 87–151, 262–290.

45. For the text of the petition, see *Perezhitoe* 1, pt. 2 (1908): 12–14. On Dik's radical youth, see Yitskhok Rivkind, "A. M. Dik's Letters," *YIVO-Bleter* 35 (1951): 222–228.

46. Indeed, the complicated relationship between the Haskalah and modern Jewish literary production has yet to be fully assessed; often, the two histories are simply conflated. See, for instance, Zinberg, *History of Jewish Literature*, vol. 12; and Joseph Klausner, *Historiah shel ha-sifrut ha-'ivrit ha-hadashah*, 6 vols. (Jerusalem: Hotsaat sefarim ahiasaf, 1952). For a recent critical review of this tendency, see Uzi Shavit, "Ha-'haskalah' ma-hi? Le-berur musag ha-'haskalah' be-sifrut 'ivrit," *Mehkarei yerushalayim be-sifrut 'ivrit* 12 (1990): 51–83.

47. On the limitations on Jewish printing during the Nicholaevan period, see P. Kon, "Di proyektirte yidishe drukeray in Kiev, 1836–1846," *Bikher-velt* 1, no. 3 (1929): 31–37; no. 4 (1929): 35–41; as well as Ginsburg, "Tsu der geshikhte fun yidishn drukvezn," in his *Historical Works*, 1:48–62; and Lederhendler, *Road to Modern Jewish Politics*, 95–97.

48. On maskilic resistance to Jewish fiction, focusing specifically on the novel, see Miron, *From Romance to the Novel*, 224–237. The most vocal opponent of Jewish literature was the "moderate" maskil, Eliezer Zweifel (1815–1888); see his collection of criticism, *Minim ve'ugav* (Vilna: Romm, 1858), 31, 52.

49. While enlightened Jewish philanthropy flourished during the era of the Great

Reforms, maskilic projects often fell victim to internal politics and rival personal agendas. See, for example, Zipperstein, "Transforming the Heder: Maskilic Politics in Imperial Russia," *Jewish History: Essays in Honour of Chimen Abramsky,* ed. Ada Rapoport-Albert and Steven J. Zipperstein (London: Peter Halban, 1988), 87–109.

50. A striking parallel may be drawn here with the literary domestication of Christianity in nineteenth-century America, which was, at least in part, the result of the social and cultural "disestablishment" of reforming clergymen; see Ann Douglas, *The Feminization of American Culture* (New York: Knopf, 1977).

51. G[rigorii] Bagrov [*sic*], "Poimannik (Byl')," *Evreiskaia biblioteka* 4 (1873): 3

52. Bagrov, "Poimannik," 6–7. On the Nicholaevan "fathers" of Jewish St. Petersburg, see Nathans, *Beyond the Pale,* 38–44.

53. Bagrov, "Poimannik," 13, 15, 17.

54. See the contemporary report in the Odessa Jewish weekly, *Den',* no. 8 (1869): 12.

55. On the economic expansion of Russia's southwestern provinces during the era of the Great Reforms, the result, in no small part, of Jewish entrepreneurship, see Alfred J. Rieber, *Merchants and Entrepreneurs in Imperial Russia* (Chapel Hill: North Carolina University Press, 1982), 219–222.

56. Bagrov, "Poimannik," 38.

57. Berdichev, ironically known as the "Jerusalem of Volhynia," was located in Kiev Province and, in the first half of the nineteenth century, was a bustling commercial town with a predominantly Jewish population of about 80 percent. Although it had a vibrant local intelligentsia — which included the famous musical family Rubinstein — Berdichev was known primarily as the capital of southwestern Hasidism. See Iulii Gessen's article on Berdichev in *Evreiskaia entsiklopediia,* 4:209–214.

58. On the link with the work of Turgenev and Dostoevsky, see Safran, *Rewriting the Jew,* 26–29.

59. On the contemporary misreading of *Notes of a Jew* as a realistic critique of Jewish mores, see N. A. Bukhbinder, "Drama pisatelia (K 35-letiiu smerti G. I. Bogrova)," *Literaturnye etiudy* (Leningrad: Nauka i shkola, 1927), 51–52; and Safran, *Rewriting the Jew,* 29–33; the most recent treatment of *Notes of a Jew* as a "naturalistic novel centered on the conflict between the protagonist and his milieu" is in Petrovsky-Shtern, *Evrei v russkoi armii,* 371–372.

60. Bogrov, *Zapiski evreia,* vols. 1–3, in idem, *Sobranie sochinenii,* 7 vols. (Odessa: Sherman, 1912–1913), 1:141.

61. Ibid., 1:198–199.

62. For a reading of "On the Jewish Question" that parallels my reading of *Notes of a Jew* as a "radical critique" of emancipation, see Julius Carlebach, *Karl Marx and the Radical Critique of Judaism* (London: Henley; Boston: Routledge & Kegan Paul, 1978), 164–182.

63. Bogrov, *Zapiski evreia,* 3:91–92.

64. Ibid., 3:159.

65. See *Di kinder-khapper fun rusland: a roman fun yidishn lebn in rusland in der tsayt fun nikolai dem ershtn* (New York: S. Kantrowitz, 1915); and a contemporary translation of this work into English, published privately in Ottawa, *The Child-Kidnappers of Russia: A Novel of Jewish Life in Russia in the Time of Nicholas I,* trans. Shoshana Dobrushin-Sharkey (Ottawa: S. D., 1996).

66. Bogrov, *Zapiski evreia,* 3:154–155.

67. Gordon *wrote* the poem in 1862–1863; it was published in Vilna's Hebrew weekly, *Ha-karmel* 6, no. 1 (1866): 1.

68. Stanislawski, *For Whom Do I Toil,* 49–51. See also Gershon Bacon, "An Anthem Reconsidered: On Text and Subtext in Yehuda Leib Gordon's 'Awake, My People!'" *Prooftexts* 15 (1995): 185–194.

69. Stanislawski, *For Whom Do I Toil*, 51.

70. See Dov Sadan, "Be-tsetekhah u-ve-ohalekhah: le-toldot sismah ve-shovrah," in his *Be-tsetekhah u-ve-ohalekhah: minyan hekrei-sifrut* (Ramat Gan: Sifriyat makor, 1966), 9–50.

71. Stanislawski, *For Whom Do I Toil*, 51.

72. Literally, "a perfect Jewish man" (Heb. *ish yehudi shalem*); see the original nineteenth-century source and discussion in Zalkin, *New Dawn*, 40–42.

73. Compare, for instance, the women martyrs who defend Jewish virtue unto death in the three narrative poems of Jewish antiquity in the collection *Songs of Judah* (1867) to the conspicuously passive female protagonist of "Tip of the Yud" (1876), victimized by misplaced rabbinic casuistry. On the tension in Gordon's work between the "romantic" heroine and the "suffering" modern woman, see Cohen, *One Beloved, the Other Hated*, chap. 8.

74. See Cohen, *One Beloved, the Other Hated*, 284–290; and Stanislawski, *For Whom Do I Toil*, 125–128.

75. *Kol mevasser* 6, no. 11 (1866): 171–173. See a partial translation in Stanislawski, *For Whom Do I Toil*, 70.

76. Stanislawski, *For Whom Do I Toil*, 70 (emphasis added). On the recruitment oath, see Sh. Gol'dberg, "Prisiazhnyi list evreiskogo rekruta 1829 g," *Perezhitoe* 2 (1910): 285–287.

77. On the pogroms of 1881–1882, see Aronson, *Troubled Waters*.

78. For the immediate, post-pogrom context of Gordon's story, see Alexander Orbach, "The Russian-Jewish Leadership and the Pogroms of 1881–82," *Perspectives on the 1881–82 Pogroms in Russia* (Pittsburgh: Russian and East European Studies Program, University of Pittsburgh, 1984), 1–37.

79. On the maskilic ambivalence toward Yiddish, see Miron, *A Traveler Disguised*, chap. 2.

80. "Ha-'atsamot ha-yeveishot," reprinted in Judah-Leib Gordon, *Kol kitvei Yehudah-Leib Gordon: prozah* (Tel Aviv: Dvir, 1960), 78–92.

81. Stanislawski, *For Whom Do I Toil*, 173.

82. Ibid., 104–105, 111–112.

83. Translation in ibid., 104.

84. The story appears in a medieval travel account of R. Petahya of Regensburg (1170s); see *Sivuv R. Petahya mi-Regensburg*, ed. Eleazar Gruenhut (Frankfurt: J. Kauffmann, 1904–1905), 9–10, cited in Avraham Grossman, *Pious and Rebellious: Jewish Women in Medieval Europe*, trans. Jonathan Chipman (Hanover, N.H., and London: University Press of New England/Brandeis University Press, 2004), 162. Translation slightly altered.

85. See, virtually, the only scholarly treatment of her life and work in Carole B. Balin, *To Reveal Our Hearts: Jewish Women Writers in Tsarist Russia* (Cincinnati, Ohio: Hebrew Union College Press, 2000), 13–50. The quotation is from an unpublished letter from Markel-Mosessohn to Gordon, cited in ibid., 13.

86. On women as readers, see the groundbreaking book by Iris Parush, *Reading Women: The Benefit of Marginality in Nineteenth-Century Eastern European Jewish Society* [in Hebrew] (Tel Aviv: Am Oved, 2001).

87. On the crucial difference between male and female reading habits, see ibid., 101–135.

88. Letter to Sheine Wolf (8 November 1881), in *'Igrot Yehudah-Leib Gordon*, ed. Y. Y. Weisberg, 2 vols. (Warsaw: Shuldberg, 1894), 2:5–6. See the citation in Balin, *To Reveal Our Hearts*, 16.

89. This dual-edged, biologically determined view of women as the "weaker sex" and therefore "morally more adept than men" pervaded nineteenth-century European culture; see Thomas Laquer's deft formulation of the dichotomy in his *Making*

Sex: Body and Gender from the Greeks to Freud (Cambridge, Mass., and London: Harvard University Press, 1990), chap. 6; here, 202–203.

90. Eugen Rispart was the pseudonym of Isaac Asher Francolm (1789–1849). The original German title of his book reads *Die Juden und die Kreuzfahrer in England unter Richard Löwenherz;* it was originally published in Leipzig in 1842. On Markel-Mosessohn's translation, see Balin, *To Reveal Our Hearts,* 33–35. The quotation is from Gordon's letter, dated 14 August 1869. See Avraham Yaari, ed., *Tsror igrot yalag el miriam markel-mosessohn* (Jerusalem: Darom, 1936), 19–20; cited in Balin, *To Reveal Our Hearts,* 32.

91. Isaac Asher Francolm, *Ha-yehudim be-angliyah: o, ha-yehudim ve-nosei-ha-tslav bi-melokh rikhard lev-ha-ari,* trans. Miriam Markel-Mosessohn, 2 vols. (Warsaw: Halter and-Eisenstadt, 1895), 2:1.

92. On Markel-Mosessohn's "fear of [presumably, male] disapprobation," see Balin, *To Reveal Our Hearts,* 35–36. The quotation is from the letter to Gordon, dated 25 December 1868–6 January 1869; cited in ibid., 36.

93. Cited in Balin, *To Reveal Our Hearts,* 45.

94. Cited in ibid., 36. For the biblical source on the law against cross-dressing, see Deut 22:5.

95. On the maskilic opposition to the traditional gender taxonomy, see David Biale, *Eros and the Jews from Biblical Israel to Contemporary America* (New York: Basic Books, 1992), chap. 7. Ironically this so-called traditional gender ideology was itself fairly new to learned Jewish elites in the nineteenth century; see Immanuel Etkes, "Marriage and Torah Study among the *Lomdim* in Lithuania in the Nineteenth Century," in *The Jewish Family: Metaphor and Memory,* ed. David Kraemer (Oxford and New York: Oxford University Press, 1989), 153–178. What we seem to have here are two competing ideologies of gender that arose in similar circumstances of rising economic pressure and increasing social differentiation.

4. RETURN OF THE NATIVE

1. On the conservative turn of the late 1870s, see Bruce W. Lincoln, *The Great Reforms: Autocracy, Bureaucracy, and the Politics of Change in Imperial Russia* (DeKalb: Northern Illinois University Press, 1990); and Alfred J. Rieber, "Alexander II: A Revisionist View," *Journal of Modern History* 43 (1971): 42–58. See also Hans Rogger, "Reflections on Russian Conservatism, 1861–1905," *Jahrbucher für Geschichte Osteuropas* 14 (1966): 195–212; and Richard Pipes, "Russian Conservatism in the Second Half of the Nineteenth Century," *Slavic Review* 30 (1971): 121–128.

2. On the conflicts within Russian educated society, see P. A. Zaionchkovskii, *Krizis samoderzhaviia na rubezhe 1870–1880kh godov* (Moscow: Moscow University, 1964); and Jonathan W. Daly, *Autocracy under Siege: Security Police and Opposition in Russia, 1866–1905* (DeKalb: Northern Illinois University Press, 1998).

3. On the expansion and increasing contentiousness of Russian public opinion during the late 1870s to the early 1880s, see Effie Ambler, *Russian Journalism and Politics: The Career of Alexei Suvorin, 1861–1881* (Detroit: Wayne State University Press, 1972); and Louise McReynolds, *The News under Russia's Old Regime: The Development of a Mass Circulation Press* (Princeton, N.J.: Princeton University Press, 1991). More specifically, on the contemporary debate over the "Jewish Question," see Klier, *Imperial Russia's Jewish Question,* chap. 17.

4. For a social profile of the Jewish university-educated intelligentsia, see Klier, *Imperial Russia's Jewish Question,* 364–369; see also Yehudah Slutsky, "Tsmihatah shel ha-intelligentsia ha-yehudit-rusit," *Zion* 25 (1960): 212–237. On the contemporary rise of the radical Haskalah, see Tsivia Nardi, "Tmurot b-tnu'at ha-haskalah be-

rusyah b-shnot ha-shishim ve-ha-shiv'im shel ha-meah ha-19," in *East European Jewish Enlightenment* [in Hebrew], ed. Immanuel Etkes (Jerusalem: Merkaz Shazar, 1993), 300–327; Israel Bartal, "Bein haskalah radikalit le-sotsializm yehudi," in Etkes, *East European Jewish Enlightenment*, 328–339; and Shmuel Feiner, "Ha-hevrah, ha-sifrut, ve-ha-haskalah ha-yehudit be-rusyah be'einei ha-bikoret ha-radikalit shel Yitshak-Ayzik Kovner," *Zion* 55 (1990): 283–316, as well as his *Haskalah and History: The Emergence of a Modern Jewish Historical Consciousness*, trans. Chaya Naor and Sondra Silverston (Oxford and Portland: Oxford University Press/Littman Library of Jewish Civilization, 2002), 274–317.

5. Feiner, "The Pseudo-Enlightenment and the Question of Jewish Modernization."

6. For the summation of the general principles of this new critical strain — materialism, the emphasis on the will to power and populism — see Feiner, *Haskalah and History*, 274–295; on Smolenskin, specifically, 317–340.

7. On the intellectual impact of the pogroms, a catalyst for the emergence of nationalism within the discourse of the radical Haskalah, see Frankel, *Prophecy and Politics*, chap. 2.

8. The idea of the modern Hebrew renaissance explicitly draws on the analogy with the European Renaissance, the "humanism" of the latter relocated to the modern Jewish street; see, for example, Nahum Slouzsch, *La renaissance de la littérature hébraïque* (Paris: Société nouvelle de librairie et d'édition, 1903); and Eisig Silberschlag, *From Renaissance to Renaissance* (New York: KTAV, 1973–1977). In one breathtaking formulation, the literary revival ensures the "humanistic growth" of the Jewish people, while Zionism provides a new political "framework" within which Judaism will play its proper historic role "as a universally significant force"; see Simon Halkin, *Modern Hebrew Literature from the Enlightenment to the Birth of the State of Israel: Trends and Values* (New York: Schocken Books, 1950), 82–83.

9. Virtually every history of modern Hebrew fiction begins with Abramovich; see, for example, Gershon Shaked, *Hebrew Narrative Fiction, 1880–1970* [in Hebrew], 2 vols. (Jerusalem: Keter, 1977–1998); as well as his tellingly titled volume of "Mendele" criticism, *Mendele, Before and After* (Heb. *Mendele, lefanav ve-aharav*) (Jerusalem: Magnes, 2004); see also Shmuel Werses, *From Mendele to Hazaz* [in Hebrew] (Jerusalem: Magnes, 1987); and Ken Frieden, *Classic Yiddish Fiction: Abramovitsch, Sholem Aleichem, and Peretz* (Albany: State University of New York Press, 1995), chap. 1.

10. Halkin, *Modern Hebrew Literature*, 45. On Abramovich's "Mendele persona," see Miron, *Traveler Disguised*, esp. chap. 7.

11. Halkin, *Modern Hebrew Literature*, 45, 52.

12. I rely here on the Bakhtinian notion of the "chronotope" which collapses the representation of time into an image of place; Abramovich created a shtetl that was always already set back in time, in the eternally frozen Nicholaevan past. This, in contrast to Sholem-aleichem's image of the shtetl as a moving target, a pit stop on the bumpy road toward Jewish modernity, signified by the railroad, an explicit foil for Mendele's ever-present horse and buggy. Cf. Sholem-aleichem, *Ayzenban geshikhtes* (Railroad Stories), vol. 28, *Ale verk* (New York: Folksfond, 1917–1923). On the chronotope as a literary device, see M. M. Bakhtin, "Forms of Time and of the Chronotope in the Novel," in his *Dialogic Imagination: Four Essays*, ed. Michael Holquist, trans. Caryl Emerson and Michael Holquist (Austin: University of Texas Press, 1981), 84–258.

13. On the problem of the contrast between the world of Mendele and the world of Abramovich in the critical literature, see Miron, *Traveler Disguised*, 148–155.

14. Ibid., 155.

15. This view of Russian-Jewish history, neatly split by the events of 1881, dominates both Israeli and American historiography. Its origins lie in the political conver-

sion narrative of M. L. Lilienblum (1843–1910), a radical maskil turned nationalist; see Moshe-Leib Lilienblum, *Way of Return* (Heb. *Derekh teshuvah*), the third part of his confessional autobiography, *Sins of Youth* (Heb. *Hat'ot neurim*), vol. 2, of his *Ktavim otobiografiyyim*, ed. Shlomo Breiman (Jerusalem: Mosad Bialik, 1970). For a summary of the contemporary scholarly consensus regarding the impact of 1881–1882 on the ideological shift from enlightenment to nationalism, see Jonathan Frankel, "The Crisis of 1881–1882 as a Turning Point in Modern Jewish History," in *The Legacy of Jewish Migration: 1881 and Its Impact,* ed. David Berger (New York: Columbia University Press, 1983), 9–22.

16. Abramovich's literary biography thus conveniently follows the same neat split as the pogrom paradigm of Russian-Jewish history; see the authoritative Klausner, *Historiyah,* 6:359–439.

17. This view of Abramovich's special "style" (Heb. *nusah*) as the "stable ground" for modern Hebrew writing originates with the poet H. N. Bialik (1873–1934); see Abramovich, "Mendeles nusekh," in idem, *Ale verk fun mendele moykher-seforim,* 17 vols. (Krakow: Farlag Mendele, 1911), 17:151–155. In contemporary criticism, see, especially, Robert Alter, *The Invention of Hebrew Prose: Modern Fiction and the Language of Realism* (Seattle: University of Washington Press, 1988), chap. 1; and idem, *Hebrew and Modernity* (Bloomington: Indiana University Press, 1994), 52–54. See also Gershon Shaked, *Bein tskhok le-dema': iyunim be-yetzirato shel mendele mokher-sefarim* (Tel Aviv: Masada, 1965); and Benjamin Harshav, *Language in Time of Revolution* (Berkeley, Los Angeles, and London: University of California Press, 1993), 37.

18. Frishman, "Mendele mokher-sefarim (Shalom Yaakov Abramovich): toldotav, 'arkho ve-safarav," in Abramovich, *Kol kitvei mendele mokher-sefarim,* 3 vols. (Odessa: Va'ad ha-yovel, 1911–1913), 2:vii; see English translations of this passage in Frieden, *Classic Yiddish Fiction,* 94; and in Miron, *Image of the Shtetl,* 7. My translation differs slightly from both.

19. See Harshav, *Language in Time of Revolution,* 25–30.

20. Dan Miron, "Le pesher ha-mvukhah be-sifrut ha'ivrit be-tekufat ha'tehiyah' shelah," in idem, *When Loners Come Together: A Portrait of Hebrew Literature at the Turn of the Twentieth Century* [in Hebrew] (Tel Aviv: 'Am Oved, 1987), 22–111.

21. The motif originated in the work of the Galician artist Ephraim Moses Lilien (1874–1925); it is associated not with the 1881–1882 pogroms but with the more politically decisive Kishinev pogrom of 1903. For an illustration, see David G. Roskies, *Against the Apocalypse: Responses to Catastrophe in Modern Jewish Culture* (Cambridge, Mass., and London: Harvard University Press, 1984), 85. See also Michael Stanislawski, "From Jugendstil to 'Judenstil': Cosmopolitanism and Nationalism in the Work of Ephraim Moses Lilien," in idem, *Zionism and the Fin-de-Siècle,* 98–115. By 1903 the ideological groundwork for Lilien's striking visual rendering of the Hebrew Renaissance had been laid by two decades of maskilic literary activity.

22. On the modern etiology of the pogroms of 1881–1882, see Aronson, *Troubled Waters.*

23. On the "ambivalent" bureaucratic response, which focused largely on containing the potential for more violence rather than on aiding the victims, see ibid., 137–144.

24. Ibid., 9–13.

25. The chief proponent of this view was the father of "spiritual Zionism" Asher Ginzberg (1856–1927), otherwise known as Ahad ha'am. See Steven J. Zipperstein, *Elusive Prophet: Ahad ha'am and the Origins of Zionism* (Berkeley and Los Angeles: University of California Press, 1993), esp. chap. 4. On the general importance of literary culture within the formation of Zionist ideology, see Iris Parush, *National Ideology and Literary Canon* [in Hebrew] (Jerusalem: Mosad Bialik, 1992).

26. In Herzl's utopian novel *Altneuland* (1902), the president of the modern

Jewish commonwealth is a learned and "venerable" Russian doctor, the pious "oculist" (read, visionary) Dr. Eichenstamm; see *Old-New Land*, trans. Lotta Levensohn (New York: Markus Wiener/Herzl Press, 1987), 77.

27. On the literary creation of the maskilic dystopia of Russian-Jewish life, see Dan Miron, "Folklore and Anti-folklore in the Yiddish Fiction of the *Haskala*," in idem, *The Image of the Shtetl*, 49–80. For a historical corrective, see B. Dinur, "Demutah hahistorit shel ha-yahadut ha-rusit u-va'ayot ha-heker bah," *Zion* 22 (1957): 93–118.

28. On the contrast between the "historical sensibility" underlying *The Fathers and the Sons* and the "abstract moral drama" at the heart of Abraham Mapu's *The Hypocrite* (Heb. *Ayit tsavu'a*, 1859–1869), which set the sole precedent for Abramovich's attempt to translate the conventions of nineteenth-century realism into maskilic Hebrew, see Miron, *From Romance to the Novel*, 223–229, 256–263.

29. Shalom Yaacov Abramovitz [*sic*], *Ha-avot ve-ha-banim, sipur ahavim* (Odessa: M. A. Beilinson, 1868), 26.

30. Miron, *From Romance to the Novel*, 50.

31. On the contemporary parallel between the peasant and Jewish emancipation, see Nathans, *Beyond the Pale*, 70–71.

32. On the differences between the first and second versions of the novel, see Dan Miron, "Der hilek fun *Limdu hetev* biz *Ha-avot ve-ha-banim*," in S. 'J. Abramovich, *Learn to Do Well* [in Hebrew] (New York: YIVO, 1969), 103–125.

33. On the providential maskilic attachment to the regime of Nicholas I, see Feiner, *Haskalah and History*, chap. 3, esp. 192–203.

34. The issue of Jewish numbers in the Russian ranks became a subject of heated polemic in the aftermath of the military reform of 1874; see Klier, *Imperial Russia's Jewish Question*, chap. 14. Recent scholarship has confirmed, on the basis of Russian military statistics, the assertion repeatedly made by Jewish publicists that the "number of Jews in the Russian army was proportionately greater than in the general population of the empire"; see Petrovsky-Shtern, *Evrei v russkoi armii*, 237. For a summary of the numbers, see M. Braginskii, "Voinskaia povinnost' v Rossii," in *Evreiskaia entsiklopediia*, 5:703–710; the quotation appears on 706.

35. Petrovsky-Shtern makes this general point about Jewish conscription literature; see his *Evrei v russkoi armii*, 359.

36. Abramovitz, *Ha-avot ve-ha-banim*, 160.

37. Ibid., 162.

38. On a mounting sense of public disappointment with the ruling persona of Alexander II between the assassination attempt of 1866 and the Russo-Turkish War (1876–1878), see Wortman, *Scenarios of Power*, vol. 2, chap. 4.

39. On contemporary readings and misreadings of Turgenev's *Fathers and Sons*, see Isaiah Berlin, "Fathers and Children: Turgenev and the Liberal Predicament," in his *Russian Thinkers*, ed. Henry Hardy and Aileen Kelly (New York: Penguin, 1994), 261–305.

40. I do not wish to strain the comparison between Turgenev and Abramovich, but the "twins" David and Shimon seem to me to be alluding to the twin sides of Bazarov's modern materialism; he is a physician whose name refers to the Russian word for "marketplace" (Rus. *bazar*).

41. Berlin, "Fathers and Children," 288. In fact, Turgenev self-consciously endowed the characterization of Bazarov's suffering with a "psychological" depth that redeemed him from caricature; see Elizabeth Cheresh Allen, *Beyond Realism: Turgenev's Poetics of Secular Salvation* (Stanford, Calif.: Stanford University Press, 1992).

42. The ambivalence registers in the unique publication history of the book. Abramovich published the Russian translation (probably by his friend and subsequent biographer, L. Binshtok) in St. Petersburg in the same year that the Hebrew original was published in Odessa; see S. Abramovich, *Ottsy i deti* (St. Petersburg: M.

Bienstock and L. P. Pestrechenko, 1868). At one end, he identified with the Russian-speaking Jewish audience to whom he addressed the translation; at the other, he maintained the proper maskilic distance, embodied in the Hebrew.

43. Abramovitz, *Ha-avot ve-ha-banim*, 7.

44. On the beginnings of Abramovich's literary career as a Yiddish writer, see Max Weinreich, *Bilder fun der yidisher literaturgeshikhte: fun di onheybn biz mendele moykher-seforim* (Vilna: Tomor, 1928); and Meir Winer, "Mendele in di zekhtsiker un zibet-sikher yorn," in idem, *Tsu der geshikhte fun der yidishe literatur in 19-tn yorhundert, etiudn un materialn*, 2 vols. (New York: YKUF, 1946), 2:74–221.

45. Abramovich entitled his translation *Toledot ha-teva'*. The first volume, on mammals, was published in Leipzig in 1862; the second volume, devoted to birds, came out in Zhitomir in 1866; and the third, and final, volume, on insects, was published in Vilna in 1872. Only the first volume was faithful to Lenz's original; the second and third borrowed freely from a variety of other German works. On the "pedagogical" significance of *Toledot ha-teva'* and on its publication history, see Klausner, *Historiyah*, 6:337–338. It seems entirely unclear to me what sort of practical benefit aspiring maskilim might have derived from Abramovich's highly idiosyncratic Hebrew versions of animals' names. My reading stresses the symbolic investment in bridging literature and natural history, involved in Abramovich's subversive attempt to recapitulate the foundational act of Genesis on the basis of modern science. See M. H. Abrams, *The Mirror and the Lamp: Romantic Theory and the Critical Tradition* (London, Oxford, and New York: Oxford University Press, 1953), 201–209; and Robert J. Richards, *The Romantic Conception of Life: Science and Philosophy in the Age of Goethe* (Chicago and London: University of Chicago Press, 2002).

46. The original title is a baroque mélange of Hebrew and Yiddish: S. Abramovich, *Kitsur mas'ot Benyamin III, dos heyst di nesiye oder a reyze-beshraybung fun binyomin dem dritten, aroysgegeben behishtadlus mendele moykher-seforim* (Vilna: Romm, 1878). The first part, in Hebrew, refers to the imaginary literary pedigree of the book: there were two other Benjamins who also wrote about their "travels," the twelfth-century Benjamin of Tudela and the nineteenth-century Israel Joseph Benjamin (1818–1864) who called himself "Benjamin II" and published a series of travel accounts about North Africa, Latin America, and the United States. See Dan Miron and Anita Norich, "The Politics of Benjamin III: Intellectual Significance and Its Formal Correlatives in Sh. Y. Abramovitsh's *"Masoes benyomin hashlishi,"* in *The Field of Yiddish: Studies in Language, Folklore and Literature*, ed. Marvin I. Herzog et al., fourth collection, 1–115 (Philadelphia: Institute for the Study of Human Issues, 1980), 26; and Klausner, *Historiyah*, 6:369–370. The second part is a Yiddish translation of the Hebrew title and explicitly includes Mendele as the fictional publisher of the "travels": "that is, a travel account of Benjamin III, published by Mendele the Bookpeddler." Abramovich's name appears in Russian as the real author of the book.

47. The trope of the "ghostlike" quality of Jewish life in exile, a form of living death, featured prominently in L. S. Pinsker's *Autoemancipation*, the first and arguably most influential political document of Russian Zionism, published in German in the wake of the pogroms. See the original *Autoemancipation!: Mahnruf an seine Stammgenossen von einem russischen Juden* (Berlin: Commission-Verlag von W. Issleib [G Schur], 1882), 4; and, in English, Leo Pinsker, "Auto-Emancipation," in Arthur Hertzberg, *The Zionist Idea: A Historical Analysis and Reader* (Philadelphia and Jerusalem: Jewish Publication Society, 1997), 184. Abramovich had a personal and direct connection to this text; like Pinsker, he was a member of Odessa's Jewish educated society, and he translated *Autoemancipation* into Yiddish in 1884. See S. Abramovich, *A sgule tsu di yudishe tsores, funem seyfer "Autoemancipation" vos iz opgedrukt in der daytsher shprakhe* (Odessa: A. Shul'tse, 1884). The relevant passage about the Jews being a "dead people, that passed away long ago" appears on page 8.

48. For a discussion of a parallel apocalyptic moment in nineteenth-century Russian culture, see Caryl Emerson, *Boris Godunov: Transpositions of a Russian Theme* (Bloomington: Indiana University Press, 1986), 14–25.

49. See Miron and Norich, "Politics of Benjamin III," 27–31.

50. On Abramovich's professional floundering between 1869 and 1881, see Klausner, *Historiyah*, 6:352–370.

51. See Miron, *Traveler Disguised*, 143–144.

52. S. Y. Abramovitsh, "The Brief Travels of Benjamin III," trans. Hillel Halkin, in *Tales of Mendele the Bookpeddler: Fishke the Lame and Benjamin the Third*, ed. Dan Miron and Ken Frieden (New York: Schocken Books, 1996), 301–302. This translation, for the most part, follows the original 1878 version.

53. On the symbolic value of the shtetl, see Miron, *Image of the Shtetl*, 1–48.

54. Abramovitsh, "Benjamin III," 375.

55. The chapters are unaccountably numbered and titled erroneously in Halkin's translation. See the original: Abramovich, *Kitsur mas'ot Benyamin ha-shlishi*, 88.

56. Abramovitsh, "Benjamin III," 382; translation altered and emphasis added.

57. See Ruth R. Wisse, *The Schlemiel as Modern Hero* (Chicago: University of Chicago Press, 1971), 33–34; and Shaked, *Bein tskhok le-dema'*, 135.

58. For this reading, see Miron and Norich, "Politics of Benjamin III," 103–104.

59. Sidra DeKoven Ezrahi, *Booking Passage: Exile and Homecoming in the Modern Jewish Imagination* (Berkeley, Los Angeles, and London: University of California Press, 2000), 53.

60. Ibid., 80.

61. Klausner, *Historiyah*, 6:372–374.

62. On the early version of *Dos kleyne mentshele*, see A. Gurshteyn, "Der yunger mendele in kontekst fun di 60-er yorn," in *Yiddish Literature in the Nineteenth Century: An Anthology of Yiddish Literary Research and Criticism in the Soviet Union* [in Yiddish and Hebrew], ed. Chava Turniansky (Jerusalem: Magnes, 1993), 485–510. The text has been reprinted in a bilingual, scholarly edition; see Mendele Mokher Sfarim, *The Tiny Fellow* [in Hebrew and Yiddish], ed. and trans. Shalom Lurya (Haifa: Haifa University, 1984). On the collected works project, see Miron, *Traveler Disguised*, 165.

63. In the 1860s and 1870s Abramovich wrote repeatedly under his own name both in Yiddish and in Hebrew; for a summary list of the titles, see Miron, *Traveler Disguised*, 314. See also the more comprehensive bibliography in Kh. Shmeruk and J. Klausner, eds., *Mendele mokher-sfarim: Bibliography of His Works and Letters for the Academic Edition* [in Hebrew] (Jerusalem: Hebrew University/Magnes, 1965). Between 1884 and 1905 Abramovich stopped writing under his own name almost entirely.

64. For the original 1879 text, see Abramovich, *Dos kleyne mentshele oder a lebensbeshraybung fun yits'hok-avraham takif. Gor in gantsn oif dos naye ibergemakht. Gedrukt behishtadlus mendele moykher-sforim* (Vilna: Romm, 1879). As in the first edition of *Benjamin III*, Abramovich's name appears separately as the author of the book, while Mendele features in the title as the fictional "publisher." The 1879 edition of *Dok kleyne mentshele* has become extremely rare; it has been reprinted, together with the notations of differences from the last version, revised in 1907, in the third volume of the incomplete Soviet critical edition of Abramovich's collected works; see [Mendele moykher-sforim], *Gezamlte verk*, ed. Meir Winer (Moscow: "Emes," 1935), vol. 3. The 1907 version considerably mutes the Nicholaevan subplot; for a comparison, see Weinreich, *Bilder fun der yidisher literaturgeshikhte*, 337ff.

65. See [Mendele Mokher Sfarim], *Ktavim be'ibam*, ed. and trans. Shalom Lurya (Haifa: Haifa University, 1994), 133–165.

66. Abramovich, *Dos kleyne mentshele*, 119–120.

67. Abramovich, *Der priziv: a drame in finf aktn* (St. Petersburg: Tsederbaum, 1884). On manuscript drafts of *The Call-Up*, the content of which shows that Abramovich

had at least a preliminary version of the play completed between 1876 and 1879, see Roskies-Wisse, "*K'minhag yud:* an umbakanter ktav-yad fun mendele mokher-sefarim," in *For Max Weinreich on His Seventieth Birthday: Studies in Jewish Language, Literature, and Society* (The Hague: Mouton, 1964), 337–342.

68. Abramovich, *Der priziv,* act 2, scene 1.

69. Abramovich to Binshtok, 16 February 1880, in "Briv fun mendele moykher sforim (fun der binshtok-kolektsiye), *Tsaytshrift* 5, pt. 2 ("Fun undzer arkhiv") (1931): 35–36.

70. Abramovich, in a dedicatory letter to "Moshe," identified by Weinreich as Moisei Yakovlevich Halpern, a friend from the author's early years in Berdichev. See Abramovich's prologue to *Der priziv.* On the identity of "Moshe," see Weinreich, "Materialn un notitsn, mendele-dokumentn," *YIVO Bleter* 10 (1936): 370–371.

71. See Klausner, *Historiyah,* 6:372–374.

72. Ben-Yosef [pseud. L. Kantor], "Ocherki novoevreiskoi literatury I: S. Ia. [*sic*] Abramovich i ego 25-let. deiatel'nost,' " *Evreiskoe obozrenie* (July 1884): 138. This was the first part of a projected two-part study of Abramovich's literary activity; here Kantor focused on Abramovich's Hebrew writing. The second part, which was supposed to focus Abramovich's Yiddish works, never appeared.

73. Ibid., 143.

74. Ibid., 138. Abraham Mapu (1808–1867) was a Vilna maskil, made famous by two popular, biblically inspired Hebrew novels, *Love of Zion* (Heb. *Ahavat tsion,* 1853) and *Guilt of Samaria* (Heb. *Ashmat shomron,* 1865); before Abramovich, he was the best-known author of original Jewish prose fiction. For a discussion of Mapu's work as a novelist and his place in the development of maskilic literature, see Miron, *From Romance to the Novel,* 17–175.

75. M. Morgulis, "K iubileiu narodnogo pisatelia Solomona Moiseevicha Abra-movicha," *Nedel'naia khronika voskhoda* 3, no. 43 (1884): 1213–1217.

76. On the celebration of Gordon's literary anniversary (29 October 1881), "the first of its kind in Russian-Jewish history," see Stanislawki, *For Whom Do I Toil?* 174–175.

77. Morgulis, "K iubileiu," 1213.

78. A. Flekser, "Feileton: prazdnik v cherte," *Russkii evrei,* nos. 45–46 (16 December 1884): 23–28.

79. Under his Russian pseudonym, Volynskii (i.e., "from Volhynia," an allusion to his southern Jewish roots), Flekser (1863–1926) established his literary reputation as a pioneer of Dostoevsky criticism and an opponent of the "social" approach to Russian literature, a mode of reading which he identified with V. G. Belinskii and his intellectual followers, N. G. Chernyshevskii and N. A. Dobroliubov; these two also inspired radical maskilic critics of Jewish literature like Abraham Paperna (1840–1919) and the wayward Abraham-Uri Kovner (1842–1909). Thus Flekser-Volynskii's interest in Abramovich marked a larger shift in Russian-Jewish literary culture, a paradoxical sign of cosmopolitanism in search of authenticity. A Jewish critic, in-spired by his philosophical understanding of Dostoevsky's humanism (at the expense of the latter's Russian Orthodox chauvinism), presumed to rescue Abramo-vich from literary obscurity as the bearer of "native" Jewish genius! For assessments (generally negative) of the inner tensions of Volynskii's work as a critic, see N. K. Mikhailovskii, "O g. Volynskom i russkom chitatele," in his *Polnoe sobranie sochinenii* (St. Petersburg: M. M. Stasiulevich, 1908–13), vol. 10; and his *Dostoevsky: A Cruel Talent,* trans. Spencer Cadmus (Ann Arbor, Mich.: Ardis, 1978). See also G. V. Ple-khanov, "Sud'by russkoi kritiki: A. L. Volynskii," in idem, *Sochineniia,* 24 vols. (Mos-cow: Gosudarstvennoe izd-vo, 1923–27), 10:164–197. The ironic affinity between modern Jewish writing and the "philosophical" (humanist) reading of Dostoevsky persisted long past Volynskii. Dostoevsky is the single most important (if often reluc-

tantly acknowledged) influence on the emergence of modern Jewish prose in both Hebrew and Yiddish, not to mention on the development of Russian-Jewish literary self-consciousness; on the latter, see Harriet Murav, *Identity Theft: The Jew in Imperial Russia and the Case of Avraam-Uri Kovner* (Stanford, Calif.: Stanford University Press, 2003), esp. chap. 6. It is also notable that, after Volynskii, the most important proponent of the "philosophical" — as opposed to both the nationalist and the strictly Marxist — approach to Dostoevsky's work was the Soviet-Jewish Dostoevsky scholar Leonid Petrovich Grossman (1888–1965) .

80. On the use of the terms *sliianie* and *sblizhenie* in the debate about Jewish emancipation in Russia, see Klier, *Imperial Russia's Jewish Question*, 72–83.

81. L. Binshtok, "Prazdnik zhargonnoi literatury (Solomon Moiseevich Abramovich i ego 25-letniaia literaturnaia deiatel'nost')," *Voskhod* 4, no. 12, pt. 2 (1884): 1–32.

82. Ibid., 19.

83. This quotation comes from a congratulatory letter that preceded a special anniversary edition of *Der prizyv*, presented as a gift to Abramovich by the author's friends who shepherded the book into print. The letter was published by Weinreich, in his "Materialn un notitsn," 371; see also the special address sent to Abramovich on the occasion of his anniversary by his friends in St. Petersburg, in ibid., 372–373.

84. Abramovich's home served as a meeting place for Odessa's maskilic society precisely at the time of the turn toward nationalism; Abramovich hosted a kind of salon devoted to the cultivation of the Hebrew Renaissance. For a description of this circle, see the memoir by one of its members, the Russian-Jewish historian Simon Dubnow, *Kniga zhizni, vospominaniia i razmyshleniia, materialy dlia istorii moego vremeni* [1934], ed. V. E. Kel'ner (St. Petersburg: PV, 1998), 245–256.

85. Compare Abramovich's own "Notes for a History of My Life," published by Nahum Sokolow in 1889, just five years after the celebration, where he talks both about the necessity of "exile" and the providential "accident" that turned him into a writer. The entire piece is shot through with allusions to writing as a form of "revelation." See Abramovich, "Reshimot le-toldotai," in *Kol kitvei mendele mokher-sfarim* (Tel Aviv: Dvir, 1959), 1–6.

86. Abramovich himself vigorously resisted any attempt to locate his work within contemporary Russian or European literature; see Klausner, *Historiyah*, 6:356–357.

87. Both *The Nag* and *Benjamin III* were translated into Polish in 1885–1886; in 1886 Polish writers invited Abramovich to Warsaw where they hosted a banquet in his honor. On this and on the conspicuous indifference of both the Hebrew and the Yiddish press to Abramovich's literary anniversary, see Klausner, *Historiyah*, 6:381.

88. Ibid., 6:384.

89. See the memoir of Abramovich's Odessa circle in Dubnow, *Fun "zhargon" tsu yidish un andere artikln: literarishe zikhroynes* (Vilna: Kletskin, 1929), 111.

90. The autobiography was variously known as *Shlomo, the Son of Reb Hayyim* (Yid. *Shloyme reb khayims*, 1899; Heb. *Hayyei shlomo*, 1903); Abramovich published the introductory section of the Hebrew version in 1900 in his first collection of Hebrew short stories.

91. Abramovich, "Ba-yamin ha-hem," in idem, *Kol kitvei mendele mokher-sfarim*, 258.

92. See Lurya's introduction, "M-*tab'at ha-mofet* el *Be'emek ha-bakha*," to Mendele Mokher Sfarim, *Ktavim be'ibam*, 21–22.

93. Abramovich worked together with the poet H. N. Bialik and the Jewish publicist and author J. Kh. Ravnitskii; only *Genesis* was eventually completed. See Klausner, *Historiyah*, 6:390.

94. There is some critical dispute about the original publication date, because it was left off the original frontispiece; see Gurshteyn, "Der yunger mendele," 486–487. On the literary context, especially on the model form of the chapbook, see Weinreich, *Bilder*, 344.

95. On the different versions of the novel, see Werses, "Mendele, ba'al ha-agadah le- or *Be'emek ha-bakhah—Dos vintshfingerl*," in his *From Mendele to Hazaz*, 11–71; and I. Nusinov, "Fun bukh tzu bukh" and "Di ershte oysgabe fun *Dos vintshfingerl*," in Turniansky, *Yiddish Literature in the Nineteenth Century*, 511–538. On *Be'emek ha-bakha*, see Jacob Fichman, "Mendele," in his *Amat ha-binyan, sofrei Odessa* (Jerusalem: Mosad Bialik, 1951), 11–52.

96. The quotation is from Fichman, "Mendele," 98–99. In private Abramovich referred ironically to the endless rewriting of *Dos vintshfingerl* as an "epic" task: see his letter to L. Binshtok, 11 June 1891, cited in Ginsburg, "Mendele moykher-sforim in zayne briv," in his *Historical Works*, 1:158.

97. For the ironic characterization of explicitly maskilic books as "poor merchandise" versus enlightenment in the form of a "tale" (Yid. *mayse*) which is a "real piece of goods for you," see Mendele Mokher Sfarim, "Dos vintshfingerl" (1866), in idem, *Ktavim be'ibam*, 30.

98. This is the function of R. Shmelke's story; see ibid., 40–41.

99. Ibid., 40.

100. On the self-conscious "distancing" of Abramovich's prophetic persona from the mundane tasks of publishing and selling books, a function ascribed to Mendele, see "Ba-yamin ha-hem," 260.

101. For a penetrating discussion of the prologue (which, in all subsequent editions of the novel, appeared as an epilogue), see Miron, *Traveler Disguised*, chap. 4. For the original text, see Sh. Y. Abramovich, "Dos vintshfingerl: a matoneh far di liebe yudishe kinder," *Di yudishe folks-bibliotek* 1 (1888): 1–9.

102. Compare this to the last section of the 1866 version that functions as a crude advertisement for Mendele's literary "goods"; its provocative title, in the Russian/Ukrainian street idiom, is "Yid, hand over your money!" (Rus. *zhid davai groshi*). See Mendele Mokher Sfarim, "Dos vintshfingerl (1866)," 50.

103. S. Y. Abramovitsh (Mendele Moykher Sforim), *The Wishing Ring: A Novel*, trans. Michael Wex (Syracuse, N.Y.: Syracuse University Press, 2003), 1. This recent translation adopts the text of the novel as it appeared in volumes 11–12 of *Ale verk fun mendele moykher-sforim (Sh. Y. Abramovits)*, 22 vols., ed. Nahman Maisel (Warsaw: Ferlag "Mendele," 1928). The revision of the Yiddish version followed in the wake of the serialization of its Hebrew counterpart, *Be'emek ha-bakha*, published in full slightly earlier than the complete *Vintshfingerl*. By 1910 both of them were complete.

104. See, for example, Miron, *Traveler Disguised*, 316.

105. Abramovitsh, *The Wishing Ring*, 31.

5. DEAD CHILDREN OF THE HEBREW RENAISSANCE

1. While the "political education" of Jewish nationalists took place in the shadow of the 1905 Revolution, it was not until the First World War that Zionism began to attract a mass following. On the formation of "party ideologies" in 1906–1907, see Frankel, *Prophecy and Politics*, chap. 3; here, 133. See also Ezra Mendelsohn, *On Modern Jewish Politics* (Oxford: Oxford University Press, 1993).

2. With few exceptions, the scholarship on Jewish nationalism is confined to political history and aims, teleologically, at Palestine; see, for instance, the recent survey by Gideon Shimoni, *The Zionist Ideology* (Hanover, N.H., and London: University Press of New England/Brandeis University Press, 1995); as well as Ben Halpern and Jehuda Reinharz, *Zionism and the Creation of a New Society* (New York: Oxford University Press, 1998). For a contrasting approach that envisions Jewish nationalism as a European cultural movement, see the pioneering article by Carl E. Schorske, "Politics in a New Key: An Austrian Trio," in his *Fin de Siècle Vienna: Politics and Culture*

(New York: Vintage, 1980), 116–180; as well as Stanislawski's *Zionism and the Fin de Siècle,* a study inspired by Schorske's work.

3. In 1906 Russian Zionists convened in Helsingfors and decided to adopt "work in the diaspora" as a key element of their platform. See the "Memorandum of the Central Committee of the Zionist Organization in Russia," trans. R. Wisse, in *The Jew in the Modern World: A Documentary History,* ed. Paul Mendes-Flohr and Jehuda Reinharz, 2nd ed. (Oxford: Oxford University Press, 1995), 555.

4. Seth Schwartz, *Imperialism and Jewish Society, 200 BCE to 640 CE* (Princeton, N.J, and Oxford: Princeton University Press, 2001), 74–87; here, 76. Schwartz offers a compelling reading of apocalypticism which privileges its ideological function over its ostensible "political" origins in "specific events," namely, the "Antiochan persecution" and "Roman oppression." A similar originary "political" bias pervades the study of modern Jewish culture as a "response to catastrophe"; see Alan Mintz, *Hurban: Responses to Catastrophe in Hebrew Literature* (Syracuse, N.Y.: Syracuse University Press, 1996); and Roskies, *Against the Apocalypse.* Like Schwartz, I am more interested in analyzing the "ethos" of nationalist "mythopoesis" than in looking for evidence of its origins in "political persecution" and "social oppression." Cf. Schwartz, *Imperialism and Jewish Society,* 75–76.

5. On this paradox, see Yaacov Shavit, "The 'Glorious Century' or the 'Cursed Century': *Fin-de-Siècle* Europe and the Emergence of Modern Jewish Nationalism," *Journal of Contemporary History* 26 (1991): 553–574. I am grateful to Nils Roemer for this reference.

6. On the fear of Jewish solidarity, a stock-in-trade theme of Russian judaeophobia at least since the mid-1870s, see Klier, *Imperial Russia's Jewish Question,* chap. 12. See also Steven G. Marks, *How Russia Shaped the Modern World: From Art to Anti-Semitism, Ballet to Bolshevism* (Princeton, N.J.: Princeton University Press, 2003).

7. On the growth of the Jewish press in the Russian Empire in the last quarter of the nineteenth century, see Zinberg, *Istoriia evreiskoi pechati v sviiazi s obshchetvennymi techeniiami* (Petrograd: Fleitman, 1915); Ivask, *Evreiskaia periodicheskaia pechat' v Rossii;* Slutsky, *Ha'itonut ha-yehudit rusit;* and Eliashevich, *Pravitel'stvennaia politika i evreiskaia pechat' v Rossii.* On Jewish literacy—in the various languages spoken and read by Jews in the Russian Empire—see Shaul Stampfer, "Yedi'at kro ukhtov etsel yehudei mizrah eiropah ba-tekufah ha-hadashah," in *Transition and Change in Modern Jewish History* [in Hebrew], ed. Shmuel Almog et al. (Jerusalem: Merkaz Shazar, 1987), 459–483.

8. See Shaul Stampfer, "Patterns of Internal Jewish Migration in the Russian Empire," in *Jews and Jewish Life in Russia and the Soviet Union,* ed. Yaacov Ro'i (Ilford, Essex: Frank Cass, 1995), 28–47.

9. On changes in the Jewish economy in the last quarter of the nineteenth century, see Arcadius Kahan, "The Impact of Industrialization in Tsarist Russia on the Socioeconomic Conditions of the Jewish Population," in his *Essays in Jewish Social and Economic History,* ed. Roger Weiss (Chicago and London: University of Chicago Press, 1986), 1–69. On urban concentration, see Dinur, "Demutah ha-historit shel ha-yahadut ha-rusit."

10. On the "profound shift" toward orthodoxy in Russian-Jewish "religious politics," see Freeze, *Jewish Marriage,* 244–251.

11. On the embourgeoisement of Russian social life, a process in which Jewish professionals—particularly lawyers and doctors but also publicists, artists, musicians, and entrepreneurs—seemed to have played a disproportionate part, see Edith W. Clowes, Samuel D. Kassow, and James L. West, eds., *Between Tsar and People: Educated Society and the Quest for Public Identity in Late Imperial Russia* (Princeton, N.J.: Princeton University Press, 1991). The Jewish "educated society" (Rus. *obshchestvo*) of late

imperial Russia still awaits its historian; for now, see Christoph Gassenschmidt, *Jewish Liberal Politics in Tsarist Russia, 1900–1914: The Modernization of Russian Jewry* (Houndmills, Basingstoke: Macmillan/St. Anthony's College, Oxford, 1995); and Nathans, *Beyond the Pale*, pt. 4.

12. On the growth of elite religious subcultures in Jewish Lithuania during the late imperial period, see Stampfer, *Ha-yeshivah ha-litait;* David E. Fishman, "Musar and Modernity: The Case of Novaredok," *Modern Judaism* 8 (1988): 41–64; as well as Immanuel Etkes, "Marriage and Torah Study among the *Lomdim* in Lithuania in the Nineteenth Century," and "The Relationship between Talmudic Scholarship and the Institution of the Rabbinate in Nineteenth-Century Lithuanian Jewry," in *Scholars and Scholarship: The Interaction between Judaism and Other Cultures,* ed. Leo Landman (New York: Yeshiva University Press, 1990), 107–132.

13. See the sources cited in Freeze, *Jewish Marriage*, 269 nn. 96–99.

14. G. B. Sliozberg, in "Otchet o soveshchanii evreiskikh obshchestvennykh deiatelei," *Evreiskii mir* 1 (1909), nos. 11–12: 35–37. On Sliozberg's career, see Nathans, *Beyond the Pale*, 325–334.

15. The quotation is from Nathans, *Beyond the Pale, 332.*

16. For the theoretical background, see the classic by V. Ia. Propp, *Morphology of the Folk-tale,* ed. Svatava Pirkova-Jakobson, trans. Laurence Scott (Bloomington: Indiana University Press, 1958). There were a number of previous attempts to write conscription folk tales in which the Nicholaevan recruit appeared as a trickster-hero; see Y. Berman, "Shnot rainu ra'ah," *Hamelitz* 1 (1861): 249–251, 269–272, 294–296, 314–316, 331–333; and L. Vladimirov, "Poimannik-chudodei," *Razsvet* 1 (1860): 660–664. Written by minor authors and published as journalistic sketches in the emergent Russian-Jewish press, these alleged eyewitness accounts from the immediate pre-reform past were actually miniature versions of the enlightenment picaresque. The historical interest involved in the literary construction of conscription "ethnography," a trend that culminated in the "cantonist songs" published in S. M. Ginsburg and P. S. Marek, eds., *Evreiskie narodnye pesni v Rossii* (St. Petersburg: "Voskhod," 1901), nos. 44–50, has never been analyzed. Historians of Jewish culture treat this material entirely as the repository of conscription history; see Roskies, *Against the Apocalypse,* 57–62; and Ofek, "Cantonists."

17. On the emergence of the "archaic avant-garde," see Terry Eagleton, *Heathcliff and the Great Hunger: Studies in Irish Culture* (London and New York: Verso, 1995), chap. 7.

18. Cf. Harold Bloom, *The Anxiety of Influence: A Theory of Poetry* (New York: Oxford University Press, 1973).

19. To this visionary company, we may also add the poets Jacob Cahan and Kh. N. Bialik, both of whom wrote or attempted to write narrative conscription poems in the apocalyptic mode. Cahan's 1904 "Ha-hotfim," in fact, rehearses the plot of Ben-Ami's "Ben-yukhid"; see *Kitvei Yaacov Cahan, shirim* (Tel Aviv: Dvir, 1960), 156–157. See also Bialik's unfinished conscription poem, "Yonah ha-hayat" —written in 1894 and published in *Ha-aretz* in 1928 —in *Collected Poems, 1890–1898* [in Hebrew], ed. Dan Miron (Tel Aviv: Dvir, 1983), 276–279.

20. On the critique of "pseudo-enlightenment," see Feiner, "Pseudo-Enlightenment." On the decadent aesthetic of the Hebrew revival, see Hamutal Bar-Yosef, *Decadent Trends in Hebrew Literature: Bialik, Berdychevski, Brener* [in Hebrew], (Jerusalem: Mosad Bialik, 1997).

21. Bar-Yosef, *Decadent Trends,* 24.

22. Compare the importance of decadence for the turn-of-the-century revival of Catholic culture in Ellis Hanson, *Decadence and Catholicism* (Cambridge, Mass., and London: Harvard University Press, 1997).

23. Compare my reading with Lederhendler's "Interpreting Messianic Rhetoric in

the Russian Haskalah and Early Zionism," *Studies in Contemporary Jewry Annual* 7 (1991): 14–33. Lederhendler contends that maskilic messianism constituted a political "myth" no one believed in, a purely "rhetorical" instrument. This is a profoundly circular argument (if no one believed it, then why was it rhetorically useful?) that fails to take into account the cultural meaning of apocalyptic writing as a style of Jewish thought and, in the words of Seth Schwartz, an "ethos" in its own right.

24. Ben-Ami, "Ben-yukhid: byl' iz vremen lovchikov," *Voskhod* 4, no. 1 (1884): 151–161; no. 2 (1884): 131–156; here, no. 1 (1884): 156–157.

25. Ibid., no. 2, 132.

26. P. Levenson, "Zakoldovannyi (byl')," *Voskhod* 4, no. 7 (1884): 16–41; here, 27.

27. M. Z. Feierberg, "Yankev the Watchman," in his *Whither? And Other Stories*, trans. Hillel Halkin (Philadelphia: Jewish Publication Society, 1973), 41–50, here; 44.

28. Roskies, *Bridge of Longing*, 125–126.

29. For the Hebrew, see "Tov!" in I. L. Peretz, *Kitvei Y. L. Peretz*, 10 vols. (Tel Aviv: Dvir, 1961), 1:5–6; for the Yiddish, see "S'iz gut!," in idem, *Ale verk* (New York: CYCO, 1947–48), 5:152–156.

30. See "Der meshulekh," in Peretz, *Ale verk*, 2:30–39.

31. "Ba-yamim ha-hem (sipuro shel zaken)," in *Kol kitvei Yehudah Steinberg* (Tel Aviv: Dvir, 1959), 230–254; here, 234.

32. Ben-Ami, "Ben-yukhid," no. 1, 151.

33. Feierberg, "Yankev," 49.

34. Peretz, "Tov!" 5.

35. On the conventional uses of railroad imagery in nineteenth-century European literature, see Marc Baroli, *Le train dans la littérature française* (Paris: Editions N. M., 1969); and Alfred Heinimann, *Technische Innovation und literarische Aneignung: die Eisenbahn in der deutschen und englischen Literatur in 19. Jahrhunderts* (Bern: Francke, 1992).

36. Levenson, "Zakoldovannyi," 19.

37. Ibid., 41.

38. Ibid., 23.

39. Steinberg, "Ba-yamim ha-hem," 253.

40. Ibid., 254.

41. Feierberg, "Yankev," 42–43.

42. Ben-ami, "Ben-yukhid," no. 1, 153.

43. For the highlights of Ben-Ami's literary career, see Zinberg's article in *Evreiskaia entsiklopediia*, 4:142–144.

44. Ibid., 4:144. See also Ginsburg, "Iz mira unizhennykh (o proizvedeniiakh Ben-Ami)," *Voskhod* 17, no. 12 (1897): 28–40.

45. See Petrovsky-Shtern, *Evrei v russkoi armii*, 186–196.

46. On *tsiyonut 'artilait*, which can also be rendered as "integral Zionism," see Stanislawski, "Vladimir Jabotinsky, Cosmopolitan Ultra-Nationalist," in his *Zionism and the Fin-de-Siècle*, 203–237; here, 210, 221.

47. Compare Roskies' literary "historicism" in *Against the Apocalypse* to Daniel Boyarin's far-reaching claim that literature does not transparently render a "reflection of its historical circumstances"; rather, a "text is the representation of a moment in the history of an *ideology.*" See Boyarin's "'Language Inscribed by History on the Bodies of Living Beings': Midrash and Martyrdom," *Representations* 25 (1989): 139–151; here, 148 (emphasis added). See also idem, "Whose Martyrdom Is This, Anyway?" in his *Martyrdom and the Making of Christianity and Judaism* (Stanford, Calif.: Stanford University Press, 1999), 93–126. In this essay, Boyarin explicitly contrasts the limited value of reading martyrological accounts in order to find out "what

happened" (in this case, to martyrs) with reading martyrology as a discursive event in the making of a polemical "ideology of death," vital to maintaining the boundaries of a living religious community. For other examples of this nuanced approach to the historical character of Jewish literature, see Cohen, *Sanctifying the Name of God;* and Einbinder, *Beautiful Death.*

48. On the expansion of radical and liberal Jewish politics as a direct result of 1905, see Frankel, *Prophecy and Politics,* chap. 3; and Gassenschmidt, *Jewish Liberal Politics.*

49. The first quotation is from Roskies's introduction to "Sholem Aleichem: The Critical Tradition," *Prooftexts* 6 (1986): 1. On the Sholem-aleichem "persona," see Miron, "Sholem Aleichem: Person, Persona, Presence," in his *Image of the Shtetl,* 128–156.

50. See the cautionary note on the importance of the "aesthetic-fictional" mediation of historical reality in Sholem-aleichem's work, in Miron, "The Literary Image of the Shtetl," in his *Image of the Shtetl,* 1–48, esp. 1–4.

51. See, for instance, Maurice Samuel, *The World of Sholom Aleichem* (New York: Vintage, 1943).

52. See the representative selection of critical approaches in "Sholem Aleichem: The Critical Tradition."

53. Technically *Der yud* was a Vienna paper; it was edited from Warsaw and published abroad because of censorship restrictions. Yiddish newspapers began to appear regularly in the capital cities of the Russian Empire only after the 1905 Revolution; see Sarah Stein, *Making Jews Modern: The Yiddish and Ladino Press in the Russian and Ottoman Empires* (Bloomington: Indiana University Press, 2004), chap. 1. For the Yiddish texts of the stories, see "Funem prizyv," in *Ale verk fun Sholem-aleichem,* 28 vols. (New York: Sholem-aleichem folks-fond, 1917–1923), 26:197–211; and "Gitl purishkevich," in ibid., 25:221–234. For English translations, see Sholem Aleichem, "The Automatic Exemption," in his *Tevye the Dairyman and the Railroad Stories,* trans. Hillel Halkin (New York: Schocken Books, 1987), 229–238; and "Goody 'Purishkevich,'" in his *Nineteen to the Dozen: Monologues and Bits and Bobs of Other Things,* trans. Ted Gorelick, ed. Ken Frieden (Syracuse, N.Y.: Syracuse University Press, 1998), 44–53.

54. For the motif of the widowed mother, see, for instance, *rekrutchina* folk song no. 49, in Ginsburg and Marek, *Evreiskie narodnye pesni:* "Zushe Rakover has seven healthy sons / Not one will be forced to carry a gun / But widow Leah's only kid will be / A scapegoat for the *kahal's* treachery." There is a translation in David G. Roskies, ed., *The Literature of Destruction: Jewish Responses to Catastrophe* (Philadelphia, New York, and Jerusalem: Jewish Publication Society, 1988), 119.

55. V. M. Purishkevich (1870–1920), a deputy of the Third and Fourth Duma, was a virulently anti-Semitic member of the Russian far right and one of the founders of the Union of Russian People, the "most numerous, noisy, intransigent and extremist of the Russian right-wing parties." See Hans Rogger, "Was There a Russian Fascism? The Union of Russian People," in his *Jewish Policies and Right-Wing Politics in Imperial Russia* (Berkeley and Los Angeles: University of California Press, 1986), 212–232.

56. Purishkevich found the entire discussion of granting "civil rights" to Jews "criminal," on the basis of the argument that the Jewish "people finds it impossible to carry out the sacred duty of defending the motherland." See his speech to the Fourth Duma (1913), cited in Petrovsky-Shtern, *Evrei v russkoi armii,* 351–352.

57. Gitl personifies maskilic gender politics; see the discussion of the ambivalent image of Jewish mothers in Dik's *Nabor* and in Gordon's "A Mother's Farewell" in chapter 3 of this volume.

58. On "creative betrayal," see Roskies, *Bridge of Longing,* 4–5.

59. Sholem-aleichem, "Funem prizyv," 202.

60. The Yiddish reads as follows: "er toig nit [. . .] (dos heyst, toygen toig er, nor far keyn soldat toyg er nit)"; see ibid., 201; and again on 202. Halkin's translation is problematic; see Sholem Aleichem, "The Automatic Exemption," 231.

61. Sholem-aleichem, "Funem prizyv," 198, 200, 201, 202.

62. Ibid., 211; idem, "The Automatic Exemption," 238.

63. The novella originally appeared in Ahad ha'am's Hebrew monthly *Ha-shiloah* 19 (1908–1909).

64. Most of Brenner's stories emerge out of a confessional impulse; there is prodigious scholarly debate on the nature of the "autobiographical" component of his fiction. For two contrasting positions, see Nurith Govrin, *Brenner: "Oved 'etsot" u-moreh derekh* (Tel Aviv: Misrad bitahon/Tel Aviv University, 1991), 123–146; and Menahem Brinker, *Narrative Art and Social Thought in Y. H. Brenner's Work* [in Hebrew] (Tel Aviv: 'Am Oved, 1990), 51. Brenner served in Orel for eighteen months; he deserted in the beginning of January 1903. See Yitzhak Bakon, *The Young Brenner: The Life and Works of Brenner until the Publication of Ha-meorer in London* [in Hebrew] 2 vols. (Tel Aviv: Ha-kibbutz ha-meuhad, 1975), 1:92–120.

65. Y. H. Brenner, "Shanah ahat," in *Kol kitvei Y. H. Brenner,* 2 vols. (Tel Aviv: Dvir, 1956), 1:106.

66. Brenner shifted his political allegiance from the Jewish Bund to its Russian rival, the Socialist Revolutionary party, during his term of service. See Bakon, *The Young Brenner,* 101–102. On the importance of the army as the seedbed of revolutionary activity, with reference to the politicization of Jewish servicemen, see Petrovsky-Shtern, *Evrei v russkoi armii,* chap. 5; for the general context, see John Bushnell, *Mutiny Amid Repression: Russian Soldiers in the Revolution of 1905–06* (Bloomington: Indiana University Press, 1985).

67. "Le- or ha-venus" was originally serialized in eleven installments in the radical weekly *Ha-po'el ha-tsair* 5 (1911), the publishing organ of the party of the same name.

68. On the connection between Brenner's move to Palestine and the ideology of the Second Aliyah, see Yosef Gorny "Hope Born of Despair," *Jerusalem Quarterly* 26 (1983): 84–95.

69. Yosef Gorny, "Changes in the Social and Political Structure of the Second Aliya between 1904 and 1940," in *Essential Papers on Zionism,* ed. Jehuda Reinharz and Anita Shapira (New York and London: New York University Press, 1996), 371–421; here, 372. See also Frankel, *Prophecy and Politics,* chap. 8.

70. Frankel, *Prophecy and Politics,* 373.

71. On the ethos of the Second Aliyah, particularly on the connection between "conquest of labor" (Heb. *kibbush ha'avodah*) and the military culture of self-defense, see Anita Shapira, *Land and Power: The Zionist Resort to Force, 1881–1948,* trans. William Templer (New York and Oxford: Oxford University Press, 1992), 62–82.

72. See the discussion of *Red Cavalry* in Petrovsky-Shtern, *Evrei v russkoi armii,* 399–403.

73. On the mirror motif, see Moshe Shamir's introduction to the *Collected Works of L. A. Arieli* [in Hebrew], ed. Milton Arfa, 2 vols. (Tel Aviv: Dvir, 1999), 1:11–12.

74. Brenner, "Shanah ahat," 108.

75. On the ambiguous representation of "barracks" in Brenner's work, see Sadan, *A Psychoanalytic Midrash: Studies in Brenner's Psychology* [in Hebrew] (Jerusalem: Magnes Press/Hebrew University, 1996), 100–105.

76. See Shapira, *Land and Power,* 72; and Frankel, "The 'Yizkor' Book of 1911 – A Note on National Myths in the Second Aliya," in *Essential Papers on Zionism,* 422–453.

77. Arieli, "Le- or ha-venus," in his *Collected Works,* 1:42.

78. Ibid., 1:69.

79. Brenner, "Shanah ahat," 107.

80. Arieli, "Le- or ha-venus," 1:64.

81. On the "absence of a father-image" in Arieli's fiction as a signifier of his "negative relationship to Judaism," see Gila Ramras-Rauch, "L. A. Arieli and the Literature of the Second Aliyah," in *From Ancient Israel to Modern Judaism, Intellect in Quest of Understanding: Essays in Honor of Marvin Fox*, ed. Jacob Neusner, Ernest S. Frerichs, and Nahum M. Sarna, 4 vols. (Atlanta: Scholars, 1989), 4:117.

82. Arieli, "Le- or ha-venus," 3.

83. The difference took the form of a polemic over of the "New Wave" of Hebrew literature, exemplified by Brenner's unmitigated Hebrew "realism"; Ahad ha'am and Peretz denounced the secular turn of the "New Wave." See the introduction to the anthology *Nitsanei ha-realizm ba-siporet ha'ivrit: kovets sipurim*, ed. Josef Even and Itzchak Ben-Mordecai, 2 vols. (Jerusalem: Mosad Bialik, 1993), 2:12. There is an extended discussion in Miron, *When Loners Come Together*, 225–260. See, in this context, the tortured attempt to rehabilitate Brenner as the "most consistent maskil" of all the Hebrew writers, in Menahem Brinker, "Brenner's Jewishness," *Studies in Contemporary Jewry Annual* 4 (1988): 232–249.

84. The quotation is from Frankel, "The 'Yizkor' Book of 1911," 448.

85. The best treatment of the ethos of "spiritual nationalism" remains Klausner's essay, *Dukhovnyi sionizm i ego glavnyi predstavitel', opyt obstoiatel'nogo izlozheniia i kharakteristiki sionistskoi doktriny Akhad gaama* (St. Petersburg: A. E. Landau, 1900).

86. See Ahad ha'am's letter in *Igrot ahad ha'am*, 6 vols. (Jerusalem: Moriah, 1923–1925), 6:228. Feierberg's response is quoted by Klausner in the latter's introduction to Feierberg's *Sefer kovets sipurav u-khtavav* (Krakow: Hevrat sefer, 1904).

87. Basic biographical information for the writers of conscription tales featured in this chapter may be found in the following sources. On Ben-ami, see L. Salmon, "Ben-ami i ego mesto v russko-evreiskoi literature," in *Evrei v Rossii: istoriia i kul'tura, sbornik nauchnykh trudov*, ed. Eliashevich (St. Petersburg: Petersburg Jewish University, 1995), 91–124. On Levenson, see the entry in *Evreiskaia entsiklopediia*, 10:66–67. On Feierberg, see Halkin's introduction to *Whither? and Other Stories*, 3–35. On Steinberg, see Jacob Fichman's introduction to *Kol kitvei Yehudah Steinberg*, 4 vols. (Krakow and Odessa: Y. Fisher, 1910–1915), reprinted in the one-volume 1959 edition, v–xiv. There is an enormous critical and biographical literature on Peretz, in both Yiddish and Hebrew; the most up-to-date synoptic treatment of his life and work in English is Wisse's *Peretz and the Making of Modern Jewish Culture* (Seattle and London: University of Washington Press, 1991).

88. See, for instance, *Kitvei ben 'ami, meturgamim me-rusit* (Odessa: Moriah, 1913–14); 2nd ed. published in Tel Aviv in 1926. See also his *Sipurim le-yaldei yisrael* (Tel Aviv: Dvir, 1930); and *Sipurim nivharim* (Tel Aviv: Dvir, 1961).

89. See Feierberg, *Polnoe sobranie sochinenii*, ed. and trans. G. Ia. Krasnyi (St. Petersburg: Sh. Bussel', 1902). This edition was included in the series "Jewish Family Library" (Rus. *Evreiskaia semeinaiia biblioteka*).

90. On Peretz's unrepentant bilingualism, see Frumah Shvarts, "Y. L. Peretz k-msaper du-leshoni," Ph.D. dissertation, Hebrew University, 1994.

91. See, for instance, *Rasskazy i skazki*, ed. S. G. Frug (St. Petersburg: "Pechatnyi trud," 1909); *Khasidskie rasskazy*, ed. M. D. Ryvkin (St. Petersburg: Sh. Bussel', 1902), vol. 8 of the "Jewish Family Library"; and *Polnoe sobranie sochinenii*, trans. Iu. Pinus, 3 vols. (Moscow: "Sovremennye problemy," 1911–1913).

92. See Parush, *National Ideology and Literary Canon*.

93. The notion of the modern Jewish "bookshelf" goes back to the title of the first Russian-Jewish literary annual, *The Jewish Library* (Rus. *Evreiskaia biblioteka*), published by A. E. Landau in St. Petersburg between 1871 and 1903; its successor was the monthly *Voskhod*. See also the most famous image of the Russian-Jewish "bookcase" in Osip Mandelshtam's memoir, *The Noise of Time*. On the connection of this

famous "bookcase" with Russian-Jewish embourgeoisement, see Michael Stanislaw-ski, *Autobiographical Jews: Essays in Jewish Self-Fashioning* (Seattle and London: University of Washington Press, 2004), 92–94.

94. On the nineteenth-century invention of "calendrical morality," inspired by the phenomenal popularity of Dickens's *Christmas Carol* (1843), see E. V. Dushech-kina, *Russkii sviatochnyi rasskaz: stanovleniie zhanra* (St. Petersburg: St. Petersburg University, 1995).

95. See, for instance, the collection of books published in St. Petersburg as part of the series Library of the Jewish School and Family" (Rus. *Biblioteka evreiskoi semii i shkoly*) in 1912–1913; this was the successor of the Jewish Family Library series, which also published a short-lived journal under the same name. These included *Bar-mitzvah: literaturno-khudozhestvennyi sbornik; Evreiskie osennie prazdniki; Khanukah; Lag ba'omer i shavuos; Paskha; Purim; Subbota;* and *Tisha b'av.* There were also a variety of other literary anthologies, published between the 1890s and the First World War, that introduced the Russian-Jewish public to the culture of the Hebrew Renaissance. These included *Novye veiiania* (Moscow: Skirmunt, 1907); *Lira siona* (St. Petersburg: Mendelevich, 1900); *Al'manakh molodoi evreiskoi literatury,* ed. S. A. Gibianskii (St. Peterburg: Sovremennaia mysl', 1908); and *Evreiskaia zhizn' v izobrazhenii evreiskikh bytopisatelei* (St. Petersburg: "Voskhod," 1903).

6. THE WRITING OF CONSCRIPTION HISTORY AND THE MAKING OF THE RUSSIAN-JEWISH DIASPORA

1. These numbers, based primarily on U.S. immigration records, have been reproduced in a variety of sources. For two slightly differing estimates, see Mark Wischnitzer, *To Dwell in Safety: The Story of Jewish Migration since 1800* (Philadelphia: Jewish Publication Society, 1948), 289; and Simon Kuznets, "Immigration of Russian Jewry to the Unites States: Background and Structure," *Perspectives in American History* 9 (1975): 39–41.

2. The cities were Warsaw, Ekaterinoslav, Lodz, Dvinsk, Lublin, Kovno, Zhitomir, Elizavetgrad, Kishinev, Kremenetz, Odessa, and Mogilev; see Dinur, "Demutah ha-historit shel ha-yahadut ha-rusit," 97. On urbanization and concentration within the Pale, see Richard H. Rowland, "Geographical Patterns of the Jewish Population in the Pale of Settlement of Late Imperial Russia," *Jewish Social Studies* 48 (1986): 207–234. On the connection between internal and external migration, exemplified in the predominantly "transitional" occupational profile of the immigrants, see Kuznets, "Immigration," 105–107.

3. See Frankel, "The Crisis of 1881–1882." Kuznets assesses the weight of the historical particulars of the Russian-Jewish situation in relation to the general economic model of mass migration ("Immigration," 86–89).

4. See the nuanced readings of the dynamics of anti-Jewish violence, with particular stress on the political significance of capitalism, in the two revisionist works on the pogroms of 1881–1882 and the Kishinev pogrom of 1903: Aronson, *Troubled Waters;* and Edward H. Judge, *Easter in Kishinev: Anatomy of a Pogrom* (New York and London: New York University Press, 1992).

5. See Hasia Diner, *A Time for Gathering: The Second Migration, 1820–1880* (Baltimore, Md.: Johns Hopkins University Press, 1992), 14.

6. The Russian-Jewish diaspora awaits its historian. For now, see the remarkable case study in Eastern European Jewish trans-nationalism by Rebecca A. Kobrin, "Conflicting Diasporas, Shifting Centers: Migration and Identity in a Trans-National Polish-Jewish Community, 1878–1952," Ph.D. dissertation, University of Pennsylvania, 2002.

7. For a summary of these developments, see Jonathan Frankel, "The Paradoxical Politics of Marginality: Thoughts on the Jewish Situation during the Years 1914–1921," *Studies in Contemporary Jewry Annual* 4 (1988): 3–21.

8. For the idea of imagined community, an idea originally derived from the study of postcolonial nationalism (not entirely irrelevant here, given that the Russian-Jewish diaspora was formed from the remains of one empire — Russia — and largely in the interstices of two others, i.e., the USSR and the U.S. — as well as in Palestine, under the British mandate), see Benedict Anderson, *Imagined Communities* (London and New York: Verso, 1983).

9. See Simon Dubnow, *Ob izuchenii istorii russkikh evreev i ob uchrezhdenii russko-evreiskogo istoricheskogo obshchestva* (St. Petersburg: A. E. Landau, 1891), also reissued in an abridged Hebrew version as "Nahpesa ve-nahkora," *Pardes* 1 (1892): 221–242. Excerpts of the Russian edition have been reprinted in *Evrei v rossiiskoi imperii XVIII–XIX vekov, sbornik trudov evreiskikh istorikov,* ed. A. Lokshin (Moscow and Jerusalem: Jewish University/Gesharim, 1995), 34–63.

10. Dubnow, "Ob izuchenii," in Lokshin, *Evrei v rossiiskoi imperii,* 57. On the impact of the famine of 1891 on Jewish migration to the U.S., see Allan Spetter, "The United States, the Russian Jews and the Russian Famine of 1891–92," *American-Jewish Historical Quarterly* 44 (1975): 236–244.

11. Dubnow, "Ob izuchenii," in Lokshin, *Evrei v rossiiskoi imperii,* 59. Emphasis in the original.

12. In 1909 Dubnow published an annotated bilingual edition of the seventeenth-century record book of the regional *kehillah* of Jewish Lithuania; see his *Pinkas ha-medinah, kovets takanot u-fesakim mi-shnat 383 'ad shnat 521,* 2 vols. (St. Petersburg: I. Lur'e, 1909–1912). On the activities of the Historical-Ethnographic Society, see the most recent appraisal by Jeffrey Veidlinger, "The Historical and Ethnographic Construction of Russian Jewry," *Ab Imperio* 4 (2003): 165–184. Dubnow's three-volume *History of the Jews in Russia and Poland,* written in Russian and translated into English by Israel Friedlander, began with the Jewish settlement of the Crimea in antiquity and ended with the reign of Nicholas II. It was published in Philadelphia by the Jewish Publication Society, between 1916 and 1920. Parts of the Russian original had appeared as articles in *Evreiskaia starina,* the journal published by the Jewish Historical-Ethnographic Society.

13. Dubnow, "Ob izuchenii," in Lokshin, *Evrei v rossiiskoi imperii,* 58.

14. On Graetz, as the proponent of a literary approach to the writing of the Jewish past, see chapter 3 in this volume. On the juridical school of Russian-Jewish historiography, with special reference to Orshanskii, see Benjamin Nathans, "On Russian-Jewish Historiography," in *Historiography of Imperial Russia: The Profession and Writing of History in a Multinational State,* ed. Thomas Sanders (Armonk and London: M. E. Sharpe, 1999), 404–407.

15. See Stanislawski, *Autobiographical Jews.*

16. See the seminal study of Jewish autobiography by Moseley, *Being for Myself Alone: Origins of Jewish Autobiography* (Stanford, Calif.: Stanford University Press, 2005).

17. See Alan Mintz, *"Banished from Their Father's Table": Loss of Faith and Hebrew Autobiography* (Bloomington: Indiana University Press, 1989).

18. See the theoretical introduction, in Moseley, *For Myself Alone,* chap. 1.

19. For biographical information, see the only scholarly work on Antokol'skii: E. V. Kuznetsova, *M. M. Antokol'skii, zhizn' i tvorchestvo* (Moscow: 'Iskusstvo,' 1989); see also, in Hebrew, David Maggid, *Ha-profesor Mordekhai ben Matityahu Antokolskii: kitsur toldotav u-farashat 'avodato bi-sdeh melekhet ha-mahshevet 'ad ha-yom ha-zeh* (Warsaw: Levinskii, 1897). For the original text of the letter, see no. 85, dated "Rome, 4 (16) December, 1873," in V. V. Stasov, ed., *Mark Matveevich Antokol'skii: ego zhizn', tvoreniia,*

pis'ma i stat'i (Moscow: M. O. Vol'f, 1905), 101–107. There is a heavily edited Hebrew translation in *Zikhronot u-tsror mikhtavim me-at Mordekhai Antokolskii,* ed. and trans. I. D. Abramsky (Jerusalem: Mosad Bialik/Betsalel Art Institute, 1952), 151–160.

20. For the publishing history of *Zikhroynes,* see David Assaf's introduction to *Journey to a Nineteenth-Century Shtetl: The Memoirs of Yekhezkel Kotik,* ed. idem, trans. Margaret Birstein (Detroit: Wayne State University Press, 2002), 30–37.

21. See, in English, Eliakum Zunser, *Tsunzers biografie, geshribn fun im aleyn: A Jewish Bard, Being the Biography of Eliakum Tsunzer,* trans. Simon Hisdarsky (New York: Zunser Jubilee Committee, 1905). For biographical information and for the original Yiddish text, see *The Works of Elyokum Zunser; A Critical Edition* [in Yiddish], ed. Mordkhe Schaechter, 2 vols. (New York: YIVO, 1964).

22. See Katz's biographical sketch, "Y. L. Katsnelson, ha-ish ve-foa'lo," in Y. L. Katsnelson, *Mah she-rau 'einai ve-sham'u 'oznai: zikhronot meyemei hayyai, me'at Buki ben yagli* (Jerusalem: Mosad Bialik, 1947), 169–277, specifically 266–269.

23. One early autobiographical sketch about conscription, Judah-Leib Levin's "Ha-hatufim," registers this connection between literature and autobiography. Levin (1844–1925), one of the poets associated with the Hebrew renaissance, turned the conscription tale of the national revival into his own personal apocalypse. See "Ha-hatufim," in Levin, *Zikhronot ve-hegyonot,* ed. Yehudah Slutsky (Jerusalem: Mosad Bialik, 1968), 30–35. The piece was originally published in 1904, in a literary anthology dedicated to the Zionist publicist Nahum Sokolow, which contained another ostensibly autobiographical sketch set "in the time of the *khappers*" and written in the apocalyptic tenor of the national revival; see Abraham-Jacob Paperna, "Ke-afikim ba-negev (roshmei tmunot u-ma'asim me-dor ha'avar)," *Sefer ha-yovel, li-kvod Nahum Sokolow* (Warsaw: Shul'dberg, 1904), 440–450. For another example of the autobiographical appropriation of the nationalist conscription tale, see Abraham Friedberg's "Zikhronot," in *Sefer ha-shanah* 3 (1902): 82–101. Because this sort of autobiographical material on conscription bears such a close literary resemblance to the national conscription tale — not only in terms of content but also in its recourse to the stylized form of the fragment — these pieces follow more closely the analytical model presented in chapter 5 than the one outlined here. The principal factor that separates the conscription sketches of Levin, Paperna, and Friedberg from the tales of Peretz, Feierberg, Steinberg, Levenson, and Ben-ami is the explicitly autobiographical mode. Here we have direct evidence of the role of nationalist conscription *literature* in the construction of a nationalist *memory* of Russian Jewry's pre-reform "childhood."

24. See Elizabeth Valkenier, *Russian Realist Art, the State and Society: The Peredvizhniki and Their Tradition* (New York: Columbia University Press, 1989).

25. Antokol'skii and Repin were roommates while they were students at the Academy. Both were members of the alternative artists' "cooperative" (Rus. *artel'*) headed by Kramskoi, the unofficial leader of the student revolt. On Antokol'skii's association with the Wanderers, see Kuznetsova, *M. M. Antokol'skii,* 27–33.

26. For the twin aspects of Antokol'skii's legacy, compare Kuznetsova, *M. M. Antokol'skii,* 7, and Mirjam Rajner, "The Awakening of Jewish National Art in Russia," *Jewish Art* 16–17 (1990–1991): 112–114.

27. See Stasov, *Mark Matveevich Antokol'skii.*

28. The letter, known primarily in its Hebrew version, became the basis for an autobiographical argument about the latent "Jewishness" of Antokol'skii's Russian art; the pioneer of Israeli art history, Mordechai Narkiss, wrote in the essay that appears at the end of *Zikhronot u-tsror mikhtavim me-at Mordekhai Antokolski* that Antokol'skii's letters testify to the "throbbing of a Jewish soul." On the basis of the intentions that Antokol'skii declared to Stasov in his conscription letter, Narkiss further argued that the maker of the "Russian epic image" secretly "yearned to

produce work on Jewish subjects" and therefore "perhaps" understood the necessity of "living in a Jewish environment." See *Zikhronot u-tsror mikhtavim*, 165–172.

29. The original was done in marble; in addition to the 1876 version, in the Tretiakov Gallery, Moscow, there is an 1878 marble copy in the Haifa Art Museum. An 1874 bronze version, poured from the original plaster cast, is at the Russian Museum in St. Petersburg. A number of smaller copies of the sculpture are housed in the collections of other Russian museums. See the index of Antokol'skii's work in Kuznetsova, *M. M. Antokol'skii*, 295.

30. Stasov, *Mark Matveevich Antokol'skii*, 99.

31. See Stasov's letter to his sister, cited in A. K. Lebedev and G. K. Burova, *Tvorcheskoe sodruzhestvo: M. M. Antokol'skii i V. V. Stasov* (Leningrad: Khudozhnik RSFSR, 1968), 59–61.

32. For a more detailed treatment of this moment in Antokol'skii's development as an artist, with special reference to the visual evidence of *Ecce homo*, see my essay, "Rome and Jerusalem: The Figure of Jesus in the Creation of Mark Antokol'skii," in *The Art of Being Jewish in Modern Times*, ed. Barbara Kirshenblatt-Gimblett and Jon Karp (Philadelphia: University of Pennsylvania Press, 2006). The quotation is from Antokol'skii's letter; see Stasov, *Mark Matveevich Antokol'skii*, 102.

33. Antokol'skii describes his plans to return to the originary scene of childhood as an inescapable, compelling "desire of the soul." See Stasov, *Mark Matveevich Antokol'skii*, 102.

34. Ibid., 106.

35. See, for example, the movement of Jesus's foot in *Ecce homo*, which plays a comparable formal function to the turning pages of the book positioned before the seated figure of *Spinoza* (1886–1887, Russian Museum, St. Petersburg) and to the rolling cup behind the reclining (dead) image of *Socrates* (1875, Russian Museum, St. Petersburg); see the discussion in my "Rome and Jerusalem."

36. Stasov, *Mark Matveevich Antokol'skii*, 106.

37. Assaf, *Journey*, 233.

38. Stasov, *Mark Matveevich Antokol'skii*, 105–106.

39. On the maskilic image of perfected Jewish manhood, see Zalkin, *A New Dawn*, 40–42.

40. Assaf, *Journey*, 103.

41. See the introduction, "Life as It Was—Yekhezkel Kotik and His Memoirs," in ibid., 25.

42. The dystopian image of traditional Eastern European Jewish society has its origins in Solomon Maimon's *Lebensgeschichte* (1792). For its subsequent history in maskilic autobiography, see Shmuel Werses, "Darkei ha-otobiografiah be-tkufat ha-haskalah," *Gilyonot* 4 (1945): 175–183.

43. See Mintz, *Hebrew Autobiography*, 3.

44. Assaf, *Journey*, 233.

45. The texts of these plays—effectively the first example of live Yiddish theatrical performance—have not survived; one, written by an otherwise unknown author named Wolf Kamrash, was called *The Communal Board in Town* (Yid. *Kahal in shtetl*). See the censor's report on the contents of this play in Avraham Yuditskii, "Vegn inhalt fun Vulf Kamrashes pyese *Kahal in shtetl,*" *Shriftn fun der katedra far yidisher kultur ba der ukrainisher akademie fun vissenshaftn* 1 (1928): 331–336. On the performance itself, see the memoirs of Menashe Morgulis, a graduate of the Zhitomir academy, "Iz moikh vospominanii," *Voskhod* 16, nos. 5–6 (1896): 177–181. See also N. Shtif, "Volf Kamrash un der 'ershter yidisher spektakl' in Rusland," in *Teatr-bukh: zamlung tsum fuftsik-yorikn yubiley funem yudishn teatr, 1876–1926* (Kiev: Kultur-lige, 1927), 21–38.

46. M. I. [*sic*] Merimzon, "Razskaz starogo soldata," *Evreiskaia starina* 5 (1912): 290–301, 406–422; 6 (1913): 86–95, 221–232.

47. See the editor's note to ibid.

48. See, especially, Itskovich, "Vospominaniia arkhangel'skogo kantonista."

49. Auerbach, *Mimesis: The Representation of Reality in Western Literature*, trans. Willard R. Trask (Princeton, N.J., and Oxford: Princeton University Press, 2003), 20.

50. Nathans, "Russian-Jewish Historiography," 419.

51. For a survey of this material, see Abraham G. Duker, "*Evreiskaia starina*: A Bibliography of the Russian-Jewish Historical Periodical," *Hebrew Union College Annual* 8–9 (1931–1932): 532–533, 535–538. For a critical overview, see Petrovsky-Shtern, *Evrei v russkoi armii*, 396–399.

52. Yearly publication was interrupted by the Russian Revolution of 1917. Between 1918 and the closing of the journal by the Jewish Section of the Communist Party in 1930, only four volumes were published.

53. See Ginsburg, "Idishe kantonistn," in idem, *Historical Works*, 3:3–135. For the original Russian version, see his, "Mucheniki-deti (iz istorii kantonistov-evreev)," *Evreiskaia starina* 13 (1930): 50–79. Considered seminal in the Russian-Jewish historiographical revival of the 1990s, it was reprinted in the 1995 anthology *Evrei v rossiiskoi imperii*, 411–439. Ginsburg's work on this subject, in either Russian or Yiddish, is consistently cited, without analysis or even qualification, in every scholarly treatment of Jewish conscription; see, for example, Louis Greenberg, *The Jews in Russia*, 2 vols. (New Haven and London: Yale University Press, 1944), 1:48–52; and Salo W. Baron, *The Russian Jew under Tsars and Soviets* (New York: Macmillan, 1964), 29–32. Until the appearance of Stanislawski's *Tsar Nicholas I and the Jews* in 1983 and Petrovsky-Shtern's *Evrei v russkoi armii* twenty years later, Ginsburg's conclusions remained unchallenged.

54. See the new reprint of the 1925–1927 edition, Iulii Gessen, *Istoriia evreiskogo naroda v Rossii*, ed. V. Iu. Gessen and V. E. Kel'ner (Moscow and Jerusalem: Jewish University/Gesharim, 1993). V. Iu. Gessen's introduction summarizes the publication information; see i–vi.

55. Nathans, "Russian-Jewish Historiography," 411. Bio-bibliographical information is handily available in a modern edition of Sophie Dubnov-Erlich's *Life and Work of S. M. Dubnov, Diaspora Nationalism and Jewish History*, trans. Judith Vowles, ed. Jeffrey Shandler (Bloomington: Indiana University Press, 1991).

56. There is very little scholarship on Lipschitz; see Israel Bartal, "'True Knowledge and Wisdom': On Orthodox Historiography," *Studies in Contemporary Jewry Annual* 10 (1994): 178–192.

57. See Yosef Hayim Yerushalmi, *Zakhor, Jewish History and Jewish Memory* (Seattle and London: University of Washington Press, 1982), chap. 3, esp. 58–59. There is considerable debate regarding certain aspects of Yerushalmi's argument, particularly regarding the question of whether 1492 was the end of the Jewish Middle Ages—which would mean that the new historiography is actually the last example of medieval Jewish "ecclesiology"—or the beginning of a Jewish "Renaissance"—in which case the historical works of the post-expulsion period are the first examples of the impact of humanism on Jewish writing. For the former position, an explicit response to Yerushalmi who argued the latter, see Robert Bonfil, "How Golden Was the Age of the Renaissance in Jewish Historiography?" in *Essential Papers on Jewish Culture in Renaissance and Baroque Italy*, ed. David B. Ruderman (New York and London: New York University Press, 1992), 219–251. There is an attendant problem regarding the relationship between historical writing and "historical consciousness," a slippery concept the usefulness of which, frankly, eludes me. See Amos Funkenstein, "Collective Memory and Historical Consciousness," *History and Memory* 1 (1989): 5–26.

58. This, of course, is not to deny the importance of the rabbinic imaginary which envisioned Sefarad as a hegemonic whole, in contrast to Ashkenaz; see Gerson D. Cohen, "The Story of the Four Captives," in his *Studies in the Variety of Rabbinic Cultures* (Philadelphia: Jewish Publication Society, 1991), 157–208. The relationship between the Sefarad of the rabbis and the Sefarad imagined by the likes of Ibn Verga, Capsali, and Ha-kohen is not at all self-evident; whether either was relevant to the way Iberian Jews actually thought of themselves, prior to the Expulsion, is even less clear. There seems to be more evidence in favor of regional or even more localized, urban consciousness. On the ironic role of the Expulsion as a catalyst for the emergence of Sefarad, see Haim Hillel Ben-Sasson, "Galut ve-geulah be'einav shel dor golei sefarad," in *Sefer yovel le-Yitshak Baer bi-melot lo shiv'im shanah*, ed. S. Ettinger et al. (Jerusalem: Ha-hevrah ha-historit ha-yisraelit, 1960), 216–227. On the parallel question regarding the ambiguous standing of Ashkenaz, see Joseph M. Davis, "The Reception of the *Shulhan 'Arukh* and the Formation of Ashkenazic-Jewish Identity," *AJS Review* 26 (2002): 251–276.

59. For the publishing record and analysis of the original Yiddish *Shevet yehudah*, see Stanislawski, "The Yiddish *Shevet Yehudah*: A Study in the 'Ashkenization' of a Spanish-Jewish Classic," in *Jewish History and Jewish Memory: Essays in Honor of Yosef Hayim Yerushalmi*, ed. Elisheva Carlebach, John M. Efron, and David N. Myers (Hanover, N.H., and London: University Press of New England/Brandeis University Press, 1998), 134–149.

60. See Werses, "Gerush sefarad u-portugal be-sifrut yidish," *Pe'amim* 69 (1997): 114–159. See also his "Gerush sefarad be-aspeklariah shel sifrut ha-haskalah," in his *Hakitsah 'ami: sifrut ha-haskalah be'idan ha-modernizatsiah* (Jerusalem: Magnes, 2001), 157–190.

61. Werses, "Gerush sefarad u-portugal," 153–154.

62. Stasov, *Antokol'skii*, 103. In light of this comment, we may discern an interesting (but entirely speculative) intersection in Antokol'skii's work. His experimental and unfinished relief, *The Attack of the Inquisition on the Jews of Spain during the Secret Celebration of the Passover* (1868–69, Tretiakov Gallery, Moscow) may have been a visual gesture toward a conscription scene. A similar, more readily perceptible connection appears in the work of the Russian-Jewish painter M. L. Maimon (1860–1924). Maimon's 1893 canvas, entitled *Marranos,* depicted a genre scene similar to that of Antokol'skii's relief. The figure posing for the patriarch was a retired artillery general named Arnol'di, himself a converted cantonist. Safran summarizes the story in the introduction to her *Rewriting the Jew,* 1–2. Maimon also painted a picture called *Khappers* (1899), the details of which clearly referenced the earlier *Marranos.* The original was housed in the Soviet Museum of Jewish Culture in Odessa. It was reproduced from an engraving, as an illustration to a Soviet edition of the novels of Abramovich. See Mendele moykher-seforim, *Geklibene verk in ayn band* (Kiev and Kharkiv: Melukhe-farlag far di natsionale minderhayten in USRR, 1936), 323. Unfortunately the current locations of both *Marranos* and *Khappers* remain unknown.

63. See Eliakum Zunser, *The Works of Elyokum Zunser: A Critical Edition* [in Yiddish], ed. Mordkhe Schaechter, 2 vols. (New York: YIVO, 1964), 2:673.

64. The conservative reading of Iberian-Jewish history characterized its "Ashkenazic" appropriation from the start; see Stanislawski, "The Yiddish *Shevet yehudah*," 145. Russian-Jewish enlighteners reproduced it faithfully; Friedberg, in his Hebrew translation of *Vale of Cedars,* turned the original *converso* protagonist into a *marrano*. See the discussion above, in chapter 3.

65. Dubnow was the founder of "diaspora nationalism," a political alternative both to socialism and Zionism; for his political credo, see "Letters on Old and New Judaism," in his *Nationalism and History*, ed. Koppel S. Pinson (New York: Atheneum, 1970), 73–241.

66. See Nathans, "Russian-Jewish Historiography," 413–414.

67. Dubnow, *History of the Jews in Russia and Poland*, trans. Israel Friedlaender, 3 vols. (Philadelphia: Jewish Publication Society, 1916–20), 2:216. In the 1890s Abramovich and Dubnow were part of the same Odessa literary circle, which also included Ahad ha'am and Ben-ami. See Dubnov-Erlich, *Life*, 92–93.

68. Dubnow, *History*, 2:27; emphasis added.

69. Wihl's poem was first published in his anthology, *Westöstliche Schwalben*, in Mannheim in 1847. The book being a "bibliographical rarity," this poem subsequently appeared in N. Samter's *Judentaufen im neunzehnten Jahrhundert* (Berlin: M. Poppenlauer, 1906), 43–44. See S. Stanislavskii, "K istorii kantonistov," *Evreiskaia starina* 2 (1909): 266–268.

70. See David Shimoni, "Doron," in his *Shirim*, 3 vols. (Tel Aviv: Masada, 1954 [1934]), 3:119–125.

71. Greenberg, *Jews in Russia*, 1:51; and Baron, *Russian Jew*, 31.

72. This revisionist view is the product of diligent and dry-eyed archival research; see Petrovsky-Shtern, *Evrei v russkoi armii*, 116–149.

73. Katsnelson, *Mah she-rau 'einai*, 15–16.

74. Jacob Ha-levi Lipschitz, *Zikhron ya'akov, historiyah yehudit be-rusiah u-folin, 1760–1896*, 3 vols. (Kovno-Slobodka: N. Lipschitz, 1924), 1:203; for Brodotskii's "signature," see 214.

75. Petrovsky-Shtern, *Evrei v russkoi armii*, 147.

76. Ibid., 87–88.

77. Ginsburg, "Mucheniki-deti," 50–51.

78. Ibid., 79.

79. See Petrovsky-Shtern, *Evrei v russkoi armii*, chap. 3. See also, above, chapter 1.

80. For recent revisions of the normative view, see Stanislawski, *Tsar Nicholas I and the Jews*, which relocates conscription from the history of anti-Jewish persecution to its immediate political context. See also Petrovsky-Shtern, *Evrei v russkoi armii*, which treats the experience of Jews in the army as an aspect of Jewish modernization in Russia.

81. Characteristically the only synthetic history that did not emerge out of the experience of migration — Gessen's 1914 *Istoriia evreev v Rossii* — does not rely on the Iberian paradigm in its treatment of conscription. Neither does Gessen talk about the deaths of cantonists as a form of martyrdom or invoke the image of extraordinary resistance to conversionary pressure. He explains what he assumes to be a high degree of mortality among Jewish recruits by reference to their "extremely difficult living conditions" as well as to "illness" and to "torment inflicted by officers." He refers to cantonists not as "child martyrs," but as "child sufferers" (Rus. *deti-stradal'tsy*), an allusion, I think, to Nikitin's reform-era history of cantonist institutions, *The Long-Sufferers* (Rus. *Mnogostradal'nye*). See Gessen, *Istoriia evreev v Rossii* (St. Petersburg: L. Ya. Ganzburg, 1914), 199–203.

82. American-Jewish immigration histories regularly refer to the *Nicholaevan* draft as a compelling motive for emigration at the turn of the twentieth century, even though, by then, Jews were subject to the universal conscription statute of 1874, cantonist institutions no longer existed, and the term of service was not twenty-five years but six. See, for example, Moses Rischin, *The Promised City: New York's Jews, 1870–1914* (Cambridge, Mass.: Harvard University Press, 1962), 19; Irving Howe, *World of Our Fathers* (New York: Schocken Books, 1976), 6–7; Gerald Sorin, *A Time for Building: The Third Migration, 1880–1920* (Baltimore, Md., and London: Johns Hopkins University Press, 1992), 21–22; and Ruth Gay, *Unfinished People: Eastern European Jews Encounter America* (New York and London: Norton, 1996), 26–28.

83. On An-sky's career, see David G. Roskies, "S. Ansky and the Paradigm of Return," in *The Uses of Tradition: Jewish Continuity in the Modern Era*, ed. Jack Werthei-

mer (New York: Jewish Theological Seminary, 1992), 243–260; and B. Lukin, "Ot narodnichestva k narodu (S. A. Ansky—etnograf vostochno-evropeiskogo evre-istva)," in *Evrei v Rossii, istoriia i kul'tura, sbornik nauchnykh trudov,* ed. D. A. Elia-shevich (St. Petersburg: Peterburgskii evreiskii universitet, 1995), 125–161.

84. For the text of the story, see "Tsvey martirer," in S. An-ski, *Oysgeklibene shriftn,* ed. Shmuel Rozhanskii (Buenos Aires: YIVO, 1964), 88–100. There is an earlier version in his *Collected Works;* see *Gezamlte verk,* 14 vols. (Vilna: Ferlag An-ski, 1928), 14:139–151.

85. See Alexander Herzen, *My Past and Thoughts,* trans. Constance Garnett (New York: Chatto and Windus, 1974), 169–170. See citations in Gessen, *Istoriia evreev,* 202; Dubnow, *History of the Jews in Russia and Poland,* 2:24–25; Ginsburg, "Mucheniki-deti," 63; Greenberg, *Jews in Russia,* 1:49; Baron, *Russian Jew,* 30–31; and Stanislawski, *Tsar Nicholas I and the Jews,* 26–27.

86. For the theoretical background of An-sky's Falk-hero, see M. M. Bakhtin, *Rabelais and His World,* trans. Helene Iswolsky (Bloomington: Indiana University Press, 1988).

87. Dina Rubina, "Nash kitaiskii biznes," in her *Nash kitaiskii biznes: roman i rasskazy* (Moscow: Eksmo, 2004), 411.

88. Boyarin, "Thinking with Virgins: Engendering Judeo-Christian Difference," in his *Dying for God,* 67–92; here, 67–73.

89. An-ski, "Tsvey martirer," 96.

90. In *The Dybbuk,* a single act of miscommunication sets in motion all the terrible events that follow; see the text of the play, in S. Ansky, *The Dybbuk and Other Writings,* ed. David Roskies (New York: Schocken Books, 1992), 1–49.

91. Baron's locution has acquired general purchase in contemporary scholarship, but the writing of Jewish *Leidensgeschichte* persists. For the initial formulation of the problem, see Baron, "Ghetto and Emancipation," *Menorah Journal* 14 (1928): 515–526.

92. On the cultural imbrication of Judaism with Christianity—no Judaization without Christianization!—see Boyarin, "When Christians Were Jews: On Judeo-Christian Origins," in idem, *Dying for God,* 1–21; Schwartz, *Imperialism and Jewish Society,* esp. chap. 6; and Peter Schäfer, *Mirror of His Beauty: Feminine Images of God, from the Bible to the Early Kabbalah* (Princeton, N.J., and Oxford: Princeton University Press, 2002), chap. 10. On the subject of martyrdom, specifically, see Israel Yuval, *"Two Nations in Your Womb": Perceptions of Jews and Christians* [in Hebrew] (Tel Aviv: Am Oved, 2000), chaps. 3–4.

93. Boyarin, *Carnal Israel: Reading Sex in Talmudic Culture* (Berkeley, Los Angeles, and London: University of California Press, 1993), esp. 197–206; see also his "Quo Vadis? or the Acts of the Tricksters," in idem, *Dying for God,* 42–66.

94. Cf. Roskies, "The Maskil as Folk-Hero," *Prooftexts* 10 (1990): 219–235.

CONCLUSION

1. Israel Aksenfeld, *Dos shterntikhl* (Buenos Aires: YIVO, 1971), 112. On Aksen-feld's literary credo, see S. M. Ginsburg, "New Material Regarding Israel Aksenfeld," *YIVO Annual of Jewish Social Science* 5 (1950): 172–183.

2. See Isaiah Trunk, *Judenrat: The Jewish Councils in Europe under Nazi Occupation* (New York: Macmillan, 1972), xxxiv.

BIBLIOGRAPHY

CONSCRIPTION LITERATURE

Abramovich [Abramovitz], Sh. J. *Der priziv.* St. Petersburg: Tsederbaum, 1884.
———. *Dos kleyne mentshele.* Vilna: Romm, 1879.
———. *Ha-avot ve-ha-banim, sipur ahavim.* Odessa: M. A. Beilinson, 1868.
———. *Kitsur mas'ot Benyomin III.* Vilna: Romm, 1878.
——— [Abramovitsh, S. Y.]. *The Wishing Ring.* Trans. Michael Wex. Syracuse, N.Y.: Syracuse University Press, 2003.
Aksenfeld, Israel. "Der ershter yidisher rekrut in rusland." In idem, *Aksenfelds verk,* ed. Meir Winer, 1: 145–196. Kiev: Melukhe-farlag literatur un kunst, 1931.
An-sky, S. "Tsvey martirer." In idem, *Oygeklibene shriftn,* ed. Shmuel Rozhanskii, 88–100. Buenos Aires: YIVO, 1964.
Arieli, L. A. "Le-or ha-venus." In *The Collected Works of L. A. Arieli* [in Hebrew], ed. Milton Arfa, 2 vols., 1: 3–70. Tel Aviv: Dvir, 1999.
Ben-Ami. "Ben-yukhid: byl' iz vremen lovchikov." *Voskhod* 4, no. 1 (1884): 151–161; no. 2 (1884): 131–156.
Berman, Y. "Shnot rainu ra'ah." *Ha-melits* 1 (1861): 249–251, 269–272, 294–296, 314–316, 331–333.
Bialik, Ch. N. "Yonah ha-hayat." In *Collected Poems, 1890–1898* [in Hebrew], ed. Dan Miron, 276–279. Tel Aviv: Dvir, 1983.
Bogrov, Grigorii. *The Child-Kidnappers of Russia: A Novel of Jewish Life in Russia in the Time of Nicholas I.* Trans. Shoshana Dobrushin-Sharkey. Ottawa: S. D., 1996.
———. *Di kinder-khapper fun rusland: a roman fun yidishn lebn in rusland in der tsayt fun Nikolai dem ershtn.* New York: S. Kantrowitz, 1915.
———. "Poimannik (Byl')." *Evreiskaia biblioteka* 4 (1873): 1–100.
———. *Zapiski evreia.* 3 vols. Odessa: Sherman, 1912–1913.
Brenner, Y. H. "Shanah ahat (reshimot)." In *Kol kitvei Y. H. Brenner,* 2 vols., 1:104–145. Tel Aviv: Dvir, 1956.
Cahan, Jacob. "Ha-hotfim." In *Kitvei Yaacov Cahan, shirim,* 156–157. Tel Aviv: Dvir, 1960.
Dik, Isaac-Meir. *Der antloyfener rekrutl.* Vilna: Widow and Bros. Romm, 1872.
———. *Der erster nabor, vos ver in dem yor 1828.* Vilna: Widow and Bros. Romm, 1871.
———. *Der soldatske syn.* Vilna: Widow and Bros. Romm, 1876.
Feierberg, M. Z. "Yankev the Watchman." In *Whither? and Other Stories,* trans. Hillel Halkin, 41–50. Philadelphia: Jewish Publication Society, 1973.

Friedberg, Abraham. "Zikhronot." *Sefer ha-shanah* 3 (1902): 82–101.
Gordon, Judah-Leib. "Der muter abshied fun ir kind im yor 1845 vos me hot opgegebn far a rekrut." *Kol mevasser* 6, no. 11 (1866): 171–173.
———. "Ha'atsamot ha-yeveishot." In *Kol kitvei Yehudah-Leib Gordon: prozah*, 78–92. Tel Aviv: Dvir, 1960.
Kaplan, Johanna, "Sickness." In *The Schocken Book of Contemporary Jewish Fiction*, ed. Ted Solotaroff and Nessa Rapoport, 136–156. New York: Schocken Books, 1992.
Levenson, P. "Zakoldovannyi (byl')." *Voskhod* 4, no. 7 (1884): 16–41.
Levin, Judah-Leib. "Ha-hatufim." In *Zikhronot ve-hegyonot*, ed. Yehuda Slutsky, 30–35. Jerusalem: Mosad Bialik, 1968.
Levinsohn, Isaac-Baer. *Di hefker-velt.* Warsaw: Shuldberg, 1902.
Matas, Carol. *Sworn Enemies.* Toronto: HarperCollins, 1993.
Nikitin, V. N. "Vek prozhit'-ne pole pereiti." *Evreiskaia biblioteka* 4 (1873): 301–358.
Orshanskii, I. G. "Istoria vykliuchki." *Evreiskaia biblioteka* 6 (1878): 15–36.
Paperna, Abraham-Jacob. "Ke-afikim ba-negev." In *Sefer ha-yovel li-kvod Nahum Sokolow*, 440–450. Warsaw: Shuldberg, 1904.
Peretz, I. L. *Ale verk fun Y. L Perets.* 11 vols. New York: CYCO, 1947–1948.
———. "Der meshulekh." In idem, *Ale verk fun Y. L Perets*, 2:30–39. New York: CYCO, 1947.
———. "S'iz gut!" In idem, *Ale verk fun Y. L Perets*, 5:152–156.. New York: CYCO, 1947.
———. "Tov!" In *Kitvei Y. L. Perets*, 10 vols., 1:5–6. Tel Aviv: Dvir, 1961.
Rabinovich, O. A. "Nasledstvennyi podsvechnik." *Razsvet* 1 (1860): 13–17, 30–33, 43–50, 57–65, 78–81, 91–98, 109–116, 130–134.
———. "Shtrafnoi." *Russkii vestnik* 21 (1859): 501–540.
Schur, M. R. *The Circlemaker.* New York: Dial Books, 1994.
Shaikevich, N. M. *Der poimannik, oder dos heldishe maydkhen.* Vilna: Levin Hofshtein, 1891.
Shimoni, David. "Doron." In idem, *Shirim*, 3 vols., 3:119–125. 1934. Reprint, Tel Aviv: Masada, 1954.
Sholem-aleichem. "The Automatic Exemption." In *Tevye the Dairyman and the Railroad Stories*, trans. Hillel Halkin, 229–238. New York: Schocken Books, 1987.
———. "Goody 'Purishkevitch.'" In *Nineteenth to the Dozen: Monologues and Bits and Bobs of Other Things*, trans. Ted Gorelick, ed. Ken Frieden, 44–53. Syracuse, N.Y.: Syracuse University Press, 1998.
Steinberg, Yehudah. "Ba-yamim ha-hem (sipuro shel zaken)." In *Kol kitvei Yehudah Steinberg*, 230–254. Tel Aviv: Dvir, 1959.
Vladimirov, L. "Poimannik-chudodei." *Razsvet* 1 (1860): 660–664.

ARCHIVAL MATERIAL

Rossiiskii gosudarstvennyi voenno-istoricheskii arkhiv (The Russian State Military-Historical Archive) (RGVIA), Moscow, Russia, Department of Military Settlements, 1810–1864, fond 405, opisi 1, 2, 4, 5, 9.

OTHER SOURCES

Abramsky, I. D., ed. and trans. *Zikhronot u-tsror mikhtavim me-at Mordekhai Antokolskii.* Jerusalem: Mosad Bialik and the Betsalel Art Institute, 1952.
Abramovich, Shalom-Jacob. *Ale verk fun Mendele moykher-seforim.* 17 vols. Krakow: Farlag Mendele, 1911–1913.

———. *Ale verk fun Mendele moykher-seforim.* Ed. Nahman Maisel. 22 vols. Warsaw: Farlag Mendele, 1928.

———. "Briv fun Mendele moykher-sforim (fun der Binshtok-kolektsiye)." *Tsaytshrift* 5, pt. 2 (1931): 1–42.

———. "Dos vintshfigerl: a matoneh far di liebe yudishe kinder." *Di yudishe folksbibliotek* 1 (1888).

——— [Mendele moykher-sforim]. *Geklibene verk in ayn band.* Kiev and Kharkiv: Melukhe-farlag, 1936.

——— [Mendele moykher-sforim]. *Gezamlte verk.* Ed. Meir Winer. 3 vols. Moscow: Emes, 1930–1936.

———. *Kol kitvei Mendele mokher-sefarim.* 3 vols. Odessa: Va'ad ha-yovel, 1911–1913.

———. *Kol kitvei Mendele mokher-sefarim.* Tel Aviv: Dvir, 1959.

——— [Mendele Mokher Sfarim]. *KTAVim be'ibam.* Ed. and trans. Shalom Lurya. Haifa: Haifa University, 1994.

———. *Learn to Do Well* [in Hebrew]. New York: YIVO, 1969.

———. *Ottsy i deti.* St. Petersburg: M. Bienstock and L. P. Pestrechenko, 1868.

———. *A sgule tsu di yudishe tsores, funem seyfer "Autoemancipation."* Odessa: Shul'tse, 1884.

——— [Abramovitsh, S. Y.]. *Tales of Mendele the Bookpeddler: Fishke the Lame and Benjamin III.* Ed. Dan Miron and Ken Frieden. Trans. Hillel Halkin and Ted Gorelick. New York: Schocken Books, 1996.

——— [Mendele Mokher Sfarim]. *The Tiny Fellow* [in Hebrew and Yiddish]. Ed. and trans. Shalom Lurya. Haifa: Haifa University, 1984.

Abrams, M. H. *The Mirror and the Lamp: Romantic Theory and the Critical Tradition.* London, Oxford, and New York: Oxford University Press, 1953.

Adams, Bruce F. *The Politics of Punishment: Prison Reform in Russia, 1863–1917.* DeKalb: Northern Illinois University Press, 1996.

Ahad ha'am. *Igrot ahad ha'am.* 6 vols. Jerusalem: Moriah, 1923–1925.

Akopova, N. I., and V. V. Berezhkov, eds. *1812 god v russkoi poezii i vospominaniiakh sovremennikov.* Moscow: Pravda, 1987.

Aksenfeld, Israel. *Dos shterntikhl.* Buenos Aires: YIVO, 1971.

Allen, Elizabeth Cheresh. *Beyond Realism: Turgenev's Poetics of Secular Salvation.* Stanford, Calif.: Stanford University Press, 1992.

Alter, Robert. *Hebrew and Modernity.* Bloomington: Indiana University Press, 1994.

———. *The Invention of Hebrew Prose: Modern Fiction and the Language of Realism.* Seattle: University of Washington Press, 1988.

Ambler, Effie. *Russian Journalism and Politics: The Career of Alexei Suvorin, 1861–1881.* Detroit: Wayne State University Press, 1972.

Anderson, Benedict. *Imagined Communities.* London and New York: Verso, 1983.

Ansky, S. *The Dybbuk and Other Writings.* Ed. David Roskies. New York: Schocken Books, 1992.

Aronson, I. Michael. *Troubled Waters: The Origins of the 1881 Anti-Jewish Pogroms in Russia.* Pittsburgh: University of Pittsburgh Press, 1990.

Assaf, David, ed. *Journey to a Nineteenth-Century Shtetl: The Memoirs of Yekhezkel Kotik.* Trans. Margaret Birstein. Detroit: Wayne State University Press, 2002.

Bacon, Gershon. "An Anthem Reconsidered: On Text and Subtext in Yehuda Leib Gordon's 'Awake, My People!' " *Prooftexts* 15 (1995): 185–194.

Bakhtin, M. M. *The Dialogic Imagination: Four Essays.* Ed. Michael Holquist. Trans. Michael Holquist and Caryl Emerson. Austin: University of Texas Press, 1981.

———. *Rabelais and His World.* Trans. Helene Iswolsky. Bloomington: Indiana University Press, 1988.

Bakon, Yitzhak. *The Young Brenner: The Life and Works of Brenner until the Publication of Ha-meorer in London* [in Hebrew]. 2 vols. Tel Aviv: Ha-kibbutz ha-meuhad, 1975.

Balin, Carole B. *To Reveal Our Hearts: Jewish Women Writers in Tsarist Russia*. Cincinnati: Hebrew Union College Press, 2000.

Bar-El, Judith. "The National Poet: The Emergence of the Concept in Hebrew Literary Criticism (1885–1905)." *Prooftexts* 6 (1986): 205–220.

Baroli, Marc. *Le train dans la littérature française*. Paris: Editions N. M., 1969.

Baron, Salo W. "Ghetto and Emancipation." *Menorah Journal* 14 (1928): 515–526.

———. *The Russian Jew under Tsars and Soviets*. New York: Macmillan, 1964.

Bartal, Israel. " 'True Knowledge and Wisdom': On Orthodox Historiography," *Studies in Contemporary Jewry Annual* 10 (1994): 178–192.

Bar-Yosef, Hamutal. *Decadent Trends in Hebrew Literature: Bialik, Berdychevski, Brener* [in Hebrew]. Jerusalem: Mosad Bialik, 1997.

Ben-Sasson, Haim Hillel. "Galut ve-geulah be'einav shel dor golei sefarad." In *Sefer yovel le-Yitshak Baer*, ed. S. Ettinger et al., 216–227. Jerusalem: Ha-hevrah ha-historit ha-yisraelit, 1960.

Ben-Yosef [L. Kantor]. "Ocherki novo-evreiskoi literatury I: S. Ia. Abramovich i ego 25-let. deiatel'nost'." *Evreiskoe obozrenie* (1884): 129–144.

Berlin, Isaiah. *Russian Thinkers*. Ed. Henry Hardy and Aileen Kelly. New York: Penguin, 1994.

Biale, David. *Eros and the Jews from Biblical Israel to Contemporary America*. New York: Basic Books, 1992.

Binshtok, L. "Prazdnik zhargonnoi literatury." *Voskhod* 4, no. 12, pt. 2 (1884): 1–32.

Blight, David W. *Race and Reunion: The Civil War in American Memory*. Cambridge, Mass.: Harvard University Press, 2001.

Bloch, Marc. *The Historian's Craft*. Trans. Peter Putnam. New York: Knopf, 1953.

Bloom, Harold. *The Anxiety of Influence: A Theory of Poetry*. New York: Oxford University Press, 1973.

Blum, Carol. *Rousseau and the Republic of Virtue: The Language of Politics in the French Revolution*. Ithaca, N.Y.: Cornell University Press, 1986.

Bonfil, Robert. "How Golden Was the Age of the Renaissance in Jewish Historiography?" In *Essential Papers on Jewish Culture in Renaissance and Baroque Italy*, ed. David Ruderman, 219–251. New York and London: New York University Press, 1992.

Borovoi, S. Y. *Evreiskaia zemledel'cheskaia kolonizatsiia v staroi Rossii*. Moscow: Izd-vo M. i S. Sabashnikovykh, 1928.

Boyarin, Daniel. *Carnal Israel: Reading Sex in Talmudic Culture*. Berkeley, Los Angeles, and London: University of California Press, 1993.

———. *Dying for God: Martyrdom and the Making of Christianity and Judaism*. Stanford, Calif.: Stanford University Press, 1999.

———. "'Language Inscribed by History on the Bodies of Living Beings': Midrash and Martyrdom." *Representations* 25 (1989): 139–151.

Bradley, Joseph. *Muzhik and Muscovite: Urbanization in Late Imperial Russia*. Berkeley: University of California Press, 1985.

Brinker, Menahem. "Brenner's Jewishness." *Studies in Contemporary Jewry Annual* 4 (1988): 232–249.

———. *Narrative Art and Social Thought in Y. H. Brenner's Work* [in Hebrew]. Tel Aviv: Am Oved, 1990.

Brooks, Jeffrey. *When Russia Learned to Read: Literacy and Popular Culture, 1861–1917*. Princeton, N.J.: Princeton University Press, 1985.

Brooks, Willis. "Nicholas I as Reformer: Russian Attempts to Conquer the Caucasus." In *Nation and Ideology: Essays in Honor of Wayne S. Vucinich*, ed. Ivo Banac, John Ackerman, and Roman Szporluk, 227–263. Boulder, Colo.: East European Monographs/Columbia University Press, 1981.

Bukhbinder, N. A. *Literaturnye etiudy*. Leningrad: Nauka i shkola, 1927.

Burds, Jeffrey. *Peasant Dreams and Market Politics: Labor Migration and the Russian Village, 1861–1905*. Pittsburgh: University of Pittsburgh Press, 1998.

Bushnell, John. *Mutiny amid Repression: Russian Soldiers and the Revolution of 1905–1906*. Bloomington: Indiana University Press, 1985.

Butterfield, Herbert. *Man on His Past: The Study of Historical Scholarship*. Cambridge: Cambridge University Press, 1969.

Carlebach, Julius. *Karl Marx and the Radical Critique of Judaism*. London, Henley, and Boston: Routledge and Kegan Paul, 1978.

Carnes, Mark C., ed. *Past Imperfect: History according to the Movies*. New York: Henry Holt, 1996.

Carr, E. H. *What Is History?* New York: Knopf, 1961.

Cesarani, David. "The Myth of Origins: Ethnic Memory and the Experience of Migration." In *Patterns of Migration, 1850–1914*, ed. Aubrey Newman and Stephen W. Massil, 247–254. London: Jewish Historical Society of England, 1996.

Chanes, Jerome A. "Anti-semitism and Jewish Security in America: Why Can't Jews Take Yes for an Answer?" In *Jews in America: A Contemporary Reader*, ed. Roberta Rosenberg Farber and Chaim I. Waxman, 124–150. Hanover, N.H., and London: University Press of New England/Brandeis University Press, 1999.

Cherikover, I. M. *Istoriia obshchestva dlia rasprostraneniia prosveshcheniia mezhdu evreiiami v Rossii*. St. Petersburg: Komitet OPE, 1913.

Clowes, Edith W., Sam D. Kassow, and James L. West. *Between Tsar and People: Educated Society and the Quest for Public Identity in Late Imperial Russia*. Princeton, N.J.: Princeton University Press, 1991.

Cohen, Gerson. "The Story of the Four Captives." In idem, *Studies in the Variety of Rabbinic Cultures*, 157–208. Philadelphia: Jewish Publication Society, 1991.

Cohen, Jeremy. *Sanctifying the Name of God: Jewish Martyrs and Jewish Memories of the First Crusade*. Philadelphia: University of Pennsylvania Press, 2004.

Cohen, Tova. "Ha-tekhnikah ha-lamdanit—tsofen shel sifrut ha-haskalah." *Mehkarei yerushalaim be-sifrut 'ivrit* 13 (1992): 137–169.

———. *"One Beloved, the Other Hated": Between Fiction and Reality in Haskalah Depictions of Women* [in Hebrew]. Jerusalem: Magnes, 2002.

Collingwood, R. G. *The Historical Imagination*. London: Oxford University Press, 1935.

Corney, Frederick C. *Telling October: Memory and the Making of the Bolshevik Revolution*. Ithaca, N.Y.: Cornell University Press, 2004.

Crews, Robert D. "Allies in God's Command: Muslim Communities and the State in Imperial Russia." Ph.D. dissertation, Princeton University, 1999.

Daly, Jonathan W. *Autocracy under Siege: Security Police and Opposition in Russia, 1866–1905*. DeKalb: Northern Illinois University Press, 1998.

Davis, Joseph M. "The Reception of the *Shulhan 'Arukh* and the Formation of Ashkenazic-Jewish Identity." *AJS Review* 26 (2002): 251–276.

Dement'ev, A. G., et al., eds. *Russkaia periodicheskaia pechat', 1702–1894*. Moscow: Izdvo politicheskoi literatury, 1959.

De-Poulet, M. P. "Khar'kovskii universitet i D. I. Kachenovskii: kul'turnyi ocherk i vospominaniia iz 40-kh godov." *Vestnik evropy* 9 (1874): 75–115, 565–589.

Derkach, B. A., ed. *Ukrain'ski poety-romantyky 20–40kh rokiv XIX st.* Kiev: Dnipro, 1968.

Dik, Isaac-Meir. *Di shtifmuter.* Warsaw: Lebensohn, 1876.

———. *Masekhet 'aniyut.* Vilna: n. p., 1878.

———. "Shtei mikhtavim le-Kh. Y. Gurland." *Reshumot* 2 (1927): 408–410.

Diner, Hasia. *A Time for Gathering: The Second Migration, 1820–1880*. Baltimore, Md.: Johns Hopkins University Press, 1992.

Dinur, Ben-Zion. "Demutah ha-historit shel ha-yahadut ha-rusit u-va'ayot ha-heker bah." *Zion* 22 (1957): 93–118.

Dohrn, Verena. "Das Rabbinerseminar in Wilna (1847–1873)." *Forschungen zur osteuropäischen Geschichte* 45 (1997): 379–400.

Douglas, Ann. *The Feminization of American Culture.* New York: Knopf, 1977.

Dubnov-Erlich, Sophie. *The Life and Work of S. M. Dubnow: Diaspora Nationalism and Jewish History.* Trans. Judith Vowles. Ed. Jeffrey Shandler. Bloomington and Indianapolis: Indiana University Press, 1991.

Dubnow, S. M. *Fun "zhargon" tsu yidish.* Vilna: Kletskin, 1929.

———. *History of the Jews in Russia and Poland.* Trans. Israel Friedlander. 3 vols. Philadelphia: Jewish Publication Society, 1916–1920.

———. *Kniga zhizni.* Ed. V. E. Kel'ner. St. Petersburg: PV, 1998.

———. *Nationalism and History.* Ed. Koppel S. Pinson. New York: Atheneum, 1970.

———. *Ob izuchenii istorii russkikh evreev i ob uchrezhdenii russko-evreiskogo istoricheskogo obshchestva.* St. Petersburg: A. E. Landau, 1891.

Duker, Abraham G. "*Evreiskaia starina:* A Bibliography of the Russian-Jewish Historical Periodical." *Hebrew Union College Annual* 8–9 (1931–1932): 525–601.

Dushechkina, E. V. *Russkii sviatochnyi razskaz.* St. Petersburg: St. Petersburg University, 1995.

Eagleton, Terry. *Heathcliff and the Great Hunger: Studies in Irish Culture.* London and New York: Verso, 1995.

Eichenbaum, Boris. *Moi vremennik.* St. Petersburg: Inapress, 2001.

Eichenbaum, Jacob. *Ga-krab.* Trans. O. A. Rabinovich. 2nd ed. Odessa: Beilinson, 1874.

Einbinder, Susan L. *Beautiful Death: Jewish Poetry and Martyrdom in Medieval France.* Princeton, N.J.: Princeton University Press, 2002.

Eklof, Ben, John Bushnell, and Larissa Zakharova, eds. *Imperial Russia's Great Reforms, 1855–1881.* Bloomington: Indiana University Press, 1994.

Eliashevich, D. A. *Pravitel'stvennaia politika i evreiskaia pechat' v Rossii, 1797–1917.* St. Petersburg and Jerusalem: Mosty kul'tury/Gesharim, 1999.

Emerson, Caryl. *Boris Godunov: Transpositions of a Russian Theme.* Bloomington: Indiana University Press, 1986.

Engelstein, Laura. *The Keys to Happiness: Sex and the Search for Modernity in Fin-de-Siècle Russia.* Ithaca, N.Y.: Cornell University Press, 1992.

Etkes, Immanuel, ed. *The Eastern European Jewish Enlightenment* [in Hebrew]. Jerusalem: Merkaz Shazar, 1993.

———. "Marriage and Torah Study among the *Lomdim* in Lithuania in the Nineteenth Century." In *The Jewish Family: Metaphor and Memory,* ed. David Kraemer, 153–178. Oxford and New York: Oxford University Press, 1989.

———. *Rabbi Israel Salanter and the Mussar Movement: Seeking the Torah of Truth.* Trans. Jonathan Chipman. Philadelphia: Jewish Publication Society, 1993.

———. "The Relationship between Talmudic Scholarship and the Institution of the Rabbinate in Nineteenth-Century Lithuanian Jewry." In *Scholars and Scholarship: The Interaction between Judaism and Other Cultures,* ed. Leo Landman, 107–132. New York: Yeshiva University Press, 1990.

Even, Joseph, and Itzchak Ben-Mordecai, eds. *Nitsanei ha-realizm ba-siporet ha'ivrit: kovets sipurim.* 2 vols. Jerusalem: Mosad Bialik, 1993.

Evreiskaia entsiklopediia. 16 vols. St. Petersburg: Brokgauz i Efron, 1906–1913.

Ezrahi, Sidra DeKoven. *Booking Passage: Exile and Homecoming in the Modern Jewish Imagination.* Los Angeles and London: University of California Press, 2000.

Fanger, Donald. "The Peasant in Literature." In *The Peasant in Nineteenth-Century Russia,* ed. Wayne S. Vucinich, 231–262. Stanford, Calif.: Stanford University Press, 1968.

Feierberg, M. Z. *Sefer kovets sipurav u-khtavav.* Ed. Joseph Klausner. Krakow: Hevrat sefer, 1904.

Feiner, Shmuel. "Ha-hevrah, ha-sifrut, ve-ha-haskalah ha-yehudit be-rusyah be'einei ha-bikoret ha-radikalit shel Yitshak-Ayzik Kovner." *Zion* 55 (1990): 283–316.

———. "Ha-ishah ha-yehudiyah ha-modernit: mikreh-mivhan be-yahasei ha-haskalah ve-ha-modernah." In *Sexuality and the Family in History: Collected Essays* [in Hebrew], ed. Israel Bartal and Isaiah Gafni, 253–303. Jerusalem: Merkaz Shazar, 1998.

———. *Haskalah and History: The Emergence of a Modern Jewish Historical Consciousness.* Trans. Chayah Naor and Sondra Silverston. Oxford and Portland: Oxford University Press and the Littman Library of Jewish Civilization, 2002.

———. "The Pseudo-Enlightenment and the Question of Jewish Modernization." *Jewish Social Studies* 3 (1996): 62–88.

———, ed. *S. J. Fuenn, from Militant to Conservative Maskil* [in Hebrew]. Jerusalem: Merkaz Dinur, 1993.

Fichman, Jacob. *Amat ha-binyan, sofrei Odessa.* Jerusalem: Mosad Bialik, 1951.

Fishman, David E. "Musar and Modernity: The Case of Novaredok." *Modern Judaism* 8 (1988): 41–64.

———. *Russia's First Modern Jews: The Jews of Shklov.* New York: New York University Press, 1995.

Flekser, A. "Feileton: Prazdnik v cherte." *Russkii evrei,* nos. 45–46 (1884): 23–28.

Foucault, Michel. *Discipline and Punish: The Birth of the Prison.* Trans. Alan Sheridan. New York: Vintage, 1995.

Frank, Stephen P. *Crime, Culture, Conflict and Justice in Rural Russia, 1856–1914.* Berkeley: University of California Press, 1999.

Frankel Jonathan. "The Crisis of 1881–1882 as a Turning Point in Modern Jewish History." In *The Legacy of Jewish Migration: 1881 and Its Impact,* ed. David Berger, 9–22. New York: Columbia University Press, 1983.

———. "The Paradoxical Politics of Marginality: Thoughts on the Jewish Situation during the Years 1914–1921." *Studies in Contemporary Jewry Annual* 4 (1988): 3–21.

———. *Prophecy and Politics: Socialism, Nationalism and the Russian Jews, 1862–1917.* Cambridge: Cambridge University Press, 1981.

———. "The 'Yizkor' Book of 1911 — A Note on National Myths in the Second Aliya." In *Essential Papers on Zionism,* ed. Jehuda Reinharz and Anita Shapira, 422–453. New York: New York University Press, 1996.

Frankel, Jonathan, and Steven J. Zipperstein, eds. *Assimilation and Community: The Jews in Nineteenth-Century Europe.* Cambridge: Cambridge University Press, 1992.

Friedberg, A. S. *Sefer ha-zikhronot.* 2 vols. Warsaw: Shuldberg, 1899.

Freeze, ChaeRan Y. *Jewish Marriage and Divorce in Imperial Russia.* Hanover, N.H., and London: University Press of New England/Brandeis University Press, 2002.

Freeze, Gregory. *The Parish Clergy in Nineteenth-Century Russia: Crisis, Reform and Counter-reform.* Princeton, N.J.: Princeton University Press, 1983.

———. "The Soslovie (Estate) Paradigm and Russian Social History." *American Historical Review* 91 (1986): 11–36.

Frieden, Ken. *Classic Yiddish Fiction: Abramovitsch, Sholem Aleichem and Peretz.* Albany: State University of New York Press, 1995.

Frierson, Cathy. *Peasant Icons: Representations of Rural People in Nineteenth-Century Russia.* New York: Oxford University Press, 1993.

Funkenstein, Amos. "Collective Memory and Historical Consciousness." *History and Memory* 1 (1989): 5–26.

Galchinsky, Michael. *The Origin of the Modern Jewish Writer: Romance and Reform in Victorian England.* Detroit: Wayne State University Press, 1996.

Gassenschmidt, Christoph. *Jewish Liberal Politics in Tsarist Russia, 1900–1914.* Houndmills, Basingstoke: Macmillan, 1995.

Gay, Ruth. *Unfinished People: Eastern European Jews Encounter America.* New York and London: Norton, 1996.

Gessen, Iulii. *Istoriia evreev v Rossii.* St. Petersburg: L. Ya. Ganzburg, 1913.

———. *Istoriia evreiskogo naroda v Rossii v dvukh tomakh.* Leningrad: Gublit, 1925.

———. *Istoriia evreiskogo naroda v Rossii.* Ed. V. Iu. Gessen and V. E. Kel'ner. Moscow and Jerusalem: Jewish University/Gesharim, 1993.

———. "O. A. Rabinovich i I. G. Orshanskii." In *Galereia evreiskikh deiatelei, literaturno-biograficheskie ocherki,* 1:77–155. St. Petersburg: A. E. Landau, 1898.

Ginsburg, S. M. *Historical Works* [in Yiddish]. 3 vols. New York: S. M. Ginsburg Testimonial Committee, 1937.

———. "Iz mira unizhennykh (o proizvedeniiakh Ben-ami)." *Voskhod* 17, no. 12 (1897): 28–40.

———. "Mucheniki-deti (iz istorii kantonistov-evreev)." *Evreiskaia starina* 13 (1930): 50–79.

———. "New Material regarding Israel Aksenfeld." *YIVO Annual of Jewish Social Science* 5 (1950): 172–183.

Ginsburg S. M., and P. S. Marek, eds. *Evreiskie narodnye pesni v Rossii.* St. Petersburg: Voskhod, 1901.

Gol'dberg, Sh. "Prisiazhnyi list evreiskogo rekruta 1829 g." *Perezhitoe* 2 (1910): 285–287.

Gorny, Yosef. "Changes in the Social and Political Structure of the Second Aliya between 1904 and 1940." In *Essential Papers on Zionism,* ed. Jehuda Reinharz and Anita Shapira, 371–421. New York: New York University Press, 1996.

———. "Hope Born of Despair." *Jerusalem Quarterly* 26 (1983): 84–95.

Gottlober, Abraham-Baer. *Memoirs and Travels* [in Hebrew]. Ed. R. Goldberg. 2 vols. Jerusalem: Mosad Bialik, 1976.

Govrin, Nurit. *Brener: "Oved 'etsot" u-moreh derekh.* Tel Aviv: Tel Aviv University, 1991.

Ó Gráda, Cormac. *Black '47 and Beyond: The Great Irish Famine in History, Economy and Memory.* Princeton, N.J.: Princeton University Press, 1999.

———. *Jewish Ireland, Gaelic Golus: The Economy and Demography of Irish Jewry, 1870s–1930s.* Princeton, N.J.: Princeton University Press, forthcoming.

Graetz, Heinrich. *Volkstümliche Geschichte der Juden.* 3 vols. Leipzig: O. Leiner, 1888.

Green, Arthur. *Tormented Master: A Life of Rabbi Nahman of Bratslav.* Tuscaloosa: University of Alabama Press, 1979.

Greenberg, Louis. *The Jews in Russia.* 2 vols. New Haven and London: Yale University Press, 1944.

Grossman, Avraham. *Pious and Rebellious: Jewish Women in Medieval Europe.* Trans. Jonathan Chipman. Hanover, N.H., and London: University Press of New England/Brandeis University Press, 2004.

Haberer, Erich E. *Jews and Revolution in Nineteenth-Century Russia.* Cambridge: Cambridge University Press, 1995.

Halbwachs, Maurice. *On Collective Memory.* Ed. and trans. Lewis Coser. Chicago: University of Chicago Press, 1992.

Halkin, Simon. *Modern Hebrew Literature from the Enlightenment to the Birth of the State of Israel.* New York: Schocken Books, 1950.

Halpern, Ben, and Jehuda Reinharz. *Zionism and the Creation of a New Society.* New York: Oxford University Press, 1998.

Halpern, Israel. "Rabbi Levi-Yitzhak mi-berdichev ugzerot ha-malkhut be-yamav." In idem, *Yehudim ve-yahadut be-mizrah eiropah,* 340–347. Jerusalem: Magnes, 1968.

Hamm, Michael F. *Kiev: A Portrait, 1800–1917.* Princeton, N.J.: Princeton University Press, 1993.

Hanson, Ellis. *Decadence and Catholicism*. Cambridge, Mass., and London: Harvard University Press, 1997.

Harshav, Benjamin. *Language in Time of Revolution*. Berkeley, Los Angeles, and London: University of California Press, 1993.

Heinimann, Alfred. *Technische Innovation und literarische Aneignung: die Eisenbahn in der deutschen und englischen Literatur in 19. Jahrhunderts*. Bern: Francke, 1992.

Hertzberg, Arthur, ed. *The Zionist Idea: A Historical Analysis and Reader*. Philadelphia and Jerusalem: Jewish Publication Society, 1997.

Herzen, Alexander. *My Past and Thoughts*. Trans. Constance Garnett. New York: Chatto and Windus, 1974.

Herzl, Theodor. *Old-New Land*. Trans. Lotta Levensohn. New York: Markus Wiener/ Herzl Press, 1987.

Hesse, Carla. *The Other Enlightenment: How French Women Became Modern*. Princeton, N.J.: Princeton University Press, 2001.

Hobsbawm, Eric, and Terence Ranger, eds. *The Invention of Tradition*. Cambridge: Cambridge University Press, 1983.

Hokanson, Katya. "Empire of the Imagination: Orientalism and the Construction of Russian National Identity in Pushkin, Marlinskii, Lermontov and Tolstoi." Ph.D. dissertation, Stanford University, 1994.

Horch, Hans Otto. "'Auf der Zinne der Zeit': Ludwig Phillippson (1811–1889) — der 'Journalist' der Reformjudentums aus Anlaß seines 100. Todestages." *Bulletin des Leo Baeck Instituts* 86 (1990): 5–21.

Hundert, Gershon. *Jews in Poland-Lithuania in the Eighteenth Century: A Genealogy of Modernity*. Berkeley: University of California Press, 2004.

Hunt, Lynn. *The Family Romance of the French Revolution*. Berkeley and Los Angeles: University of California Press, 1992.

Hunter, J. Paul. *Before Novels: The Cultural Contexts of English Fiction*. New York and London: Norton, 1990.

Iggers, George G., and James M. Powell, eds. *Leopold von Ranke and the Rise of the Historical Discipline*. Syracuse, N.Y.: Syracuse University Press, 1990.

Il'in, N. I. *Velikodushie, ili rekrutskii nabor, drama v trekh deistviiakh*. St. Petersburg: Tip. Imperatorskogo teatra, 1807.

Itskovich, I. "Vospominaniia arkhangel'skogo kantonista." *Evreiskaia starina* 5 (1912): 54–65.

Ivanova, N. I. "Goroda Rossii." In *Rossiia v nachale XX veka*, ed. A. N. Sakharov et al., 111–136. Moscow: Novyi khronograf, 2002.

Ivask, U. G. *Evreiskaia periodicheskaia pechat' v Rossii*. Tallinn: Beilinson, 1935.

Johnston, Máirín. *Dublin Belles: Conversations with Dublin Women*. Dublin: Attic, 1988.

Jost, I. M. "Schilderungen aus Rußland von herrn Rabinowitsch." *Jahrbuch für die Geschichte der Juden und des Judentums* 1 (1860): 9–66.

Judge, Edward H. *Easter in Kishinev: Anatomy of a Pogrom*. New York and London: New York University Press, 1992.

Kahan, Arcadius. *Essays in Jewish Social and Economic History*. Ed. Roger Weiss. Chicago and London: University of Chicago Press, 1986.

Kaiser, Friedhelm Berthold. *Die russische Justizreform von 1864: zur Geschichte der russischen Justiz von Katharina II. bis 1917*. Leiden: Brill, 1972.

Kammen, Michael. *The Mystic Chords of Memory: The Transformation of Tradition in American Culture*. New York: Knopf, 1991.

Katsnelson, Y. L. *Mah she-rau 'einai ve-sham'u 'oznai*. Jerusalem: Mosad Bialik, 1947.

Katz, Jacob, ed. *Toward Modernity: The European Jewish Model*. New Brunswick, N.J., and Oxford: Transaction Books, 1987.

Keep, John L. H. *Soldiers of the Tsar: Army and Society in Russia, 1462–1874*. Oxford: Oxford University Press, 1985.

Kestenberg-Gladstein, Ruth. *Neuere Geschichte der Juden in den böhmischen Ländern.* Tübingen: Mohr, 1969.

Kimerling [Wirtschafter], Elise. "Soldiers' Children, 1719–1856: A Study in Social Engineering in Imperial Russia." *Forschungen zur osteuropäischen Geschichte* 30 (1982): 61–136.

King, David. *The Falsification of Photographs and Art in Stalin's Russia.* New York: Metropolitan Books, 1997.

Kipp, Jacob W. "Consequences of Defeat: Modernizing the Russian Navy, 1856–1863." *Forschungen zur osteuropäischen Geschichte* 20 (1972): 210–225.

Klausner, Joseph. *Dukhovnyi sionizm i ego glavnyi predstavitel'.* St. Petersburg: A. E. Landau, 1900.

———. *Historiyah shel ha-sifrut ha'ivrit ha-hadashah.* 6 vols. Jerusalem: Hotsa'at sefarim ahiasaf, 1952.

Klier, John. "The Dog That Didn't Bark: Anti-Semitism in Post-Communist Russia." In *Russian Nationalism, Past and Present,* ed. Geoffrey Hosking and Robert Service, 129–147. Basingstoke, Hampshire: Macmillan, 1998.

———. *Imperial Russia's Jewish Question, 1855–1881.* Cambridge: Cambridge University Press, 1995.

———. *Russia Gathers Her Jews: The Origins of the "Jewish Question" in Russia, 1772–1825.* DeKalb: Northern Illinois University Press, 1986.

Kobrin, Rebecca. "Conflicting Diasporas, Shifting Centers: Migration and Identity in a Trans-National Polish-Jewish Community, 1878–1952." Ph.D. dissertation, University of Pennsylvania, 2002.

Kon, P. "A. M. Dik as a Teacher in the Government School for Jewish Children in Vilna" [in Yiddish]. *YIVO Bleter* 3 (1932): 84–85.

———. "Di proyektirte yidishe drukeray in Kiev, 1836–1846." *Bikher-velt* 1, no. 3 (1929): 31–37; no. 4 (1929): 35–41.

———. "When Was I. M. Dik Born?" *Filologishe shriftn fun YIVO* 2 (1928): 329–344.

Kostomarov, Nikolai. *Avtobiografiia.* Moscow: Zadruga, 1922.

Kotsonis, Yanni. *Making Peasants Backward: Agricultural Cooperatives and the Agrarian Question in Russia, 1861–1914.* Houndmills: Macmillan, 1999.

Kuznets, Simon. "Immigration of Russian Jewry to the United States: Background and Structure." *Perspectives in American History* 9 (1975): 35–124.

Kuznetsova, E. V. *M. M. Antokol'skii, zhizn' i tvorchestvo.* Moscow: Iskusstvo, 1989.

Laquer, Thomas. *Making Sex: Body and Gender from the Greeks to Freud.* Cambridge, Mass., and London: Harvard University Press, 1990.

Layton, Susan. *Russian Literature and Empire: Conquest of the Caucasus from Pushkin to Tolstoy.* Cambridge: Cambridge University Press, 1994.

Lebedev, A. K., and G. K. Burova. *Tvorcheskoe sodruzhestvo: M. M. Antokol'skii i V. V. Stasov.* Leningrad: Khudozhnik RSFSR, 1968.

Lederhendler, Eli. "Interpreting Messianic Rhetoric in the Russian Haskalah and Early Zionism." *Studies in Contemporary Jewry Annual* 7 (1991): 14–33.

———. *The Road to Modern Jewish Politics: Political Tradition and Political Reconstruction in the Jewish Community in Tsarist Russia.* Oxford and New York: Oxford University Press, 1989.

LeDonne, John P. *The Russian Empire and the World, 1700–1917: The Geopolitics of Expansion and Containment.* New York: Oxford University Press, 1997.

Leerssen, Joep. *Remembrance and Imagination: Patterns in the Historical and Literary Representations of Ireland in the Nineteenth Century.* Notre Dame, Ind.: Notre Dame University Press, 1997.

Levanda, Lev. *Goriachee vremia.* St. Petersburg: A. E. Landau, 1875.

———, ed. *Polnyi khronologicheskii sbornik zakonov i polozhenii kasaiushchikhsia evreev ot ulozheniia tsaria Aleksaia Mikhailovicha do nastoiiashchego vremeni, 1649–1873.* St. Petersburg: K. V. Trubnikov, 1874.

Lilienblum, Moshe-Leib. *KTAVim otobiografiyyim.* 2 vols. Ed. Shlomo Breiman. Jerusalem: Mosad Bialik, 1970.

Lincoln, Bruce W. *The Great Reforms: Autocracy, Bureaucracy and the Politics of Change in Imperial Russia.* DeKalb: Northern Illinois University Press, 1990.

——. *In the Vanguard of Reform: Russia's Enlightened Bureaucrats, 1825–1861.* DeKalb: Northern Illinois University Press, 1982.

Lipschitz, Jacob Lippman Ha-levi. *Zikhron ya'akov.* 3 vols. Kovno-Slobodka: N. Lipschitz, 1924.

Lipstadt, Deborah E. *Denying the Holocaust: The Growing Assault on Truth and Memory.* New York: Free Press, 1993.

Litvak, Olga. "The Literary Response to Conscription: Individuality and Authority in the Russian-Jewish Enlightenment." Ph.D. dissertation, Columbia University, 1999.

——. "Rome and Jerusalem: The Figure of Jesus in the Creation of Mark Antokol'skii." In *The Art of Being Jewish in Modern Times,* ed. Barbara Kirshenblatt-Gimblett and Jon Karp. Philadelphia: University of Pennsylvania Press, forthcoming.

Loewenthal, Naftali. *Communicating the Infinite: The Emergence of the Habad School.* Chicago: University of Chicago Press, 1990.

Lokshin, A., ed. *Evrei v rossiiskoi imperii XVIII–XIX vekov, sbornik trudov evreiskikh istorikov.* Moscow and Jerusalem: Jewish University/Gesharim, 1995.

Lotman, Yu. M. *Semiosfera.* St. Petersburg: Iskusstvo SPb, 2000.

Lowenthal, David. *The Past Is a Foreign Country.* Cambridge: Cambridge University Press, 1985.

Lukin, B. "Ot narodnichestva k narodu (S. A. Ansky — etnograf vostochno-evropeiskogo evreistva." In *Evrei v Rossii, istoriia i kul'tura,* ed. D. A. Eliashevich, 125–161. St. Petersburg: Petersburg Jewish University, 1995.

McReynolds, Louise. *The News under Russia's Old Regime: The Development of a Mass Circulation Press.* Princeton, N.J.: Princeton University Press, 1991.

Maggid, David. *Ha-profesor Mordechai ben Matityahu Antokolskii: kitsur toldotav u-farashat 'avodato b'sde malekhet mahshevet 'ad ha-yom ha-zeh.* Warsaw: Levinskii, 1897.

Mann, Iu. *Dinamika russkogo romantizma.* Moscow: Aspekt, 1995.

Margolies, Morris B. *Samuel David Luzzatto, Traditionalist Scholar.* New York: KTAV, 1979.

Markish, Simon. "Osip Rabinovic." *Cahiers du monde russe et sovietique* 21 (1980): 5–30, 135–158.

Marks, Steven G. *How Russia Shaped the Modern World, from Art to Anti-Semitism, Ballet to Bolshevism.* Princeton, N.J.: Princeton University Press, 2003.

Mendelsohn, Ezra. *On Modern Jewish Politics.* Oxford: Oxford University Press, 1993.

Mendes-Flohr, Paul, and Jehuda Reinharz, eds. *The Jew in the Modern World: A Documentary History.* 2nd ed. Oxford: Oxford University Press, 1995.

Merimzon, M. "Razskaz starago soldata." *Evreiskaia starina* 5 (1912): 290–301, 406–422; 6 (1913): 86–95, 221–232.

Mikhailovskii, N. K. *Dostoevsky: A Cruel Talent.* Trans. Spencer Cadmus. Ann Arbor, Mich.: Ardis, 1978.

——. *Polnoe sobranie sochinenii.* 10 vols. St. Petersburg: M. M. Stasiulevich, 1908–1913.

Miller, Forrestt. *Dmitrii Miliutin and the Reform Era in Russia.* Nashville: Vanderbilt University Press, 1968.

Mintz, Alan. *"Banished from Their Father's Table": Loss of Faith and Hebrew Autobiography.* Bloomington: Indiana University Press, 1989.

——. *Hurban: Responses to Catastrophe in Hebrew Literature.* Syracuse, N.Y.: Syracuse University Press, 1996.

Miron, Dan. *From Romance to the Novel: Studies in the Emergence of the Hebrew and Yiddish Novel in the Nineteenth Century* [in Hebrew]. Jerusalem: Mosad Bialik, 1979.

———. *The Image of the Shtetl and Other Studies of Modern Jewish Literary Imagination.* Syracuse, N.Y.: Syracuse University Press, 2000.

———. *A Traveler Disguised: The Rise of Modern Yiddish Fiction in the Nineteenth Century.* New York: Schocken Books, 1973.

———. *When Loners Come Together: A Portrait of Hebrew Literature at the Turn of the Twentieth Century* [in Hebrew]. Tel Aviv: Am Oved, 1987.

Miron, Dan, and Anita Norich. "The Politics of Benjamin III: Intellectual Significance and Formal Correlatives in Sh. Y. Abramovitsh's *Masoes benyomin hashlishi.*" In *The Field of Yiddish: Studies in Language, Folklore and Literature,* ed. Marvin I. Herzog et al., 1–115. 4th collection. Philadelphia: Institute for the Study of Human Issues, 1980.

Mironov, B. N. *Sotsial'naia istoriia Rossii perioda imperii (XVII–nachalo XX v.).* 2 vols. St. Petersburg: Dmitrii Bulanin, 1999.

Morgulis, M. "Iz moikh vospominanii." *Voskhod* 16, nos. 5–6 (1896): 177–181.

———. "K iubileyu narodnogo pisatelia Solomona Moiseevicha Abramovicha." *Nedel'naia khronika voskhoda* 3, no. 43 (1884): 1213–1217.

Moseley, Marcus. *Being for Myself Alone: Origins of Jewish Autobiography.* Stanford, Calif.: Stanford University Press, 2005.

———. "Jewish Autobiography in Eastern Europe: The Prehistory of a Genre." Ph.D. dissertation, Oxford University, 1990.

Murav, Harriet. *Identity Theft: The Jew in Imperial Russia and the Case of Avraam-Uri Kovner.* Stanford, Calif.: Stanford University Press, 2003.

Nakhimovsky, Alice Stone. "Mikhail Zhvanetskii: The Last Russian-Jewish Joker." In *Forging Modern Jewish Identities: Public Faces and Private Struggles,* ed. Michael Berkowitz, Susan L. Tananbaum, and Sam W. Bloom, 156–179. London: Vallentine Mitchell, 2003.

Nathans, Benjamin. *Beyond the Pale: The Jewish Encounter with Late Imperial Russia.* Berkeley, Los Angeles, and London: University of California Press, 2002.

———. "On Russian-Jewish Historiography." In *Historiography in Imperial Russia: The Profession and Writing of History in a Multinational State,* ed. Thomas Sanders, 397–432. Armonk, N.Y., and London: M. E. Sharpe, 1999.

Neuberger, Joan. *Hooliganism: Crime, Culture and Power in St. Petersburg, 1900–1914.* Berkeley: University of California Press, 1993.

Niger, Sh[muel]. "A maskils utopie: araynfir tsu Ayzik Meir Diks a manuskript on a nomen." *YIVO Bleter* 36 (1952): 136–190.

———. "Ayzik Meir Dik and His Hebrew Works." *He-'avar* 2 (1918): 140–142.

———. "To the Question of A. M. Dik's Birthday." *Pinkes fun amopteyl fun YIVO* 1 (1927–1928): 380–382.

Nikitin, V. N. *Evrei-zemledel'tsy.* St. Petersburg: Novosti, 1887.

———. *Mnogostradal'nye: ocherki byta kantonistov.* St. Petersburg: Otechestvennye zapiski, 1872.

———. "Vospominaniia." *Russkaia starina* 127–128 (1906): 582–669, 54–61, 312–396; 129 (1907): 87–106, 289–307.

———. *Zhizn' zakliuchennykh.* St. Petersburg: Izd-vo Kolesova i Mikhina, 1871.

Nora, Pierre, ed. *Les lieux de mémoire.* 7 vols. Paris: Gallimard, 1984.

———. *Realms of Memory: Rethinking the French Past.* Ed. Lawrence Kritzman. Trans. Arthur Goldhammer. 3 vols. New York: Columbia University Press, 1996–1998.

Novick, Peter. *The Holocaust in American Life.* Boston: Houghton Mifflin, 1999.

———. *That Noble Dream: The "Objectivity" Question and the American Historical Profession.* Cambridge: Cambridge University Press, 1988.

Ofek, Adina. "Cantonists: Jewish Children as Soldiers in Tsar Nicholas' Army." *Modern Judaism* 13 (1993): 277–308.

Orbach, Alexander. *New Voices of Russian Jewry: A Study of the Russian-Jewish Press in Odessa in the Era of the Great Reforms, 1860–1871.* Leiden: Brill, 1980.

———. "The Russian-Jewish Leadership and the Pogroms of 1881–82." In *Perspectives on the 1881–82 Pogroms in Russia,* 1–37. Pittsburgh: Russian and East European Studies Program, University of Pittsburgh, 1984.

Orshanskii, I. G. *Russkoe zakonodatel'stvo o evreiakh.* St. Petersburg: A. E. Landau, 1877.

"Otchet o soveshchanii evreiskikh obshchestvennykh deiatelei proiskhodivshii v Kovne, 19–22go noiabria, 1909 goda." *Evreiskii mir* 1, nos. 11–12 (1909): 32–61.

Parush, Iris. *National Ideology and Literary Canon* [in Hebrew]. Jerusalem: Mosad Bialik, 1992.

———. *Reading Women: The Benefit of Marginality in Nineteenth-Century Eastern European Jewish Society* [in Hebrew]. Tel Aviv: Am Oved, 2001.

Pelli, Moshe. *Kinds of Genre in Haskalah Literature: Types and Topics* [in Hebrew]. Tel Aviv: Ha-kibbutz ha-meuchad, 1999.

Penslar, Derek J. *Shylock's Children: Economics and Jewish Identity in Modern Europe.* Berkeley and Los Angeles: University of California Press, 2001.

Petrovsky-Shtern, Yohanan. *Evrei v russkoi armii, 1827–1914.* Moscow: Novoe literaturnoe obozrenie, 2003.

Phillipson, Ludwig. "Aufforderung an alle deutsch-lesenden Israeliten." *Allgemeine Zeitung des Judentums* 19 (1855): 87–89.

———. "Der Fortbestand des Judenthums: An einer Freund in F." *Allgemeine Zeitung des Judentums* 43 (1879): 625–627, 657–659, 673–675, 705–707.

Pinsker, Leo. *Autoemancipation! Mahnruf an seine Stammgenossen von einem russischen Juden.* Berlin: Commission-Verlag von W. Issleib (G. Schur), 1882.

Pipes, Richard. "Catherine II and the Jews." *Soviet-Jewish Affairs* 5, no. 2 (1975): 3–20.

———. "Russian Conservatism in the Second Half of the Nineteenth Century." *Slavic Review* 30 (1971): 121–128.

———. "The Russian Military Colonies, 1810–1831." *Journal of Modern History* 22, no. 3 (1950): 205–219.

Plekhanov, G. V. "Sud'by russkoi kritiki: A. L. Volynskii." In *Sochineniia,* 24 vols., 10:164–197. Moscow: Gosudarstvennoe izd-vo, 1923–1927.

Propp, V. Ia. *Morphology of the Folk-Tale.* Ed. Svatava Pirkova-Jacobson. Trans. Laurence Scott. Bloomington: Indiana University Press, 1958.

Rabinovich, O. A. *Sochineniia.* 3 vols. St. Petersburg and Odessa: Izdaniie Odesskago obshchestva "Trud," 1880–1888.

Raeff, Marc. "The Political Philosophy of Speranskij." *American Slavic and East European Review* 12, no. 1 (1953): 1–21.

Rajner, Mirjam. "The Awakening of Jewish National Art in Russia." *Jewish Art* 16–17 (1990–1991): 98–121.

Ramras-Rauch, Gila. "L. A. Arieli and the Literature of the Second Aliyah." In *From Ancient Israel to Modern Judaism, Intellect in Quest of Understanding: Essays in Honor of Marvin Fox,* ed. Jacob Neusner, Ernest S. Frerichs, and Nahum M. Sarna, 4 vols., 4:115–123. Atlanta: Scholars, 1989.

Ransel, David L. *Mothers of Misery: Child Abandonment in Russia.* Princeton, N.J.: Princeton University Press, 1988.

Riasanovsky, Nicholas V. *A Parting of Ways: Government and the Educated Public in Russia, 1801–1855.* Oxford: Clarendon, 1976.

Richards, Robert J. *The Romantic Conception of Life: Science and Philosophy in the Age of Goethe.* Chicago and London: University of Chicago Press, 2002.

Rieber, Alfred J. "Alexander II: A Revisionist View." *Journal of Modern History* 43 (1971): 42–58.

————. *Merchants and Entrepreneurs in Imperial Russia.* Chapel Hill: North Carolina University Press, 1982.

Rischin, Moses. *The Promised City: New York's Jews, 1870–1914.* Cambridge, Mass.: Harvard University Press, 1962.

Rivkind, Yitskhok. "A. M. Dik's Letters" [in Yiddish]. *YIVO Bleter* 35 (1951): 222–228.

Roemer, Nils. *Jewish Scholarship and Culture in Nineteenth-Century Germany: Between History and Faith.* Madison: University of Wisconsin Press, 2005.

————. "Provincializing the Past: Worms and the Making of a German-Jewish Cultural Heritage." *Jewish Studies Quarterly* 12 (2005): 80–100.

————. "Turning Defeat into Victory: *Wissenschaft des Judentums* and the Martyrs of 1096." *Jewish History* 13 (1999): 65–80.

Rogger, Hans. *Jewish Policies and Right-Wing Politics in Imperial Russia.* Berkeley and Los Angeles. University of California Press, 1986.

————. "Reflections on Russian Conservatism, 1861–1905." *Forschungen zur osteuropäischen Geschichte* 14 (1966): 195–212.

Roskies, David G. *Against the Apocalypse: Responses to Catastrophe in Modern Jewish Culture.* Cambridge, Mass., and London: Harvard University Press, 1984.

————. "Ayzik-Meir Dik and the Rise of Yiddish Popular Literature." Ph.D. dissertation, Brandeis University, 1975.

————. *A Bridge of Longing: The Lost Art of Yiddish Storytelling.* Cambridge, Mass., and London: Harvard University Press, 1995.

————, ed. *Literature of Destruction: Jewish Responses to Catastrophe.* Philadelphia, New York, and Jerusalem: Jewish Publication Society, 1988.

————. "The Maskil as Folk-Hero." *Prooftexts* 10 (1990): 219–235.

————. "S. Ansky and the Paradigm of Return." In *The Uses of Tradition: Jewish Continuity in the Modern Era,* ed. Jack Wertheimer, 243–260. New York: Jewish Theological Seminary, 1992.

Roskies-Wisse, Ruth. "*K'minhag yud:* an umbakanter ktav-yad fun Mendele mokhersfarim." In *For Max Weinreich on His Seventieth Birthday: Studies in Jewish Language, Literature and Society,* 337–342. The Hague: Mouton, 1964.

Rowland, Richard H. "Geographical Patterns of the Jewish Population in the Pale of Settlement of Late Imperial Russia." *Jewish Social Studies* 48 (1986): 207–234.

Rubina, Dina. *Nash kitaiskii biznes: roman i rasskazy* (Moscow: Eksmo, 2004).

Sadan, Dov. *Be-tsetekhah u-ve-ohalekhah.* Ramat Gan: Sifriyat makor, 1966.

————. *A Psychoanalytic Midrash: Studies in Brenner's Psychology* [in Hebrew]. Jerusalem: Magnes, 1996.

Safran, Gabriella. *Rewriting the Jew: Assimilation Narratives in the Russian Empire.* Stanford, Calif.: Stanford University Press, 2000.

Salmon, Laura. "Ben-ami i ego mesto v russko-evreiskoi literature." In *Evrei v Rossii: istoriia i kul'tura, sbornik nauchnykh trudov,* ed. D. A. Eliashevich, 91–124. St. Petersburg: St. Petersburg Jewish University, 1995.

Samter, N. *Judentaufen im neunzehnten Jahrhundert.* Berlin: M. Poppelauer, 1906.

Samuel, Maurice. *The World of Sholom Aleichem.* New York: Vintage, 1943.

Saunders, David. *The Ukrainian Impact on Russian Culture, 1750–1850.* Edmonton: Canadian Institute of Ukrainian Studies, 1985.

Schäfer, Peter. *Mirror of His Beauty: Feminine Images of God from the Bible to the Early Kabbalah.* Princeton, N.J., and Oxford: Princeton University Press, 2002.

Schirmann, Jefim [Ephraim]. *The History of Hebrew Poetry in Christian Spain and Southern France* [in Hebrew]. Ed. Ezra Fleischer. Jerusalem: Merkaz Shazar, 1997.

Schorsch, Ismar. *From Text to Context: The Turn to History in Modern Judaism.* Hanover,

N.H., and London: University Press of New England/Brandeis University Press, 1994.

Schorske, Carl E. *Fin-de-Siècle Vienna: Politics and Culture.* New York: Vintage, 1980.

Schwartz, Seth. *Imperialism and Jewish Society, 200 BCE to 640 CE.* Princeton, N.J.: Princeton University Press, 2001.

Serchuk, Vance F. "Continuity and Crisis: The Development of the Moscow Choral Synagogue, 1869–1906," BA thesis, Princeton University, 2001.

Serkov, S. R., ed. *Kliatvu vernosti sderzhali: 1812 god v russkoi literature.* Moscow: Moskovskii rabochii, 1987.

Shaked, Gershon. *Bein tshok le-dema' "iyunim be-yetzirato shel Mendele mokher-sefarim.* Tel Aviv: Masada, 1965.

———. *Hebrew Narrative Fiction* [in Hebrew]. 2 vols. Jerusalem: Keter, 1977–1978.

———. *Mendele, lefanav ve-aharav.* Jerusalem: Magnes, 2004.

Shapira, Anita. *Land and Power: The Zionist Resort to Force, 1881–1948.* Trans. William Templer. New York and Oxford: Oxford University Press, 1992.

Shatskii, Jacob. "Haskalah in Zamosc." *YIVO Bleter* 34 (1952): 24–61.

Shavit, Uzi. "Ha-'haskalah' ma-hi? Le-berur musag ha-'haskalah' be-sifrut 'ivrit." *Mehkarei yerushalaim be-sifrut 'ivrit* 12 (1990): 51–83.

Shavit, Yaacov. "The 'Glorious Century' or the 'Cursed Century': *Fin-de-Siècle* Europe and the Emergence of Modern Jewish Nationalism." *Journal of Contemporary History* 26 (1991): 553–574.

Shcherbina, Nikolai. *Izbrannye proizvedeniia.* Ed. I. D. Glikman. Leningrad: Sovetskii pisatel', 1970.

Shimoni, Gideon. *The Zionist Ideology.* Hanover, N.H., and London: University Press of New England/Brandeis University Press, 1995.

Shmeruk, Khone, and Joseph Klausner, eds. *Mendele mokher-sfarim: Bibliography of His Works and Letters for the Academic Edition* [in Hebrew]. Jerusalem: Hebrew University Magnes Press, 1965.

Shohet, Azriel. *Mosad "ha-rabanut mi-ta'am" be-rusyah.* Haifa: Haifa University, 1976.

"Sholem Aleichem: The Critical Tradition." *Prooftexts* 6 (1986).

Sholem-aleichem, *Ale verk fun Sholem-aleichem.* 28 vols. New York: Sholem-aleichem folks-fond, 1917–1923.

Shpigel', M. "Iz zapisok kantonista." *Evreiskaia starina* 4 (1911): 249–259.

Shtif, N. "Volf Kamrash un der 'ershter yidisher spektakl' in Rusland." In *Teatr-bukh: zamlung tsum fuftsik-yorikn yubiley funem yudishn teatr, 1876–1926,* 21–38. Kiev: Kultur-lige, 1927.

Shvarts, Frumah. "Y. L. Peretz k-msaper du-leshoni." Ph.D. dissertation, Hebrew University, 1994.

Silberschlag, Eisig. *From Renaissance to Renaissance.* New York: KTAV, 1973–1977.

Slouzsch, Nahum. *La renaissance de la littérature hébraïque.* Paris: Société nouvelle de la librairie et d'édition, 1903.

Slutsky, Yehuda. *Ha'itonut ha-yehudit-rusit ba-meah ha tesha' esreh.* Jerusalem: Mosad Bialik, 1970.

———. "Tsmihatah shel ha-intelligentsia ha-yehudit-rusit." *Zion* 25 (1960): 212–237.

Sokolov, N. I. *Russkaia literatura i narodnichestvo: literaturnoe dvizhenie 70kh gg. XIX v.* Leningrad: Leningrad University, 1968.

Sorin, Gerald. *A Time for Building: The Third Migration, 1880–1920.* Baltimore, Md., and London: Johns Hopkins University Press, 1992.

Sorkin, David. *The Transformation of German Jewry, 1780–1840.* Oxford: Oxford University Press, 1987.

Spetter, Allan. "The United States, the Russian Jews and the Russian Famine of 1891–92." *American-Jewish Historical Quarterly* 44 (1975): 236–244.

Spicehandler, Ezra. "Odessa as a Literary Center of Hebrew Literature." In *The Great*

Transition: The Recovery of the Lost Centers of Modern Hebrew Literature, ed. Glenda Abramson and Tudor Parfitt, 75–90. Totowa, N.J.: Rowan and Allanheld, 1985.

Stampfer, Shaul. "Patterns of Internal Jewish Migration in the Russian Empire." In *Jews and Jewish Life in Russia and the Soviet Union*, ed. Yaacov Ro'I, 28–47. Ilford, Essex: Frank Cass, 1995.

———. *Ha-yeshivah ha-litait be-hithavutah.* Jerusalem: Merkaz Shazar, 1995.

———. "Yedi'at kro ukhtov etsel yehudei mizrah eiropah ba-tekufat ha-hadashah." In *Transition and Change in Modern Jewish History* [in Hebrew], ed. Shmuel Almog et al., 459–483. Jerusalem: Merkaz Shazar, 1987.

Stanislavskii, S. "K istorii kantonistov." *Evreiskaia starina* 2 (1909): 266–268.

Stanislawski, Michael. *Autobiographical Jews: Essays in Jewish Self-Fashioning.* Seattle and London: University of Washington Press, 2004.

———. *For Whom Do I Toil? Judah Leib Gordon and the Crisis of Russian Jewry.* Oxford: Oxford University Press, 1988.

———. "Jewish Apostasy in Russia: A Tentative Typology." In *Jewish Apostasy in the Modern World,* ed. Todd Endelman, 189–205. New York and London: Holmes and Meier, 1987.

———. "Russian Jewry, the Russian State and the Dynamics of Emancipation." In *Paths of Emancipation: Jews, States and Citizenship,* ed. Pierre Birnbaum and Ira Katznelson, 262–283. Princeton, N.J.: Princeton University Press, 1995.

———. *Tsar Nicholas I and the Jews: The Transformation of Jewish Society in Russia, 1825–1855.* Philadelphia: Jewish Publication Society, 1983.

———. "The Yiddish *Shevet Yehudah:* A Study in the 'Ashkenization' of a Spanish-Jewish Classic." In *Jewish History and Jewish Memory: Essays in Honor of Yosef Hayim Yerushalmi,* ed. Elisheva Carlebach, John M. Efron, and David N. Myers, 134–149. Hanover, N.H., and London: University Press of New England/Brandeis University Press, 1998.

———. *Zionism and the Fin-de-Siècle: Cosmopolitanism and Nationalism from Nordau to Jabotinsky.* Berkeley: University of California Press, 2001.

Stanton, Rebecca J. "Odessan Selves: Identity and Mythopoesis in Works of the 'Odessa School.' " Ph.D. dissertation, Columbia University, 2004.

Starr, Frederick S. *Decentralization and Self-Government in Russia, 1830–1870.* Princeton, N.J.: Princeton University Press, 1972.

Stasov, V. V., ed. *Mark Matveevich Antokol'skii: ego zhizn', tvoreniia, pis'ma i stat'i.* Moscow: M. O. Vol'f, 1905.

Stein, Sarah. *Making Jews Modern: The Yiddish and Ladino Press in the Russian and Ottoman Empires.* Bloomington: Indiana University Press, 2004.

Steinschneider, Moritz. "Schach bei der Juden." In idem, *Geschichte und Literatur des Schachspiels,* ed. Antonius van der Linde, 1:155–202. Berlin: J. Springer, 1874.

Sumarokov, A. P. *Stikhotvoreniia.* Ed. A. S. Orlov. Moscow: Sovetskii pisatel', 1935.

Sviiasov, E. V., ed. *Russkaia voennaia proza XIX veka.* Leningrad: Lenizdat, 1989.

Trunk, Isaiah. *Judenrat: The Jewish Councils in Europe under Nazi Occupation.* New York: Macmillan, 1972.

Tsederbaum, Alexander. *Di geheymnise fun berditchev.* Warsaw: n.p., 1870.

Turniansky, Chava, ed. *Yiddish Literature in the Nineteenth Century: An Anthology of Yiddish Literary Research and Criticism in the Soviet Union* [Yiddish and Hebrew]. Jerusalem: Magnes, 1993.

Tynianov, Iu. *Arkhaisty i novatory.* Leningrad: Priboi, 1929.

Valkenier, Elizabeth. *Russian Realist Art, the State and Society: The Peredvizhniki and Their Tradition.* New York: Columbia University Press, 1989.

Van Dyke, Carl. *Russian Imperial Military Doctrine and Education, 1832–1914.* New York: Greenwood, 1990.

Veidlinger, Jeffrey. "The Historical and Ethnographic Construction of Russian Jewry." *Ab Imperio* 4 (2003): 165–184.

Venturi, Franco. *Roots of Revolution: A History of the Populist and Socialist Movements in Nineteenth-Century Russia.* Trans. Francis Haskell. London: Weidenfeld and Nicolson, 1960.

Violette, Aurele J. "The Grand Duke Constantine Nikolayevich and the Reform of Naval Administration, 1855–1870." *Slavonic and East European Review* 52 (1974): 584–601.

Walicki, Andrzej. *The Controversy over Capitalism: Studies in the Social Philosophy of the Russian Populists.* Oxford: Oxford University Press, 1969.

Weiner, Amir. *Making Sense of War: The Second World War and the Fate of the Bolshevik Revolution.* Princeton, N.J.: Princeton University Press, 2001.

Weinreich, Max. *Bilder fun der yidisher literatur-geshikhte.* Vilna: Tomor, 1928.

———. "Materialn un notitsn, mendele-dokumentn." *YIVO Bleter* 10 (1936): 167–180, 364–375.

Werses, Shmuel. *Criticism of Criticism: Evaluations in Development* [in Hebrew]. Tel Aviv: Hotsa'at yahdav, 1981–1982.

———. "Darkei ha-otobiografiah be-tkufat ha-haskalah." *Gilyonot* 4 (1945): 175–183.

———. *From Mendele to Hazaz* [in Hebrew]. Jerusalem: Magnes, 1987.

———. "Gerush sefarad be-aspeklariah shel sifrut ha-haskalah." In idem, *Hakitsah 'ami: sifrut ha-haskalah be'idan ha-modernizatsiah,* 157–190. Jerusalem: Magnes, 2001.

———. "Gerush sefarad u-portugal be-sifrut yidish." *Pe'amim* 69 (1997): 114–159.

White, Hayden. *Metahistory: The Historical Imagination in Nineteenth-Century Europe.* Baltimore, Md.: Johns Hopkins University Press, 1973.

Wilensky, Mordecai. *Hasidim and Mitnaggedim: A Study of the Controversy between Them in the Years 1772–1815* [in Hebrew]. 2 vols. Jerusalem: Mossad Bialik, 1970.

Winer, Meir. *Tsu der geshikhte fun der yidisher literatur in 19tn yorhundert.* 2 vols. New York: YKUF, 1945–1946.

Winter, Jay. *Sites of Memory, Sites of Mourning: The Great War in European Cultural History.* Cambridge: Canto, 1995.

Wirtschafter, Elise Kimerling. *From Serf to Russian Soldier.* Princeton, N.J.: Princeton University Press, 1990.

Wischnitzer, Mark. *To Dwell in Safety: The Story of Jewish Migration since 1800.* Philadelphia: Jewish Publication Society, 1948.

Wisse, Ruth R. *The Modern Jewish Canon: A Journey through Language and Culture.* New York: Free Press, 2000.

———. *Peretz and the Making of Modern Jewish Culture.* Seattle and London: University of Washington Press, 1991.

———. *The Schlemiel as Modern Hero.* Chicago: University of Chicago Press, 1971.

Wortman, Richard S. *The Development of Russian Legal Consciousness.* Chicago: University of Chicago Press, 1976.

———. *Scenarios of Power: Myth and Ceremony in Russian Monarchy.* Vol. 2. Princeton, N.J.: Princeton University Press, 2000.

Yaney, George L. *The Systematization of Russian Government: Social Evolution in the Domestic Administration of Imperial Russia, 1711–1905.* Urbana: Illinois University Press, 1973.

Yerushalmi, Yosef Hayim. *Zakhor, Jewish History and Jewish Memory.* Seattle and London: University of Washington Press, 1982.

Yuditskii, Avraham. "Vegn inhalt fun Vulf Kamrashes pyese *Kahal in shtetl.*" *Shriftn* 1 (1928): 331–336.

Yuval, Israel. *"Two Nations in Your Womb": Perceptions of Jews and Christians* [in Hebrew]. Tel Aviv: Am Oved, 2000.

Zaionchkovskii, P. A. *Krizis samoderzhaviia na rubezhe 1870–1880kh godov.* Moscow: Moscow University, 1964.

———. *Voennye reformy 1860–1870 godov v Rossii.* Moscow: Moscow University, 1952.

Zalkin, Mordechai. *A New Dawn: The Jewish Enlightenment in the Russian Empire, Social Aspects* [in Hebrew]. Jerusalem: Hebrew University Magnes Press, 2000.

Zinberg, Israel. *A History of Jewish Literature.* Trans. Bernard Martin. 12 vols. Cincinnati and New York: Hebrew Union College Press/KTAV, 1978.

———. *Istoriia evreiskoi pechati.* Petrograd: Fleitman, 1917.

Zipperstein, Steven J. *Elusive Prophet: Ahad ha'am and the Origins of Zionism.* Berkeley and Los Angeles: University of California Press, 1993.

———. *Imagining Russian Jewry: Memory, History, Identity.* Seattle: University of Washington Press, 1999.

———. *The Jews of Odessa, a Cultural History, 1794–1881.* Stanford, Calif.: Stanford University Press, 1986.

———. "Transforming the Heder: Maskilic Politics in Imperial Russia." In *Jewish History: Essays in Honour of Chimen Abramsky,* ed. Ada Rapoport-Albert and Steven J. Zipperstein, 87–109. London: Peter Halban, 1988.

Zunser, Eliakum. *Tsunzers biografie, geshribn fun im aleyn; A Jewish Bard, Being the Biography of Eliakum Tsunzer.* Trans. Simon Hisdarsky. New York: Zunser Jubilee Committee, 1905.

———. *The Works of Elyokum Zunser: A Critical Edition* [in Yiddish]. Ed. Mordkhe Schaechter. 2 vols. New York: YIVO, 1964.

Zweifel, Eliezer. *Minim ve'ugav.* Vilna: Romm, 1858.

INDEX

OLGA LITVAK

teaches European and Jewish history at Princeton University.
She writes and lectures on the cultural life of Eastern European Jewry.
Born in Soviet Russia and educated in the United States,
she is a New Yorker by conviction.